T0276442

"Communication is the central challenge for activists of all stripes to rally support, pressure politicians. In this fascinating history of a life spent in advertising, Jerry Mander shows how he connected people and groups championing various progressive issues with print media and funders. Today, when social media gives life to corporate greenwashing, whacko conspiracists, and people out to make a quick buck, *70 Ads to Save the World* is filled with inspiring stories of ad campaigns in which failures are as important as the successes to show what works and what doesn't."

— David Suzuki, Author of *The Legacy: An Elder's Vision for Our Sustainable Future*

"With profound wisdom and deep experience, Jerry Mander speaks truth to power and the powers of advertising, ultimately responsible for pollution, waste, consumerism, climate catastrophe, and human discontent. *70 Ads* empowers readers to transform the way they look at the world, shifting our focus from glamor to grace and from greed to gratitude."

—Satish Kumar, Editor Emeritus, Resurgence & Ecologist and Founder, Schumacher College

"Jerry Mander has been on the leading edge of every major environmental and justice issue of our time. Thankfully for us all, he used his creative genius to teach the world about these urgent issues through these magnificent ads. A wonderful book, full of rich history and gorgeous visuals. Highly recommended!"

— Maude Barlow, Activist and Author of *Still Hopeful: Lessons from a Lifetime of Activism*

"Anyone wanting to sway public opinion, influence policymakers and reverse legislation needs to read this book. I'm talking about anyone interested in what has worked and not worked when educating the public about the issues that define our times. I'm talking about professors of environmental studies, Indigenous rights, reproductive rights, animal rights, the impact of computers on social structures, military impacts on nature, globalization of corporate power, and restoring local economies. I'm talking about our thinking. This is your textbook. This is Jerry Mander's brilliant, generous offering to save the world."

— Katie Singer, author of *An Electronic Silent Spring* and *Our Web of Inconvenient Truths*

"Outrageous, provocative, vastly entertaining, *70 Ads* follows Jerry Mander's work as an advertising wizard, depicting the most memorable and effective environmental and political campaigns during his lengthy career. Want to stop the "all-but-certain" government plans to dam the Grand Canyon? Here are the ads that scuttled the whole damned scheme! Well-known as a social activist, political thinker, anti-globalist organizer, and friend to the world's most inspired change agents, Mander shares his vision of how shrewd, often impish craftsmanship can produce a better world."

— Langdon Winner, Professor Emeritus of Humanities, Arts and Social Sciences at Rensselaer Polytechnic Institute, Author of *Autonomous Technology* and *The Whale and The Reactor*

"Imagine combining advertising genius with deep ecology with radical transformation of our economic institutions with bold global organizing. Impossible. You can't find these in a single individual... until Jerry Mander got behind a typewriter and changed the game."

—John Cavanagh, Former Director of Institute for Policy Studies

"The advertisements that Jerry Mander created are, like his mind, both deep and nimble. Forget about advertising as a degraded tool of commerce, and instead view it as a literary genre. Some of these ads spring with condensed power, some beguile the mind with unexpected charm and nuance, and some read like a page from *The Onion*. What characterizes them all is irreverence, playfulness, and a sense of surprise. While the corporate world has used advertising to sell people unwanted products, Jerry uses it as a lance to poke holes in pieties and to get at the heart of truths."

— Malcolm Margolin, Executive Director of California Institute for Community, Art, and Nature

"Jerry Mander's illustrated memoir is a phenomenal trove of social history, communications brilliance, and moral clarity. However much media may change, Mander's genius endures—to inform the public and act for justice; to speak with intelligence, respect, and wit. Take heart! Through these pages you'll meet a remarkable elder, a great friend of the Earth."

— Stephanie Mills, author of *In Service of the Wild* and *Epicurean Simplicity*

70 ADS TO SAVE *the* WORLD

{ *AN ILLUSTRATED MEMOIR OF SOCIAL CHANGE* }

JERRY MANDER

SYNERGETIC PRESS
SANTA FE • LONDON

Published by Synergetic Press
1 Blue Bird Ct. Santa Fe, NM 87508 &
24 Old Gloucester St. London, WCIN 3AL, England

Library of Congress Control Number: 2022937351

ISBN 9780907791812 (paperback)
ISBN 9780907791997 (ebook)

Book design: Daniela Sklan | Hummingbird Design Studio
Managing Editor: Amanda Müller
Editor: Carrie Pilto

Printed in Canada

Contents

"Cop-killer bullets, mail-order handguns, machine guns... has the N.R.A. gone off the deep end?"

—George Napper, Public Safety Commissioner Atlanta, Georgia

"Lee Harvey Oswald clipped a coupon from *The American Rifleman*, the National Rifle Association's journal, to buy the mail-order gun he used to murder President John F. Kennedy.

Yet it took the murders of Dr. Martin Luther King Jr., and Senator Robert F. Kennedy for Congress to muster the political courage to pass a national law which stopped mail-order gun sales.

Now the NRA's leadership is lobbying to turn back the clock—to repeal not only national laws, but state and local controls aimed at keeping handguns out of the wrong hands. Just imagine mail-order gun sales again... easy access to new machine guns... or more people carrying handguns in public!

America's handgun violence problem is enormous, costing the lives of over 20,000 of us each year. For black Americans, gun violence and homicide has reached epidemic proportions. We need tougher laws, not weaker ones.

We in law enforcement are working hard to prevent violence in America. A part of the answer is a prohibition on the sale of undetectable handguns and the enactment of the "Brady Bill" which would require a seven-day national waiting period before a handgun purchase to allow background checks.

Georgia doesn't have such a law state-wide. Recently a police officer was gunned down by a felon who easily purchased a handgun in the next county. A waiting period with a background check could have made the difference. That peace officer could be alive today.

Evidence shows that waiting periods do work. My own city of Atlanta enacted a 15-day waiting period and background check in 1982, and that year we stopped 42 criminals from purchasing handguns. Last year, 16 of the 270 applicants for handguns were rejected for criminal records; three were disqualified for mental disorders. If Georgia had a state-wide program, even more prohibited persons could be stopped from purchasing handguns.

Waiting periods also mean a cooling-off period to deter crimes of passion and suicide. A cooling-off period could have prevented a combined shooting and suicide incident which occurred just across the street from my office. The .38 caliber revolver used in the shootings was purchased the *day before* in one of Atlanta's neighboring jurisdictions which does not require a waiting period.

This tragedy points out that our system of laws is only as strong as the weakest link. Law enforcement studies show handguns used in violent crime flow from states with weak handgun laws to those with strong laws. My colleagues in New York, a state with a strong

handgun law, report that many handguns seized in violent crime there originate here in Georgia. We need a national, uniform minimum standard of handgun laws. But the NRA has a $54 million budget to spend against us and is working at all levels of government to dismantle existing handgun control laws and to prevent the passage of any new measures.

Let's mark the anniversaries of the deaths of President Kennedy, Dr. King, and Senator Kennedy this year by sending Congress a message—America wants sane handgun laws now!"

Sale of cop-killer ammo would be legal if the N.R.A. had its way.

Help me fight the N.R.A.!

John Hinckley pulled a $29 revolver from his pocket and shot the President, a secret service man, a police officer, and my husband. I'm not asking for sympathy, I'm asking for your help. Tens of thousands of Americans have joined Handgun Control, Inc., for the reason I did—because, together, we can take on the N.R.A. and win. Please pick up a pen, fill out the coupon, add a check to aid our work, and mail it to me today. Thank you.

Sarah Brady

There are already more than 100,000 rapid-fire machine guns in private hands. The latest models are light and concealable. Congress passed a law to block their sale. The N.R.A. is trying to get that law repealed.

It's time to break the N.R.A.'s grip on Congress once and for all. Here's my contribution to Handgun Control, Inc., the national nonprofit citizens group you help direct:
☐ $15 ☐ $25 ☐ $35 ☐ $50 ☐ $100 or $_____.
☐ Tell me more about how I can help.

NAME

ADDRESS

CITY   STATE   ZIP

HANDGUN CONTROL

1400 K Street, N.W. Washington, D.C. 20005, (202) 898-0792

Contributions to Handgun Control, Inc. are not tax deductible.

This exotic sea turtle may be headed for extinction, but it's still available as a Japanese cigarette lighter.

The purchase of sea turtles by Japan is responsible for the greatest killing of endangered species in the world today.

Almost a quarter of a million hawksbill turtles have been made into eyeglass frames, cigarette lighters and combs since 1980.

Another 500,000 olive ridley

Endangered sea turtles are shot or clubbed, then cut out of their shells.

sea turtles have been skinned for handbags, belts and matching high heels since 1970.

Japan is an official signatory of the Convention on International Trade in Endangered Species (CITES) but has used a loophole to support the illegal slaughter of

Stop the trade. And save the turtles.

sea turtles in Mexico, Brunei, the Comoros Islands, Jamaica, the Maldives, Grenada, St. Vincent, and Panama. Populations of these exotic, protected creatures are declining worldwide. This ad is their S.O.S.

Japan will give up this sickening trade if enough people notice. Please mail the coupons immediately.

Mr. Hikaru Matsunaga
Minister of International Trade & Industry
1-3-1 Kasumigaseki, Chiyoda-Ku
Tokyo, JAPAN

Your import of hawksbill turtle shell is in violation of international conventions. To safeguard Japan's reputation abroad, you should halt all trade in endangered wildlife immediately — not only sea turtles, but whales, dolphins, and monitor lizards. You can't afford to let Japan even appear to profit from the extinction of defenseless creatures.

NAME

ADDRESS

President George Bush
The White House
Washington, D.C. 20500

Undermining international protections for endangered sea turtles, Japan is profiting from extinction. Symbolic gestures are not enough. It's time to get tough and impose meaningful trade sanctions, as required by the Pelly Amendment. Japan's exports of cultured pearls to the U.S. market are worth over $100 million. That's a good place to start...and would get quick results.

NAME

ADDRESS

Todd Steiner, Sea Turtle Restoration Project
Earth Island Institute
300 Broadway, San Francisco CA 94133

Last year, coupons like these helped stop the sea turtle slaughter in Mexico. Yet sea turtles will not really be safe until the international trade is halted, shrimp fleets no longer net them, countries develop conservation programs, and nesting beaches are fully protected. [ ] Keep me up-to-date. [ ] I'm enclosing my support for this urgent battle against extinction: __$15 __$35 __$50 __$100 or $_____.

NAME

ADDRESS

Note: Coupon to Japan takes 50c postage

Prepared by Public Media Center   Photo (top): James D. Watt

ix

TO MANY OF OUR DAUGHTERS, THIS LOOKS LIKE A COAT HANGER.

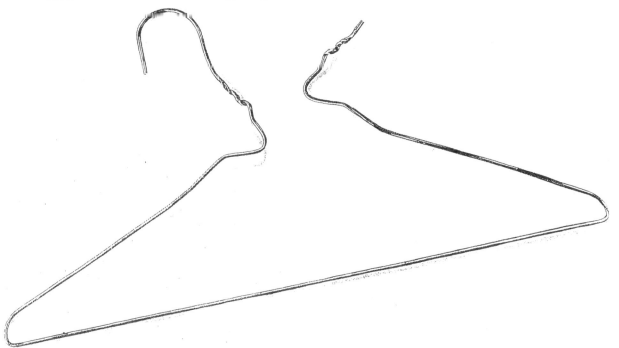

PLEASE. SIGN THE PLEDGE TO KEEP IT THAT WAY.

Just sixteen years ago, a coat hanger was more than a coat hanger.

For countless desperate women, it looked like the only way out of a crisis pregnancy.

Infection, uncontrolled bleeding, a perforated uterus, sterility, abuse at the hands of back-alley butchers, these are just some of the horrendous risks women were forced to endure. Thousands died.

Then the Supreme Court acted to protect women's private medical decisions. Abortion was made legal and safe. And the women of America stopped dying.

It's frightening that anyone could seriously propose returning to the bloody, brutal, desperate past.

Yet the *Webster* case, to be heard by the post-Reagan Supreme Court in ninety days, could make it practically impossible for millions of American women to obtain a safe, legal abortion.

Already anticipating victory, an extremist, vocal minority, personally opposed to abortion, has launched a savage nationwide assault on our right to decide for ourselves.

Their view of women does not allow for personal choice. They block the doors to health clinics. Lobby to limit birth control methods. Impose obstacles to abortion unlike any other medical procedure. Try to withhold information about abortion from poor patients. And unceasingly demand that abortion be outlawed. Under all circumstances...at any cost.

They would involve lawyers and politicians in a decision now made between a woman and her doctor. They would make women and their doctors into criminals. Most shocking of all, they just might win.

Your right to choose has never been in greater danger. Sixteen years after safety was assured, a single Supreme Court decision could rip away protections now taken for granted. Please act now. Sign the pledge. Defend every woman's right to choose.

We know restrictive abortion laws kill women.

Must we learn the same lesson twice in a lifetime?

"ADD YOUR NAME TO MINE. AFTER SIXTEEN YEARS OF SAFETY, TIME IS RUNNING OUT."

KATE MICHELMAN
Executive Director, NARAL.

MY STATEMENT OF PRINCIPLE AND PLEDGE:

I believe our Constitution protects every woman's right to make her own decision about abortion, according to her own personal convictions, free from the dictates and intrusion of government. Others want to take away this right. They seek to impose their beliefs on the rest of us by making abortion illegal. The women of America must never be thrown back to that degrading and dangerous time of illegal abortions when they risked their lives and health, and thousands died. I therefore pledge to oppose any attempt to interfere with the fundamental right of a woman to make her own decision about abortion.

NAME _____

ADDRESS _____

CITY _____ STATE ____ ZIP ____

I enclose my tax-deductible donation of __$15 __$25 __$50 __$100 __More

National Abortion Rights Action League and the NARAL Foundation
1101 14th Street, N.W., Washington, D.C. 20005

x

Monocultures of the mind

Ours is the first culture in history to have moved inside media—to have largely replaced direct contact with people and nature for simulated versions on TV, sponsored by corporations. Now it's happening globally, with grave effects on cultural diversity and democracy.

The ultimate goal of economic globalization is that every place on earth should be more or less like every place else. Whether in the U.S., Europe, Africa or Asia, all countries should have the same franchise fast-food, the same films and music, the same jeans, shoes and cars, the same urban landscapes, and the same personal, cultural and spiritual values. *Monoculture.* Such a model serves the marketing and efficiency needs of global corporations.

Free trade agreements and bureaucracies like the World Trade Organization, NAFTA *et al.* have the job of enforcing rules that accelerate globalization by *preventing* countries from regulating corporations to protect scarce resources, labor, culture or small business. *But, this is only part of the story.*

There is also the crucial role of television, *which carries the homogenization mandate to another level entirely—directly inside people's brains.* By its ability to speak identical imagery to *billions* of people on earth, TV is capable of unifying thoughts, feelings, values, tastes and desires to match the needs of the institutions who send the images. These are giant corporations, whose ideals of Utopia are invariably commodity-oriented, urban, technology-oriented, and indifferent to nature. The net result is a homogenized *mental* landscape that nicely conforms to the franchises, freeways, suburbs, highrises and clearcuts of an homogenized physical world.

The process really began a generation ago in the U.S. when TV became ubiquitous. Here are some details:

1. TV in the U.S.

98% of the homes in the U.S. have TV sets. 88% have at least two sets. 95% of the population watches TV every day.

According to Nielsen Media Research, the average American home keeps the TV going for 7.5 hours per day. The average *adult* watches more than four hours daily.

Kaiser Family Foundation reports the average child (age 2-4), watches about 2.5 hours per day. The average child (8-13) watches about 4 hours. More than 50% of kids have TV in their bedrooms.

The more one considers them, the more shocking these numbers become. If the average viewer watches four hours, this means that roughly half the population watches more than four hours per day. You may ask, how is this even possible? (By heavy viewing every night, and then on weekends.) The advent of computers has not altered these figures by much; it has actually added to the time that people spend immersed in electronic activity.

Americans spend more time watching TV than doing anything else in life besides working, sleeping or going to school. TV has replaced community life, family life and the environment. In fact, for most people, TV now is the everyday environment. Ours is the first generation to have essentially moved inside media; to have replaced direct contact with people and nature for simulated versions. Television was the original "virtual reality."

The situation is bizarre. Just imagine that a team of anthropologists came from another planet to study the U.S. Their report back home might go like this: "The main thing this culture does is sit night after night in dark rooms, eyes not moving, not talking, brains inactive, staring at a light! Images pour into their brains from thousands of miles away. Once inside these brains, the images remain permanently. This is odd. Maybe it's a kind of brainwashing."

(*Do you doubt the permanence of TV imagery?* Let us ask you this: Can you get a mental picture of Ronald McDonald? Or, the Energizer Bunny? How about Dave, the owner of Wendy's, or Colonel Sanders? Or the Taco Bell Chihuahua? Did you know you had these commercial images stored in your brain? Can you erase them?)

One more statistic: The average American viewer sees about 21,000 commercials per year; that's 21,000 repetitions of an *identical* message. Some advertise cosmetics, others drugs, or cars or beer. But they all say the same thing: *Buy something. Do it now. Commodities are the answer.*

2. Global TV

Around the world, the situation is little different. In Canada, England, France, Germany, Italy, Russia, Greece, Poland, and other countries in Europe and South America, the average person watches 3-4 hours per day. In Japan and Mexico, they watch *more* than here.

From New York to Africa, most people spend hours every day watching TV. With global TV controlled by few companies, people see lots of "Baywatch," "Jerry Springer" and CNN, plus billions in advertising. It's a kind of mental re-training; the cloning of cultures to all be alike.

Even in places on earth where there are still no roads—tiny tropical islands, icy tundras of the north, or in the mountains of the Himalayas—people are sitting in their grass houses or log cabins watching Americans in Dallas driving sleek cars, or standing around swimming pools drinking martinis, plotting ways to do-in one another. Or, they are seeing "Baywatch," the most popular series in the world. Life in Texas, California, New York is made to seem the ultimate in life's achievements while local culture, even where it is still extremely vibrant and alive—can seem backward. *(In many places, locally produced TV is almost non-existent.)*

The act of sitting and watching TV is quickly replacing other ways of life and other value systems. People are carrying the same images that we do, and craving the same commodities, from cars to hairspray to Barbie dolls. Television is turning everyone into everyone else. It's cloning cultures to be like ours.

Next question: *Who sends these images?*

3. The Operators of the System

Most alarming about global TV is how few corporations operate it. The degree of concentration of media ownership rivals that of the oil industry. A small number of huge companies dominate global TV, *as well as* films, newspapers, books, cable systems, music, theatres, advertising *et al.*

The situation is made worse by global bureaucracies like WTO and NAFTA whose rules make it nearly impossible for national governments to *keep out* foreign media interests who gain control of domestic media, leaving little voice for local culture and values. Now we see a fierce round of global acquisitions and mergers in this field (notably AOL Time Warner) making the biggest corporations even bigger. We may soon see the day when the same few companies

dominate *all* media, and thus effectively control information dissemination *everywhere on* the planet.

Can democracy survive such a condition? Cultural diversity surely cannot.

Right now, the biggest three global media giants are AOL Time Warner, The News Corporation, and Disney. Here is an *abbreviated* list of their holdings:

- *AOL Time Warner:* Warner Brothers Films and Television, CNN, TNT, TBS, Court TV, HBO, Cartoon Network, Cinemax, New Line Films, and magazines including *Time, Fortune, People, Sports Illustrated.* They own the Atlanta Hawks and Atlanta Braves, the Hanna Barbera animation studio, as well as major shares in movie theatre companies, dozens of TV stations, satellites, cable systems, *et al.* in Asia, Europe, Africa and elsewhere.

- *Disney:* Disneyland, Disney World, Euro Disney, Disney Channel, ABC Television, ABC Radio, ESPN, A&E, Entertainment and History channels. They own Miramax, Touchstone and Walt Disney Pictures as well as the Anaheim Angels and Anaheim Mighty Ducks. They have large holdings in TV stations, cable systems, satellites throughout the world.

- *The News Corporation:* Fox TV Network, Fox News Channel, 20th Century Fox Studios, Golf TV Channel, 22 U.S. TV stations, 130 daily newspapers, 23 magazines, Harper Collins publisher, and the Los Angeles Dodgers. They have large interests in satellite companies, TV stations and other media in Europe, China, Australia, New Zealand, Canada, and many more places.

(Source: *Rich Media, Poor Democracy* by Robert McChesney)

Of course all of these media giants, among other competitors, share common commercial values. So we are left with the most powerful and pervasive communications system in history, dominated by a few corporations with similar views about how life should be lived?

Is this good? Is it okay for billions of people to be receiving non-stop doses of powerful images and information, controlled by few sources, essentially telling them to be unhappy about how they live and who they are, to get on to the commodity treadmill, to put their trust in corporations, and to embrace a global homogenization of values?

Many groups think not. They are working on these issues in the context of globalization, democracy, cultural diversity, the environment, human rights and human health. If you want to know more about them please contact us.

The Center for Commercial-Free Public Education
TV Turnoff Network
Public Media Center
Independent Press Association
Cultural Environment Movement
Adbusters Media Foundation
Center for Media and Democracy
International Center for Technology Assessment
International Forum on Globalization
Institute for Policy Studies/Global Economy Project
Media Alliance
Earth Island Institute
Yes! Magazine
Planet Drum Foundation
Collective Heritage Institute/Bioneers Conference
The Nature Institute/NetFuture

Signers are all part of a coalition of more than 80 non-profit organizations that favor democratic, localized, ecologically sound alternatives to current practices and policies. This advertisement is #2 in the Megatechnology series. Other ad series discuss extinction crisis, genetic engineering, industrial agriculture and economic globalization. For more information, please contact:
Turning Point Project, 310 D St. NE, Washington, DC 20002
1-800-249-8712 · www.turnpoint.org · email: info@turnpoint.org

PREAMBLE

Free Speech & The Privatization of Consciousness

A.J. LIEBLING put it this way: "In the United States, freedom of the press is guaranteed, but only to those who own one." He might have added that "freedom of speech" is also guaranteed. But only some speakers get to actually amplify their voices using mass media. Most people cannot.

Very few of us can match the tens of millions of dollars that global oil companies spend annually in lobbying and advertising campaigns about how oil drilling is good for all of us. Drilling brings jobs, they say, as well as business development, and economic growth. Cutting down forests is also good, the corporations tell us, and so are GMO farms, driverless cars, robots on the assembly line, and guns for all.

Corporations express their "free speech" every day, spending hundreds of millions of dollars in mass media advertising. In fact, they deliver their free speeches multiple times per day, and then again tomorrow and the day after. They might repeat their free speech message a thousand times a week on television, on the internet, and in ten or eleven newspapers each day, pouring out elaborate imagery that flies into the brains of 30-40 million people.

Meanwhile, some of us, working in our neighborhoods or our non-profit organizations, can get together and write press releases. We send those to newspapers, or hold press conferences, saying, "No, do not dig up the Alaska wildlands to get gas and oil. Stop killing dolphins to get tuna fish. Outlaw all handguns now. Don't put dams in Grand Canyon. Do not outlaw abortion. Do not spend half the US budget on the military," etc.

If we get lucky, a bit of our own free speech might produce a short story on page 18 of the newspaper. We can also use Facebook and tweet, hoping to be re tweeted. But our powers to take effective action are clearly limited by control over the algorithm, and measly budgets. "Free speech" in the United States can be *very* expensive. For example, one "free speech" page in *The New York Times* in 2021 costs about $165,000. In *The Wall Street Journal*, it's $195,000. That may work for large, rich corporations, but for the rest of us, it's difficult. And that's just print media. It's not the only problem.

In 2017, total commercial advertising spending in the world, in all media, was roughly $700 *billion* dollars. About 30% of this global expenditure was made in the United States (i.e., about $225 billion). Total advertising spending by *non*-commercial, non-profit communities in the US was below ten *million* dollars that same year. In other words, commercial "free speech" advertising interests in the United States outspent non-corporate free speech, arguing contrasting views, by roughly 20 million-to-one. (20,000,000-1). That's the approximate ratio by which corporate or commercial interests dominate mass-media, "free-speech" ad expressions in the US (tweet media notwithstanding).

As my late partner in the commercial ad business in the 1960s, the amazing, brilliant, Howard Gossage often argued: "To appreciate the full consequences and powers of mass media advertising, it's important to understand the impacts of directed media imagery." Gossage was especially appalled by advertising on television. He explained it this way: "Once TV images are directed through your eyes and into your brains, they *never* leave. The images are permanent." Gossage liked to cite particular mid-1960 commercial images: "Did you know you had the Jolly Green Giant still living in your brain? Or the Geiko Gekko? Or, the Marlboro Man? Go ahead, try to erase them," he'd say.

The images you ingest from repetitive TV advertising—and now social media "influencers"—will permanently occupy your mind. Forever. You cannot get rid of them. This brings astounding advantages to the senders of mass-media imagery. It confirms their ability to permanently implant and to "occupy" mass consciousness. The power relationship is profoundly, insidiously inequitable.

A further example of the powers of image retention is the high percentage of TV/movie performers who get elected to high public office: Ronald Reagan, Arnold Schwarzenegger, Jesse Ventura, Sonny Bono, Clint Eastwood, Al Franken, Clay Aiken, George Murphy, and alas, Donald Trump! They are also, usually, re-elected.

Some lawyers argue that this situation violates the First Amendment to our Constitution. "Free speech" is obviously *not* "free." This cannot be what the First Amendment intended. Television, for example, did not even exist at the time the First Amendment was written. It came along two centuries later. So, considering the First Amendment's obvious intention to guarantee equal rights to "free speech" for all Americans and to sustain a democratic flow of information, the question becomes this: *Should advertising qualify as legal?* Doesn't it violate our Constitution? The "free speech" concept could obviously only have been meant to protect citizens handing out books, or printed flyers, or speaking at meetings, and from soap boxes.

There were no "mass media" in the 1780s; no TV or film, or any moving-image medium. The potentials for the domination of personal and national consciousness via media in the country, except perhaps by government, were minimal. But today, we have commercial advertising interests outspending non-commercial voices by *20 million to one,* with similar distortions in every medium.

Non-corporate campaigners—environmentalists, or health, or rights activists, et. al.—have exquisitely small budgets, if they have any budgets at all—by which to try and offset such a terribly one-sided information environment. Very few activist organizations have enough money to buy any advertising, leaving their campaign possibilities often reduced to protest marches, sign-holding, large rallies (if possible), online petitions, webinars, and tweets.

So, this book displays some remarkable efforts of those who, despite these distorted odds, *do* try to use mass media advertising for "free speech," seeking to offset the astounding advantages of corporate speech. It's the one vs. the 20 million; hoping to breakthrough and reach the public, along with pressuring the powers-that-be on major issues affecting society.

Amazingly, these counter efforts have often met with startling success. Despite the gigantic dominating expenditures by corporate interests, they are sometimes overcome by the fact that the actual truth has a "ring" to it. If people hear it, they often recognize it! Once an alternate point of view gets out on the table, victory suddenly becomes possible. And, some activists have learned ways to present truly effective counterpoint advertising, as we will see.

In this book, we display several dozen examples of successes, but also some non-successes, to reveal the true dynamics of the situation we face. And, to help us understand that it's sometimes possible to breakthrough, against great odds, against an otherwise overwhelming commercial domination of media and public consciousness.

★　　★　　★

THANK YOU

Many talented people over the last 40 years had key roles in writing, designing, or producing the examples shown in this book. I can't name them all, but a few are especially important. One of the greatest political ad writers in the world is Jono Polansky, who authored a dozen of the ads in this book. Special thanks also goes to several people who, over decades, helped produce and promote the key agencies that created these works. I speak especially of Herb Chao Gunther, who founded Public Media Center and was its Chief Executive over three decades, as well as Barbara Grob and Katie Kleinsasser, who were key operatives from the 1980s through the early 2000s. And, such designers as Daniela Sklan (who also did this book!), Marget Larsen, George Dippel, Elizabeth Garsonnin, and so many others. Thank you to all. Thanks especially to my wife and soul-mate, Koohan Paik-Mander. Her creative ideas and enthusiasm were important at every stage . . . and repeatedly helped carry us over difficult spots.

1

FROM ADMAN TO ANTI-ADMAN

The Committee Theatre
Howard Gossage: Ads for Cars, Beer & Paper Airplanes
Marshall McLuhan & Leopold Khor
David Brower, the Sierra Club, Grand Canyon & Personal Transformation

I GRADUATED FROM New York's Columbia University Graduate Business School in 1959, with a master's degree in International Economics. I was living in Greenwich Village at the time. Right after graduation, I tried to get a job with a New York Park Avenue ad agency, but was told "Your hair is too kinky; try Seventh Avenue."

I took my first full-time job commuting daily to Newark, to work for Worthington Corporation, a giant international industrial company. I worked in their public relations department, but I didn't like the commute and wasn't happy with the job. After a year, I decided to resign and join friends of mine who had moved to San Francisco.

I *loved* San Francisco!—the open Mediterranean feel of the place in those days; the light, the informality. It felt like living in the south of France.

My first California job was in 1960, working for Irving ("Bud") Levin in the publicity department of his San Francisco International Film Festival. Maybe that was the best decision of my life. My "job" was to promote the films that were being shown, and to meet and host media celebrities—visiting directors, movie stars, etc. —as they were coming through town. That included greeting and talking with such people as Norman Lear, George Peppard, Candice Bergen, Lenny Bruce, among many others. Not a tough task. I had to take them out to nice restaurants. I found most of them charming, interesting, smart, friendly, and of course, entertaining.

Besides hosting, my job was also to arrange interviews and press conferences and to write some promotional background stories. After learning the skills for a year and a half or so, I opened my own public relations firm, *Jerry Mander & Associates*, joined after a while by Zev Putterman to continue that kind of PR work—promotion, films, entertainers, and the like—all of which I enjoyed very much.

One of my most remarkable clients was the amazing *avant-garde* dancer Anna Halprin and her Dancers' Workshop Company. I had the pleasure of helping her arrange, and then accompanying the group on their tour of Europe in 1962. It included a full month's performance schedule at Teatro La Fenice in Venice, and then dates in Rome, Zagreb, and Paris. We were joined in those travels by several other *avant-garde* performance stars, featuring musicians John Cage, Mort Subotnick, Terry Reilly, and a long list of dancers including Daria and Rana Halprin, and John Graham. It was wonderful. All of it. Life was good.

THE COMMITTEE THEATRE

Another theatrical client that came along soon after Anna Halprin was "The Committee," a new satirical improvisational theatrical review company and night-club that opened in 1963 on Broadway in San Francisco's North Beach. They were an instant sensation. The Committee was an offshoot of prior improvisational satirical theatres like "Second City" in Chicago, and "Beyond the Fringe" in London. It was conceived, produced, and performed by Second City veterans, notably Alan Myerson, who managed and directed the new San Francisco team, joined by his wife, Jessica Myerson, who co-produced, and also performed on stage.

Being a publicist for The Committee was *very* easy work. The press was always ready and eager to meet and talk with members of the Committee's cast, at that time including the great Garry Goodrow, Larry Hankin, Hamilton Camp, Kathryn Ish, Dick Stahl and Peter Bonerz. Then a bit later came Carl Gottlieb, Scott Beech, Mimi Farina (sister of Joan Baez) and many others. They were all attention-grabbing, smart, and hilarious.

Within weeks of its launch, The Committee had become the toast of San Francisco and sold out almost every night. In the daytime, many of the actors volunteered their improvisational skills and humor to aid some of the public protests that were going on. This *was* the sixties! Especially in Berkeley. Students on campus, led by Mario Savio, had just shut down the University. At night, back in San Francisco, The Committee's lobby, with its appealing bar and lounge chairs, became a hangout for activists, celebrities, and notables of the period. Janis Joplin was often there, hanging out, holding court, and entertaining the crowd. Sometimes, she was joined by members of the Grateful Dead and other musicians as well as other celebrities passing through. This was non-stop fun!

It was on behalf of "The Committee" that I wrote and produced my very first full-page advertisement, which was notably successful. And it changed my life.

FIRST ADVERTISEMENT (1966)

So, here's how I got started in advertising. After a few months at The Committee, Alan Myerson told me about a weird public statement just issued from Washington, DC. The Pentagon had announced a new "heart-felt" program intended to make life more pleasant for thousands of Vietnamese children who'd lost their parents or relatives in the war, usually from US bombings and military actions. The US military didn't want those poor parentless Vietnamese kids to remain angry at the US once the war was over. So, the generals came up with a "brilliant" idea: to collect huge piles of toys and then *air-drop* the toys from military helicopters directly down to the kids. Instead of bombs, toys! What a great humanistic plan.

Myerson and I agreed that The Committee should announce its patriotic support of the program, and start collecting toys for the Pentagon. Then, we could gather the toys, put them in a helicopter, and deliver the toys to DC by *air-dropping them on the Pentagon!*

We decided we could help stimulate this patriotic plan by running a full-page advertisement in the *San Francisco Chronicle*. The ad would ask the public to participate in our humanitarian endeavor by bringing their spare toys to the Committee lobby. We'd then donate all the toys to this marvelous loving Pentagon effort. But . . . what kind of toys would be appropriate?

Given the kids' recent experiences, the most familiar toys would obviously be war toys. So, the Committee announced it would offer prizes for the best war toys, and then gather them all together. Then, in the spirit of the whole campaign, we'd save taxpayer dollars by renting our own helicopter to air-drop the cargo on the Pentagon.

I had only once before ever produced an advertment. It was a half-page one, months earlier, for a friend who ran a local bar. Where there'd once been San Francisco National Bank, he opened "San Francisco National Bar." That was kinda fun, but The Committee ad—full page in the *Chronicle*—was a life-changing experience. (*See opposite page*)

The War Toys ad announced our efforts to collect the greatest war toys we could find and to send them to the Pentagon to bring happiness to the unfortunate parentless kids in Vietnam.

The ad ran in the *Chronicle* in 1966. It was designed by my close friend Barbara Stauffacher, already a celebrated print designer in San Francisco. Stauffacher placed that beautiful toy shoulder bazooka in the ad. It was a very appealing instrument with which Vietnamese kids were surely familiar. They would certainly love to have a machine gun.

The response to the ad was gigantic; big newspaper and media stories; war toys arriving by the hundreds. Within days, The Committee lobby was overflowing with a mountain of toys. We held a press conference announcing that once we'd collected the toys over the following three weeks, we would deliver them free of charge, by helicopter, dropped onto the Pentagon.

Everyone thought that was an excellent idea! Except the FBI. Two agents visited us and threatened us with arrest, which unfortunately killed our delivery system plan. We sent them instead by truck. But…the point had been made. The Pentagon ultimately did

(text continued on page 4)

Give Now! Help American Efforts In Vietnam!
You May Win $100!

CONTEST:

Will Yours Be War Toy of the Week?

In the public service, an event sponsored by the Committee:
Helping collect war toys for our Pentagon.

eviewing Mr. Johnson's efforts in his struggle for peace, we were moved by this news item:

Pentagon Orders Air Drop of Toys To Viet Children

Washington

A shrewd move. After all, there is evidence the American image is declining.

Toys Will Help

Our leaders feel toys will help; for, our Pentagon reasons that toys will brighten the children's days and demonstrate our concern.

But what sort of toys? Barbie Dolls would clearly be in poor taste. Toy Cadillacs likewise. What then would Mr. Johnson, or say, General Westmoreland send? Training toys! They would doubtless choose toys to help train the young Viet for the life he can expect under our guidance.

Cash Prizes!

So, this contest (with cash prizes) is being held to collect toys of the kind our leaders would prefer.

For example, the plastic bazooka (pictured above) costs $11.00 and shoots a blast of air capable of dismantling cardboard structures at 40 feet. Auxiliary features are a three-stage rocket, a shoulder recoil pad, and a target which collapses when hit.

For the training of children on how to do-in the enemy, we doubt it has a peer.

Your Favorite

But then, you too have a favorite which might win First Prize, and it needn't be specific to Vietnam. As the salesgirl in the toy store told us, "These toys are good for ten years, and you never know who the enemy will be by then."

Napalm

You may want to enter the atomic tank which ejects napalm, thereby scorching the crops and starving the enemy ($11.95) or, the emergency hospital kit, featuring crutches, plasma, bandages, and stethoscope (only $1.20 plus tax) or maybe your taste runs to toys which train for jungle warfare.

Enter Now!

Whatever your special favorite enter our contest now. Deposit your toy at The Committee, 622 Broadway, during the next three weeks and become eligible for the War Toy of the Week prize, $100.00!

And the greatest satisfaction will be in knowing that on February 28 at Noon, we will deliver your entry and all others we collect, directly to the people to whom they will mean the most...our Pentagon Generals.

Delivery Device

Our delivery device will be parachute from a helicopter and can you think of a more apt one, considering the recipients? For our Pentagon Generals, removed as they are from the excitement of battle—consigned to mere statistics and the deciding of who will live and who will die—this should provide at least some of the thrill gifts delivered this way can bring.

Let Us Continue

So let us continue. And if you worry that a Vietnam accord will be reached before we can deliver our gift, remember there is always the Dominican Republic.

CONTEST RULES AND REGULATIONS

Entries must all be war toys and will be accepted February 1-20, between 6 and 11 P.M., excluding Mondays. They become the property of The Committee and will be used solely for purposes of delivery to The Pentagon. Mail entries accepted. Each Sunday evening during this period, a weekly winner of $100 will be selected by The Committee cast and announced. In case of ties prize will be divided. Entries will be judged on the basis of originality and aptness of thought.

The Committee

622 BROADWAY, SAN FRANCISCO - EX2-0807

not continue with its program, for still unannounced reasons. We thought we might have had something to do with it.

ENTER: **HOWARD GOSSAGE**

In the midst of all that tumult, I received a surprise telephone call from a well-known advertising iconoclast, Howard Gossage. I had read many impressive articles about Gossage, including his critiques of commercial advertising, but I had never met him. *That phone call changed my life!*

Gossage told me that he loved The Committee's War Toy ad. He laughed all the way through it, he said, and appreciated its political intentions. Gossage suggested that I drop by his ad agency—Freeman & Gossage—to talk things over. We got along very well. A couple more meetings followed, and he suggested that I move my whole publicity office inside his agency and start spending some of my time writing ads on a regular basis. He put me in charge of several clients, notably KLH audio systems, a very high-quality radio/stereo speaker company from Cambridge, Massachusettes. We were all so pleased at our new partnership, that I invited Gossage and his beautiful wife, the actress Sally Kemp, to appear as models in the upcoming advertisement for KLH audio (see opposite page). It was a notable success. Within a few years, Freeman & Gossage became Freeman, Mander & Gossage.

★   ★   ★

Howard Gossage ran his ad business like none other. He was already famous for being as much a critic of the advertising world as a proponent. He would publicly state that spending his days promoting corporate sales through advertising was "too trivial a pursuit for a grown man." He tried hard to change the deal, though he continued to work very successfully for many commercial clients, notably Eagle Shirt-makers, Rover & Land-Rover cars, Rainier Brewing Co., KLH audio systems, et. al., and *Scientific American* magazine, among others.

His ad campaigns were always unusual and entertaining, and would sometimes not even mention a client's product sales interests. And yet everyone loved working with him. His genius and humor were transparent and lively. For example, Gossage's advertising plan for Rainer Beer & Ale—which had come to the agency seeking new markets among "upscale" customers—was to promote the beer by offering great deals on new Beethoven Sweatshirts. That became a national sensation. In the 1960s, the sweatshirts were suddenly everywhere. Rainer was getting credit and doing well.

Gossage also suggested we promote Rover and Land-Rover cars by running ads with the headline: *Computer Commuting.* These would present an argument in favor of *less* use of cars, not more. It was to be a computer-organized ride-sharing scheme based on environmental concerns; too many cars on the road, and too much pollution. Keep in mind, this was five decades before the effects of cars on air quality became a big public issue in the US (And computers? They had just barely come on the scene.)

Gossage argued that if there were fewer, better, *smaller* cars on the road—like Rover—the environment would be aided. It was an extraordinary idea for the 1960s. But the client didn't like it! So, Gossage then organized a "car painting" competition instead, to see if the smaller Rover cars were easier to paint than big ones. And he ran a variety of ads asking questions like, *How Do You Feel About Billboards?* And another one focused on the fact that so many police departments, and also some criminals, used Rover cars to benefit their efforts. The headline for the first of those ads was *The Land-Rover and Crime.* It garnered a lot of friendly response.

As for *Scientific American Magazine,* Gossage's ad strategy was to launch *The Great International Paper Airplane Competition.* Here's the back-story on that campaign.

(text continued on page 9)

(This "Subjective value" analysis pertains to another remarkable, if controversial, feature of KLH stereo equipment.)

KLH & LOVE

A recent survey sponsored by KLH has proven beyond doubt that when you buy KLH stereo equipment you will love your wife (or husband) more.

Admittedly this is a flamboyant claim. However, let us review the facts:

This survey asked each respondent to assume that he was for some reason to be deprived of his wife (or husband), and to assume that dollars could somehow prevent the catastrophe.

We asked *how many* dollars it would be worth to keep her (him). Well gentlemen, the findings showed that owners of KLH equipment said, on the average, $541,616.23.

Owners of other sorts of equipment said a mere $362,615.59. There is, then, a difference of $179,000.64 in favor of the average KLH spouse.

Now if this difference in marital value is not attributable to the fact that KLH owners become more loving people, then what is it attributable to? The statistics offer us no other answer.

Oh, there will be cynics who will rationalize that these scientific findings are inconclusive.

But to us it is abundantly clear that when you buy a Model Twenty Four three piece stereo system at $320†, or a Model Twenty at $400†, and the full dynamic range of a symphony orchestra or a rock and roll group, as the case may be, or a crooner, even, is heard, as if for the first time, throbbing out from our famous speakers, you are bound to be a happier and more loving person for it, aren't you? You certainly are.

Yes.

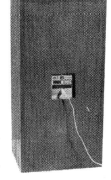

ADDENDUM: *For complete survey data (scientific findings on other things: toothpaste, wives, mechanics, tv programming, etc.), drop us a line, saying, "Love," at KLH, 30 Cross Street, Cambridge, Mass., 02139. (If you also would like a catalog, put it this way: "Love" "Catalog.")*
Yes.

†SUGGESTED RETAIL PRICE

Special Report:

"THE LAND-ROVER AND CRIME"

◆

PREFERRED BY THE POLICE OF 37 COUNTRIES
AND THE BANDITS OF AT LEAST 1

"THE
LAND-ROVER
AND CRIME"
(*cont. from previous page*)

DUE TO THE GROWING POPULARITY of the Land-Rover in the commission of grand theft, an interim report seems in order. Apparently our 4-wheel drive vehicle has latent virtues which may be of interest to the prospective owner.

It is not our intent here to point out raffish ways for one to pick up a great deal of extra money in one's spare time. Rather the opposite: to abet law and order by useful suggestion.

For instance: in two recent major crimes Land-Rovers were most helpful in hauling away £2,500,000 ($7,000,-000) and £90,000 ($252,000), respectively. Now, although it is well-known that the police of the United Kingdom also employ Land-Rovers, *nowhere is it reported that they employed them on these occasions for hot pursuit of the brigands.* Perhaps that was their mistake.

NEAR LEIGHTON BUZZARD, BEDS.

The first theft, widely if grudgingly admired for its sheer bulk of loot, was, of course, the Great Train Robbery which brought the title back to England.

This Olympics of knavery took place, you recall, at Cheddington, just five miles out of Leighton Buzzard, Bedfordshire, on August 8 last, a Thursday.

Nearly a week passed before any clues turned up. Then, on Tuesday, August 13, a Times of London article datelined Brill, Buckinghamshire, reported:

"A lonely farmhouse near here, twelve miles from Oxford, was the hideout for the mail train gang and their haul of £2,500,000 in bank notes. Mailbags in three abandoned vehicles—an Army type truck and two Land-Rovers—have been found but no money."

NOT LIKE DARTS

Dismissing the Army lorry, one surmises that the Land-Rovers were given the arduous getaway assignment not only for their rugged dependability, but for their capacious rear doors, as well.

Bank notes in excess of so many tend to be cumbersome. When you are trying to on-load literally bags and bags of the stuff you simply haven't got the time to aim nicely; it's not like darts.

No, robbing a train is a very near thing at best and one has got to have the tools to do the job.

FOUND BY MUSHROOMER

Paradoxically, another Land-Rover feature, its outstanding over-all height, caused the thieves to flee the farm, it is thought. According to The Times:

Left Profile . Rear View

"On Sunday afternoon a local man went mushrooming near the farm and noticed the top of a Land-Rover sticking out of a dilapidated outhouse among the trees." This he duly reported.

The Times account continues: "Police believe that the gang fled in haste. In the garden, near a row of runner beans, was a partly dug hole about 3 ft. deep, a spade still standing in a mound of clay.

"Detective Superintendent Fewtrell,

head of Buckinghamshire's C.I.D., surveyed the hole and commented. 'Presumably they intended burying the evidence. We know they got out before they intended...they must have got the wind up'."

Naturally we are pleased that, having been an accessory to the crime, the Land-Rover was also helpful in its solution.

LAND-ROVER STRIKES AGAIN

Though piddling by comparison, the latest Land-Rover effort—the Longfield, Kent, job of September 27—was respectable by county competition standards. It also illustrated an entirely different aspect of the Land-Rover's amazing versatility.

Under the headlines "£90,000 Stolen In Bank Van Ambush" and "Getaway By 8 Masked Men: Guard Felled By Cosh", The London Times describes how the armoured car was high jacked. The bandits lay in wait with their vehicles along a hedgelined road at the T-junction leading off to Horton Kirby and South Darenth. And then:

"A brick was hurled through the windscreen of the bank van, forcing the driver to stop. The bank van was hemmed in by the Land-Rover and the lorry." Whereupon the bandits leaped from the ambush vehicles armed with pick-axe handles, enveloped the bank van, carried the day, and drove off towards Horton Kirby.

To our knowledge this is the first time the Land-Rover has been used in the actual *commission* of a stick-up of this magnitude. While this dubious demonstration of its versatility would seem conclusive, one wonders: what would the

(*cont. on next page*)

outcome have been had the victim-vehicle *also* been a Land-Rover (Model 109 Bank Van)? An interesting conjecture.

LAW-FEARERS ASK

"Why," decent law-fearing people may ask, "do you sell Land-Rovers to chaps who are going to use them to rob trains and banks?"

Actually, we can't always tell.

We've sold Land-Rovers to all sorts of customers in over 160 countries, including the armed services of 26, the police forces of 37, veritable legions of country squires, desert chieftains, titled persons, oil and gold prospectors, light and heavy sportsmen; and to multitudes of nice families for skiing, beach buggy-ing and other pleasant things. With this limitless range we often don't know precisely how a buyer intends to use his Land-Rover.

NEW OWNER OFTEN CLUELESS

More often than not the new owner doesn't know himself until he's tested its enormous virtuosity. For all we know, the recent bandits were ordinary citizens who only turned to lives of crime *after* they found their Land-Rovers were just the thing for sticking up trains.

As a matter of fact, we can give you what appears to be a character reference on one of our customers; this one also from The London Times of August 13. A member of the Mail Train Mob got the key to the farmhouse hideout from a neighboring housewife (he said he was the new owner).

She describes him thus: "He was a well dressed, well spoken, and charming man. I have not seen him since."

Neither have we; we do hope he's keeping it serviced.

■ ■ ■ ■ ■ ■ ■ ■ ■ ■ ■ ■ ■ ■

BORED WITH YOUR
PRESENT LIFE?

IF YOU STILL TRUST THE MAILS, MAIL THIS COUPON TODAY!

Rover Motor Co. of N. America Ltd.
Section 009
405 Lexington Ave., N. Y. 17.

My name is:

_____

Address_____

City_____State_____

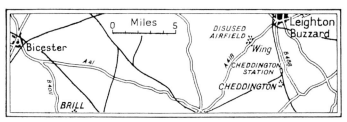

9

[*Scientific American Calls For Entries: Can It Be There's A Paper Plane Which Makes The SST 30 Years Obsolete?*]

1st International Paper Airplane Competition

SCIENTIFIC AMERICAN primarily concerns itself with what Man is up to these days, and our readership is known for travelling more than that of any other magazine. So it is little wonder we have spent considerable time studying the two designs for the supersonic SST airplane recently announced by Boeing and Lockheed. (See Fig. 1 and Fig. 2.)

Soon we'll all be flying around in thin air at Mach 2.7, i.e., from New York to London in 150 minutes. Quite a prospect!

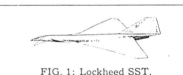

FIG. 1: Lockheed SST.

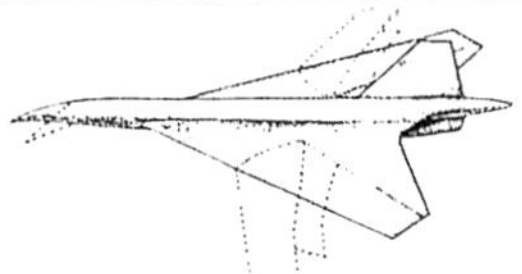

FIG. 2: Boeing SST.

Still, at the close of our inquiry there remained this nagging thought: Hadn't we seen these designs somewhere before?

Of course. Paper airplanes. Fig. 3 and Fig. 4 illustrate only the more classical paper plane designs, in use since the 1920's or so, having a minimum performance capability of 15 feet and four seconds.* (See over)

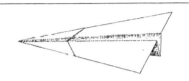

FIG. 3: Paper plane circa 1920, the classic paper plane. Smoothness of flight, grace.

FIG. 4: First developed among paper airplane designers in the 1930's. Known for spectacular darting motions. Note hooked nose.

We do not mean to question the men at Boeing and Lockheed, or their use of traditional forms. But it seems to us unjust that several million paper plane designers around the world are not also given their due, a credit which if it had been extended some years ago would have saved the pros quite some straining at the drawing boards.

Well anyway, with design having caught up with itself, we can now postulate that there is, right now, flying down some hallway or out of some moviehouse balcony in Brooklyn, the aircraft which will make the SST 30 years obsolete. No?

Consider this: Never since Leonardo da Vinci, the Patron Saint of paper airplanes, has such a wealth of flight

research and experimentation remained untouched by cross-disciplinary study and publication. Paper airplane design has become one of those secret pleasures performed behind closed doors. Everybody does it, but nobody knows what anyone else has learned.

Many's the time we've spied a virtuoso paper plane turn the corner of the office hallway, or suddenly rise up over

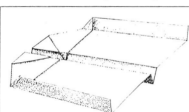

FIG. 5: Drawn from memory, this plane was last seen in 12th floor stairwell at 415 Madison Avenue. Do you know its designer? Where is he?

the desk, or on one occasion we'll never forget, veer first down the stairs to the left, and suddenly to the right, staying aloft 12 seconds in all. (See Fig. 5.)

But who is its designer? Is he a Board Chairman or a stock boy? And what has he done lately?

All right then. In the interests of filling this information gap, and in light of the possibility that the future of aeronautics may now be flying in a paper plane, we are hereby calling for entries.

[*Leonardo Papers Found; Other Developments Analyzed*]

1ST INTERNATIONAL PAPER AIRPLANE COMPETITION; A LAST BACKWARD GLANCE

Fig. 1. Six members of the Panel of Jurors at the 1st International Paper Airplane Competition shown during Final Flyoffs observing one of 43 finalists launched for their study and the press. The particular entry they are watching was entered in the distance category, and flew some 87 feet before crashing into a CBS camera, at one foot three inches above ground. It was reflown.

By now, most of you are acquainted with the names, performances and other details of the Final Flyoffs held Washington's Birthday Eve at the New York Hall of Science. (As one news account put it, the event "drew international press coverage not seen since the visit of Pope Paul.")

For ready reference, however, we record the winners elsewhere on this page, together with performance data where applicable.

Our *primary* purpose now, is to review with you what we have learned from this experiment.

This much *is* certain. At long last the hitherto uncelebrated and uncatalogued achievements of aircraft design's "underground" have had their day in the sky.

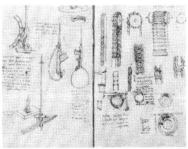

Fig. 2. The Leonardo. Proud possession of 7 winners whose paper planes were judged best of 11,851 entries.

And, there's this: A mere eight weeks after our competition was formally announced the long lost notebooks of Leonardo da Vinci, the Patron Saint of Paper Airplanes, whose name graces our winner's trophy (see Fig. 2 and Fig. 3), were suddenly discovered.

If no further benefit accrued to science during this project, would not this discovery be ample?

But, going on....

One of our distinguished panel of jurors, Prof.

Fig. 3. Two pages of drawings by Leonardo da Vinci, Patron Saint of Paper Airplanes, discovered eight weeks after competition was announced. This development alone is said to have made the entire project worthwhile.

David Hazen of Princeton's Aeronautics Dept., when asked if indeed we *had* found the key to the SST of the year 2000 flying about in a paper airplane, stated categorically, "No, we have learned nothing new at all."

BERKELEY PROTEST

Not wishing to excite controversy within academia, we must yet observe that another juror, Prof. Edmund Laitone of Berkeley protested, believing Prof. Hazen may have spoken hastily.

Fig. 4. Entry from Mr. P. W. Swift of Xerox Corp., considered by Prof. Edmund Laitone, Chairman of the Aeronautics Dept. at the Univ. of California, Berkeley, so interesting aerodynamically, as to warrant "serious additional study."

Several of the entries need further study, Prof. Laitone indicated, particularly one dart-like object distinguished by flight-perpendicular ring air foils (hoops) both forward and aft. (See Fig. 4.) Prof. Laitone felt "it raises important questions concerning an aspect of aerodynamics that has had virtually no study."

"I would like to know," he added, "exactly what the optimum diameter-length ratio for cylindrical lifting surfaces would be at various Mach and Reynolds numbers? We may find it demonstrates lift characteristics and stability potentials applicable to *both* supersonic and subsonic speeds."

An exciting prospect to be sure.

And now on to the statistical data.

U. S. GOVERNMENT

In all, 5,144 people entered 11,851 airplanes. They came from 28 countries including Liberia and Switzerland, though the largest number of foreign entries were from Japan (some 750), mostly in origami categories. The U. S. government, while not admitting that it considered the winning of this competition vital to national interests, was represented by entries from 18 of its agencies.

Fig. 5. Actual size study of smallest entry. Entered in the distance category with instructions to drop straight down from upstretched hand. It was decided, however, that distance would be judged on horizontal rather than downward vertical, as that measure would be limited by the inherent size of the individual dropping it. Furthermore, entry was discovered to be made from foil, not paper.

The smallest entry received measured .08 x .00003 inches (see Fig. 5) submitted by the Space Particles and Field Dept. of Aerospace Corp. The largest entry was 11 feet. Entered in the distance flown category, it flew two times its length.

DR. SAKODA

The most interesting statistic, we believe, is that against an estimated 5,000 entries from children, the seven winners were all grownups and between them have devoted 314 years to paper airplane design and experimentation. All seven are engaged in science and engineering, even the ori-

gami winner, Dr. James Sakoda, a professor of anthropology who specializes in computer programming.

Frederick Hooven, of Ford, whose flying wing (see Fig. 6) won in duration aloft, learned his aerodynamics as a student of Orville Wright's, using Mr. Wright's own wind tunnel for early testing.

And Capt. R. S. Barnaby, an aerobatics winner, was founder of the N. Y. Model Aero Club back in 1909.

ENGLAND, 1934

Captain Barnaby presented us with the startling news that the very model that won him first place in our competition won him second place in a paper plane competition in England, 1934.

Does this suggest that aerodynamics has retrogressed over the years? It is hard to say since who knows *what* won first place in '34?

Fig. 6. Flying wing which won duration aloft category. It is shown here in stroboscopic illumination taken at 17 images per second.

You see, without continuously available data, we have merely our imaginations to guide us, which brings us to this special good news:

Commander Richard Schreder, another of our jury who is also national Soaring Champion, has suggested that the American Soaring Society will be pleased to keep our effort aloft, as it were, by sponsoring the 2nd International Paper Airplane Competition, a suggestion we heartily endorse.

For, even as a magazine whose readership is devoted to technological advance and for whom air travel is a way of daily life, we still remain convinced that there is a world of discovery, pleasure and satisfaction in all manner of subsonic activity, from the walking through forests to the flying of paper airplanes. Or as Capt. Lee Cermak, still another of our judges and pilot of the Goodyear blimp Mayflower put it:

"I don't care how much you fly, you won't ever see a jet stop, just to take a better look at the sharks."

WINNERS OF THE LEONARDO

Duration aloft Nonprofessional*	Jerry A. Brinkman Assistant Sales Manager Globe Industries, Dayton, Ohio	9.9 seconds aloft
Duration aloft Professional**	Frederick Hooven, Special Consultant to the General Manager, Ford Motor Co., Detroit	10.2 seconds aloft
Distance flown Nonprofessional	Louis W. Schultz, Engineering Group Manager, Stewart Warner Corp., Oak Brook, Illinois	58 feet, 2 inches
Distance flown Professional	Robert B. Meuser, Lawrence Radiation Lab., Univ. of California, Berkeley	91 feet, 6 inches (At this point, while still aloft entry hit rear wall of Hall of Science.)
Aerobatics Nonprofessional	Edward L. Ralston, University of Illinois, (and Clark, Dietz & Associates, Consulting Engineers) Urbana, Illinois	
Aerobatics Professional	Capt. R. S. Barnaby, USN (Ret.), Exhibits Consultant to the Director, Science Museum, Franklin Institute, Philadelphia, Penn.	
Origami Nonprofessional	Prof. James Sakoda, Professor of Sociology and Anthropology, Brown University, Providence, Rhode Island	
Origami Professional	The judges did not consider that any entry in this category was worthy of The Leonardo.	

*"Nonprofessionals" were defined in our rules as those not involved professionally in air travel.

**"Professionals" were defined as "people employed in the air travel business, people who build non-paper airplanes, and people who subscribe to Scientific American, because they so much."

NOTE: All entries were pre-tested by students of the NASA Goddard Inst. of Space Studies who reported that entries performed considerably better in preliminary testing than in the finals. The reason for this was not nervousness before the judges, but rather that the TV lights created severe thermals invariably hazardous to paper plane flight.

Gerard Piel, the publisher of *Scientific American*—himself a major intellectual leader in the scientific world at that time—had come to the agency to ask if we could help him. Piel was frustrated that he had not been able to attract more advertisers' interest in *Scientific American* from the aeronautics and travel industries. Those ads were noticeably absent from *Scientific American*. Piel couldn't understand why, and he wanted us to help.

We had a great series of very entertaining meetings, and elaborate elongated lunches. Gossage and Piel got along great, and during one of the meetings Howard burst forth with one of his typically unanticipated brilliant ideas. "If you want to attract the aeronautics and airline advertisers," he said, "just run a *paper airplane* contest! That will surely get attention from the aeronautics industry," Gossage said. The ads would invite the industry people (and the general public) to express their latest design wisdoms…via paper airplanes. The public will love it, Howard said, and "so will the aeronautics industry," as he burst out laughing, "and some great ideas might emerge."

Piel laughed too, and then said, "Okay." Howard then turned to me and asked me to write the ads, fast. George Dippel, one of the agency's brilliant art directors, designed them, and he also drew some very provocative paper plane designs as stimulants.

The first *Scientific American* paper airplane ads ran in the *The New York Times* and *The New Yorker* in December 1966, and were an instantaneous hit. The campaign was greeted with enormous enthusiasm, and brought more than 11,000 mailed-in responses from 28 countries: actual packages of folded paper airplanes, sometimes very complex and ingenious.

The judging committee included a couple of well-known aeronautic scientists, augmented by sky-diving champions, glider pilots, and the pilot of the Goodyear Blimp! The finalists were flown before the judges and a sold-out audience at the New York Hall of Science. The event received more media attention than a simultaneous visit to New York City by the Pope, though . . . . I frankly never did find out to what degree sales increased. That became almost secondary; *Scientific American* was all over the press at that point, and Gerard Piel and his ad department and everyone else were very happy.

ENTER: MARSHALL MCLUHAN

Well, I could go on with stories like that based on Howard Gossage's unique creative instincts, but there was another side to working with him that was equally important. While all that advertising stuff was going on, Howard was simultaneously devoting much of his time doing what he *really* loved. That was to launch and celebrate new political and philosophical ideas. Howard himself became most famous, in the 1960s, for nationally launching two little-known iconoclastic philosophers: Marshall McLuhan *("Understanding Media"),* and Leopold Khor *("The Breakdown of Nations").* These were not "clients." They were emerging intellectual visionaries that Howard wanted to help make famous. Because, well, he loved doing that.

In each case Gossage hosted large three-day private, invitational seminars in our office conference room, for an invited audience of 50 or so national intelligentsia, intending to introduce these still unrecognized intellectuals to a literary public. This is where Tom Wolfe met McLuhan for the first time, kicking off Wolfe's series of famous articles about McLuhan, and thus began their very long public relationship. Gossage also hosted Leopold Khor, a brilliant economic radical from Ireland, and a group of activists who decided to travel to Anguilla to support a burgeoning independence movement there that Khor was advocating. Howard went too.

That latter effort did *not* succeed in saving Anguilla, except that Gossage's advocacy definitely put Khor's great book on the best-seller list, alongside McLuhan's. They both became among the most important, radical intellectuals of the mid-1960s.

And then, soon after that, walking in the front door of the agency without any appointment, came yet another man who changed *my* life!

ENTER: DAVID BROWER & THE SIERRA CLUB

Of all the big revelations and turning points in that remarkable decade, the one that directly affected my life the most came on the day when David Brower, who was then Executive Director of the Sierra Club, decided to visit our agency. He had no appointment. And he didn't come to see either Howard Gossage or me. Brower was an admirer of the *style* of our agency, he said, and he was particularly eager to meet Marget Larsen, the agency's chief graphic designer.

Brower was carrying in his pocket a full text he had already written for an advertisement that he wanted us to run, "to save the Grand Canyon." His goal was to somehow stop the US government (Lyndon Johnson administration) from proceeding with its plans to build two giant dams inside the Grand Canyon walls. The dams would have flooded the Grand Canyon to a depth of 800 feet—deeper than the Statue of Liberty is tall—thus destroying 150 million years of natural history and incredible beauty, visited and loved by millions of Americans.

A third dam, further upstream at Glen Canyon, but not technically part of the Grand Canyon, had already been built. Brower was miserable about that, furious with himself for not having managed to block it. He pledged his life to block these next two dams. Nonetheless, in 1966, the Grand Canyon dam plan was on the verge of approval by Congress.

The government's argument in favor of the dams was that they would generate sufficient electricity to greatly expand real estate and industrial development in the gorgeous surrounding desert region, thus supporting power companies and developers in Arizona, New Mexico, Utah, Colorado, and California. A secondary argument that the Interior Department used to aggressively promote the dams was that with 800 foot deep rivers, tourists in power boats "would be better able to view the ancient canyon walls more closely." I'll come back to that one in a moment.

Desperate to build resistance to the dams, Brower had already written his own version of an advertisement he wanted to place, and he came to the agency to beg Marget Larsen to design it for him. Dave was a big fan of Larsen's unusual classical design approach, which entirely characterized the agency's ad style. He felt that kind of design would be perfect to provide a conservationist feeling.

Marget appreciated Brower's compliments but told him he'd have to first meet with Howard and me. Brower resisted, but then finally agreed. It began a long collaboration between us, actually lasting over 20 years, including work on dozens of ads about many different issues.

But on this first occasion, the mood was difficult. Brower asked us to accept and insert *his* version of the anti-dams ad. Howard and I read it and argued vociferously with Brower about it. We warned Brower that his ad as written would not be effective.

We were getting nowhere with him. But then Howard proposed yet another of his non-stop brilliant ideas. He suggested that we should have a competition in the *The New York Times*—one ad that we would quickly write vs. the ad that Brower had written. Marget Larsen would design them both in the same style.

In those days, *The New York Times* offered ad agencies a competition option, to test out which of two ads might perform better. *The Times* called it "A–B" and it meant that each "hit" of the paper on the presses would be rotated, one hit for each ad. In the end, we could measure (by the number of coupon responses from each ad) which one was most effective.

Brower burst out laughing at the proposed competition, but cheerfully agreed. Gossage then turned to me and said I should please immediately go home. I had 48 hours to draft a competitive ad, closer to our own standards. Here's the straight-forward headline I wrote:

> *"NOW ONLY YOU CAN SAVE GRAND CANYON FROM BEING FLOODED . . . FOR PROFIT."*

Then came another brilliant idea from Howard. Each of the competing ads should include a series of *six* response coupons; cut-outs, addressed to key administration officials, including President Johnson, Secretary of the Interior Stewart Udall, as well as Chairman of the House Interior Committee, Wayne Aspinall, plus three others, demanding that they immediately drop the project. Flooding the Grand Canyon was a terrible plan. *(see pages 12-13)*

This idea of "multiple response coupons" was actually a *first* for the advertising world. Ads did often appear with one coupon, to send money or seek rewards, etc. But never before had multiple coupons been used for urgent messaging, to urge an administration toward serious policy change. It was a technique we used over and over again for many decades, as we found it to be an excellent device on many grounds.

(Later in this book, I will argue that 5,000 coupons delivered this way is far more powerful and impressive than 500,000 two-second tweets. Another effect is that having to make a physical effort to mail them radicalizes the sender as much as it impresses the receiver.)

So, going back to the 1966 competition between Brower and us: the *Times* test showed that our ad was out-pulling Brower's ad by 2-1. Over the next 20 years that I worked with him, Brower never again proposed that he should write his own ads.

"SISTINE CHAPEL"

We did not stop with just one ad. Six weeks later, we ran another ad in *The New York Times*. That ad contained a specific response to the bizarre argument that people in the Bureau of Reclamation were using. The Bureau was asserting that the public *wants* to flood the rivers in Grand Canyon so they can get into small boats high up in the canyon and be able to touch its beautiful walls! That dumb argument was killed off forever in one afternoon's public testimony before Congress, by one of Brower's key Sierra Club assistants, the brilliant Hugh Nash. Hugh responded to that statement by asking the congressional committee: "Well, should we also flood the Sistine Chapel, so tourists can get nearer the ceiling?" *(see page 17, point 4)*

Hugh Nash's line stopped that argument cold, and it later became the headline of our most successful and famous advertisement.

The "Sistine Chapel" ad and the prior newspaper ads produced an unprecedented public outcry. Wayne Aspinall, Chairman of the House Interior Committee, who had been a strong advocate of the Grand Canyon dam proposals, announced he would withdraw his support. He specifically cited that ad and quoted its headline as causing a huge public outcry.

Soon after, Secretary of the Interior Stewart Udall also indicated that he had never received such a huge written protest on any project he'd worked on. It lead Secretary Udall to publicly credit the ad series as being the primary reason that he, and the Johnson administration, were reversing field. They announced they would *permanently* halt advocacy or production of the Grand Canyon dams, a policy that has sustained to this day, six decades later.

Even more important was that this victory on a major controversial national environmental battle in the 1960s played a major role in transforming what had been a relatively moderate, quiet movement of "companions on the trail," as Gossage liked to put it, into an expanding, aggressive, activist environmental movement that retains great power today.

Brower and the Sierra Club suddenly became celebrated national heroes, and the club's membership quickly *doubled*, thus bursting out a new politically oriented national and international environmental movement that had never existed before and continues today.

Brower was quick to recognize the momentum of the moment. He seized the opportunity to immediately and aggressively move forward onto several more issues. We quickly did two more very successful ads toward the establishment of the first Redwood National Park in Northern California, thus preventing the logging of one of the few remaining intact redwood forests in the world. That was soon followed by a successful push for a North Cascades National Park, and an attack on the proposed "Peripheral Canal" that was planned to bring California's abundant water supply to desert regions in southern California that developers hungered after.

But then, only a few years after this burst of successful advertising, a shocking event took place within the Sierra Club: Dave Brower was suddenly *fired* for doing one ad that was not officially authorized by the club's Board of Directors.

That ad, *"Earth National Park,"* was the first notable national effort to bring forward a major argument that Brower had been wanting to make: the case against *anthropocentrism*. The ad, partly written by Brower himself, focused on disputing the belief that human beings are some kind of natural royalty of the Earth, and should be the unquestioned rulers of the planet, and of evolution itself. In fact, as the "Sistine Chapel" ad pointed out, modern humans had just recently emerged—a few hundred thousand years ago—as compared with elephants (60 million years), reptiles (275 million years), corals (575 million years)—and the living planet itself (about 4 billion years). And yet our modern system operates under the clear assumption that human beings represent a kind of superior status *above* nature and all other living creatures. We were just learning to call this "anthropocentrism," the belief that we embody a Divine Right to rule over the rest of the natural world—despite its billions of years' tenure—and if possible, the cosmos as well.

Brower hated this idea/assumption (as do I), and he hoped that "Earth National Park" would at least enable some new discussions. In the late 1960s, any oncoming global environmental breakdown still seemed a long way off, though it was already becoming obvious that humans were doing a god-awful job of managing evolution. Rachel Carson's ground-breaking best-selling book a few years earlier, *Silent Spring*, had already set off huge alarms. But they were not yet sufficiently heeded.

Brower was eager to accelerate the discussion. He decided he would "roll the dice" on his Earth National Park idea. Fearful that this subject might involve too

(text continued on page 15)

FOR EARTH'S SAKE

THE NEW YORK TIMES, THURSDAY, JUNE 9, 1966.

ADVERTISEMENT

Now Only You Can Save Grand Canyon From Being Flooded.... For Profit

(If they can turn Grand Canyon into a "cash register" is any national park safe? You know the answer.)

Yes, that's right, *Grand Canyon!* The facts are these:

1. Bill H.R. 4671 is now before Rep. Wayne Aspinall's (Colo.) House Committee on Interior and Insular Affairs. This bill provides for two dams—Bridge Canyon and Marble Gorge—which would stop the Colorado River and flood water back into the canyon.

2. Should the bill pass, two standing lakes will fill what is presently 130 miles of canyon gorge. As for the wild, running Colorado River, the canyon's sculptor for 25,000,000 years, it will become dead water.

3. In some places the canyon will be submerged five hundred feet deep. "The most revealing single page of the earth's history," as Joseph Wood Krutch has described the fantastic canyon walls, will be drowned.

The new artificial shoreline will fluctuate on hydroelectric demand. Some days there will only be acres of mud where the flowing river and living canyon now are.

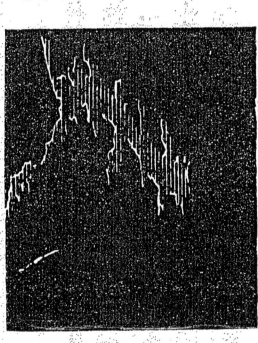

The Grand Canyon: How man plans to improve it. *(Newsweek, May 30, 1966)* U. S. Bureau of Reclamation.

9. What to do? Letters and wires are effective, and so are the forms at right once you have signed them and mailed them. (You will notice that there is also one in the box below to the Sierra Club; that's us.)

4. Why are these dams being built, then? For commercial power. They are dams of the sort which their sponsor, the Bureau of Reclamation of the Department of the Interior, calls "cash registers."

In other words, these dams aren't even to store water for people and farms, but to provide *auxiliary* power for industry. Arizona power politics in your Grand Canyon.

Moreover, Arizona doesn't need the dams to carry out its water development. Actually, it would have more water without the dams.

5. For, the most remarkable fact is that, as Congressional hearings have confirmed, seepage and evaporation at these remote damsites would annually *lose* enough water to supply both Phoenix and Tucson.

As for the remainder, far more efficient power sources are available right now, and at lower net cost. For the truth is, that the Grand Canyon dams will cost far more than they can earn.

6. Recognizing the threat to Grand Canyon, the Bureau of the Budget (which speaks for the President on such matters) has already suggested a moratorium on one of the dams and proposed a commission consider alternatives.

This suggestion has been steadily resisted by Mr. Aspinall's House Committee, which continues to proceed with H. R. 4671. It has been actively fought by the Bureau of Reclamation.

7. At the same time, interestingly, other Bureaus within Secretary Udall's domain (notably National Parks, Fish and Wildlife, Indian Affairs, Mines, Outdoor Recreation, Geological Survey) have been discouraged from presenting their findings, obtained at public expense. Only the Reclamation Bureau has been heard.

8. Meanwhile, in a matter of days the bill will be on the floor of Congress and—let us make the shocking fact completely clear—it will probably pass.

The only thing that can stop it is your prompt action.

10. Remember, with all the complexities of Washington politics and Arizona politics, and the ins and outs of committees and procedures, there is only one simple, incredible issue here: This time it's the Grand Canyon they want to flood. *The Grand Canyon.*

WHAT THE SIERRA CLUB IS FOR

The Sierra Club, founded in 1892 by John Muir, is nonprofit, supported by people who sense what Thoreau sensed when he wrote, "In wildness is the preservation of the world." The club's program is nationwide, includes wilderness trips, books, and films—and a major effort to protect the remnant of wilderness in the Americas.

There are now twenty chapters, branch offices in New York, Washington, Albuquerque, Seattle, and Los Angeles, and a main office in San Francisco.

This advertisement has been made possible by individual contributions, particularly from our Atlantic, Rocky Mountain, Rio Grande, Southern California and Grand Canyon chapter members, and by buyers of Sierra Club books everywhere, especially the twelve in the highly praised Exhibit Format Series, which includes books on Grand Canyon, Glen Canyon, the Redwoods, the Northern Cascades, Mount Everest, and the Sierra.

David Brower, Executive Director,
Sierra Club
Mills Tower, San Francisco, California

☐ Please send me more of the details of the battle to save Grand Canyon.

☐ I know how much this sort of constructive protest costs. Here is my donation of $_____ to help you continue your work.

☐ Please send me a copy of "Time and the River Flowing," the famous four-color book by Philip Hyde and François Leydet which tells the whole story of Grand Canyon and the battle to save it. I am enclosing $25.00

☐ I would like to be a member of the Sierra Club. Enclosed is $14.00 for entrance fee and first year's dues.

Name _____
Address _____
City _____ State _____ Zip _____

Note: All contributions and membership dues are deductible.

Address _____
City _____ State _____ Zip _____

No. 3

REPRESENTATIVE WAYNE ASPINALL
HOUSE OF REPRESENTATIVES
WASHINGTON 25, D.C.

I URGE YOU TO HALT PROCEEDINGS ON H.R. 4671, NOW IN YOUR COMMITTEE, AND TO SEEK EXPERT TESTIMONY FROM THE MANY INTERIOR DEPARTMENT AGENCIES THAT HAVE NOT YET APPEARED BEFORE YOU. THANK YOU.

Name _____
Address _____
City _____ State _____ Zip _____

No. 4 (To your Congressman)

REPRESENTATIVE _____
HOUSE OF REPRESENTATIVES
WASHINGTON 25, D.C.

PLEASE JOIN IN THE FIGHT TO SAVE GRAND CANYON BY URGING DELETION OF BOTH DAMS PROPOSED IN H.R. 4671. THANK YOU.

Name _____
Address _____
City _____ State _____ Zip _____

No. 5 (To one of your U.S. Senators)

SENATOR _____
UNITED STATES SENATE
WASHINGTON 25, D.C.

PLEASE JOIN IN THE FIGHT TO SAVE GRAND CANYON BY URGING DELETION OF BOTH DAMS PROPOSED IN H.R. 4671. THANK YOU.

Name _____
Address _____
City _____ State _____ Zip _____

No. 6 (To your state's other Senator)

SENATOR _____
UNITED STATES SENATE
WASHINGTON 25, D.C.

PLEASE JOIN IN THE FIGHT TO SAVE GRAND CANYON BY URGING DELETION OF BOTH DAMS PROPOSED IN H.R. 4671. THANK YOU.

Name _____
Address _____
City _____ State _____ Zip _____

SHOULD WE ALSO FLOOD THE SISTINE CHAPEL SO TOURISTS CAN GET NEARER THE CEILING?

EARTH began four billion years ago and Man two million. The Age of Technology, on the other hand, is hardly a hundred years old, and on our time chart we have been generous to give it even the little line we have.

It seems to us hasty, therefore, during this blip of time, for Man to think of directing his fascinating new tools toward altering irrevocably the forces which made him. Nonetheless, in these few brief years among four billion, wilderness has all but disappeared. And now these:

1) There is a bill in Congress to "improve" Grand Canyon. Two dams will back up artificial lakes into 148 miles of canyon gorge. This will benefit tourists in power boats, it is argued, who will enjoy viewing the canyon wall more closely. (See headline). Submerged underneath the tourists will be part of the most revealing single page of earth's history. The lakes will be as deep as 600 feet (deeper for example, than all but a handful of New York buildings are high) but in a century, silting will have replaced the water with that much mud, wall to wall.

There is no part of the wild Colorado River, the Grand Canyon's sculptor, that will not be maimed.

Tourist recreation, as a reason for the dams, is in fact an afterthought. The Bureau of Reclamation, which backs them, prefers to call the dams "cash registers." They are expected to make money by sale of commercial power.

They will not provide anyone with water.

2) In Northern California, four lumber companies are about to complete logging the private virgin redwood forests, an operation which to give you an idea of its size, has taken fifty years.

Soon, where nature's tallest living things have stood silently since the age of the dinosaurs, the extent of the cutting will make creation of a redwood national park absurd.

The companies have said tourists want only enough roadside trees for the snapping of photos. They offer to spare trees for this purpose, and not much more. The result will remind you of the places on your face you missed while you were shaving.

3) And up the Hudson, there are plans for a power complex —a plant, transmission lines, and a reservoir on top of Storm King Mountain—destroying one of the last wild and high and beautiful spots near New York City.

4) A proposal to flood a region in Alaska as large as Lake Erie would eliminate at once the breeding grounds of more wildlife than conservationists have preserved in history.

5) In San Francisco, real estate developers are day by day filling a bay that made the city famous, putting tract

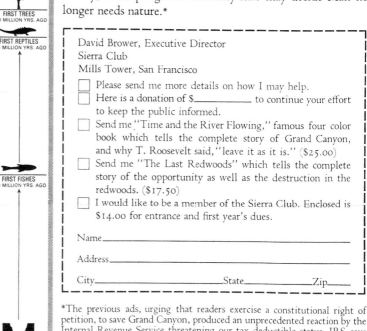

houses over the fill; and now there's a new idea—still more fill, enough for an air cargo terminal as big as Manhattan.

There exists today a mentality which can conceive such destruction, giving commerce as ample reason. For 74 years, the 40,000 member Sierra Club has opposed that mentality. But now, when even Grand Canyon can be threatened, we are at a critical moment in time.

This generation will decide if something untrammelled and free remains, as testimony we had love for those who follow.

We have been taking ads, therefore, asking people to write their Congressmen and Senators; Secretary of the Interior Stewart Udall; The President; and to send us funds to continue the battle. Thousands *have* written, but meanwhile, the Grand Canyon legislation has advanced out of committee and is near a House vote. More letters are needed and more money, to help fight a mentality that may decide Man no longer needs nature.*

David Brower, Executive Director
Sierra Club
Mills Tower, San Francisco

☐ Please send me more details on how I may help.
☐ Here is a donation of $_____ to continue your effort to keep the public informed.
☐ Send me "Time and the River Flowing," famous four color book which tells the complete story of Grand Canyon, and why T. Roosevelt said, "leave it as it is." ($25.00)
☐ Send me "The Last Redwoods" which tells the complete story of the opportunity as well as the destruction in the redwoods. ($17.50)
☐ I would like to be a member of the Sierra Club. Enclosed is $14.00 for entrance and first year's dues.

Name_____

Address_____

City_____ State_____ Zip____

---

*The previous ads, urging that readers exercise a constitutional right of petition, to save Grand Canyon, produced an unprecedented reaction by the Internal Revenue Service threatening our tax deductible status. IRS says the ads may be a "substantial" effort to "influence legislation." Undefined, these terms leave organizations like ours at the mercy of administrative whim. (The question has not been raised with any organizations that favor Grand Canyon dams.) So we cannot now promise that contributions you send us are deductible—pending results of what may be a long legal battle.

The Sierra Club, founded in 1892 by John Muir, is nonprofit, supported by people who, like Thoreau, believe "In wildness is the preservation of the world." The club's program is nationwide, includes wilderness trips, books and films—as well as such efforts as this to protect the remnant of wilderness in the Americas. There are now twenty chapters, branch offices in New York (Biltmore Hotel), Washington (Dupont Circle Building), Los Angeles (Auditorium Building), Albuquerque, Seattle, and main office in San Francisco.

big a leap for the Sierra Club Board, Brower skipped over the usual request for board approval for his ad. Instead, he decided to pay for this ad insertion with separate funds from his publishing program, an account which operated free of Board approval.

That independent act by Brower, and the advertisement he placed, were *not* okay with the Board. So, only a few years after the club's spectacular victories, saving Grand Canyon, the Redwoods, et. al., Brower was formally reprimanded for running the Earth National Park ad. And he was *fired*. What a shock! And right in the midst of a sensational winning streak.

But there's also good news. Typical of Brower, getting fired didn't slow him down for one minute. Without missing a step, Brower immediately formed Friends of the Earth International. I was pleased and flattered when he asked me to become part of the first FOE Board, which I happily accepted. Meanwhile, Howard Gossage stepped forward and said his ad agency would host and house Brower and his new FOE organization on the second floor of our building. *Free*. So, Dave moved right in together with his right-hand colleagues Tom Turner, Hugh Nash, and Ken Brower, Dave's son. Soon after, Joan McIntyre joined the team.

In the next chapter, I will come back to Brower and his later work with FOE—notably his collaborations with McIntyre on issues of animal rights and anthropocentrism—and later with Earth Island Institute.

But before getting to all that, I think it's necessary for me to interrupt the story to say a bit more about the ultimate transformative effects upon *me* of working with Dave Brower, as well as with Howard Gossage, through all of this!

TRANSFORMATION: COMMERCIAL ADMAN TO ANTI-ADMAN

Directly because of my experiences with David Brower and the Sierra Club, and other non-profit organizations, as well as with the astonishing, paradoxical genius of Howard Gossage, my personal interests were rapidly fleeing *commercial* advertising.

By the late 1960s, it had become obvious to me that commercial advertising—which I realized mainly celebrates commodity life, waste, growth, and the vast overuse of all resources embodied within the corporate processes—did not match my own evolving environmental worldview. As always, Howard Gossage was in total agreement with that critique

and understood it well. In fact, he taught me a lot of it, though he'd always managed to find a way to work with and around it.

But my doubts were overwhelming me, and I'd even begun going public with them, speaking out and writing. I began to understand I was probably no longer suited for the commercial advertising business, not even the extraordinary version that Gossage created. I needed to find a way out of it. And then one *terrible* event decided matters.

I had known that Gossage was in a long struggle with Leukemia, which began when he was an air force jet pilot during WWII. By the end of the 1960s, his medical problems suddenly became truly intrusive. And finally, in 1969 Gossage died. He was 52 years old! For me, that was the last straw; the end of the line. *The fun was gone*. Gossage was my last connection to the commercial ad world. I knew I had to get out. So, closing down the agency became the plan.

★   ★   ★

It took about a year and a half to complete our agency's contracts and other obligations and campaigns. We needed to unravel the finances, and figure out what was next for our great, faithful employees. After so many dedicated years, they did not deserve to be quickly abandoned.

The transition proceeded into 1970, when, because of our well-known environmental campaigning, I was asked to be a keynote speaker at a major environmental conference at Aspen Institute in Colorado. In the presence of many of the environmental leaders of the time, including several Nobel Prize winners, and some key figures in the Nixon White House (John Ehrlichman, et. al.), I spoke about the *inherent* conflict between consumerism and environmentalism, and the extremely negative impact of hundreds of millions of advertising dollars overwhelming public consciousness within our so-called democratic free speech society.

All of this led to a lengthy *Wall Street Journal* interview with ace *Journal* reporter Henry Weinstein, inquiring about our agency's environmental campaigns. I admitted to Weinstein that I felt guilty about doing commercial advertisements for an automobile client, Rover and Land-Rover cars. By 1970, when the interview took place, it was already clear, as Gossage had openly suggested, that autos were among the leading causes of a rapidly advancing global environmental crisis. To save the world we should be promoting *less* use of cars, not more, which would have challenged the primacy of corporate profit over all other values under capitalism.

I told Weinstein about how Gossage had already proposed to Rover a full campaign on "Computer Commuting," a "ride-sharing" idea that was 50 years ahead of its time. But, could a car company in the 1960s get away with promoting *less* use of cars, instead of more? Actually, no! Rover declined that campaign idea. And yet word had gotten around the advertising world and was causing some ruckus. Automobile advertisers had always been considered the most desirable clients. How could our agency seem to be tossing that away?

Weinstein's interview of me appeared in the *The Wall Street Journal* a few days later on page one of the newspaper. The outcome was predictable. The very morning that the interview appeared, our Rover client telegrammed to say that the company was relieving me of my worries about advertising for cars. We were fired. The following morning's *Wall Street Journal* carried the full story about the firing with the headline: *"West Coast Ad Man Need Worry No More About Rover Account."* I was relieved. Finally, the die was cast.

I continued to write articles and give speeches about the negative role of advertising, and went so far as to convene a conference of public interest attorneys, at my house, to seek a legal pathway to challenge the constitutionality of advertising itself, as a distortion of the intentions of the First Amendment. That effort did not materialize, though it's still a good idea. I'd love to start that again.

A year later at the Sandage Symposium on Advertising at the University of Illinois—an annual ad industry event—I was invited to deliver a speech which I called "Four Arguments for the Elimination of Advertising." This was several years before I began work on my television book with a similar name.

The speech was widely reported in the advertising trades, once again setting me apart as an ad man who wished there was no advertising. By then I was

actively proceeding to close the ad agency. With the help of Alice Lowe, who had managed most of the agency's daily operations for 20 years, we dissolved Freeman, Mander & Gossage. I then set out to form the country's first *non-profit* ad agency, Public Interest Communications (PIC). I was joined in this endeavor by Dugald Stermer, the Art Director of *Ramparts Magazine,* business man Alvin Duskin (more about him in the next chapter), and King Harris, former president of Campbell Ewald Advertising.

At PIC, our rule was to work only for non-profit organizations or private individuals wanting to address specific controversial issues. We developed principles about how to do effective advertising for very low budget clients, basically following one of Gossage's rules: "Try for a hole in one with every shot."

Many of the relevant attitudes and teachings of Gossage applied every day. We quickly demonstrated that newspaper ads, constructed in a certain manner could successfully compete against much bigger budget advertising on television and in print.

A few years later, PIC evolved into Public Media Center (PMC) under the visionary leadership of Herb Chao Gunther, joined by a talented staff of writers and designers. *(more on that in Chapter Three)*

Meanwhile I managed to complete *"Four Arguments for the Elimination of Television,"* published by William Morrow Co. in 1978, in which I articulated my negative feelings about the impacts of that medium on society and the planet, especially as a primary means for challenging public thought, imagery, and awareness. The public seemed ready to think about this. The book sold more than a million copies.

(Chapter 2 starts on page 25)

Dinosaur and Big Bend. Glacier and Grand Teton, Kings Canyon, Redwoods, Mammoth, Even Yellowstone and Yosemite. And The Wild Rivers, and Wilderness.

How Can You Guarantee These, Mr. Udall, If Grand Canyon Is Dammed For Profit?

1) A bill will soon be voted in Congress (H.R. 4671) which would put two dams into Grand Canyon, maiming for all time the wild river that has been the canyon's sculptor for 25,000,000 years.

2) If the bill passes, two artificial lakes will back up into 133 miles of canyon gorge. And hardly a century later, silting will have created wall to wall mud and tangled growth.

3) In some places, the inner gorge will be submerged five hundred feet. A vital part of "The most revealing single page of the earth's history," as Joseph Wood Krutch has described it, will be drowned.

4) It is argued that artificial lakes will be an "improvement" because tourists will be nearer the walls.

Should we flood the Sistine Chapel, so tourists can float nearer the ceiling?

5) Between the lakes, the Colorado's depth will vary fifteen feet from day to day, depending on hydroelectric demand.

Shoreline campsites will become suddenly dangerous. Wildlife will be disrupted, as will the ecology of one of history's treasures.

There is no part of the Colorado River within Grand Canyon that would not be affected.

6) The dams will not be used for water. They are called "cash registers" by the Bureau of Reclamation. They are expected to make money by sale of commercial power.

7) But for even the making of money, Grand Canyon dams will soon be as obsolete as they are unnecessary. Congressional testimony established they are fantastically expensive and wasteful of water. Still the alternatives are ignored.

8) The real push for the dams is political—an attempt by the seven states in the Colorado Basin to finance diversion of water from the Columbia River to the Colorado, at a cost of an undetermined number of billions of dollars to the other states.

9) If the bill does pass, no national park will be safe. With the unthinkable precedent set in Grand Canyon, it will be simple to approve dams or other commercial projects *already proposed* in a dozen national parks.

10) If the bill passes, America will have violated a treaty obligation signed at the International Convention on Nature Protection and Wildlife Preservation, that it would never subject a national park to exploitation for commercial profit.

Our entire National Park System, so brilliant it has been a model for every nation in the world, would suddenly be meaningless.

11) Secretary of the Interior Stewart Udall could do much to save the day.

Taking advantage of the important new evidence presented in the House hearings, he could urge the dams be deleted from H.R. 4671. He could urge that Congressional committees at least hear the findings of his National Park Service, Bureaus of Recreation, and Mines and Geological Survey, instead of only Reclamation.

By failure to act, Mr. Udall is assisting the demise of the great park system he was pledged to protect.

12) It is an accident of history, but it is this generation which must assure that something untrammeled and free remains in the American earth as testimony that we had love for the people who follow.

13) It is for all the above reasons that we ran the two advertisements on June 9th—protesting the destruction of Grand Canyon—that produced an unprecedented reaction by the Internal Revenue Service.

By 4 P.M. the next day, an IRS messenger delivered a letter to us in San Francisco. It cast a cloud over our tax deductible status, effectively stopping major financial assistance for our public service program.

IRS read the ads as a sudden attempt to "influence legislation" in a "substantial" way. (They do not define those terms, leaving organizations like ours at the mercy of administrative whim.) *And they do not even raise the question with organizations that favor the dams.*

Vasey's Paradise at Marble Gorge, where a fantastic natural spring gushes out of the sheer rock canyon wall, will be submerged by 270 feet of water. The Statue of Liberty and its base, placed at this spot, would have only its upper arm and torch showing above the water. If the dams are built in Grand Canyon, 133 miles of inner gorge will be submerged by water as deep as *500 feet,* and later by that much mud.

14) The Sierra Club has been in the business of helping people enjoy and save natural beauty for /4 years. Nothing new has been added to this goal in that time, except that the battle to save Grand Canyon is now in its critical phase.

If the IRS succeeds in slowing us down, it will also have slowed every organization which chooses to work for the saving of our resources. And this is no time to slow down.

15) Therefore, tax deductible or not, we intend to continue. After all, as astonishing as it may seem, it *is* the Grand Canyon that's in danger this time. *The Grand Canyon.*

16) Possibly within the next two weeks, the House Committee on Interior and Insular Affairs will have reported out the bill and it will be ready for a floor vote in the House.

You can stop it by adding your coupons to those that have been sent already, or better still, your own letters.

And while we cannot now promise that any contributions you send us are deductible, a determination still in the hands of IRS, we *can* promise the funds will help fight the remaining battles against a technology that feels it no longer needs nature.

WHAT THE SIERRA CLUB IS FOR

The Sierra Club, founded in 1892 by John Muir, is nonprofit, supported by people who sense what Thoreau sensed when he wrote, "In wildness is the preservation of the world." The club's program is nationwide, includes wilderness trips, books, and films—and a major effort to protect the remnant of wilderness in the Americas.

There are now twenty chapters, branch offices in New York, Washington, Albuquerque, Seattle, and Los Angeles, and a main office in San Francisco.

This advertisement has been made possible by individual contributions, particularly from our Atlantic, Rocky Mountain, Rio Grande, Southern California and Grand Canyon chapter members, and by buyers of Sierra Club books everywhere, especially the twelve in the highly praised Exhibit Format Series, which includes books on Grand Canyon, Glen Canyon, the Redwoods, the Northern Cascades, Mount Everest, and the Sierra.

(Better Hold Up On The Flowers and Cheery Wires, Just A Bit Longer)

"Grand Canyon National Monument Is Hereby Abolished"

—From a bill submitted to Congress 15 days ago by Rep. Wayne Aspinall

Had You Thought The Battle Against Dams In Grand Canyon Was Over?

I "GOLIATH AND THE PHILISTINES"

ON FEBRUARY 1, Secretary of the Interior Stewart Udall, speaking for the Administration, announced that the President had withdrawn all support for the Marble Canyon Dam, which would have altered irrevocably the wild Colorado River and ruined a large part of Grand Canyon. In fact, the Secretary reported, the Administration was now advocating expansion of Grand Canyon National Park to *include* this dam site (see map).

A great victory, everyone felt, and the Sierra Club offices were inundated with wires, letters, flowers, and pleasant encomiums praising us, as one note said, "for having slain Goliath and turned away the Philistines."

Naturally enough, most people assumed the *whole* struggle was over. But, as usual, it is not so simple. By now, we have several "Goliaths" and as for the Philistines, they're coming back over the hill.

II "CASH REGISTERS"

III TOURISTS IN POWER BOATS

SUPPORTERS of the dams suggest that building them in Grand Canyon is only good sense.

They point out that the new "recreational lakes" will benefit tourists in power boats who will enjoy viewing the upper canyon walls more closely.

Should we flood the Sistine Chapel, so tourists can get nearer the ceiling?

And, to express their "willingness to compromise," some of the dam builders have lately suggested just one dam in Grand Canyon instead of two. Like one bullet in the heart instead of two. (The point, you see, is that if you alter the river's flow at *any* point you interfere with the life force of the canyon, the element which has made it what writers have called "a museum of the history of the world.")

In some quarters, even Mr. Aspinall's bill (see headline) is considered a "compromise," as it would extend Grand Canyon National *Park* upstream while eliminating Grand Canyon National *Monument* (to make room for a 93 mile reservoir). It is felt that if what you are flooding is no longer part of the park system, the public will no longer think it important.

But changing official names around doesn't change the fact that it is all part of Grand Canyon, and once flooded, whatever is under the water is gone forever.

No.
The President
The White House
Washington 25, D.C.
Dear Mr. President:

I wish to congratulate you for your Administration's position opposing the Marble Canyon Dam and the suggestion that Grand Canyon National Park be extended upstream.

However, I am still concerned that the Hualapai Dam may be built *downstream*, thereby flooding 93 miles of canyon gorge and marring forever what Joseph Wood Krutch described as "the most revealing single page of Earth's history." I ask therefore that you speak out as forcefully on the dangers of *this* dam, lest special interest groups be able to push a bill containing it through Congress.

Your's sincerely,

Address

City _____ State _____ Zip

No. 2
Hon. Wayne Aspinall, Chairman
House Committee on Interior and Insular Affairs
House Office Building
Washington 25, D.C.
Dear Mr. Aspinall:

As I am irrevocably opposed to the sacrifice of *any* part of Grand Canyon to commercial interests, I therefore urge that you reconsider your oft stated support for proposals to dam Grand Canyon.

Testimony has proven that dams are completely unnecessary, even wasteful, and that alternate power sources are available. And *new* testimony is also available substantiating that Grand Canyon dams are unneeded.

I urge that your committee invite *this* test mony and consider it carefully, and I urge that you refrain from back ng these dam bills.

Your's sincerely,

Address

City _____ State _____ Zip

No. 3
Hon. John Saylor
House Committee on Interior and Insular Affairs
House Office Building
Washington 25, D.C.
Dear Mr. Saylor:

I congratulate your forthright opposition to efforts which would

FOR while we can now look forward to Administration support, this must be understood:

A number of special interest groups are *still* planning to push dam bills through Congress (and several have already been submitted). Or, failing that, Arizona could build them itself — with or without Administration support.

The key advocates of Grand Canyon dams are these:

1) Commercial interests within the Colorado Basin states, who see these dams (commonly called "cash registers") as a hypothetical means of financing an altogether different project: the turning of part of the Columbia River southward, benefiting themselves, particularly California.

The Grand Canyon itself is of no interest; it is merely an expedient.

2) Southern California real estate developers also gain from presumed dam revenues. (They would like to create still more of Los Angeles.)

3) And the Arizona Power Authority favors the dams. It contends they will provide cheap new sources of power to subsidize Arizona agriculture. (Two-thirds of Arizona's water goes to cattlefeed and cotton, *already* subsidized products.)

The dams will not provide anyone with water. In fact, through seepage and evaporation they will waste enough water to supply Phoenix.

IV MENTALITY

So in summary, while the President's action is heartening, and the Grand Canyon struggle is beginning to turn, we remain in the same essential position, and that is this:

There exists today a mentality which condones destruction done in the name of commerce.

Commercial interests claim we who love the land refuse their "reasonable compromises." But it is forgotten that nearly the whole natural landscape has *already* been compromised ... tract houses creep over the hillsides, concrete covers the landscape, forests are gone, waters are fouled, and even the air is heavy with waste.

It is not much to ask that some things at least be left "unimproved" to show we have love for those who follow.

If we can't even save Grand Canyon for them, is there hope for saving whatever else of nature our planet still offers?

We have been taking ads, therefore, suggesting that there is something one can do. Thousands have already responded by writing letters (especially important), sending coupons, and also funds to continue the effort; and prospects have thereby improved. But as Grand Canyon legislation still stands a good chance of passage, please don't stop now.

Thank you.

THE GRAND CANYON

The Grand Canyon, measured along the Colorado River that created it, is 280 miles long, and includes Grand Canyon National Park (shown in black), Grand Canyon National Monument (dark grey), and the large surrounding Grand Canyon region (light grey) that is currently unprotected. The river is shown in white.

The proposed Hualapai Dam (A) would raise the water level at that point by 659 feet; or by 354 feet *more* than the height of the Statue of Liberty and its base. (See inset.)

Water will back-up all the way to Kanab Creek (B) 93 miles upstream, effectively flooding most of the inner gorge to that point, and some of the most elaborate, beautiful and valuable exhibits of natural history in the world. Furthermore, within about 100 years, silting will have replaced even this water with that much mud.

The upstream Marble Canyon Dam (C) would back water into an equally spectacular region of Grand Canyon, located above the park, all the way to Lee's Ferry (D). Furthermore, it would release river water irregularly according to hydroelectric demand, so that daily, the river would rise and fall as much as 15 feet, destroying natural exhibits, making river traveling prohibitively dangerous and leaving, where the river bank had been, a wasteland where nothing will grow.

250,000 ACRES	500,000 ACRES	750,000 ACRES	1,000,000 ACRES	1,250,000 ACRES	1,500,000 ACRES	1,750,000 ACRES	2,000,000 ACRES

ABOUT 2 MILLION, B.C., WHEN THE FIRST MAN APPEARED

115 YEARS AGO, THE 1ST LOGGING

THE REDWOOD TREES THAT HAVE NOT YET BEEN CUT

ALL WE ASK TO SAVE

"History will think it most strange that America could afford the Moon and $4 billion airplanes, while a patch of primeval redwoods—not too big for a man to walk through in a day—was considered beyond its means."

EARTH BEGAN four billion years ago, and Man two million. The Age of Technology on the other hand is hardly two hundred years old, and to give you an idea of just how little relative time *that* is, imagine a line an inch long, and then one from New York to Japan.

Yet, during this inch of time, Man has become so impressed with his brand new power as to alter his world irrevocably.

For instance:

1) By the time Man appeared on this planet a forest of

9) The real heart of the matter is simply this: A logger will resist his job being changed from logging to running a park; a local businessman will fear a decline for a time, and the companies believe they've an inalienable right to cut down trees for money.

But this planet is all we non-loggers have, and any other will forever feel strange.

It seems to us, therefore, we should not be so hasty about removing all our natural environment: the element which

HERE ARE SOME STEPS YOU CAN TAKE:

HON. RONALD REAGAN
Governor, State of California
Sacramento, California

Dear Governor Reagan,

I urge that you join in support of a meaningful redwood national park in your state: 90,000 acres at Redwood Creek, saving but 2½ more of what once grew.

It is an accident of geography that the redwoods are in California. They are the property of every American; even of every person in the world, and of future generations as well. And you giant redwood trees already covered about two million acres of Northern California. (See chart.)

2) They were there in the age of the dinosaurs and when Rome was built. They were there when Christ was alive, and when Columbus discovered America. They were still there during the Gold Rush just a hundred fifteen years ago; a reminder, to those who've walked through them, of how we all started.

3) But in the last 115 years (a half-inch on your mental chart) nearly all of the forest has been logged.

4) Of that which remains a few are in small state parks. The rest is scheduled for cutting.

5) A national park has been proposed for Redwood Creek which could, at any rate, save 2% more of the old trees.

6) But lumber interests, having cut so much and taken the rest for granted, are eager to get on with business. They see little reason why they should not.

7) Tourists, they point out, want only enough old trees for the snapping of photos, and they have offered to leave "enough." (The result would remind you of the places on your face you missed while you were shaving.)

8) The companies add that redwood forests are dark and gloomy, and furthermore clearing out old-growth trees is good for the forest. "Overmature" timber they like to call it.

*It's hard to say how the forest grew so well before the loggers were there to protect it.**

makes Earth feel like home.

Deciding what is *too much* destruction in the name of commerce is not always easy, but in the case of the redwoods it is.

By default, the world has given up the rights to 97% of what has been growing for 2 million years. That is surely more than enough. Buying 2% back ought hardly be thought much to ask, on behalf of our children's children.**

History will think it most strange that America could afford the Moon and $4 billion airplanes while a patch of primeval redwoods—not too big for a man to walk through in a day—was considered beyond its means.***

This generation will decide this question and hundreds of others just like it; questions that will determine whether or not something untrammelled and free will remain to prove we had love for those who follow. To impress people with that, and to suggest they *do* have some say in what happens, the Sierra Club (now with 47,000 members), has been taking ads such as this.

We have been asking that people write letters, mail coupons and that they send us funds to continue our efforts.

Thousands *have* written, but meanwhile, in this session of Congress, a bill which will propose a park at Redwood Creek—the only possible location for a meaningful, varied redwood park—will face its greatest and probably its last test.

More letters expressing your view are needed, and more dollars to help fight the notion that man no longer needs nature.

*Lumber companies who own the redwood forests have spent tremendous sums to suggest that even when the land is cut completely clear of trees, as is often the case, no permanent harm is done the forests; as the cut-over area is immediately reseeded, and is then designated a "tree farm." However, because the special growing conditions that redwoods require are often impaired by modern tractor logging, the "tree farms" are most often not seeded with redwoods, but douglas fir, spruce, and Monterey pine.

**The arithmetic on the acreage goes this way: At present, 85% of the two million virgin acres has been cut. 3% of the original virgin acreage is left to cut, while the other 12% that's left is scheduled for cutting; which would make a total of 97% of the virgin growth as well as a lovely, remote beach area, a number of spectacular wooded hills where redwoods are displayed in the variety of growth conditions in which they thrive, and a navigable river which includes The Emerald Mile, a stretch of huge redwoods running along both sides of the stream. The net effect, then, would be that instead of 97% of the original redwoods going to cutting, only 95% would be gone and we would then have a real sweep of forest large enough for people to walk in without it seeming like a parking lot outside a baseball game.

***A redwood national park of 90,000 acres in the Redwood Creek area would cost $150 million. That is, about 75 cents per American. Or, if amortized into the future, a few pennies from our children as well. Considering it will last their lifetime, and THEIR children's and grandchildren and so on, it would seem to qualify, in economic jargon, as a "steal."

The Sierra Club, founded in 1892 by John Muir, is nonprofit, supported by people who, like Thoreau, believe "In wildness is the preservation of the world." The club's program is nationwide, includes wilderness trips, books and films—as well as such efforts as this to protect the remnant of wilderness of the Americas. There are now twenty chapters, branch offices in New York (Biltmore Hotel), Washington (Dupont Circle Building), Los Angeles (Auditorium Building), Albuquerque, Seattle, and main office in San Francisco.

(Our previous ads, urging that readers exercise a constitutional right of petition to save Grand Canyon from two dams which would have flooded it, produced an unprecedented reaction by the Internal Revenue Service threatening our tax deductible status. IRS called the ads a "substantial" effort to "influence legislation." Undefined, these terms leave organizations like ours at the mercy of administrative whim. [The question has not been raised with organizations that favor Grand Canyon dams.] So we cannot now promise that contributions you send us are deductible—pending results of what may be a long legal battle.)

---

are the steward of this inheritance.

I ask that you do your utmost to assure that they are preserved not only as isolated museum-like groves, but in their original magnificent sweep; so that walking through them will remain among Man's most moving experiences.

Yours sincerely,

Name _____
Address _____
City _____ State _____ Zip _____

MR. C. DAVIS WEYERHAEUSER
Chairman of the Board
Arcata Redwood Company
Tacoma Building, 1015 "A" St., Tacoma, Washington 98402

Dear Mr. Weyerhaeuser,

Yours is one of the two companies that presently own almost all the virgin redwood forests within the proposed Redwood Creek Park.

Therefore, you are in a rare position to singlehandedly assure that one of Mankind's great heritages will be preserved.

Considering that, 1) a meaningful redwood park would return to public hands only 2% of the forest that once grew, and 2) the government would then reimburse your shareholders more than amply, I urge that you join in supporting a 90,000 acre park at Redwood Creek.

Future generations will thank you even more than I do today.

Yours sincerely,

Name _____
Address _____
City _____ State _____ Zip _____

MR. OWEN CHEATHAM
Chairman of the Board
Georgia-Pacific Corporation
Executive Offices, 375 Park Avenue, New York, N.Y. 10022

Dear Mr. Cheatham,

Yours is one of the two companies that presently own almost all the virgin redwood forests within the proposed Redwood Creek Park.

Therefore, you are in a rare position to singlehandedly assure that one of Mankind's great heritages will be preserved.

Considering that, 1) a meaningful redwood park would return to public hands only 2% of the forest that once grew, and 2) the government would then reimburse your shareholders more than amply, I urge that you join in supporting a 90,000 acre park at Redwood Creek.

Future generations will thank you even more than I do today.

Yours sincerely,

Name _____
Address _____
City _____ State _____ Zip _____

Also, write:

The President, Secretary of the Interior Stewart Udall, Your Senators and Congressman.

Urge them to support a 90,000 acre national park at Redwood Creek, in *this* session of Congress.

EDGAR WAYBURN
Vice President, Sierra Club
Mills Tower, San Francisco

☐ Please send me more details on how I may help.

☐ Here is a donation of $_____ to continue efforts such as this to keep the public informed.

☐ Send me "The Last Redwoods" which tells the complete story of the opportunity as well as the destruction in the redwoods. ($17.50.)

☐ I would like to be a member of the Sierra Club. Enclosed is $14.00 for entrance and first year's dues.

Name _____
Address _____
City _____ State _____ Zip _____

Legislation by Chain-saw?

While Congress has been considering the exact boundaries for a great Redwood National Park, Georgia-Pacific Corp. has begun logging within two spectacular regions which should be selected. The company says it is doing this (potentially reducing the park's size and quality with its chain-saws) "...in the interests of our stockholders." QUESTION: How many G.-P. stockholders disapprove of such behavior in their names? (The coupons below offer them and everyone else an opportunity to help delay the logging, so that Congress, not Georgia-Pacific, may define the optimum park borders.)

Above is Redwood Creek country that belonged in a national park. Arcata Redwood Co. moved before Congress did. However, Arcata (and also Simpson and Miller-Rellim companies) are now withholding further cutting in critical areas until final park boundaries are determined by Congress. Corporations, it would seem, *can* behave responsibly.

Georgia-Pacific on the other hand, the second largest lumbering concern in the world, a company with timber holdings so vast (3,500,000 acres) it could easily cut profitably elsewhere, has refused the direct appeal of 35 congressmen to *temporarily* refrain from logging

within park boundaries under consideration by the House of Representatives. Instead G.-P. has begun logging in two areas of the finest redwood forest left on Earth, one of which is the Emerald Mile, where trees soar in an incredible 300 foot wall (see photo right), along both sides of Redwood Creek. (How tall is a 300 foot tree? Imagine a football field; these trees would reach from goal to goal.)

The fear is this: Unless we all object, G.-P. will effectively limit the choices of Congress and the photo above at right will resemble the photo above at left.

1. In November, the Senate passed a bill (S.2515) which would establish a redwood national park. It is a small park — narrow enough to walk across in a few hours — but as a compromise plan it represents a gain. Conservation minded people support it, and hope it may be improved.

2. The bill permits 2,346 acres to be added to the park by the Secretary of the Interior. The House of Representatives has this option as well, and the many park supporters in the House have made clear their intention of fighting for this addition. But this can happen only if, a) the bill moves through quickly and, b) if Georgia-Pacific does not cut the trees down meanwhile.

3. Georgia-Pacific began cutting in the McArthur-Elam Creek area in late October, and then, about December 11, in the Emerald Mile. (See map.) The first logging there is for access roads, landings, and other clearing operations preliminary to full scale clear-cut logging.

4. Georgia-Pacific, in committing these acts, may not be violating any laws. Nor is it violating the wording of promises it has made. To explain:

A year ago, after tremendous public pressure, G.-P. and three other logging concerns agreed to halt logging within redwood areas proposed as parks, until the Senate had acted to define the boundaries. Now the Senate has done so. *But the House has not.* G.-P., therefore (unlike the other three redwood companies) feels it may now quickly cut down everything beyond the Senate lines. Then, you see, there will be no point in having the House, or Secretary Udall add the Emerald Mile or the McArthur-Elam Creek area, or others. The trees will already have become patio furniture.

5. On Dec. 4, Rep. Jeffery Cohelan reported, with outrage, his exchange with G.-P. on this question. (From the Congressional Record):

Cohelan: Adjacent to the Senate park boundaries are virgin redwoods lovely enough to grace the best redwood national park...These trees are now being fed to the sawmills of the Georgia-Pacific Corp., forever blocking the opportunity for us to choose them to dignify a park worthy of its name...We thus wrote the following letter to Georgia-Pacific (signed by Cohelan and 34 other congressmen):

"...Since the entire question of the precise lines and acreage of the proposed park should be finally determined some time next spring, we hope that this request to suspend further logging [in some 3,000 acres adjacent to the Senate boundary] will be favorably considered."

Georgia-Pacific answered:

"...it is necessary for us to do some harvesting in this area in order to run our plants on an economically sound basis. For the above reason and in the interest of our employees, our stock holders and good forest management and indeed as a corporate citizen, we respectfully must decline your request."

6. Mr. Cohelan then said, "The second largest lumbering concern in the world says it cannot accord the House the same concern it voluntarily gave the Senate...I deplore this indifference to the public interest."*

7. It is important to place G.-P.'s urgent desire to proceed into the proper context:

The company's profits last year were 50 million dollars. This year, by all reports, prospects are better still. The redwood land it says it must cut represents *less than one one-thousandth of G.-P. holdings.* It's not as though there are no other trees to cut for a few months, so Congress can do its work. We are speaking of 3,000 acres among three and one-half million.

8. Can anyone believe that by briefly refraining from logging one one-thousandth of its acreage

Georgia-Pacific will be doing a disservice to its employees and its stockholders?

If this were true, and the company's profit picture were so dependent upon these few acres, then the stock exchange might well be flooded with "Sell G.-P." orders any day now, whether G.-P. logs redwoods or not.

9. What can be done?

If you are a G.-P. shareholder, let your management know what you think of its actions, which if not in formal contempt of Congress, are by any standard, contemptuous of it.

The dark area shows the main body of the private lands to be acquired in the South Unit of S.2515 (22,474 acres). Shaded area indicates private holdings which might still be included in the park. Circled areas show where Georgia-Pacific has begun logging operations, which if allowed to continue, will effectively deny the Congress and Secretary of the Interior the options of adding spectacular acreage in a condition worthy of park status.

Or, if you are just a concerned citizen, write G.-P.; write your Congressmen; write the President...and let them know you consider that a redwood national park worthy of your children should not be sacrificed for one company's few pennies of profit per share.

Thank you.

* Perhaps anticipating a public outcry, G.-P. recently spent $50,000 on ads in 11 newspapers, saying incredibly, "Yes, America's majestic redwoods have already been saved." We had intended to provide here a list of the factual errors and misleading innuendos in the G.-P. ad, but found it would have required nearly the entire page. (However, for those who wish to have it, a point by point refutation *is* available; you have only to check the appropriate box in coupon #5.) Suffice it to say here, the ad implied that the redwoods are growing virtually as before and that somehow lumber companies deserve much credit for saving them. Well. The first point is hardly worth comment considering the state of the redwood region. As for the latter, it is much as though the U.S. Cavalry took credit for saving whatever Indians remain.

An International Program, Before it's Too Late, to Preserve Earth
as a "Conservation District" within the Universe

"EARTH NATIONAL PARK"

I. The Moon, Mars, Saturn…nice places to visit, but you wouldn't want to live there.

ANY MOMENT NOW, Man will find himself hurtling around in an Outer Space so enormous that descriptions of its size only boggle the mind. (One attempt has put it this way. The size of the Earth is to the size of the known Universe as a germ is to our entire solar system.)

Yet, we already hear excited talk of locating, out there, a planet that duplicates the natural environment on Earth, i.e., trees, flowers, water, air, people; you get our meaning.

The fact is that if we do find such a duplicate Earth out there, it may be some thousands of years from today. Until then, the only place in the Universe that will feel like home is Earth, unless *your* idea of home life could include setting up house on space platforms, or the Moon or taking your evening walk with oxygen helmet and space suit.

We haven't got used to thinking about it this way yet, but, as Astronaut Borman pointed out—for us people, Earth is a kind of inhabitable oasis in an unimaginably vast desert.

Also, Earth is a strange sort of oasis, in that quite apart from providing us what we need to live—water, air, sustenance, companionship—this oasis actually *grew* us and every other life form. We are all related.

Darwin, during his famous Galapagos journey, found all life on Earth from plankton to people—to be part of an incredibly complex interwoven and interdependent blanket spread around the globe. There is no loosening one thread in the blanket without changing the stresses on every other thread, or worse, unraveling it.

So then, if it is life on Earth that most of us are stuck with for the next little while, we had better consider the consequences of what has recently been going on here.

II. Toward a more Moon-like Earth.

There was not always enough oxygen to support the existence of Man. It wasn't until green plants and certain ocean plankton had evolved that the natural process was begun by which oxygen is maintained in the atmosphere: photosynthesis.

Man, one would think, has a stake in assuring that this process continues. Consider then, these bits of news:

—*In the U. S. alone, oxygen-producing greenery is being paved over at a rate of one million acres per year and the rate is increasing. Also, paving is contagious. Other countries are following suit.*

—*The oceans have become the dumping ground for as many as a half million substances, few of which are tested to see if the plankton we need can survive them.*

—*New factories, autos, homes, and jet airplanes have incredibly increased the rate at which combustion takes place—i.e., at which oxygen is used and replaced in our atmosphere by carbon dioxide and carbon monoxide.*

The result is a kind of Russian roulette with the oxygen supply. Dr. Lamont C. Cole, ecologist, Cornell University, New York, has said this:

"When and if we reach the point where the rate of combustion exceeds the rate of photosynthesis, the oxygen content of the atmosphere will decrease. Indeed there is evidence that it may already have begun to decline around our largest cities."

There is a bright side: If we should continue what we're doing, overpopulation will cease to be a problem.

Sterile

In only 25 years, traces of DDT have found their way into the average American to the extent of eleven parts per million. They are also found in animals, birds, fish and recently, in notable quantity, in the fatty tissues of Antarctic penguins. (If you wonder about the consequences, similar pesticides have already made sterile a species of hawk and owl in England. Here is the way it works: insects eat sprayed plants, small birds eat them, and then big birds eat *them*. By that time, the insecticide has been concentrated many-fold and the big birds are in big trouble. Now, if we humans were in the habit of eating owls and hawks…)

Aside from the toxic effects on Man and other animals, pesticides like DDT and newer more voguish chemicals eliminate whole populations of certain bacteria and pest organisms.

However, and here is the shocker, *no one in the world knows, when we aim at a particular pest, which other organisms may be eliminated by ricochet.* Someone had better find out.

If some pesticide. herbicide, or defoliant should by inadvertence kill too many of the "nitrogen-fixing" organisms—those organisms that enable living things *to make use of* the nitrogen in the atmosphere—*then life on Earth could end.*

It is that dependent and fragile.

Rampant Technology

The Aswan High Dam was dreamed up to prevent the Nile from overflowing its banks as it had yearly throughout history. (It was thought such a great idea that countries vied for the honor of helping build it; the U.S. foremost among them.) The goals were electricity and year-round irrigation, thus greater productivity. No one, including the U.S., thought much about certain *side* effects, which may ultimately prove the most important:

—Since the natural floods have been halted, lifegiving nutrients that were formerly delivered to the land and the Mediterranean sea are now piling up in a reservoir above the dam, unusable.

As a result the Eastern Mediterranean sardine fishery is already doomed.

As for the land, the lack of nutrients, plus the waterlogging caused by old irrigation, plus salinization, *may actually decrease productivity.* Newly irrigated lands have the same fate in store.

—A particular snail has begun to thrive in the warm irrigation canals. The snail hosts a worm which causes schistosomiasis, a debilitating, often fatal disease. In one region around the dam, the incidence of this disease used to be 2%. It has now risen to 75%.

—At Aswan, we may also see repeated the awful developments at Kariba Dam, East Africa. At Kariba, rafts of hyacinths and reeds have spread over much of the reservoir's surface. It has been estimated that if this growth should cover just 10% of the reservoir at Aswan, the plants could actually transpire into the desert air enough water to stop *all* flow into the lower Nile.

Looking at the bright side again: In a few centuries, the dam will fill up with silt, and end its useful life. Then, the river will flow right over it, creating a huge, perhaps lovely, waterfall. Tourists will enjoy the view.

More Improvements

Engineers are improving things everywhere:

—In Alaska, a $2 billion dam is proposed—to bring power to non-existent industry—which would flood a wilderness and nesting region the size of Lake Erie.

—In Brazil, engineers propose an Amazon dam that would flood a green area as big as Italy.

—In Southeast Asia, a series of proposed Mekong River dams may do for Laos, Thailand, and Vietnam what Aswan is doing for Egypt. *Every* country should be spared such improvements.

III. A wildlife preserve where *we* are the wildlife.

The speed with which our world is being altered is so rapid that there is no cataloguing it; it is everywhere…forests are gone, hillsides eroded and bulldozed, waters filled, and air and water polluted. The implicit assumption is that Man is the Master of Nature, and that losing a wild place or species or plant is of no great importance to us, and never mind the esthetics. But as we have shown, tinkering with the natural order of things can be a dangerous business, *for there is a need to think of the organic wholeness of nature, not man apart from that.* Man's vanity notwithstanding, he is irretrievably intertwined with everything on his planet and therefore must proceed with a degree of caution, until, at last, he has the option of actually leaving Earth.

If, before then, we should so alter our environment that we rid it of ingredients we need for life, then *we* will merely pass the way of other life forms that have become extinct for one reason or another. And, as humbling a thought as it may be, Nature might scarcely miss the people. Things might eventually get back into their own pattern, the natural order reviving. Plankton might evolve; oxygen might re-form in the atmosphere; grass might grow through the pavement and among tumbled columns as it has before.

With all this in mind, you may see that we, the 70,000 member Sierra Club, the groups we work with, and the critical publishing project you see outlined at right, are not so much proselytizing on behalf of Nature. In due course, Nature will take care of itself.

Our motives are more selfish, in fact. They are on behalf of our very own lives and the lives of our children who, we feel, have not only the right to live but also the right to live in a world that maintains the natural order enough to continue to feel like home.

We find therefore, that it is not tenable to confine our activities to local crises in the United States. The problems are everywhere and are doubling by the decade.

And so, we have embarked upon an antidotal new international publishing program to export the view that it is now the entire planet that must be viewed as a kind of conservation district within the Universe; a wildlife preserve of a sort, except we are the wildlife, together with all other life and environmental conditions that are necessary constituents of our survival and happiness.

If you wish to participate and support this approach, general means to do so are suggested at the right.

Thank you.

— David Brower, *Executive Director*
Sierra Club, Mills Tower
San Francisco, Calif. 94104
or
15 E. 53rd St., New York City

(The California Water Project is illegal. Nobody told the voters that.)

Suing California

WHEN *Californians voted on Proposition 7 the other day, most were not aware that they were actually voting on the California Water Project. There was no way of knowing this from the way the thing was worded—a Yes vote just seemed like a harmless bit of legalese. But in fact we voted to support, through a bond issue, a project which is costing a minimum of $4½ billion; is benefiting no one save 50 or 100 of Southern California's largest real estate operators; would dam the last of our wild rivers; and, according to a recent Federal report, would destroy life in San Francisco Bay as surely as paving it over with asphalt.*

On top of all that, it is illegal. A lawsuit was filed yesterday. More suits will follow shortly, as more money is raised. You are invited to help.

Here are the details:

1) A few months ago I placed an advertisement pointing out that, in the judgment of every leading conservation group in the state, the California Water Plan is potentially the most destructive single project in our history.

2) The plan includes damming our last free-flowing rivers, and diverting water from them and from the Sacramento River southward to Los Angeles. Just incidentally, it would flood lands of the Round Valley and the Wintu Indians in the Dos Rios area. It would deprive fishermen, other sportsmen, and people who just like to look, of some of the most scenic country we still have left. And it would reduce the natural "flushing action" of fresh water through San Francisco Bay, killing the birds and fish as effectively as shooting each one with a gun. (See Fig. A.)

3) Once it arrives down south, at a cost of some $4½ billion, the water will not be used for drinking. It will be used to benefit private real estate operators needing greater water flows to turn what is now open space into more of Los Angeles. The effect will be to increase crowding, smog, water pollution and the sort of creeping, random ugliness that have made California not nearly as marvelous or as healthy a place to live as it used to be.

4) Thirty-six thousand people responded to the earlier anti-Water Plan advertisement, sending opinion coupons to Mr. Unruh, Mr. Reagan, and others.

Mr. Unruh took the occasion to denounce the plan on its merits. But when a reporter asked Mr. Reagan's press secretary what the Governor thought of this outpouring of feeling about the California environment, all he could manage was this already famous remark: "We have better things to do than count silly coupons."

While perhaps not on a par with the Governor's classic "bloodbath" remark, the "silly coupon" comment has its own special place in the Hall of Fame of anti-democratic remarks.

5) One of the "better things" they had to do in Sacramento was to prepare ballot Proposition 7, which, without ever mentioning the Water Project, would allow the state to finance it with high-interest bonds. Californians, unaware that the entire project was being conducted in an illegal manner, making the bond issue a dubious one at best, voted Yes. But that's not the end of the story.

6) About the time of the voting, the United States Geological Survey submitted a report to Secretary of the Interior Walter Hickel on environmental effects of California's water diversion plan. The report reads like an autopsy after the death of our state. The U.S.G.S. said that if things went as planned, the bay would "turn into another Lake Erie...a dead sea." It said that because of the lower rate of fresh water flow into the bay, chemicals would collect in the south bay and elsewhere, causing algae blooms which would suffocate all aquatic life.

7) If that isn't sufficient reason to stop the project, then there is also the recent independent report by the Rand Corporation, the famous Santa Monica "think tank." It reported, amazingly, that in fact there is *no* shortage of water in southern California, nor will there be in the foreseeable future. "A political water coalition," said the report, "has created what appears to be an already excessive and costly supply; the coalition continues to seek out vast new increments [the California Water Plan] although supplies now arranged for cover gross needs for 30 to 50 years."

And after that time, as everyone must surely realize by now, California will be so jammed with people and tract houses that accommodating any further growth, with its companion crowding and crime, would be nothing short of suicide.

8) So, misleading ballot measures notwithstanding, I have formed a non-profit committee which is currently planning a number of lawsuits against the state, intending to point out the variety of illegalities in the project, and stop it once and for all. We have been raising money for this purpose,

and to date have raised $18,000. We will need, in all, some $50,000 for these suits, and we ask that you use the coupon below to help us if you agree with the cause. The money will be used for the legal struggle, ads to finance litigation, and for no other purpose.

The first suit was filed in Federal District Court in San Francisco yesterday.

9) This particular suit is based upon Federal reclamation law which states that, when Federal funds are used for water projects—as some are in this project—no individual beneficiary may achieve a financial gain upon more than 160 acres of land. The law was intended to support small landowners, you see. Yet the accompanying Fig. B will show you how the *big* promoters are doing, in what appears to our attorneys to be an obvious violation of the law.

Fig. **B**

THE REAL REASON FOR THE CALIFORNIA WATER PROJECT

Because the California Water Project would provide sufficient water to make it profitable for big developers to turn farm land and other open space into subdivisions and industrial developments, huge corporations have been busily buying up California land and waiting for Mr. Reagan to bring home the bacon. Already, simply because of the prospect of the project's being completed, land values have made spectacular increases. This chart indicates how a few companies have already made out:

Land Owner	Amount of Land	Approximate Economic Gain Thus Far
Tenneco	162,560 acres	$93,797,120
Standard Oil	101,120 acres	58,346,240
Tejon Ranch	54,400 acres	31,388,800
Southern Pacific	37,120 acres	21,033,240
Miller & Lux	25,000 acres	14,405,000

All this despite the fact that Federal reclamation laws prohibit the use of such water to achieve profits upon more than 160 acres. The purpose of the law is to disallow just the sort of rampant big company speculation that is going on here and now.

Furthermore, to the extent that large corporations have bought up the land, and the land is substantially appreciated in value, it is unavailable for purchase by family farmers at reasonable prices. This is also contrary to the intent of the reclamation laws.

And, while they wait for the opportune time to subdivide, the big landowners compete unfairly with small raisin and almond growers, glutting their markets. Or they raise un-needed crops, such as cotton, which are subsidized still further by us taxpayers.

10) Among others, the California Water Project is in violation of the following Federal and State laws:

5th and 14th Amendments U. S. Constitution
Federal Reclamation Laws 43 USC Sections 423, 430, 523-525
The San Luis Act 74 Stat. 156
Rivers and Harbors Act of 1899 33 USC Section 403
National Environmental Policy Act of 1969 83 Stat. 852
Fish and Wildlife Coordination Act 16 USC Sections 661-663
Migratory Bird Acts 16 USC Section 701
Anadromous Fish Act of 1965 16 USC Section 757
Federal Water Pollution Control Act, as amended by Federal Water Quality Improvement Act 33 USC Section 466 et seq.
Federal Administrative Procedure Act 5 USC Sections 500-559
National Estuarine Areas Act 16 USC Section 1221 et seq.
Act of September 22, 1959 16 USC Section 760
California Counties of Origin Act, California Water Code Section 10505
California Watershed Protection Act, California Water Code Sections 11460-11463

11) We will be backing at least two and possibly seven other suits against the state, based on some of these violations. So, if you agree with our position, and can afford to help us fight the legal battle, please do.

Thank you.

Alvin Duskin for the Legal Committee
To Stop The California Water Plan
510 Third Street, San Francisco, CA 94107

Fig. **A**

HOW THE CALIFORNIA WATER PROJECT WILL DESTROY THE DELTA AND THE BAY

The California Water Project will reduce the flow of fresh water into San Francisco Bay from 15½ million acre feet per year to as little as 2½ million. The United States Geological Survey says the effect will be to decrease the natural "flushing action" of the fresh water, which removes from the Bay the variety of chemicals and pollutants that otherwise kill life in the water, as well as other life which feeds upon it, such as birds and animals. When the flow of the river is reduced, the inflow of the ocean will increase, thereby drastically altering the natural ecology not only of the Bay but of the Delta, pushing far upstream the salinity, and a lot of dangerous chemical garbage, that was formerly swept out through the Golden Gate. The Geological Survey reports that the result of all this, if the project is not stopped, will be to make San Francisco Bay as "dead as Lake Erie."

Blocked sewage outflow from San Francisco and elsewhere drifts here. Stinks. Kills aquatic life.

Blocked agricultural run-off (pesticides, chemical fertilizers) drifts here, causing algae blooms, killing fish.

Sea water intrudes into what are presently fresh water channels. Ruins farming, fishing, water sports, and land values.

2

"NON-PROFIT" AD AGENCY: PUBLIC INTEREST COMMUNICATIONS (P.I.C.)

Alvin Duskin & The San Francisco Opposition
David Brower (2) & Friends of the Earth International
Joan McIntyre & Project Jonah—Saving Whales and Dolphins

At the end of 1969, San Francisco Mayor Joseph Alioto announced that Alcatraz Island, the former prison site which sits right in the middle of an inspirationally gorgeous San Francisco Bay—visible everywhere in the city and from Marin County—would soon be blessed by a giant new project. It was to be designed, built, paid for, and operated by a right-wing Texas billionaire, Lamar Hunt. The plan was to build a giant "space museum" with military dimensions, on Alcatraz, to become the new focal point of San Francisco Bay!

The Alcatraz deal had been quietly approved without *any* public discussion and very little public awareness, but doubtless with considerable financial promises from Hunt toward Mayor Alioto's political fantasies—which were then substantial. Alioto was clearly contemplating his run for governor.

But suddenly, things changed! San Francisco's celebrated, iconoclastic newspaper columnist, Herb Caen—who was read every day by anyone in the Bay Area who followed local goings-on, insider gossip, and social and political happenings in San Francisco—wrote a *blistering* attack on the Alcatraz project, and denounced the Mayor and Board of Supervisors for supporting it.

Caen then reassured his readership, adding this: "Concerned citizens… yesterday organized The Committee for a Politically Independent Alcatraz and will commence firing through all known media." That committee, said Caen, was comprised of celebrated best-selling author Jessica Mitford, Warren Hinckle, the editor of *Ramparts* magazine, and…*me!*

The problem with that committee, however, was that Herb Caen just made it up. No such committee existed. Caen understood that by mentioning it, he could make it happen. Fortunately, we three "committee members" at least knew each other. We had participated together in various political campaigns over the years. But we had never discussed the Alcatraz issue.

Yet in those days, if Herb Caen launched you, you'd best stay launched! So, Warren Hinckle and I quickly decided to meet and talk things over. Jessica was away, temporarily residing in Europe. After talking with her on the phone, Warren and I scheduled our own lunch meeting to discuss the matter further.

Hinckle and I met at Enrico's Café in the heart of North Beach, a popular hip restaurant/cafe and hangout in the 1960s and 1970s. We completely agreed with Caen about the need to fight that dumb Texas space museum idea. But how?

Over a lunch of multiple martinis, Warren and I had a great time sharing our horror stories about the mayor and figuring out the best way to follow Caen's lead. We decided that we'd at least quickly write and place an advertisement in the *San Francisco Chronicle* to amplify the furor and to give an outraged public a way to express its irritation. If we beat the Alcatraz development, it might provide momentum to take on other growing problems of over-development in the city.

But a full-page ad in the *SF Chronicle?* That was so expensive! Warren and I could write it and get it designed. *But where could we find the money to actually run it in the newspaper?*

ENTER: ALVIN DUSKIN

We brainstormed about who out there might be willing to join us in this new oppositional movement. And just minutes later, as if sent from heaven, in walked Alvin Duskin, a very successful, progressive, and charismatic local dress designer and marketer. I had gotten to know Alvin socially a bit because he was then dating a woman who worked for me. "Hey, let's ask Alvin," we instantly decided. "He's smart, he's a good speaker, he's good-looking, he's got tons of money and he *loves* attention."

I stood up from our table, waving my arms: "Yo Alvin! Come on over; we've just been talking about you. How would you like to be *really* famous?" Alvin walked over, laughing. "Sure," he said, with a big smile. We told him it would only cost enough to pay for a full-page ad in the *Chronicle.* "Look," we said, "we're pretty sure you can't stand that horrible Texas Alcatraz space museum thing that Alioto has just pushed through, right?" He nodded, and we discussed how it all related to the broader issues of overdevelopment and too many high-rise buildings in the city. We explained how we wanted to draft a big ad to attack the Mayor and the Texas billionaire about their crazy idea "and the ad could be signed by you, *only* you," we said, "as an expression of your personal outrage. You could demand that the public rise up, express its own outrage, and let the Mayor know what they think of him for backing that awful idea."

We told Duskin, "The campaign will be all yours. You organize the public opposition. You deal with the press. You get all the credit." And if it feels useful, we said, we could do some quick follow-up ads to be sure to get a 100% win. "You'd become instantly famous and head the campaign," we added, "and be in a good position to build a movement against what's going on all over the city. Let someone else run your dress business for awhile."

By then Alvin was laughing loudly, and joyfully. For about five minutes. Then he got very quiet. Finally he said, "Okay, when do you need the money?"

Warren and I worked quickly on the ad, passing it back and forth a few times daily, and sharing it with Alvin, who added some of his own ideas. We got it inserted into the paper within a week. The ad had five clip-out coupons: one each to the mayor and the Board of Supervisors, one back to Alvin, *plus* one coupon to the US Secretary of the Interior, Walter Hickel; and one to Robert Kunzig of the US General Services Administration. These latter two coupons demanded that Alcatraz be given protected status as a National Park or Recreation Area, rather than be ruined by a Texas billionaire for his ego purposes. We thought that request would probably never be honored, but we wanted everyone to think of Alcatraz that way.

The response to the ad was *instantaneous* and gigantic. Eight thousand envelopes arrived in the Mayor's office immediately after the ad ran. Even more important was that Alioto played right into our hands.

That morning, the Mayor immediately called a press conference. He was furious. He attacked Duskin (whom he didn't know) as some kind of crazy, out of town, New York low-life. "A small-time New York dress guy who doesn't know anything about the needs of our great city." Alvin quickly advised the press that he was born and raised in San Francisco, as were his parents, and his three children, who all went through San Francisco schools. He had never lived anywhere else. And his dress company had been employing hundreds of San Franciscans for many years. The mayor looked ridiculous.

By the following morning, more than 18,000 coupons had been cut out, filled out and mailed by outraged SF citizens, collected in giant mailbags and dumped onto the desks of the Mayor and the Board of Supervisors. The following day more coupons streamed in.

Only 48 hours later, the Mayor and the Board of Supervisors *cancelled* the whole project! Less than a month later, Alcatraz was invaded by several hundred Indigenous activists, primarily from local California tribes, notably the *Ohlone*, who demanded recognition of *their* prior sovereignty over that island, and the right to determine whatever would become of it.

Duskin announced his full support for the invasion, and they remained camped out on Alcatraz for 19 months. Eventually they backed off when the island was given full, permanent protected status as part of the new Golden Gate National Recreation Area— just as the ad had demanded. *That* was a 100% victory!

(text continued on page 29)

(A LITTLE BIT OF TEXAS IN SAN FRANCISCO BAY?)

As Big A Steal As Manhattan Island

If you feel as I do, that our Mayor is rushing us into a bad deal, economically and otherwise, then raise your voice NOW.

On Monday it may be too late.

Alcatraz, July, 1904. From a glass negative, courtesy the San Francisco Maritime Museum.

1) Alcatraz, the focal point of San Francisco Bay, the center of our most precious resource, will soon become a "space museum" and the site of a "period re-creation of San Francisco." This is the plan of Texas millionaire Lamar Hunt, which the Board of Supervisors passed by one vote.

2) Everyone had thought *that* plan was already defeated and then we awoke one day to find we might spend our lives looking out at Hunt's island. Yet no one (except the Mayor and Mr. Hunt) actually *liked* the plan much, and the Planning Commission discredited it utterly. One commissioner said, "We don't need a new chamber of horrors."

3) The plan is touted by Mayor Alioto because of the money. Mr. Hunt promised, you see, to pay the $2,000,000 to buy the island for us; to give the city 1% of the island's gross revenue (which he said would come to $30-40,000 per year); and to pay $1,800 per month for maintenance to the Federal government until the deal is complete.

Yet numerous reports (including one by Planning Commissioner Jacobs) indicated the government might *give* the island to San Francisco for *nothing* if "the city decided to use the island solely for the public benefit." The Mayor should be getting Alcatraz *free!*

As for the 1% we would get, remember this: Mr. Hunt would get 99%! (If we got 2%, he would get 98%, 3% for us is 97% for him, etc. etc.) And he's already richer than we are. In any event, for Mr. Hunt to be talking about $30,000 to $40,000 a year is absurd. We get almost that much income from Coit Tower. It is far less than the income from Kezar or Brooks Hall, or the Union Square Garage ($650,000). And it is a *lot* less than from Mr. Trieschmann's plan for Alcatraz. (Not that we should go for that one either, but at least it *does* produce income.)

The $1,800 per month maintenance? It seems inconceivable that *that* amount could have had any bearing on any decision, but if it did, here is my offer: If Mayor Alioto will work to delay this decision for six months, try to get Alcatraz free, and come up with a better plan—in other words, if he will act like the Mayor of San Francisco and not like a lobbyist for Lamar Hunt—I will take care of the $1,800 a month for six months.

4) The Mayor also said he likes the Hunt plan for its "open space" provisions.

That plan provides "open space" in the sense that Candlestick Park provides "open space." The structures don't cover the whole area, true, but who feels like he's in open space when he's standing in the middle of a stadium or on top of a "space museum"?

5) Real open space, of course, could only be provided on Alcatraz by tearing down the buildings and then leaving it completely alone—giving it back to the Pelicans the Spanish named it for—and frankly that is the plan I personally favor. That would be the most pleasing view of all in our Bay. And it could be a step towards making the whole Bay a National Park.

6) But never mind *my* ideas, there have been many other good ones. My point in placing this ad is not to promote my own plan, but to stop Mr. Hunt's. If my plan is only a dream, then his is a nightmare.

A SPACE MUSEUM. What will be in this space museum? A "song" to American victory? An America-first polemic? Who will write the copy inside and plan the fittings? H. L. Hunt? It is worth noting that NASA will likely supply most of the rockets and capsules—and *free*—because it openly acknowledges its desire to "promote" public support for more space expenditures. Will Hunt's island be a gigantic propaganda pavilion? In *our* Bay?

And as for "re-creating San Francisco"—*on Alcatraz?* That idea is in a league with plastic redwood trees. It may be a nice facsimile, but the real thing is just nearby.

7) How could this have happened, that Mayor Alioto is rushing us into a contract with Lamar Hunt to execute a dreadful plan that no one has considered carefully?

The reason is that we—all of us out here in Citizenland—thought its passage so unlikely that we didn't bother to oppose it. The only one really trying was Mr. Hunt—and Mayor Alioto, for some reason. As The Chronicle put it, "...the millionaire and his aide have spent days and nights talking with supervisors. They were evidently persuasive."

8) The above is history. It is not quite too late. Use the coupons on the right. Write letters to the supervisors, or call them on the phone. Go to the Board meeting this coming Monday. Think up your own ideas and send them in, or send them to me. Don't only oppose the Bad Guys (listed in coupon #1), but support the Good Guys who voted against the Hunt plan. (Boas, Pelosi, Morrison, Mendelsohn, Tamaras.)

Find out: What do the city's architects favor? Planners? What ideas do poor people have for Alcatraz? (Here is a thought: Whatever the plan there will be demolition and construction jobs a-plenty, and jobs in concessions when the island is finished. Why doesn't the city seek a Federal grant and take this wonderful opportunity to set up on-the-job training, and continuing jobs, for its unemployed?)

Further: Where is the Sierra Club in all this? Why isn't there a referendum? Do other Bay cities have anything to say? Do we really have to make money from the most vital spot in the Bay? Why isn't anyone pushing the Feds to get the island free? For some meaningful purpose, or some beautiful one? What on Earth is the rush? The election?

I am as much of a novice in big city politics as you are—I spend most of my days manufacturing dresses—but I feel sure that if we rally on this one we can stop Mr. Hunt. And in the process, create something great in the Bay.

Alvin Duskin
984 Mission Street
San Francisco 94103

No. 1

To: The Clerk, Board of Supervisors, City Hall, San Francisco, California

Dear Sir:

Kindly inform Supervisors Von Beroldingen, Blake, Ertola, Francois, Gonzales, and Mailliard that I oppose their rushing into the Hunt plan for Alcatraz. There are good alternatives, including some pressure on the Feds to give it to the city free. I ask that one of them move for a six month delay of approval for this plan which nobody seems to like very much, except Mr. Alioto and Mr. Hunt.

Name
Address
City _____ State _____ Zip

No. 2

Mayor Joseph Alioto, City Hall, San Francisco

Dear Sir:

I oppose your support of the Hunt plan for Alcatraz, at least until it is considered by the people along with other possibilities. Also, I disagree with your apparent view that no one would go over there if it were only rocks, sea and birds. Plenty of people would go over there, if a commercial ferry would take us. The view is the greatest in the world, so they say. Please stop pushing so hard for the Hunt plan.

Name
Address
City _____ State _____ Zip

No. 3

Robert Kunzig, Administrator, General Services Administration, General Services Building, 18th and "F" Street N.W., Washington, D.C. 20405

Dear Sir:

Traditionally, in deals involving public property and public agencies responsible only to taxpayers, the price of one dollar is exacted. Under what conditions and uses would you agree to a free transfer of title to Alcatraz from the Federal government to the city of San Francisco? Park usage? Public housing? Cultural benefit? Conservation? We want Alcatraz back, and perhaps the only price for it ought to be the one we've already paid: looking at a Federal prison out there all these years.

Name
Address
City _____ State _____ Zip

No. 4

Walter J. Hickel, Secretary, Department of the Interior, C Street between 18th and 19th Streets N.W., Washington, D.C. 20240

Dear Sir:

I wish to propose an idea to you. San Francisco Bay, which is in increasing danger of being destroyed by fill and pollution like Lake Erie and most of our rivers, is one of the country's great scenic resources. I propose that you ask the General Services Administration to grant the Department of the Interior title to Alcatraz Island, as a first step in the eventual declaration of San Francisco Bay as a National Park or National Monument. Development in the Bay has gone far enough.

Name
Address
City _____ State _____ Zip

No. 5

Alvin Duskin
984 Mission Street
San Francisco, California 94103

Dear Sir:

I support your efforts to stop the Hunt plan for Alcatraz.

☐ I agree with you that the buildings should be torn down and the island left to the birds.
☐ I believe that Alcatraz should be left alone. That nothing be done to change it.
☐ I propose the attached plan.

Name
Address
City _____ State _____ Zip

YOU CAN HELP DECIDE IF OUR CITY WILL BECOME A SKYLINE OF TOMBSTONES.

PHOTO: STEWART BLOOM

Both the above pictures are of downtown San Francisco. Same spot, same weather conditions. The top one was twelve years ago. The bottom one, last year.

In only twelve years the downtown area has taken on the closed, forbidding look and feel of most other American cities. And now the high-rises are beginning to spread throughout the city, ruining views, changing the character of the landscape, and what's more, increasing property taxes city-wide.

New studies have shown that the more we build high-rise, the more expensive it becomes to live here. They are as great a disaster economically as they are esthetically. Ask a New York taxpayer.

In the next five years, 40 more skyscraper office buildings are due to be built and nearly as many high-rise hotels and apartments.

Many of them are going into new areas of town which so far have been spared. You can help slow them down.

A petition is being circulated which would stop construction on all new buildings taller than six stories until each of them is studied by the voters of this city and approved.

Tall buildings could still be built, but only after the people of the city wanted them. The pressure would be on the big developers to **prove** that these buildings bring money into the city, and that they mean long-term jobs for San Franciscans, not only commuters. Thank you.

Alvin Duskin

HOW YOU CAN HELP:

1) Sign a petition or circulate one (only registered San Francisco voters may do this);
2) help with mailings, phone calls and organizational work;
3) donate money to accelerate the campaign.

Use the coupon, or come personally anytime from 9-6, Monday through Saturday: 520 Third St., Second Floor. (397-9200)

To: The San Francisco Opposition, Alvin Duskin Factory,
520 Third Street (Second Floor), San Francisco, CA 94107
☐ I would like to sign a petition and will be coming down to do so. (Only registered San Francisco voters may sign; if you are **not** registered, we **can** register you.)
☐ I would like to circulate a petition, or man a signature table. ☐ I will be down to pick them up. ☐ I can't come down, but please mail them to me at the address below. (Registered San Francisco voters only.)
☐ I am not eligible to vote in San Francisco, but would like to help the campaign with volunteer work at your office, or elsewhere. ☐ I will come down to talk to you about it between 9-6, Monday through Saturday. ☐ I can't come down, so will you please call me at the number below.
☐ Here is a donation of $_____ to help with the costs of running this campaign: staff, mailings, printing, ads, etcetera. (Checks payable to: San Francisco Opposition.)

Name_____ Phone number_____
Address_____
City_____ State_____ Zip_____

28

"THE SAN FRANCISCO OPPOSITION"

So, from out of nowhere, Alvin Duskin had quickly and successfully stepped forward to launch and assume the reigns of a tremendously powerful local urban environmental movement in San Francisco. He organized the emerging activists under the name of the San Francisco Opposition. Once the Alcatraz issue had simmered down, Alvin continued with new campaigns against urban overdevelopment and other issues. I will return to those shortly.

I was so pleased by the ease and intelligence that Duskin had displayed in the Alcatraz campaign, and his apparent interest in doing future ads on a variety of urban environmental issues, that I asked Alvin if he'd like to join the startup Board of a new *non-profit* ad agency I was putting together, Public Interest Communications. PIC would launch as soon as we finished dissolving Freeman, Mander & Gossage. The Board included Dugald Stermer, the fabulous Art Director of *Ramparts* magazine in its heyday years, and King Harris, the progressive, retired former president of Campbell Ewald, a commercial ad agency in the city.

Public Interest Communications (PIC) would become the first strictly not-for-profit ad agency in the US, as far as I knew. It was during transition to that venue, over the next five years, that Alvin initiated a new series of very effective protest campaigns.

The first ad in the new series was a protest against the horrific overdevelopment of high-rise architecture throughout the city, destroying its small-scale Mediterranean character and pastel beauty. The ad shows two marvelous photos of the San Francisco skyline taken from across the Bay, one picture twelve years earlier than the latter (by Stewart Bloom).

The main demand of the ad was that the Board of Supervisors enact a city-wide six story height limit. Alioto and other officials were aghast. They made the ridiculous rejoinder that high-rise buildings aided "economic development" and were good for everybody. Yet it was obviously a lie, as the ads explain. As high-rise buildings spread through the city, the rents rapidly increased throughout formerly affordable neighborhoods. There was suddenly an advance of homelessness among people who could no longer afford the rents. Alvin proposed and sponsored more ads on the subject, including this:

"YOU CAN HELP DECIDE IF
OUR CITY BECOMES A SKYLINE
OF TOMBSTONES."

The uprisings in response to the Duskin campaigns were very strong, and the city finally *did* pass a city-wide six story height limit that lasted for several years.

Throughout these battles, Alvin Duskin led his movement with great ease, charm and joy; and the San Francisco Opposition was able to achieve a series of staggering victories. For a full decade, the San Francisco Opposition campaigns had a major role in maintaining San Francisco's appealing look and character.

Meanwhile, Duskin and the movements he had helped launch were enthusiastically expanding beyond their San Francisco Bay Area base to deal with some broader negative developments in the state of California. I helped Alvin produce two explosive attacks opposing the planned California Water Project and the Peripheral Canal. These monstrous projects, built at public expense, were designed to divert northern California wild river waters to southern California to feed more overdevelopment. While claiming that the purpose of the water diversion was to provide drinking water to the south, the real goal was to benefit large scale industrialized corporate farming in southern California, and to service industrial development and population growth east of Los Angeles. Those were new battle territories for all of us.

Unfortunately, those latter campaigns against on-coming state-wide rapid commercial development proved less successful than the earlier rounds in San Francisco where one or two ads in the local paper were able to shock a local population into focusing on human and environmental needs before serving a wealthy few. The latter Duskin ads were not sufficient to change the dynamics of statewide issues. We would have needed much larger budgets. However, the statewide ads did help to diminish, to some degree, the extent of the water diversion process. But huge corporate opposition spending and campaigns by corrupt state officials continued to dominate state-wide media.

Looking back now, a half century after our great local victories, I regret to report that the situation in San Francisco is now even worse than when we started our early campaigns. A massive "techie" takeover of San Francisco has rapidly undermined our victories from four decades earlier. The tech industry and its self-interested, and self-aggrandizing campaigns are rapidly advancing, taking full control of the city. After 50 years of local resistance, one of the world's most appreciated and appealing urban environments is disappearing.

Alcatraz, The Bay, Water And The Imminent Death of California

FOUR MONTHS AGO, being personally outraged over the plans for a mindless commercialization of Alcatraz, I placed an ad in these pages.

To my amazement, it produced a tremendous public outcry and we were all treated to the spectacle of officials trampling each other in a race to deny that they had ever voted the way they *had* in fact voted.

The Hunt Plan for Alcatraz is dead, and now it seems that the island will either become a park (which almost all of the 8,000 respondents wanted it to be) or else it may be given to the Indians.

Both solutions are acceptable as far as I am personally concerned, the more so because my own preference—a bird sanctuary—has begun to seem to me inadequate. Recent terrifying facts have made me realize that the birds may soon have nothing to eat from bay waters [dead fish] and when the situation for birds, and trees, and by the way for people is reaching the point where we are all as nearly extinct as the brown pelican.

In order to save Alcatraz for wildlife, it is necessary to keep life in the Bay, and if any of you think that struggle has been won by the Save the Bay people then you haven't heard of a creation called The California Water Plan. Listen to this:

1. The idea is to take water which is presently in ample supply in Northern California and move it south, via one of the most complex (and expensive) series of canals, dams, pipelines and tunnels ever accomplished in the world (see map). The result will be terrible destruction to scenic areas, but that's the least of it.

2. The water is to be used to encourage new industry and more population on the presently undeveloped outskirts of Los Angeles. In other words, to make more Los Angeles .

3. The water will produce profits for (a) real estate developers eager to turn the countryside into suburbs (b) industry, which wants the water for development, and (c) some mechanized agriculture, principally subsidized cotton.

4. On the other hand, the accelerated development will dramatically increase smog, traffic, people and poisonous chemicals. It will encourage everything *bad* about Los Angeles.

While helping some business it will do so at the expense of 99% of the population.

5. So much for L.A. Here is what will happen

I. THE POLLUTION "BODY COUNT"

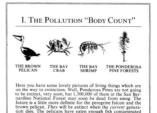

THE BROWN PELICAN THE BAY CRAB THE BAY SHRIMP THE PONDEROSA PINE FORESTS

Here you have some lovely pictures of living things which are on the way to extinction. Well, Ponderosa Pines are not going to be extinct, very soon, but 1,300,000 or them in the San Bernardino National Forest may soon be dead from smog. The future is a little more definite for the peregrine falcon and the brown pelican. *They* will be extinct when the *current* generation dies. The pelicans have eaten enough fish contaminated with pesticides that as a result, when they lay eggs, the shell is not thick enough to support its own weight. It cracks open and all the offspring die. No next generation. We don't know what happens to the human reproductive process from digesting these same fish, but it isn't good, that much we know.

up here. After the water is diverted, the fresh water outflow of the Sacramento River will be reduced from 18 million acre feet per year to 2 million. (See Box II.)

II. THE SACRAMENTO

Fresh water flow of the Sacramento River today [A], and when and if the California Water Plan is completed [B]. All the fresh water between gets shipped to Southern California to help make more of Los Angeles.

6. With less fresh water flowing through the rivers and delta, the pesticides, nitrates and industrial chemicals that wash into it will have much greater destructive power than even now. They are likely to kill off millions of fish (as happened recently in Germany), species which eat the fish, plantlife along the shores, birds which need the plantlife, and finally, the marine plankton along California's continental shelf, which produce 70% of the oxygen we breathe.

It's a chain reaction. Everything needs the next thing, you see; that is the miracle of nature. We are busily destroying the chain, forgetting that if *it* is disrupted, so are we. A few too many chemicals in the plankton, or the fish and birds *we* eat, and we can forget Alcatraz forever.

7. These same chemicals flow into San Francisco Bay and eventually we will have a bay as dead as Lake Erie. Which is why what happens to the birds on Alcatraz starts with what happens to the California Water Plan in Sacramento. But there's one other little point. Poison Lake.

8. As it heads south some water will be used for irrigation. Eventually this water will be leached from the land into a giant ditch (San Joaquin Drain) because it will be so filled with nitrates and pesticides that it could begin to poison the soil.

9. Originally, the plan was to take this poisoned water and, by a marvel of engineering creativity, dump it back into San Francisco Bay. This technological advance has since been discredited, but as nobody can figure just what *can* be done with such a deadly water supply, the solution that's been devised is this one: collect it all in what the engineers call Kesterton Reservoir, but I call "Poison Lake," and then leave it there until someone figures out how to clean it all up. That's the solution!

10. Now all this imaginative thinking is not free. You and I voted in 1960 (during the administration of Governor Brown) to pass the $1.75 billion Water Bonds Act to execute this wonderful thing. What did *we* know? But this water is not for drinking, it turns out, and the real cost is more nearly $3 billion and guess who is going to foot the bill for the difference? You know the answer. (See Box III.)

11. There's a lot more to this, of course, than I can possibly tell you on this page, and I'm not the expert anyway. If any of you want the full technical story, please check the appropriate box above, and I'll tell you where to find reports which all discuss alternative less expensive and less destructive ways of getting water where and when it is really needed, and which also contain reports by scientists who *are* experts and who will scare you more than I have.

It should be obvious that the time for placing prime importance on commercial development of anything in this state has long since passed. We have already reached the point where life in California is hardly the pleasant experience it used to be. What's the use of a nice house in the countryside when there's damn little countryside anymore? Where do *you* go to escape people or traffic or aircraft noise? Or to find unpoisoned air, or food that's not killing you slowly as you eat it?

In Los Angeles, things are so bad that mothers are keeping their children indoors to keep them from breathing the air. (In Tokyo, by the way, they have vending machines which provide a few minutes worth of oxygen. Put in a coin, out drops a face mask. That's what it's come to there.)

Industrial growth may have been a good idea when California was an underdeveloped state, but now it's an overdeveloped state. We cannot afford any longer to give commerce and industry

first say-so over the environment, not if we once get it in our heads that we are also wildlife; we are only one strand of the web of life on this planet and in order to survive we have got to save everything else.

III. MONEY

The California Water Plan is not the brainchild of Governor Reagan though he has been doing his part in promoting it. It was hatched during the administration of Governor Brown who said it would cost no more than the $1.75 billion we authorized in the 1960 Water Bonds Act. [See A on chart] However, according to the Daily Commercial News, he knew even then that it would cost more, but didn't say so because of "political realities." The Daily Commercial News reported: "Without telling the public that the cost was [then] estimated at $1.94 billion with no consideration for inflation, [See B] 'in light of political realities' the voters [that's us] were induced to vote the $1.75 billion." The real costs are *now* estimated by the state at $2.75 billion, [C] and on the upcoming June ballot we are all probably going to be asked to approve a constitutional amendment upping the interest rate so that the state can unload $800 million worth of unsold water bonds. "Upping the interest rate" means that you and I get to pay more so the state can continue this disaster. Actually, no one has any definite idea of what the whole thing will cost by the time it is finished, since so much of the technology that is needed to pull it off hasn't yet been developed. Some organizations have said it will wind up costing at least twice what Governor Brown said it would [D].

The California Water Plan will accelerate development at a time when we're choking from what we already have. Just because, in our naivete, we supported it ten years ago, does not change that it's a disaster in today's world and should be scrapped.

A critical element of the project—the Peripheral Canal—is now on Gov. Reagan's desk. Hailed by the State as a "compromise," this canal would divert water from above the Delta instead of from the Delta itself which makes it about as much of a compromise as one bullet in the heart instead of two. The *entire plan* is out of date and all work on it must be stopped, if we want a livable California.

Please join me in trying to halt this project, by mailing the coupons above and encouraging others to do likewise. Thank you.

Alvin Duskin, 510 3rd St., San Francisco 94107

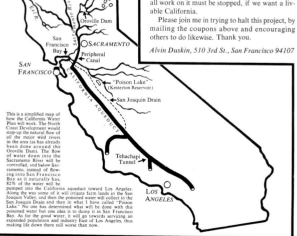

This is a simplified map of how the California Water Plan will work. The North Coast Development would stop-up the natural flow of *all* the major wild rivers in the area (as has already been done around the Oroville Dam). The flow of water down into the Sacramento River will be controlled, and below Sacramento, instead of flowing into San Francisco Bay as it naturally has, 82% of the water will be pumped into the California aqueduct toward Los Angeles. Along the way some of it will irrigate farm lands in the San Joaquin Valley, and then the poisoned water will collect in what I have called "Poison Lake." No one has determined what will be done with this poisoned water but one idea is to dump it in San Francisco Bay. As for the *good* water, it will go towards servicing an expanded population and industry East of Los Angeles, thus making life down there still worse than now.

Long-time San Franciscans are now fleeing the city in droves to escape sky-rocketing rents, non-stop traffic jams at all hours, and the ugly high-rise buildings that now dominate the city, reminding us all, every day, who is now in charge. San Francisco is now ranked among the world's most expensive cities.

The most awful techie building of all, and by far the tallest in San Francisco, is the Sales Force Tower, 65 stories high, rising above the formerly gorgeous low-rise Mediterranean skyline. The top several floors of the building are a monstrous *LED screen* projecting its technocratic imagery every night in four directions across the entire city and the Bay as well. There is no escape from it. It expresses a degree of arrogance, ugliness, and self-importance that defy belief, except as a statement emanating from a worldview that believes only in its own powers. And the joys of utter dominion over a local landscape. In fact, that building represents an appropriate celebration of self-interested, techie-channeled arrogance, demonstrating a desire and ability to capture everything and everyone.

Meanwhile, Marc Benioff, who runs Sales Force, gave interviews in the *The New York Times* saying how much he loves San Francisco, and how much work he is doing to help San Francisco's homeless. The reality is that he and Sales Force and the rest of the techie takeover crews were the main *cause* of the homelessness, the flight of long-term residents, and the ugly-fication of San Francisco. We now have a citywide celebration of techie arrogance.

The historic diversity of San Francisco's residents is a thing of the past. Down on street level, thousands of twenty-something white boys have captured the sidewalks, walking pridefully among their giggling groups, many of them sporting fashionable little beards, talking into their iPhones, appreciating themselves while driving long-time residents out of that dying city.

Here's the terrible reality that we have to admit. The great urban battles that we won 30 years ago, have *not* been sustained. Dave Brower had it right: *"There are no environmental victories, only holding actions."* Money interests always come back. They never get old. There's always a Marc Benioff to lead the invasion.

Meanwhile, Alvin Duskin fled San Francisco. In his late eighties, Alvin moved an hour north of the city, near the ocean. So did I. Herb Caen was gone. Jessica Mitford and Warren Hinckle are gone too. But Alvin and I were still hanging out, discussing the matters until his death in 2021.

So, was anyone else out there who'd join us to fight this battle over again?

ENTER: DAVID BROWER (2)
Friends of the Earth, International

Following his departure from the Sierra Club in 1969, Dave Brower immediately founded Friends of the Earth. At Howard Gossage's invitation, Brower moved FOE into the second floor of Freeman, Mander & Gossage, soon joined by his favorite staff members: Tom Turner, Hugh Nash, and then Ken Brower, Dave's son, as well as Joan McIntyre. Within a few years, FOE became Friends of the Earth, International. It quickly expanded with affiliates in 30 countries and still remains one of the few most internationally important and globally focused environmental groups.

Brower had been fired by the Sierra Club Board because he had placed the *Earth National Park* ad without explicit permission, which led him to start a new organization with his own hand-picked Board. This assured that he could openly advocate a much broader view of global environmental crises. Brower's rhetoric and his new projects made clear his intentions. Now he was openly suggesting that the entire planet needed to be conceived as "an environmental conservation district within the Universe." He was ready to do battle on a much broader terrain, including critiquing certain new technological advances, and the environmental consequences of militarism.

The four ads from FOE that I have shown here are good examples of his new terrain. Brower's first ad at FOE was directed against an awful new technology, the proposed US Super-Sonic air transport (SST) that the Nixon government was supporting. SST promoters celebrated the possibility of two-hour flights from New York to Paris. But they did not discuss the SST's long list of environmental impacts. With an assist from FOE's anti-SST ad campaign, the project was dropped.

Alas, that is another case where an environmental victory in the first round is challenged again a decade or two later. David Brower successfully fought the SST forty years ago on environmental grounds, but Donald Trump tried hard to revive it.

★　　★　　★

From its beginnings, Friends of the Earth viewed global environmental crises as multi-faceted and multi-dimensional. Besides the battles for parklands

(text continued on page 35)

(SST: "Airplane of Tomorrow")

BREAKS WINDOWS, CRACKS WALLS, STAMPEDES CATTLE, AND WILL HASTEN THE END OF THE AMERICAN WILDERNESS

FRIENDS OF THE EARTH is a conservation organization and we have been reading, with mixed feelings, all the recent reports about threats to our environment and the "massive efforts to win the War on Pollution."

It's a good thing, clearly, to recognize that we've only a few years to meet such problems. However we have the sinking feeling that what we've witnessed so far is only *apparent* activity; *cosmetic* solutions which are creating an impression in the public mind that things are somehow being taken care of.

But things are *not* being taken care of.

For example, this:

1) In the same message that he spoke so eloquently about environmental pollution, President Nixon announced that he was budgeting $275 million for this year's work toward a commercial supersonic transport (SST).

2) Mr. Nixon said that he made that decision in order to (a) create jobs, (b) help the balance of payments, and (c) add to our national prestige. He did not say anything about the virtues of the plane itself. It is easy to understand why.

3) The SST has been a subject of controversy mainly because it produces a "sonic boom." If you've ever heard one (from the much quieter military supersonic fighters that occasionally fly by) you'll remember it as a shattering experience. Something in the magnitude of a factory explosion down the block. It is that sudden and scary.

4) Sleeping through a sonic boom is out of the

RELATIVE NOISE LEVELS

	Perceived decibel level
Room in a quiet city dwelling at midnight	32
Average city residence	40
Small 2-engine private plane (sideline noise @ 1,500 feet)	80-85
Heavy truck, 25 ft. away	90
Train whistle, 500 feet away	90
Subway train, 20 feet away	95
DC-3 (sideline noise @ 1,500 feet)	95-100
Loud outboard motor	102
Loud motorcycle	110
Boeing 707, DC-8 (sideline noise @ 1,500 feet)	110-115
Rock 'n' Roll band playing at loudest moments	120
Large pneumatic 3" riveter	125
SST (sideline noise @ 1,500 feet)	122-129

Increases in decibels, by the way, are not arithmetic, they are logarithmic. Therefore every increase of ten decibels is a ten-time increase in noise!
According to the FAA, 100 decibels is a level that a high percentage of the population will find intolerable, and to which they'll react strongly. Yet, the FAA's new noise standards permit 108. The first question, then, is why they are permitting noise standards above what the population will find tolerable? And secondly why are they supporting the SST which will be many times worse than is now permissible? If the argument is that most of this urban noise – during take-off and landing – will be right around the airport we should point out that the SST's take-off noise won't be confined to the airport vicinity. It will produce over 100 decibels for 13 miles in either direction from its flight path.

question. Booms can break windows, crack walls, and stampede cattle and have done so throughout the country. If they're used for everyday commercial travel, stay off of operating tables at boom-time.

5) The boom affects an area 50 miles wide for the entire length of a flight. If the SST flew the usual air routes in this country, the boom zones would cover practically everything. (See map.) In some places – Cape Cod for example – the

average day might be punctuated by twenty bangs loud enough to make you duck for cover. Even wilderness areas – the one place where man's technological feats give way to nature's quiet – will offer no escape.

6) Boeing Aircraft – which is receiving a 90% subsidy to build the thing – likes to call it the "airplane of tomorrow." As for the boom, they call that "a 20th Century sound."

People in Oklahoma City, however, don't call it that. In 1964 they put up with five months of military supersonic testing and reacted this way: 15,000 complaints to authorities, 4,000 damage suits and the declaration by a quarter of the population that they could never live with it.

7) Mr. Nixon, apparently sensitive to this point, said we shouldn't worry, that the SST would fly at boom speeds only over the oceans, or other sparsely populated areas.

But the FAA has *not* said that, though if it did, it wouldn't mean much. Its membership changes, remember, and so by the way does the President. Ten years hence, if SSTs prove unprofitable without high speed land routes which do you think the airlines will do: scrap them? Or lobby to change the ruling? You know the answer.

8) But *what about* the oceans?

No one knows the effect of sonic booms upon sea life. If the enormous vibrations should disperse the fish concentrations off Newfoundland (over which most trans-Atlantic SSTs would fly), it could disturb the fish industries there. That's 40% of the U.S. fish catch and 12% of the world's.

We *do* know what happens to animals living under the boom. They panic. A boom killed 2,000 mink in Minnesota during 1966; a boom drove a herd of cattle off a cliff in Switzerland in 1968; and simulated booms have significantly changed the birth patterns of test rats at the University of Oklahoma.

9) As for the sparsely populated areas, *those* are what we now call wilderness; places still free of the crunch of technology.

Or they're farmlands, or reservations, or else national park lands where a visit would no longer be the same. Not with a boom every little while, and the trees rattling, and animals going crazy from the shock.

So much for sonic booms. They are a terrible prospect, but they're only part of the story.

10) Before making his decision, Mr. Nixon established a committee of many of the top figures in his own administration to advise him concerning whether he should cancel the whole SST project.

They said yes, he should.

The feeling of their report is typified by the remark of Mr. Hendrik S. Houthakker of the President's Council of Economic Advisors who, on the question of prestige, put it this way: "…we do not believe that our prestige abroad will be enhanced by a concentration on white elephants." (See also Footnote.)

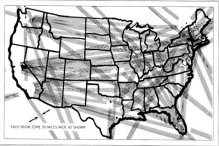
This map shows the air routes across the continental United States. If SSTs used these routes, boom zones 50 miles wide would effectively cover most of the country. (See also item 7 in text.) Some say it is possible to learn to live with the boom. Oklahoma City citizens who had bitter taste of this kind of "living" in 1964 rose in outrage against it. And many doctors have indicated that, psychological effects aside, we already have much more noise in our daily lives than is healthy for our hearts and nervous systems. Dr. Samuel Rosen of the Mt. Sinai School of Medicine put it this way: "Any loud noise, whether we like it or not, constricts blood vessels. Eventually, this could cause permanent damage." And Dr. Chauncey Leake of the Univ. of Calif. Med. Center has said : "Noise is a stress, an insult…It affects the nervous, endocrine and reproductive systems. It may damage unborn children."

EACH BOOM ZONE 50 MILES WIDE AS SHOWN

11) There is evidence that the SST will pollute the upper atmosphere in such a way as may result in terrible alterations of global weather.

12) It will be far more dangerous than present aircraft because of severe problems of metal fatigue, landing speed, visibility and maneuverability.

13) It will have a relatively short range (4,000 miles). And despite the fact that it will be *more* expensive to build than the 747, it will use *three times* the fuel.

As a result, it will be much more expensive to fly in. It will be an elitist's flight.

That's your "airplane of tomorrow!"

Notwithstanding all the talk, it appears that *basic* attitudes remain unaltered.

The SST is being built because people continue to believe that there's an advantage to being able to get from N.Y. to Paris two hours sooner than at present; that if technology can do a thing, then it ought to be done.

But this attitude – the tendency to place technology ahead of considerations of our living environment – has gotten us into this mess. More luxury technology may have seemed a good idea at one time in history, when we were an underdeveloped country. But now we are an over-developed country.

The little bits of wilderness that still exist are being threatened daily by our *more, faster, bigger* attitudes. Industry needing more space, or trees, or ore; ever more people buying more of what industry makes and then seeking a place to escape from it.

Talking about "pollution" is not sufficient. If industry, "newly awake to its responsibilities," as the media like to say, *does* come up with a non-polluting auto engine, will it then be okay to cover-up the rest of America with highways and cars? (Mr. Nixon's budget also contains $5½ billion for highway construction. The result will be more damage than all of his anti-pollution programs could possibly correct.)

And even if there were no boom, the more noise we have in cities and over America's parkland, the more it will confirm the nightmarish

feeling: *We are locked in a small room, and the walls and ceiling are closing in on us.*

Friends of the Earth is interested in promoting the proposition that we had better come up with alternatives to endless technological expansion, considering that we live on a planet of fixed size.

We have established a number of task forces to investigate the implications of an economy in which growth of exploitive industries is curtailed; a society which doesn't measure "progress" as an outgrowth of GNP. We wish to build for a system which you might call microdynamic, while macrostatic.

Meanwhile, we are also opposing specific government and industry projects that seem to us to typify the sort of thinking that will lead our species into an unnecessarily short and miserable life. The SST is one. New highway construction is another. Nuclear power. Water diversion. The Alaska Pipeline. Pesticides. Airport expansions. The killing of wildlife for furs. Etc., Etc.

Coupon #6 above will permit you to learn more about what we are up to. The others contain messages to specific individuals who can be effective in stopping the SST. But please do not stop there. The congressional vote on the SST will be coming up *within the next few weeks*. Write, telephone and wire your own congressmen, the Department of the Interior, the Department of Transportation, the FAA, and urge others to do likewise.

Thank you.

David Brower, *President*
Gary Soucie, *Executive Director*
Friends of the Earth
451 Pacific Ave., San Francisco, CA 94133, *or*
30 East 42nd St., New York, NY 10017

FOOTNOTE
On the other two issues Mr. Nixon felt were paramount in his decision in favor of the SST, his advisory committee felt as follows:
JOBS: "The net employment increase from SST production would likely be negligible and would occur in the professional and technical categories where shortages already exist. The project would have practically no employment benefits for the disadvantaged hardcore unemployed." BALANCE OF PAYMENTS: "If the U.S. overall balance of payments is considered, there is substantial reason for delay in proceeding to the next stage of SST development." [The reasoning went this way: Mostly Americans, and mainly rich ones, would fly on SSTs. They would spend large sums abroad, thereby *worsening* the balance of payments.] FOR A COMPLETE COPY OF THE PRESIDENT'S ADVISORY COMMITTEE REPORT ON THE SST, SEE COUPON #6.

THE NEW YORK TIMES, MONDAY, AUGUST 23, 1982

("...The need is now for a gentler, a more tolerant people than those who won for us against the ice, the tiger and the bear. The hand that hefted the ax, out of some old blind allegiance to the past, fondles the machine gun as lovingly. It is a habit we will have to break to survive, but the roots go very deep." [Loren Eiseley])

Ecology & War

THIS ADVERTISEMENT is placed by Friends of the Earth, a conservation organization, but it concerns war. Until recently we were content to work for our usual constituency: life in its miraculous diversity of forms. We have spoken for the trees and plants, the animals, the air and water, and for the land itself. We have argued that human well being cannot be separated from the health of the natural world from which we all emerged. We have left it for others to argue about war.

But the nuclear war contemplated by the U.S. and Russia would kill life of *all* kinds, indiscriminately, on a scale and for a length of time into the future that is so great that it qualifies as the major ecological issue of our time. In fact, from an ecological point of view, the war has already begun, as the mere preparations for it are causing illness and deprivation to humans, bringing harm to the planet's life-sustaining abilities, and casting a deathly pall over life on Earth.

I

We have been living with the nuclear threat too long. That nations continue to threaten each other does violence to the human spirit. Among the young, expectations of an early death have placed a vise on their hearts and creative energies. A deadening blow has been struck against the future. Just *thinking* about war as much as we've had to is stifling the human imagination.

We're told *not* to think about it, but to leave it to national security planners. These people talk "counterforce targeting," "equivalent megatons," "industrial survivability"...phrases which avoid the actuality of millions of dead children, vaporized forests, disappeared cities.

We have heard this kind of language before. To the people who do-in nature, forests are "board feet," rivers are "acre feet," nature itself is a "resource." No sense of awe of the natural world. No connection or caring. It's the same mentality that can plan the death of whole populations. They sit before their computers plotting war scenarios and missile trajectories, dazzled by automated weapons and computer targeting—are we supposed to trust these people? To them it's just blips on a video screen like some kind of hot game of Missile Command. Except at the end there are 500 million dead bodies and a world laid waste for eons. In behalf of what? A competition among computer programmers?

II

Even if the shooting war never actually starts, every stage in preparation for it brings danger to human beings and the planet. Digging uranium from the ground causes lung cancers among miners at ten times the national average. The transit of nuclear materials on roads brings the chance of deadly accident. Nuclear plants make disaster or terrorism a present danger. The continued testing of weapons releases radiation into soil and air. *All* nuclear production adds to the stockpiles of atomic wastes, some deadly to life for 250,000 years or more.

Meanwhile, countries obsessed with the glamour of militarism remain blind to other ecological perils. The recent *Global 2000 Report to the President* states that catastrophe awaits if nations don't stop what they're doing and turn to the following: 1) an imminent worldwide shortage of water, 2) the loss of forest cover, 3) the rapidly expanding deserts and the deterioration of the world's topsoil, affecting the food supply, 4) the ravaging of the world's remaining fuel and minerals, 5) the reckless increase of CO_2 in the atmosphere, 6) the destruction of animal habitats and with them the planet's genetic reserves. These are symptoms of breakdown of the Earth's life support system, a *holocaust*, except in slow motion, without the fireball.

President Reagan responded to the report by firing its authors. He dismantled U.S. agencies that research these problems. And he has increased the rate at which we devour energy and minerals to feed the military machine.

III

The political adage says, "The public is always ahead of the politicians." And so it is now. Millions of people are demonstrating for an end to the arms race, an end to belligerence, and a turn toward something "higher" in human affairs. The leaders of most governments have not understood this call. Perhaps they are not equipped to grasp it.

Take Mr. Reagan and Mr. Brezhnev. Both men see the world in terms of power, domination, national interest, spheres of influence, "massive retaliation." They both seek to "negotiate from strength," i.e., by intimidation. Can this possibly succeed? ("You don't increase your security by decreasing the security of your opponent."
—Richard Barnet)

Mr. Reagan wants peace, he says, but he budgets more for war than anyone in history, at the expense of the economy, suffering Americans, and the environment. He is exporting more than $25 billion in arms to other nations. He is also increasing exports of nuclear technology, bringing bomb capability to many small countries. He speaks of "freedom" but supports governments that oppress their own people (El Salvador, South Africa) and he doesn't seem to understand the contradiction in this. As for the peace movement, he discounts it as "orchestrated" by Russia.

Mr. Brezhnev seems the same. He speaks of peace but builds arms at the expense of his own people and economy. He exports weapons to warring nations and nuclear technology too. He supports governments that oppress their own people (Afghanistan, Poland). And the peace movement? He's for it in Europe and the U.S., but suppresses it in Russia.

Both men view disarmament in public relations terms. The goal is to seem as if you are interested in disarming, while pointing the finger at the other. *The world is sick of watching this!! Two bullies, facing each*

other down, acting out of pride, machismo, and insincerity. And apparently willing to bring all the rest of us down with them to defend their stuck positions. How do you get through to men like this?

The prognosis is not good unless, somehow, both Reagan and Brezhnev can be made to feel the gravity of the moment, are willing to identify with the other, recognize the amazing historical opportunity that is theirs, and, most important, deeply wish to succeed. We must insist they see things that way. The coupons may help. But we cannot leave it at that.

IV

In the short run, we must support *all* activities toward *fewer* arms. Nuclear freeze. SALT II. The test ban treaty. Get after your elected representatives—by mail or personally. Tell them you are outraged by the military budget and that your vote is going to disarmament candidates. But even this is not enough.

We need a profound change. A new political language which recognizes that real security emerges only when nations befriend each other. Belligerency, competition for resources on a finite planet, exploitation of people and nature are behaviors that have failed. They're out of date. We need to seek people skilled in the arts of peace, accommodation, compromise. Not shy to speak of love for all creatures and for whom war is a violation of natural law, a breakdown of the civilized experiment. We need to articulate a system of values that reflects this.

To encourage this process, Friends of the Earth is initiating the First Biennial Conference on the Fate of the Earth: Conservation and Security in a Sustainable Society. (The Cathedral of St. John the Divine, New York, Oct. 19-21.) Also, we have created new task forces on disarmament, the elections, and other related activities. For more information on these, please check the boxes below. Thank you.

FRIENDS OF THE EARTH
David Brower, *Chairman*, Rafe Pomerance, *President*

33

Ronald Reagan, the Health of Humans & the Natural World

Environmentalists were reluctant to criticize the President during his first year. We concentrated instead on Interior Secretary James Watt. But, let's face it, Mr. Reagan is the real James Watt. It's time to say so. ❦ Our President is taking apart nearly every institution that protects planetary and human health. His actions and his rhetoric are consistent: Destructive, disdainful and uncomprehending of environmental values. We've got a sad and serious problem. You can help turn it around.

The ecology movement began during the 1950s at the first signs of environmental breakdown: Pesticides in human tissue, dangerous levels of air pollution, strontium 90 in milk, sharp growth of cancer rates, loss of animal species, and the rapid depletion of wilderness.

For the first time, Americans sensed that the interdependence between humans and the natural world had to be taken seriously. We were not above the laws of nature. Despoiling our nest, we would eventually kill ourselves. Meanwhile, life itself would lose joy and meaning.

Presidents Kennedy, Johnson, Nixon, Ford and Carter were all, in varying degrees, responsive. New institutions emerged that had promise for preserving the health of the planet, of human beings, of future generations, and of the land, air and water.

A year ago, all that abruptly changed.

During his campaign, Mr. Reagan equated environmentalism with "extremism." We shook it off, but he has since repeated that word. By now it's obvious that Mr. Reagan sees environmentalists as some kind of enemy. From a President, this is something new and tragic. It comes at a moment when increased human passion toward the natural world might be the one thing that could save it, and us.

I. Mr. Reagan's Appointees
The new Assistant Secretary of Agriculture, John Crowell, used to work for Louisiana Pacific, the largest buyer of federal timber. He wants our national forests cut at three times the present rate.

Dr. John Todhunter used to *fight* pesticide regulations. Now he's supposed to regulate pesticides.

William A. Sullivan, Jr., was a lobbyist for the steel industry. Now he oversees enforcement of environmental law. "If I were an environmental activist," he said of his own appointment, "I'd be scared to death."

James Edwards, Energy Secretary, says ecologists are being "used by subversives." We think he means the Russians. He's fired a third of the solar energy staff. He plans a 93% cut in solar and conservation. Meanwhile, 100% of the *nuclear* budget remains.

James Watt used to sue the government for mining and energy companies. He is still carrying towels for them. His zeal has led more than one million Americans to sign petitions to fire him. Mr. Reagan's response? Watt is his "favorite" cabinet member.

The new head of the Environmental Protection Agency is Anne Gorsuch. Of her first 19 appointees, 15 were business executives. No environmentalists.

When these people think "environment" their images run to oil, minerals, lumber. To them, the environment is something you dig up, cut down, take apart or pave. "The regulated have captured the regulators," said William Butler of the National Audubon Society.

II. Industrializing Wilderness
Is Mr. Reagan a friend of nature? That's the image he's created, as he owns a ranch, rides horses and chops wood on national television. But back at the office…

Mr. Reagan fights to block additions to the national park system, even where Congress has okayed the funds. The President prefers to leave the land with private interests who want to develop it. Dozens of our national

ACID RAIN AND "DEAD LAKES"
It's hard to imagine a more ominous sign than the death of life in wilderness lakes and streams, from "acid rain." In the Adirondacks alone, there are 212 "dead lakes" and many more lakes and streams where wildlife — fish, snails, frogs, birds — is rapidly diminishing. ❦ Acid rain is from sulfur dioxide and nitrogen oxide emitted by fossil fuel power plants, autos and industry. It's very bad in the East, but also in the Rockies and California. Where it doesn't kill fish, it often malforms them. It also affects trees, crops and humans! When this water gets into our drinking water pipes, it leaches copper and lead. Then we drink it. ❦ Despite urgent appeals, Mr. Reagan is ignoring this problem. Rather than strengthening the Clean Air Act, he has been working to gut it. What can you do? Start with the coupons.

parks may be affected. If prior presidents had this attitude, there'd now be dams and lakes in Grand Canyon.

Then there's drilling and mining in our National Wilderness. Recent headlines reported Mr. Reagan would ban wilderness development until the year 2000. The President had fooled the press! Not mentioned: (1) 36,000,000 acres of proposed wilderness could be *released* from protection, (2) a *permanent* ban, already set by Congress to begin next year, would be *superseded.* Far from preserving wilderness, Mr. Reagan would open it to more corporate exploitation.

Mr. Reagan has stopped additions to the Endangered Species List, a first step in their protection. He's in favor of poisoning wild coyotes with a deadly bait that kills scores of other animals. He wants more powerboats on wild rivers, more snowmobiles in national parks. And he's for the most massive offshore oil and gas drilling in

history. Included are the rich Georges Bank fishing grounds, and east coast shores from Long Island to Cape Hatteras. Oil rigs 20 stories tall looming off the beach, with the prospect of gooey sands. On the west coast, only a huge outcry stopped oil drilling off Northern California. Pt. Reyes. Mendocino. Some of the most beautiful coast in the world. So *there's* your rancher President. In favor of nature? Mainly for those who own some.

III. Dismantling Environmental Institutions
In 1980, the President's Council on Environmental Quality (CEQ) released "The Global 2000 Report to the President," following three years' work. It's a listing of the dangers awaiting humanity by 2000 AD if governments do not face some facts — Loss of forests, expanding deserts, water shortages, deterioration of soil, depletion of fuels and minerals, increased carbon dioxide in the atmosphere, increased radioactivity, loss of animal habitats. The report asked for urgent conservation efforts and emphasis on renewable resources.

Mr. Reagan responded by cutting the budget of CEQ by 64%, and firing the staff that produced the report.

The Crippling of the EPA. The main agency charged with protecting the quality of our lakes, rivers and air, as well as protecting human beings, is the EPA. This agency once led in efforts to make business obey the law. Apparently, this is no longer desirable.

Toxic waste enforcement is down by 48%. Expect more Love Canals. Air pollution enforcement is down by 48%. Clean water enforcement, down by 55%. In fact, the Office of Enforcement itself has been dismantled

and the activities dispersed. All this is done in the name of efficiency. But the actual purpose is clear. Under Nixon, Ford and Carter the average number of violations referred to prosecution was 150-200 per year. Under Reagan it's 66. So much for law and order.

EPA's research into toxic substances is being cut by 30%. Research into asbestos is eliminated. Same for the health effects of synfuels and diesel fuel. (When research teams and experiments are dismantled, it takes years to restart them. Meanwhile, the cancer rates soar.)

Overall, the EPA budget will be cut by 50-60% in real dollars by 1983. If Mr. Reagan has his way, the EPA will no longer be functional.

Occupational Health and Safety (OSHA). Some of the most poisonous environments in the world are factories where millions of Americans work. Mr. Reagan's OSHA has reversed its role, from protecting workers to protecting management. It is planning to ease controls on cotton dust and lead inhalation, and labeling of dangerous products. And, amazingly, OSHA has cut workers' access to their own medical records, making it harder for them to know if their job is making them sick.

Others. The Coastal Zone Management Program may soon be gone. The U.S. contribution to the UN Environment Program, cut by 29%. The Office of Surface Mining and the entire Interior Dept. have been reoriented toward favoring the industry view. Hundreds of professional staff — people who have been preparing programs for years — have been driven from their jobs. The "institutional memory" is being destroyed. Three more years of this and the whole apparatus for protecting our children's future will have been wiped out.

❦   ❦   ❦

The rationale for this performance is Mr. Reagan's "economic recovery" goal. He says he has a "mandate" to do what he's doing. But what "mandate" can he possibly mean? Did you vote to trade your children's heritage for poisonous air and water and a growing cancer rate? Did you vote to overfeed the Pentagon and starve public health, transportation, education and housing? In fact,

NUCLEAR POWER AND NUCLEAR WEAPONS
*The ultimate environmental problem is nuclear destruction. The President seems oblivious to that. While chopping environmental safeguards, he's gung-ho to subsidize nuclear power, an industry so inefficient and dangerous it could never survive on its own. Worse, he wants to export nuclear technology. More nations will be able to build nuclear bombs than ever before. We're in a much more dangerous world. ❦ Mr. Reagan speaks casually of "limited nuclear war." And he's spending more on weapons than anyone has before — $2 trillion over the next five years. 100 B-1 bombers at $300-400 million each. A new Trident sub each year, at $2 billion apiece, equal to the **combined** budgets of EPA, the national parks, and the solar energy program. Then there are MX missiles, lasers in space and the neutron bomb, all in the name of "security." Do you feel more secure?*

only 28% of eligible voters cast their vote for Mr. Reagan.

The President has a "theory" that by giving the largest corporations more of the public resource, they will become richer, with a little left over to "trickle down" to us. Do you believe this theory works? Is 9% unemployment some kind of great achievement?

Anyway, a recent CBS/NY Times poll found that 67% of Americans were against any relaxation of environmental laws. And a Harris poll found that 80% want clean air laws as tough or tougher than they are now. *That* is the President's mandate.

Enough is enough. It's time we informed Mr. Reagan he may *not* trade away America's future; that this generation demands a healthy, untrammeled natural world as living testimony of our love for those who follow. You can begin by using the coupons, writing letters, getting active. Thank you.

FRIENDS OF THE EARTH
David Brower, *Chairman,* Rafe Pomerance, *President*
Washington DC: 530 7th St. SE, 20003. **San Francisco:** 1045 Sansome St. CA 94111
(Prepared by Public Media Center, San Francisco)

and conservation, the FOE program included trade issues, technology issues, and broad economic and conceptual frameworks. So it was not surprising to me when David Brower indicated he was eager to prepare an advertisement citing the broad array of anti-environment policies that emerged from the Ronald Reagan- James Watt (Interior Secretary) government. High on Brower's list was the battle against the rapidly expanding US offshore oil drilling and production in Alaska. Brower proposed very broad ad messages on the long-term implications of massive oil development in pristine areas of Alaska and elsewhere. His ads helped articulate the range of issues involved, including devastation of the Alaska National Wildlife Refuge, and a long list of off-shore ocean explorations. Those issues later returned with Donald Trump.

But to me, the most unusual and remarkable of David Brower's campaigns in the 1970s was captured by his ad, *"ECOLOGY & WAR."* This was yet another of Dave's very broad-brush conceptual efforts, exactly in the spirit of *"EARTH NATIONAL PARK."* The specific goal of this campaign was to introduce the general public to a too-little-noted environmental problem: *war*. But this time Brower didn't get fired by anyone.

Dave Brower also deserves immense credit for recognizing and helping to elevate and launch the genius of Joan McIntyre, who worked at FOE in the early 1970s. Brower was very supportive and encouraging of all her efforts to complete, launch, and promote an astonishing ground-breaking book, *"Mind in the Waters."* The book advocated on behalf of the wisdom of certain animals, notably large-brained intelligent whales and dolphins.

Like McIntyre, Brower himself often argued against the prevailing assumptions that human beings have an intrinsic superiority and a justified authority over the rest of life on earth. That distortion of reality, he argued, and the inflation and expansion of our powers, was a major root cause of environmental devastation. Joan McIntyre brought a brilliant, articulate new voice to this argument, as follows.

ENTER: JOAN MCINTYRE

PROJECT JONAH, SAVING WHALES & DOLPHINS & ANTI-ANTHROPOCENTRISM

The purpose statement of Stewart Brand's celebrated *Whole Earth Catalog* (1969) opens: "We are as gods and might as well get good at it." It took me decades to get past that suggestion, and realize what was wrong with it. Joan McIntyre had grasped the absurd contradiction all along: "Anthropocentrism."

That is the term that describes a prevailing attitude among human beings, especially those from industrial and technologically advanced nations, that our species represents a kind of ruling class, or "royalty" over the rest of nature. With that goes an innate feeling of superiority and justified authority, largely rooted in the widely held belief that we are the most "intelligent" creature on Earth.

Such matters are exquisitely discussed in Joan McIntyre's magnificent and beautifully presented 1974 book, *"Mind in the Waters."*

McIntyre succeeds in confirming enormous tangible doubt about the accuracy of our assumptions of human "superiority" and "authority." She makes a beautifully argued, *very* convincing case. Even by using prevailing scientific ways of measuring capacity for intelligence, McIntyre argues that whales and many dolphin species' brain capacities and abilities may arguably *surpass* humans.

Several other creatures appear to be nearly as gifted. These include octopuses and at least one land animal (elephants) and possibly others, including certain chimpanzees, apes, and monkeys.

In her discussion, McIntyre describes the scientific assumption that inherent intelligence capacity is derived and expressed by brain *size* and *convolutions* within the brain. Yet most scientists manage to ignore that, by those prevailing measures, whales' and some dolphin's brains are actually larger as well as more convoluted and complex than human brains are, even relative to the size of their bodies.

The size and shapes of both human and animal brains apparently result from their long-term use. In the case of whales and dolphins, brain size and convolutions result from 30 million years of constant use. On the other hand, human beings in our evolved form have only functioned as such for about 20 *thousand* years.

So, it should really come as no shock that these big-brained sea creatures would exhibit a great intelligence, comparable to, or conceivably beyond, the capacities of humans. Human brains, which emerged much more recently, actually *do not* display greater size or complexity. So, why has this not been more recognized? Why is this not more widely discussed?

McIntyre points out that, as sea creatures, whales and dolphins actually bring an entirely *different* set of daily experiences, and likely alternative values and world-views. Yet these attributes remain mostly opaque to human beings—including scientists. Or perhaps they are deliberately ignored. It would be entirely inconvenient to confirm that some sea creatures—by the standards that are generally applied—might actually be as smart as we are.

As far as we can tell, these animals spend most of every day swimming around, eating a lot, and socializing. Modern science has acknowledged that whales, for example, are in the habit of having long underwater conversations with other whales that may be 20-30 miles away. How do they manage this? And they sing a lot! For hours at a time.

But the biggest question that Joan McIntyre asks is this: Uninhibited by gravity and the difficulties of life on land—and without any apparent interest in building cars or computers or bombs—*what exactly do we suppose that whales and dolphins, with their very large and complex brains, are thinking about and talking about?*

★ ★ ★

Modern science has a difficult time grasping the value, importance, and implications of any similarities or differences between those smart sea creatures and humans. Our species continues to assume that our own mental capacities and abilities are unique and far superior in all ways. We tend to laugh away observations that whales or dolphins just might have comparable or possibly higher intelligence than humans.

Per Stewart Brand's famous line ("we are as gods"), we invariably assume the wisdom and righteousness of our decision-making on all matters affecting Nature. We do this even though current circumstances—pollution, depletion, wastes, war, and a coming planetary climate breakdown—certainly seem to bely our assumptions of superior human intelligence and behavior on these matters. Sea creatures have not caused similar problems.

In my opinion, we must *repeatedly* focus on that biggest question of all, the one that I would expect modern science to take great interest in studying: Given the obvious size and complexity of whales' brains yet their apparent disinterest in inventing cars or planes or guns or technologies or cities or societies similar to ours, what are those highly intelligent creatures thinking about? *What do they know that we may not?*

★ ★ ★

Joan McIntyre founded Project Jonah in the early 1970s, and she pledged to devote her entire life—much of it lived close to the ocean on Lanai, Hawaii—to studying, working with, attempting to advocate for, and save wildlife of *all* kinds from the suffering and other grave impacts of excessive, indulgent human expansion and behavior.

McIntyre's first major effort to use media for these efforts was her campaign to de-popularize fashions that involved wild animal furs and skins. She wrote a wonderful statement, presented in a national advertisement that our agency prepared and placed for her, asking for pledges and promises that human beings would stop purchasing and/or wearing any products made from wild or endangered animal skins, furs, or feathers.

She managed to gain 100 celebrity signatories to that statement, including from the likes of Robert Redford, Lauren Bacall, Ali McGraw, Dick Cavett, Huntington Hartford, Mrs. Norman Mailer, John Lindsay, Neil Simon, Betsy von Furstenberg, Mrs. Leonard Bernstein, and 90 others.

That ad *(see page xiv)* was met with surprisingly enthusiastic response. *It launched a national movement that remains largely viable to the present day.*

Meanwhile, McIntyre also continued to work tirelessly to get human beings to recognize our deadly impacts upon whales and dolphins, and our failure to acknowledge the profound importance of our destructive behaviors toward them. When we kill whales, she argued, we might be murdering the most intelligent creatures on the planet.

In the two ads that she produced in the 1970s, and in her marvelous book, Joan went so far as to directly challenge the fundamental belief of most human beings, especially those from the industrial world—and most recently especially applicable to the ultra-arrogant techie world—that human beings should be confirmed as the *royalty* of life on earth. Our celebrated complex brains and our ability to invent instruments for dominating and rearranging nature form the bases and expressions of our anthropocentrist superiority.

Meanwhile our tech and military achievements also enable the dominion of *some* humans over other apparently different or "inferior" humans. This notably includes the many Indigenous peoples and societies who have mostly chosen to live well *within* nature, rather than above it. One might argue that choosing this may be an obvious clear sign of *greater* Indigenous intelligence and understanding.

Can it be that most other present-day humans are simply *not* sufficiently intelligent to grasp the answer to the urgent questions that might explain whale thinking? Asking such questions might involve admitting that we actually know very little. We continue to think that our own big brains make it all okay and even appropriate for us to express our assumptive authority to reshape tens of millions of years of planetary systemic processes. All of this, in order to serve our own perceived interests, even if it will likely kill all other life on the planet—including ourselves. If "we are as gods," we are definitely not good at it.

(Chapter 3 starts on page 41)

KILLING-OFF THE WHALES AND DOLPHINS

"We needn't wait for the galaxies to send us intelligent, non-human life so that we might begin communications. *Intelligent non-human life* exists in this planet's oceans, right now, and we are making it into pet food, car wax, machine oil and lipstick." [see BOX I, below]

NO ONE KNOWS when the human being appointed itself "superior" to the other animals but, by now, among technological cultures, there is little questioning of that assumption. Being the animal with the brains and machinery, so goes the argument, we represent the final flowering of the natural process . . . some kind of de facto royalty on the planet.

We therefore feel justified doing-in this living thing or that one, even on behalf of ridiculous trivia. That we could be suffering a failure of perception never occurs to us.

In the past, human beings have had to rethink other widely held assumptions about the nature of things—the shape of the planet is one, or that some kinds of people are superior to other kinds. And in Box I (below) you'll find there's reason to question things again, especially in light of research on cetaceans (whales and dolphins) First, however, there's some information you should have:

1] Contrary to popular assumption, international whaling is not an industry out of some heroic past. More whales were killed during the last ten years than ever before, and the five largest species are nearing extinction.

2] Take the blue whale, one hundred feet long, the largest creature to have ever inhabited this planet. (That's twice the size of the largest dinosaur; longer than ten cars.)

Humility, one supposes, might restrain humans from destroying such an animal. Not so.

Blue Whale

3] As the largest whales disappear, the industry goes after the next largest, etc. Now, it's sperm whales, 60 feet long, 60 tons. (Moby Dick was a sperm whale.) Last year 22,407 sperm whales were killed; this year, nearly 25,000.

4] The killing is not nearly as personal as in the old days when Ahab was at it in small boats. Technology has provided spotter helicopters, radar, and harpoons that explode inside the body, causing an awful death. Then gigantic "factory ships" move in and a 60-ton creature is reduced to so many barrels of oil and flesh in 30 minutes. On to market.

5] Whales are made into machine oil, margarine, shoe polish, transmission fluid, lipstick, car wax, fertilizer, perfume, soap, candles, crayons and pet food. In Japan, whale meat is also eaten, as a delicacy. *But there is no product made from whales for which an adequate, inexpensive substitute does not exist.*

6] Two countries, Japan and Russia, account for most of the whales killed, with Norway, South Africa and Peru next. Doubtless you will

your heart, please note what our furs industry is doing to dolphins. (Box II.)

And then there's the U.S. Navy. It is attempting to train dolphins in the following endearing tasks: to stab "enemy" frogmen, using knives affixed to their muzzles; to perform kamikaze attacks on "enemy" facilities; and to attach bombs to the hulls of Chinese ships. (*Note: Dolphins can tell a Chinese ship from ours via the dolphin's own sonar system which "sees" through the alloy construction of the metal; neat trick for a lower life form.*)

7] There's only one organization with power to protect cetaceans—the Int'l. Whaling Commission—and a more short-sighted handful of men would be hard to find. They come from the commercial fishing world. They speak of these animals as "resources," never magnificent, aware beings. They bar the press from meetings and "protect" a species only after it's been so depleted that hunting becomes too costly. The IWC did nothing to protect the blue whale until too late, and it has now authorized a terrible

THERE ARE MORE details we could share with you, but you've probably got the idea : Something very stupid is going on out at sea. Just as researchers learn the first amazing lessons about whales and dolphins, they are being destroyed for products of no intrinsic value.

Project Jonah, the sponsor of this ad, is working to save the whales by pushing for a ten-year moratorium on all commercial whaling (a plan which the U.N. has approved but the IWC rejected), and also by encouraging research with free living wild whales and dolphins; killing animals to study them has got to go.

Here are ways you can help:

Coupons and letters: Nothing works better than huge outpourings of mail. Please use the coupon below; write letters as well.

International Childrens' Campaign: To children, live animals offer more than the products made from them. And so, not surprisingly, we have been receiving, lately, many letters, poems, and drawings from children (see illustration).

mans from destroying such an animal. Not so. The U.S. Bureau of Fish & Wildlife estimates the blue whale population is down to about 3,000 today, from 300,000 only forty-five years ago. So much for humility.

South Africa and Peru next. Doubtless you will be pleased to hear that for once the U.S. is not involved in some mindless slaughter. In 1971 this country outlawed whale hunting and banned whale products. But before patriotism grips

depletion of fin whales, sei, and sperm whales. The next meeting of this august body is in London, June 25. It is necessary they realize they're no longer alone.

We need whales! Whales have always been great to see!

We are now encouraging more, and plan to present them to the IWC. Failing there we will personally take the material, and some children, to the highest officials of the whaling nations. Please discuss this project with your kids.

Money: We have placed this ad in several publications at a cost of more than $20,000. We can scarcely afford that. If you can make a *tax-deductible* donation it will help pay for the ad, accelerate our work, and help protect the remaining whales and dolphins.

Thank you.

Joan McIntyre, *President*
Project Jonah

Board & Advisors: *Joan McIntyre, Jerry Mander, Maxine Mc-Closkey, Gail Madonia, Candice Bergen, Judy Collins, Francis A. Martin, Jr., Peter Dohrn (Mediterranean), Alain Herve (Europe), Farley Mowat (Canada), Peter Poynton (Australia).* Offices: *1300 Sansome, San Francisco 94111; France—25 Quai Voltaire, Paris 7e; Canada—12 Dacoiah Ave., Toronto 128; Australia—72 Studley Park Rd., Kew 3101, Victoria.*

BOX I. Various Animals Compared as to Brains, Other Qualities

*Brains, in scale:
Adult Human (L),
Sperm Whale (C),
Bottlenose Dolphin*

By the same standards science uses to judge human brains, cetaceans (dolphins and whales) seem to have brains as remarkable as our own celebrated faculties. This may disturb many human beings wishing to remain officially the "smartest" animal on the planet, but there you have it.

The usual measurements are these: 1) brain size, 2) convolutions (folds) of the brain, and 3) relative size of the neo-cortex as compared to the motor cortex. The bibliography (Box III) will tell you where to find complete studies, but here are some highlights:
• Many cetaceans have larger brains than humans do. A human brain weighs about 3 lbs. Some dolphin brains weigh more than that, and an adult sperm whale brain weighs 19 lbs., largest on the planet.
• The dolphin brain is as convoluted as the human brain, and many whale brains are much more so. This means a greater brain surface area, more brain cells, and therefore more potential for new thought combinations.
• As for the third measurement, neo-cortex vs. motor cortex, the point is this: As the mammalian brain grew bigger over millions of years, the portion devoted to motor functions—walking, breathing, seeing—remained the same. The part that grew was the neo-cortex, where thinking (model making) takes place, imagination, creativity, etc. It's *this* that humans have made such a fuss about.
Yet Dr. Myron Jacobs of the N.Y. Aquarium reports: A kangaroo cortex is 69% neo-cortex. A macaque monkey cortex is 93% neo-cortex. A human cortex is 96% neo-cortex. But one dolphin species has 98% of its cortex in neo-cortex.
It is believed that findings for whales will be at least as impressive.

Such large, complex brains do not develop in animals for no reason, but rather through millions of years of creative use. However, living in the ocean rather than on land as we do, there is no reason to believe that cetaceans have been using their brains in the way we have. With abundant food and few natural enemies (humans have been a major threat for a bare two generations, whaletime), it seems they've had to pay less attention to objective pursuits like food, shelter, clothing, safety.

Then too, water being a supportive medium, unlike air, cetaceans don't have gravity to deal with. They sleep very little. And have lots of free time. So to get this picture: For millions of years, these creatures have been gliding through a supportive medium, without our particular concerns, and all this time their brains have been evolving into the largest and most complex on the planet.

The question, of course, is this: If whales and dolphins are not using those gigantic brains to "do" things the way we do, then what are they using them for?

We don't know. Although scientists who have worked with them are prepared to conjecture.

Dr. Gregory Bateson, for example, believes that dolphins may devote their brains to working out more complex social and sexual relationships than humans do. Dr. John Lilly believes that they are into advanced forms of communication, and, Dr. Karl-Erik Fichtelius wonders if the other great brained animals might not offer us a new conception of life, proving, finally, that *we* don't "own" the planet.

It's clear, anyway, that whales and dolphins are not into organized vio-

lence, power, money or ego, but, rather, something quite a bit more playful.

Of course, guessing about whales' thought can only be anthropomorphic, and therefore uncertain. Even describing *human* "intelligence" is difficult, let alone transposing it to a creature that lives in such a subjective world.

Other animals may operate more on something like sheer "knowing" rather than analytical processes like thinking. And then there's "instinct." We have been taught that "instinct" is "lower" than thought. But is that true? Is "knowing" or "feeling" how to care for an infant, say, a "lower" thing than deducing it in your head?

In our whole approach to animal abilities we find a human-invented hierarchy of qualities. Thinking is better than sensing. Invention is better than instinct. We stick to this rank-order even when research shows, for example, that dolphins do innately what we've invented sonar for. Whales communicate across hundreds of miles of ocean, and dive to 3,000 feet, somehow controlling their breathing and adjusting to the water pressure. And *many* animals cannot.

One *could* make the case that human technology is a substitute for abilities even small-brained animals already have. But we'd best not get further into that one today.

We *can* conclude this much: We needn't wait for the galaxies to send us intelligent non-human life with which to begin communications. *Intelligent non-human* intelligence exists in this planet's oceans right now, and we are making it into pet food, car wax, machine oil, and lipstick.

BOX II. Killing Dolphins for Tuna

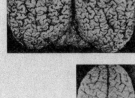

Pacific White Sided Dolphins

Every year, the American tuna industry kills some 250,000 dolphins. Here's how:

Tuna enjoy the company of dolphins so they habitually swim just below them in the water. Therefore, when fishermen see dolphins they surround them with gigantic "purse sein" nets which snare the tuna, but also the dolphins. As dolphins are not fish but are air-breathing animals like ourselves, they suffocate under water.

This technique is a recent innovation. It used to be that when fishing for tuna you just fished for tuna and let the other creatures live. But someone figured that you could increase the tuna per man-day of boat-time, or some such standard. The assumption, of course, is that human beings have a perfect right to waste the life of an intelligent, playful, friendly animal for an abstraction like corporate profit.

There are other techniques available which would spare the dolphins, while still getting the tuna. But so far the people in the industry, blinded by the balance sheet, have resisted all attempts to re-institute them.

You can do this: Write a tuna company. Tell them you don't want a public relations story, just an answer—When are they going to quit killing dolphins?

BOX III. Recommended Bibliography

Fichtelius, K. E., *Smarter Than Man?*, Pantheon, '72.
Filimonov, I., "Comparative Anatomy of Cerebral Cortex of Mammals," Off. of Scientific Info., U.S Dep't. Interior, '64.
Hillaby, J., "Genocide at Sea: New Scientist, 7/4/68.
Jacobs, M. S., "Intelligence in the Large Brained Cetacea," Cetacean Brain Inst., Mar. Aquarium, '72.
Kellogg, W. N., *Porpoises & Sonar*, U. of Chicago Press, '61.
Lilly, J. C., *Man and Dolphin*, Pyramid, '61.
Lilly, "Interspecies Communication," McGraw Hill, '62. *Yearbook of Science and Technology*, McGraw Hill, '62.
Lilly, *The Mind of the Dolphin*, Discus/Avon, '67.
Melville, H., *Moby Dick*, New Amer. Library, '61.
McVay, S., "Can Leviathan Endure ..." Nat'l. History, 1/71.
Montagu, A. & Lilly, *Dolphin in History*, Clark Lib., UCLA, '63.
Morgane, P. J. & Jacobs, M. S., "The Comparative Anatomy of the Cetacean Nervous System," *In: Functional Anatomy of Marine Mammals*, ed. by Prof. R. J. Harrison, Academic Press, '73.
Mowat, F., *A Whale for the Killing*, Little, Brown, '72.
Norris, *Whales, Dolphins & Porpoises*, U. of Cal. Press, '66.
Payne, R., "Swimming with Right Whales," Nat'l Geog., 10/72.
Payne & McVay, "Songs of Humpback Whales," Sci., v.173, '71.
Pilleri, G., *Investigations on Cetacea*, Vol. 1-4, Brain Anatomy Institue, U. of Berne, Switzerland.
Scheffer, V., *The Year of the Whale*, Scribner's, '68.
Small, G., *The Blue Whale*, Columbia U. Press, '71.
Slijper, E. J., *Whales*, Basic Books, '62.
Tavolga, W., ed. *Marine Bio-Acoustics*, Pergamon, '64.
Tschernezky, "Dolphins & Mind of Man," N.w. Sci.St., 3/22/68.
Wooldridge, D., *Machinery of the Brain*, McGraw Hill, '63.

Nine Reasons Why Abortions Are Legal:

Abortion is never an easy decision, but women have been making that choice for thousands of years, for many good reasons. Whenever a society has sought to outlaw abortions, it has only driven them into back alleys where they became dangerous, expensive and humiliating. Amazingly, this was the case in the United States until little more than a decade ago when abortion was legalized. Thousands of American women died. Thousands more were maimed. For this reason and others, women and men fought for and achieved women's legal right to make their own decisions about abortion.

However, there are people in our society who still won't accept this. Some argue that even victims of rape or incest should be forced to bear the child. And now, having failed to convince the public or the lawmakers, certain of these people have turned to bombs. Since January of 1984, more than thirty bombings and burnings have been reported at family planning and abortion clinics. (See photo.)

Some say these acts will stop abortions, but that is ridiculous. When the smoke clears, the same urgent reasons will exist for safe, legal abortions as have always existed. No nation committed to individual liberty could seriously consider returning to the days of back alley abortions; to the revolting specter of a government forcing women to bear children against their will. Still, amid such attacks, it is worthwhile to repeat a few of the reasons *why* our society trusts each woman to make the abortion decision herself.

1 Laws against abortion kill women.

To prohibit abortions does not stop them. When women feel it is absolutely necessary, they will choose to have abortions, even in secret, without medical care, in dangerous circumstances. In the two decades before abortion was legal in the U.S., it's been estimated that *nearly a million women per year* sought out illegal abortions. Thousands died. Tens of thousands were mutilated. *All* were forced to behave as if they were criminals.

2 Legal abortions protect women's health.

Legal abortion not only protects women's lives, it also protects their health. For tens of thousands of women with heart disease, kidney disease, severe hypertension, sickle-cell anemia and severe diabetes and other illnesses that can be life-threatening, the availability of legal abortion has helped avert serious medical complications that could have resulted from childbirth. Before legal abortion, such women's choices were limited to dangerous illegal abortion or dangerous childbirth.

3 A woman is more than a fetus.

There's an argument these days that a fetus is a "person" that is "indistinguishable from the rest of us" and that it deserves rights equal to women's. On this question there is a tremendous spectrum of religious, philosophical, scientific and medical opinion. It's been argued for centuries. Fortunately, our society has recognized that each woman must be able to make this decision, based on her own conscience. To impose a law defining a fetus as a "person," granting it rights equal to or superior to a woman's—a thinking, feeling, conscious human being—is arrogant and absurd. It only serves to diminish women.

4 Being a mother is just one option for women.

Many hard battles have been fought to win political and economic equality for women. These gains will not be worth much if reproductive choice is denied. To be able to choose a safe, legal abortion makes many other options possible. Otherwise an accident or a rape can end a woman's economic and personal freedom.

ELAINE SHAW, M.D.,
SAN FRANCISCO, CALIFORNIA

"I wonder if young women today can fully identify with the situation only two decades ago. When I was a young doctor at a New York hospital, there would scarcely be a week go by that some woman wouldn't be brought to the emergency room near death from an illegal abortion. I saw some wonderful women die, and others reproductively crippled. Then, I too became pregnant, by accident, and though I was a doctor I could not ask any other doctor for help. In those days, if known, it would have cost us both our jobs. So I drove secretly to a Pennsylvania coal-mining town and was led to a secret location. I was lucky. I wasn't injured. But I'm so glad that times have changed. I have five daughters and a son now. I hope they never have to make the agonizing decision about abortion, but if they do, I would hate for them to have to act like criminals and to risk their lives to do what they feel is right for their future."

SHERRY MATULIS,
PEORIA, ILLINOIS

"I have been married for 35 years, I'm the mother of five children, grandmother of three. In the mid-1950s I was brutally raped and left for dead. I later discovered I was pregnant. I was horrified. I would not have that child. Our family doctor couldn't help. An abortion could have cost him and me 20 years in prison. I tried home remedies—like scalding myself, and falling down stairs—but they didn't work. Finally I found a local abortionist. I will always remember walking up those dark stairs. The incredible filth. The man had a whiskey glass in one hand and a knife in the other. The pain was the worst I have ever felt, but the humiliation was even worse. Hemorrhaging and hospitalization followed. I thought I would never be with my family again. I had no choice but I resent what I had to go through to terminate that pregnancy. And I resent the people who now say that women should be forced to endure such experiences."

5 Outlawing abortion is discriminatory.

Anti-abortion laws discriminate against low-income women, who are driven to dangerous self-induced or back-alley abortions. That is all they can afford. But the rich can travel wherever necessary to obtain a safe abortion.

6 Compulsory pregnancy laws are incompatible with a free society.

If there is any matter which is personal and private, then pregnancy is it. There can be no more extreme invasion of privacy than requiring a woman to carry an unwanted pregnancy to term. If government is permitted to compel a woman to bear a child, where will government stop? The concept is morally repugnant. It violates traditional American ideas of individual rights and freedoms.

7 Outlaw abortion, and more children will bear children.

Forty percent of 14-year-old girls will become pregnant before they turn 20. This could happen to your daughter or someone else close to you. Here are the critical questions: Should the penalty for lack of knowledge or even for a moment's carelessness be enforced pregnancy and childrearing? Or dangerous illegal abortion? Should we consign a teenager to a life sentence of joblessness, hopelessness and dependency?

8 "Every child a wanted child."

If women are forced to carry unwanted pregnancies to term, the result is unwanted children. Everyone knows they are among society's most tragic cases, often uncared-for, unloved, brutalized, and abandoned. When they grow up, these children are often seriously disadvantaged, and some-

times inclined toward brutal behavior to others. This is not good for children, for families, or for the country. Children need love and families who want and will care for them.

9 Choice is good for families.

Even when precautions are taken, accidents can and do happen. For some families, this is not a problem. But for others, such an event can be catastrophic. An unintended pregnancy can increase tensions, disrupt stability, and push people below the line of economic survival. *Family planning* is the answer. All options must be open.

❦ ❦ ❦

At the most basic level, the abortion issue is not really about abortion. It is about the value of women in society. Should women make their own decisions about family, career and how to live their lives? Or should government do that for them? Do women have the option of deciding when or whether to have children? Or is *that* a government decision?

The anti-abortion leaders really have a larger purpose. They oppose most ideas and programs which can help women achieve equality and freedom. They also oppose programs which protect the health and well-being of women *and* their children.

Anti-abortion leaders claim to act "in defense of life." If so, why have they worked to destroy programs which *serve* life, including pre-natal care and nutrition programs for dependent pregnant women? Is this respect for life?

Anti-abortion leaders also say they are trying to save children, but they have fought against health and nutrition programs for children once they are born. The anti-abortion groups seem to believe life begins at conception, but it ends at birth. Is this respect for life?

Then there are programs which diminish the number of unwanted pregnancies *before* they occur: family planning counselling, sex education and contraception for those who wish it. Anti-abortion leaders oppose those too. And clinics providing such services have been bombed. Is this respect for life?

Such stances reveal the ultimate cynicism of the compulsory pregnancy movement. "Life" is not what they're fighting for. What they want is a return to the days when a woman had few choices in controlling her future. They think that the abortion option gives too much freedom. That even contraception is too liberating. That women cannot be trusted to make their own decisions.

Americans today don't accept that. Women can now select their own paths in society, including when and whether to have children. Family planning, contraception and, if need be, legal abortion are critical to sustaining women's freedom. There is no going back.

❦ ❦ ❦

If you agree with this, you can help. Please mail the coupons. (One supports the Reproductive Health Equity Act which would restore federal abortion funding to 43 million women dependent on the government for their health care. Another asks for further investigation of clinic harassment and violence.) Also, clip this ad and post it in a public place. And if you can, support our work with a contribution and by contacting Planned Parenthood in your area. Thank you.

BOMBINGS & HARRASSMENT

There have been more than 30 arsons and bombings at family planning and abortion clinics in the past 17 months. Just as insidious is the harassment inflicted on women attempting to enter these clinics. Anti-abortion leaders have just announced plans to inflict a "year of fear and pain" on women seeking legal abortions and on their health care providers. A more aggressive investigation of this conspiracy is needed. Please send the coupon to Mr. Meese.

Ⓟ Planned Parenthood®

3

PUBLIC MEDIA CENTER (PMC)

—◆—

Enter: Herb Chao Gunther, Jono Polansky et. al. (PMC)
Faye Wattleton—Planned Parenthood vs. Reagan
Enter: David Brower (3), at Earth Island Institute
Against Globalization of Corporate Powers, Lori Wallach, Public Citizen
and The International Forum on Globalization (IFG)

B Y THE 1970s, a massive shift was taking place in domestic life everywhere, particularly in the US. The powers of mass media had been rapidly globalizing and accelerating since the 1950s, especially after the arrival of television, which prompted Marshall McLuhan to write this warning: "Ours is the first age in which many thousands of the best-trained individual minds have made it a full-time business to get inside the collective public mind." He observed that society was entering a "helpless state engendered by prolonged mental rutting," the effect of our immersion in thousands of television ads and entertainment alike.

Then came McLuhan's 1964 blockbuster, *"Understanding Media"* which argued that the world was being enveloped by mass media, notably television, bringing unforeseen negative characteristics. "The medium is the message," said McLuhan. And the message was that centralized corporate control of public consciousness had never been greater. By the 1970s, the mass shift to television as the world's primary communications instrument became obvious. And that medium's unique powers—to implant "moving image media" into peoples' brains, over and over was something print media couldn't match. Television enabled unprecedented enclosure of public consciousness and understanding by powers whose motives were exclusively self-interested: growth and profit. This was bad. What to do?

Personally, I remained strongly supportive of the extraordinary capabilities of *print* media. But, I also felt it was crucial to understand and react to the new realities. Ad campaigns in print media *were* still effective in particular ways, as confirmed in the following decades. But, the unique, massive, invasive impacts of global television created a new problematic intrusive information environment. And, it was not being sufficiently critiqued.

That's when I decided to take a couple of years off from writing ads to complete the book on the negative consequences of global television; especially its abilities to "occupy" mass consciousness *and* implant its own imagery (see p. 16). Meanwhile, however, an amazing crew of creative, dedicated media activists burst onto the scene and filled the void.

ENTER: HERB GUNTHER (PMC) & PLANNED PARENTHOOD

In 1974, a dynamic new non-profit ad agency was born: Public Media Center (PMC), directed by Herb Chao Gunther. PMC went instantly into over-drive and kept at it till the end of the century. Under Gunther's leadership, PMC produced *hundreds* of high-impact *winning* advocacy ad campaigns.

Probably the most famous and consequential campaign was the work in behalf of Faye Wattleton,

"Then I got that awful phone call."

"SHE'D NEVER CALLED ME BEFORE. We'd just been together a couple of times.

So she tells me she's pregnant.

I mean, I didn't know what to say. There's just this silence on the phone until she asks if I died.

She sounds like she's burnt out on crying and you don't know what to do. It's like you're a blank.

The worst part is I wake up in the morning and it just rushes at me. Quit school. Get married. Run away from it. I don't know.

I didn't know then and I don't know now.

All I know is all the ways it shouldn't have happened. All those easy ways. But it's a little too late for that, I guess. Too late this lifetime, for me."

Nobody has all the answers about sex. But keep in mind that a million teen girls get pregnant every year. Which means a million guys don't hear the end of it. Here's your choice. You can take responsibility when it's easy or you can wait until it's impossible. Don't make a big mistake. Buy a condom. You can get them at any drugstore or from your local Planned Parenthood. If you need help or information, call us. That's what we're here for.

Planned Parenthood®
Federation of America

810 Seventh Avenue,
New York, NY 10019

IF THEY'RE OLD ENOUGH TO GET PREGNANT, THEY'RE OLD ENOUGH NOT TO.

There's a forty percent chance she'll get pregnant before she's nineteen. One of the million teens who get pregnant each year.

That's the highest teen pregnancy rate in the industrialized world. And you don't have to look far for the reason: two-thirds of sexually-active teens in America use no method of birth control or fail to use it consistently.

The personal consequences of teen pregnancy are tragic and the social costs are staggering. Over $16 billion each year. That's the price we pay for misinformation and ignorance about the facts of life.

We need to equip our children with basic information about the risks of pregnancy and about contraception.

Most teens know less about such things than you might think. Few people realize that only two states and the District of Columbia require sex education programs in schools. And the mass media, marketing sex with no mention of precautions, only make matters worse.

Even parents who care the most may fail to make sure their children are informed—fearing they might appear to condone behavior they wish to discourage. But research shows that when parents hesitate, teens tend not to.

Studies also find that teens who've been thoroughly informed about the facts of life are much more likely to say no to peer pressure. And to start later.

That's why Planned Parenthood encourages better parent-child communication. Works to improve sex education. And maintains that all sexually-active people, including teens, should be able to get the birth control help they need and want.

Given the facts, teens can make responsible decisions. Denied the facts, all they can make are mistakes.

Biologically, after all, any teenage girl *can* get pregnant. The only question is whether she won't.

You can help. Write us for more information. Use the coupon.

The soaring teen pregnancy rate is everybody's problem. I want to help:

☐ Please send me information about Planned Parenthood's POWER (Parents Organized to Win Educational Rights) Campaign so I can make a difference where I live.

☐ Send me a copy of the booklet, "How to Talk with Your Child about Sexuality" (one dollar enclosed).

☐ Here's my tax-deductible contribution to support all of Planned Parenthood's programs encouraging responsible decisions by teens and adults: ☐ $25 ☐ $35 ☐ $50 ☐ $75 ☐ $150 ☐ $500 or: $_____.
Send your check to 810 Seventh Avenue, New York, NY 10019

NAME _____

STREET/CITY/ZIP _____

Planned Parenthood®
Federation of America

then president of Planned Parenthood, as it fought against Ronald Reagan's anti-women programs. That very urgent campaign played out throughout the 1980s and was astonishingly successful. Working closely with Wattleton, PMC's ads directly helped express a mass opposition that successfully *blocked* Reagan's aggressions. (It's hard to believe that three decades later, Mr. Donald Trump tried to repeat *exactly* what Reagan was trying for in the 1970s and 1980s.)

Herb Gunther assembled a great staff of activists, writers, and artists, led by the brilliant, high-speed copy-writer, Jono Polansky, who wrote hundreds of ads on a variety of themes. And, I was personally very pleased and flattered that once my TV book was finally done and published, Gunther invited me back into the group to re-join the fray. I was anointed "Senior Fellow," and started producing ads again. Of the many dozens of PMC's ads in behalf of Planned Parenthood, I personally authored only

five. Two of these, including "*FIVE WAYS TO PREVENT ABORTION (And One Way That Won't)*" and "*NINE REASONS WHY*" (page 40), kicked off the 1985 campaign defending abortion rights. Both ads appeared full-page in the *NY Times* and in newspapers across the country—PMC's largest media buy to date—and continued to be used in later years. The following year, a new series focused on teen pregnancy, targeting the hypocritical, irresponsible ban on birth control during sex scenes on television. Coupons addressing the network presidents asked them to reverse their dangerous policies. One of the headlines read: "*THEY DID IT 20,000 TIMES ON TELEVISION LAST YEAR. HOW COME NOBODY GOT PREGNANT?*" The provocative nature of the contraceptive ads generated terrific publicity. More than one hundred articles on the issue appeared, and Wattleton was invited to speak on television programs nationwide, multiplying their reach considerably.

(text continued on page 50)

Some women are silent on the horrors of illegal abortion.

The rest of us can't be.

Not now. Not when every woman's right to choose a legal and safe abortion is threatened.

On July 3, five Justices of the Supreme Court voted to let state legislatures interfere in a woman's most personal and private decisions. And this fall, the Court will hear three more challenges to your right to decide for yourself.

In Florida, the attack on women's health and privacy is spearheaded by Governor Bob Martinez. He has ordered a special session of the state legislature to enact laws that may block thousands of women in Florida from safe, legal abortions.

We must never forget what happens when abortion is criminalized.

Women die.

By the thousands, they are maimed and killed.

It was true in America before 1973.

In nations where it's still illegal, unsafe and clandestine abortions are among the leading causes of death for women of childbearing age (the global death toll is over 200,000 a year).

Those who ignore this horror, or

Half a million marched in Washington this spring. Ignoring majority support nationwide for legal abortion, Gov. Martinez wants to impose his personal beliefs on the women of Florida. Help us stop him.

choose to forget it, pretend that outlawing abortion will stop it.

Polls show that 20% of women think abortion has **already** been outlawed. It's only a matter of time before desperation and fear lead to tragedy and death.

Does the Governor truly care? If he did, he'd support more family planning, sex education and birth control research to reduce the basic cause of abortion: unintended pregnancy.

But he doesn't.

Some women are silent on the horrors of illegal abortion. But those of us who survive them can't be silent. We must speak out. We must act.

Governor Bob Martinez:
The Capitol, Tallahassee, FL 32399
(904) 488-2272

Governor Martinez:

Your call for special legislation restricting legal abortion is a dangerous betrayal of American values: freedom of conscience, respect for privacy, and religious tolerance. You have no mandate to impose your personal beliefs on the people of Florida. And no right to endanger innocent women. If you want to stop abortion, support efforts to prevent unwanted pregnancy.

NAME

ADDRESS

State Legislator
The Capitol, Tallahassee, FL 32399
(904) 488-1234

Dear State Legislator:

On behalf of all women forever silenced by illegal abortion, please speak out now against Governor Martinez's attempt to restrict legal abortion and impose his personal beliefs on the people of Florida. Tell the Governor if he really wants to stop abortion, he should support efforts to end unwanted pregnancy.

NAME

ADDRESS

I'm speaking out for all women who no longer can. I believe abortion should remain a personal and private matter between a woman and her doctor. We can't allow Governor Martinez to pass special legislation imposing his personal beliefs on the people of Florida. [ ] I've contacted the Governor and my state legislator. [ ] Here's my contribution to all of Planned Parenthood's programs: __ $25 __ $50 __ $100 __ $250 __ $500 or __.

NAME

ADDRESS

Ⓟ Planned Parenthood®

Don't wait until women are dying again.

Robert Bork's Position on Reproductive Rights:

I f your senators vote to confirm the Administration's latest Supreme Court nominee, you'll need more than a prescription to get birth control. It might take a constitutional amendment. Robert Bork is an extremist who believes you have no constitutional right to personal privacy. He thinks the government is free to dictate what you can and can't do in highly personal and intimate matters such as marriage, childbearing, parenting. If he wins a lifetime seat on the Supreme Court, Bork could radically change the way Americans live. Here's how to stop him, and why...

For years, "moral majority" extremists—with the active support of the White House—have been trying to impose their beliefs on the rest of us. They think they have the right to tell you how to live your life. So far, our democratic system has blocked them.

But now, in the waning days of the Reagan Administration, they just might succeed after all.

They've been given their very own Supreme Court nominee—an ultra-conservative judicial extremist named Robert Bork—who has repeatedly attacked important Court decisions which protect your right to privacy and freedom from government interference in your most personal and private decisions.

Bork has long been known in legal circles for his highly unusual ideas on civil rights, free speech and personal privacy.

Claiming to possess the only correct

For right-wing extremists to claim Bork shouldn't be rejected on ideological grounds, when ideology got him nominated in the first place, is absurd.

The Senate historically has rejected one out of every five nominations to the Supreme Court. The Senate has a responsibility to consider nominees on the basis of how they think and what they believe—not just their narrow technical qualifications. Would Robert Bork preserve the Court's social consensus or spark disastrous conflict? Safeguard our liberties or threaten their very existence? Balance the Court or throw it dangerously out of kilter, into the hands of extremists eager to tell us how to live our lives?

Bork has acknowledged, "There are areas properly left to individual freedom, and coercion by the majority in these aspects of life is tyranny."

Decades of Supreme Court decisions uphold your freedom to make your own decisions about marriage and family, childbearing and parenting. But Robert Bork is convinced that government has the power to interfere in the most intimate areas of all:

■ He attacks as "utterly specious" the landmark Supreme Court decision striking down a ban by the state of Connecticut on the use of birth control by married couples in the privacy of their own homes.

STATE-CONTROLLED PREGNANCY? It's not as far-fetched as it sounds. Carrying Bork's position to its logical end, states could ban or require any method of birth control, impose family quotas for population purposes, make abortion a crime, or sterilize anyone they choose. The way he reads it, nothing in the U.S. Constitution—including long-standing Supreme Court decisions—protects Ameri-

method for interpreting the Constitution (he says he can discern the "original intent" of the men who wrote it two centuries ago), Bork uses obscure academic theory to arrive at positions that he himself admits may appear "bizarre."

As a law professor, Bork's opinions were a private matter. But as a Supreme Court justice, he would have the power to change your life.

Of the eight justices now on the Supreme Court, four have generally been part of a moderate and balanced consensus protecting Constitutional rights and liberties.

And if confirmed, Bork wouldn't hesitate a moment to use that power.

In his own words, Justices have a "duty" to "require basic and unsetting changes...despite any political clamor, when the Constitution, fairly interpreted, demands it." Bork sees the Court not as a problem-solver, guided by past decisions, but as a reckless trouble-maker, aggressively seeking ways to upset past rulings he thinks are wrong. Regardless of the social havoc that may result. Or the pain and suffering of innocent people.

What unsettling changes would Bork make in your personal life, if the Senate confirms him?

■ In a case involving a company which produced dangerous amounts of toxic lead, Bork refused to strike down a company policy which required female employees to become sterilized, or to be fired from their jobs.

■ He denounces the Supreme Court decision recognizing a woman's right to choose abortion—to make a private medical decision about her own pregnancy—as "wholly unjustifiable" and "unconstitutional."

■ Stripped of privacy protections, we couldn't even choose our own relationships or living arrangements without fear of government intrusion. Bork agreed with a local zoning board's power to prevent a grandmother from living with her grandchildren because she didn't belong to the "nuclear family."

Is this the sort of closed-minded extremism we want on the Supreme Court? Are we ready to turn back the clock to a time when "moral majorities" choked off almost all family planning options through a welter of state and local laws?

It has happened before. Deprived of your constitutional right to privacy, it can happen again. Presidents serve four years, senators serve six. But Robert Bork—if confirmed by the U.S. Senate—will be on the Supreme Court for life.

Four more justices (two named by Reagan) generally vote against expansion of our basic freedoms. Retired Justice Powell was the pivot...

...but right-winger Bork would throw the Court off balance.

' But Bork's record proves beyond any doubt that he fiercely believes the most private and personal aspects of our lives—marriage, childbearing, parenting—are *not* protected by the Constitution from government intrusion.

cans from these and other barbaric violations of basic human rights.

The Senate vote on Bork may be more important than the next presidential election. Make sure your senators know where you stand.

If you don't have the right to make life's most important decisions—free of outside interference—what are the rest of your rights worth?

If the Senate confirms Robert Bork, it will be too late. Your personal privacy, one of the most cherished and unique features of American life, has never been in greater danger. Please, mail the coupons immediately.

Do the court justice. Block Bork.

Mail now or CALL your Senators (202) 224-3121.

"Forty years ago I had a back-alley abortion. I almost died from it."

If you wonder whether legal abortion is a good idea, ask a woman who survived an illegal one.

She'll tell you how painful, dirty, humiliating and horribly dangerous a back-alley abortion was.

Despite the incredible risks, millions of American women had abortions before they were legalized in 1973. An untold number were maimed for life.

Thousands were literally slaughtered, packed off bleeding and infected to die in abject terror.

Today, the threat to women's lives no longer comes from abortion. It comes from those who want to outlaw it. People who argue that abortions should be banned — even if the result is as horrible as it was in the past.

This increasingly vocal and violent minority will stop at nothing.

They've resorted to harassment, physical threats, even bombings.

They're attacking the U.S. Constitution. And they're pressuring legislators and the courts to make abortion illegal again. For all women. Regardless of circumstances.

Even if her life or health is in danger. Even if she's a victim of rape or incest. Even if she's too young to be a mother.

Speak out on November 12.

Or they just might succeed in turning back the clock to when women had no choice.

Except the back alley.

Here's my urgent contribution to support Planned Parenthood's Campaign to Keep Abortion Safe and Legal, 810 Seventh Avenue, New York, NY 10019-5818.

_____

NAME

_____

ADDRESS

_____

CITY   STATE   ZIP
                                    MS 1189

A copy of our latest financial report is available from the New York Department of State, Office of Charities Registration, Albany, New York 12231, or from Planned Parenthood Federation of America, 810 Seventh Ave., New York, New York 10019. Please write PPFA for a description of our program and activities and/or a list of the organizations to which PPFA has contributed in the last year. © 1989 PPFA, Inc. This ad was paid for with private contributions.

Mobilize for women's lives Nov. 12 in Washington, D.C. and across America

Planned Parenthood®
Federation of America

ALEX MURAWSKI

When JR took Mandy for a little roll in the hay, which one had the condom?

It's no secret that a lot of TV characters have sex. The only mystery is how they keep from getting pregnant.

Official TV network policy keeps birth control out of sight and out of mind. In fact, the networks usually won't allow the word "contraception" on the air unless it's part of a news report.

No wonder America's young people have gotten the wrong idea. If their parents never mention birth control, schools in 48 states don't refer to it, and TV censors any reference to it–our kids don't have a clue.

Bombarded by thousands of messages promoting sex but omitting a few crucial facts of life, a million teens get pregnant each year. Their ignorance is absolutely appalling (see box above). And it doesn't stop there. Poorly informed teens grow up to be poorly informed adults–accounting for the sad fact that one half of all pregnancies are unintended.

Given this ignorance, censorship is certainly NOT the answer. Young people need more information, not less. And the more straightforward, the better. Where hypocritical attitudes don't prevail, it turns out young people are much safer (see box below).

WHAT TEENS DON'T KNOW
- A high percentage of teens think you can't get pregnant the first time, or when you're bleeding. It's true you can't get pregnant during your period. But some girls bleed when they ovulate and think it's their period.
- Lots of kids don't know where to buy contraceptives, or how to use them. Many teens believe withdrawal is a safe method.
- Some kids think it's impossible to get pregnant if you're not married...if you don't have an orgasm...if you have sex standing up.
- 75% of teenagers think if you get a case of VD, you can never get it again. 87% think you don't need treatment if the outward symptoms disappear. 91% feel that VD isn't really dangerous to one's health.

WHERE TEENS DO KNOW
- The United States has a higher teen pregnancy rate, teen childbirth rate, and teen abortion rate than Canada, England, the Netherlands, Sweden or France.
- Not because America is "sexier": teens in these countries are just as active as U.S. teens.
- "Race" is no explanation: a white American teen is twice as likely to get pregnant as a sexually-active English teen. (In fact, the black teen pregnancy rate in the U.S. is declining, while the rate among white teens continues unabated.)
- Countries which accept teenage sexuality as a fact of life–and consequently provide more contraceptive services and sex education than the U.S.–all have lower teen pregnancy rates.

To begin with, we hope the TV networks will catch up with their audience. Eight out of ten adults who are aware of the teen pregnancy crisis in the U.S. would like to see more birth control messages on TV, for example.

To make this point yourself, forcefully and directly, use the coupons, write a letter or call. Let the three men who run the TV networks know what you think.

If they're going to show sex on TV, after all, the least they can do is do it right.

Ⓟ Planned Parenthood®
Federation of America, Inc.

They did it 20,000 times on television last year.

*T*eenage pregnancy in the U.S. has reached epidemic proportions, shattering hundreds of thousands of lives and costing taxpayers $16 billion per year. Instead of helping to solve this problem, the TV networks have virtually banned any mention of birth control in programs and advertising. We need to turn this policy around. *You can help.*

I. On television, sex is good, contraception is taboo.

There's a lot of sex on television. We all know that. What most people don't realize is that while the networks have been hyping sex, they've banned all mention of birth control in advertising, and censor information about it in programming. (It is permitted in the news.) Millions of dollars in sexually alluring ads are okay. Ads for

Finally, after long negotiations, the three networks agreed to let the spots run. But only after the dreaded "C-word" –"contraception"–was censored. Instead, the networks substituted this dynamic phrase: "There are many ways to prevent unintended pregnancy."

As for network policies censoring "birth control" within programs? No change. As for the rejection of commercials for contraceptive products like condoms, foams, the pill? No change. As for the reduction of irresponsible sexual imagery? No change. As for a sense of balance between sexual hype and realistic useful information? No change.

III. Blaming the public tastes

Network executives argue that they've a responsibility to uphold high standards of public taste. The mention of birth control (except in the news) would somehow violate that. Is that true? Does the public really

How come nobody got pregnant?

here and there to sell products. And characters like J.R. Ewing have been seducing women a few times an hour for eight years.

In 1978, researchers counted 20,000 sexual scenes on prime-time network television (which does not include soap operas), with nary a mention of consequences or protection. It's even higher today. The only sexual mystery left seems to be how all these people keep doing it without contraception while nobody gets pregnant.

With all that worry-free hot action on television, it's no wonder American youngsters are having sex earlier and more often. *And* getting pregnant. Kids watch an average of four hours every day. That's more time than they spend in school or doing anything else in life, except sleeping. That's four hours per day inside a world where no one ever says "no," where sex is loose and often violent, and where sexual responsibility is as out-of-date as hula-hoops. Today's TV message is this: "GO FOR IT *NOW*. GO FOR IT AGAIN. AND DON'T WORRY ABOUT ANYTHING."

But there is plenty to worry about. The teen pregnancy rate in this country is now the highest of any country in the industrialized world. In the U.S. more than a million teens get pregnant every year. The consequences are tragic: high rates of school drop-outs, broken families, welfare and abortion. Who pays the tab? You do. About $16 billion yearly.

Of course television is *not* the only cause. When it comes to sex, there's a terrible breakdown of communications between parents and kids. There's also an appalling lack of timely, comprehensive sex education in schools. So kids are learning about sex the hard way–by experience. But television is making matters worse. Both because of what's on TV, and because of what is not.

II. Censorship by the Networks

The television industry is very sensitive about people telling them what they cannot broadcast. But the TV industry itself feels free to censor content.

Last year, the American College of Obstetricians and Gynecologists (ACOG)–a most prestigious physicians organization–prepared an ad campaign to educate kids about how to prevent pregnancy. They wanted to use print media, radio, and television. The brochure for the campaign said this: (1) Kids *can* resist peer pressure. They can take the option of postponing sex until they're ready. (2) The pill *is* a safe contraceptive for young women. And (3) sexually active young *men* should also be responsible–use condoms. These were useful statements.

The TV commercials ACOG prepared were even milder. All they suggested was that *unintended pregnancy* can interfere with career goals for women, and they offered to send the brochure. But, amazingly, the network execs said the ads were too "controversial," because they made mention of the word "contraceptives." These are the same networks which routinely show thousands of murders, rapes and acts of kinky sex. And 94% of the sexual encounters in soap operas are among people not married to each other. Are *those* presentations non-controversial? Do *those* represent some kind of higher moral value?

A recent Louis Harris Poll showed exactly what the public wants. Most Americans believe that television portrays an unrealistic and irresponsible view of sex. And 78% would like to see messages about contraception on TV. A similar percentage wants more sex education in schools. So it's not the public which resists more responsible sexual imagery. It's the television executives who resist it. Why? Maybe it's just a creative problem for them. We think they can solve it. Right now they don't even mention birth control when it's exactly appropriate. Why can't J.R. ask his latest conquest if she is prepared? Why can't she ask him? The screenwriters can work it out.

The television industry once said the public couldn't handle images of people wearing seatbelts, and they figured that one out. The case of birth control should be simpler than seatbelts, since 90% of adults already accept its use. It's mainly teenagers who don't.

IV. What you can do

Television executives keep trying to avoid their own responsibility, telling us that TV imagery has nothing to do with shaping teens' attitudes, that television doesn't influence them. But this is ridiculous. Television is the most powerful medium ever invented to influence mass behavior. It's on that basis that the networks sell their advertising.

Television influences all of us every day. And it is a major influence on teenagers about sexuality and responsibility. It may now be a more important influence than school, parents, or even peers. The problem is that television is putting out an unbalanced view which is causing *more* problems for teenagers and society. The situation has got to change.

It's time we turn to the small number of men who control this medium and tell them they have a responsibility to the public beyond entertainment, titillation, pushing products and making money.

They need to know you are out there, and that you are concerned. It will make a tremendous difference. Use the coupons. Write letters and make phone calls. And join Planned Parenthood's efforts in your area.

Thank you.

Planned Parenthood®
Federation of America, Inc.

This ad paid for by private contributions. ©Copyright 1986 Planned Parenthood Federation of America, Inc.

Guess Which of These Are in "Good Taste"
(According to the Networks)

VAGINAL SPRAY

CONDOMS

PREP-Z

TAMPONS

The tv network execs have decided that all advertisements for contraceptive products are in "bad taste" and they have banned them. Vaginal sprays, hemorrhoidal products, tampons are all in "good taste," according to them. So are toilet paper ads, underwear ads and nudity in everything from soap and cosmetic ads to beer ads. As for network drama and comedy programs which emphasize sexual doings? "Good taste." But mentioning "contraception" or "birth control" within programming (except news) is censored. ☙ The networks have not yet got the message. Our country is suffering a major problem of teen pregnancy, and television network policy is making it worse. Hyping sexuality while censoring information about responsibility is giving a terrible double message. ☙ The networks need to hear from you. Now. Please use the coupons above, write letters, phone. Your response can turn things around.

As for the many dozens of other ads on these subjects (as are displayed in the surrounding pages) primary credit belongs to Jono Polansky. He will surely go down in media history as the world's most prolific author of effective and persuasive public interest ad writing, ever. During his tenure at PMC, Polansky wrote nearly all the winning Planned Parenthood campaigns and also authored the excellent ads from NARAL and dozens of others. His work was spectacularly successful, both for its political impact and ability to raise much-needed funding. And then came David Brower.

ENTER: DAVID BROWER (3) AT EARTH ISLAND INSTITUTE

If Dave Brower had any flaw, it would have been his inability to sustain long term agreements within his own organizational leadership teams, even among the organizations he helped invent. As noted earlier, he was fired by the Sierra Club in 1969—despite his astonishingly sensational series of victories for Grand Canyon and Redwood National Park, North Cascades National Park, et. al. But, he had defied authority by running an advertisement *("EARTH NATIONAL PARK")* that the Sierra Club's Board of Directors had never authorized, and which they felt exceeded the club's mandate.

No matter. Suddenly on the loose, Brower had leaped forward to found Friends of the Earth, appointing his own Board of Directors. There, for a time, he had complete freedom and authority. But as the years progressed beyond the decade, and the organization became global and far more complex, Brower again ran into the problem of failing to effectively communicate or collaborate with his own management team. There's no question he continued to do spectacular things at Friends of the Earth, but sometimes they were not part of the broader management scheme.

So, after ten years with FOE, Brower again decided to leave and to help create yet a third important non-profit activist agency: Earth Island Institute.

At Earth Island, Brower's relationships with management and staff were much easier and very productive. Perhaps it was simply that Dave was getting older and more compliant—and the management team at Earth Island was especially compatible, flexible, radical, and similarly dedicated to Brower's brand of issues. Dave Phillips and John Knox had co-managed the organization from its founding, and worked with Brower with great ease, commitment, and success. Brower passed away in 2000, but Phillips and Knox continued to do remarkable, dedicated work right to the present.

Earth Island's emphasis was always clear and powerful, remaining largely focused on lesser known but profoundly important *international* environmental issues. These included threats to the massive murder of sea life caused by irresponsible behaviors of several countries, most notably the United States and Japan. Several Earth Island ads, displayed in these pages, are good examples of that organization's condemnations of horrific *international* behavior toward endangered sea-life; all in behalf of trivial, doubtful human pleasures and corporate profits. These range from the aggressive Asian marketing of "Tiger Penis Soup," to the ecocidal needs of the Bumble Bee Tuna's corporate management seeking to locate herds of tuna. (They would often find the tuna by spotting herds of dolphins that tended to hover above the tuna tribes. Commercial fishermen still today routinely kill dolphins to get to the tuna.)

The first ad in the following section (featuring TIGER PENIS in the heading) attacks *Taiwan* for being the world's leading killer of some of the last wild tigers on the planet, to get at certain tiger body parts. The second ad attacks *Japan* for financing a massive international sea turtle hunt to provide raw materials used globally for "eyeglass frames, cigarette lighters, and combs." *(See ad on page v)*

The third ad attacks *Norway*—usually considered an environmentally conscious and caring society—but which has lately revived its deplorable whale-harvesting programs.

The fourth and fifth ads attack *US* policy and corporations for supporting the vast hunt for undersea herds of tuna fish, spotted and caught because of their proximity to dolphin herds—thus netting and killing tens of thousands of both species together. All of this in behalf of providing millions more cans of Bumble Bee Tuna!

And the sixth ad criticizes *Mexico* for joining the US assault on the remaining dolphins, newly encouraged by the pathetic rules of the General Agreement on Tariffs and Trade (GATT).

Before we finish reporting on Earth Island, we must also mention that David Brower, just as he had done at the Sierra Club and Friends of the Earth, could not resist one further expression of his broad personal philosophies. This was expressed by his attacks on the over-riding worldviews and systems of value that drove the horrible behaviors that Brower's organizations fiercely opposed. At the Sierra Club, Brower used an ad to propose *Earth National Park*. At Friends of the Earth, it was *Ecology & War*. And then at Earth

(text continued on page 58)

50

A BOWL OF TIGER PENIS SOUP SELLS FOR $320 IN TAIWAN. ONLY WHILE SUPPLIES LAST.

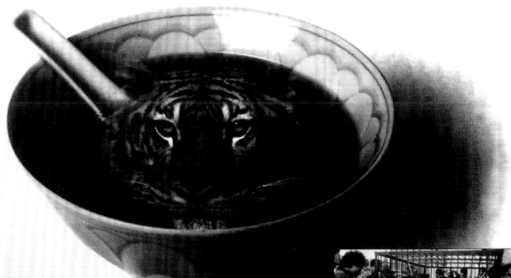

Taiwan has become a giant Black Hole sucking endangered species toward extinction. This island nation is the world's #1 market for tigers from Asia (sold for parts) and rhinos from Africa (their horns are worth their weight in gold).

But if a Taiwanese businessman thinks $320 for a bowl of tiger penis soup is costly, wait until he gets the real bill. Under U.S. law, the White House can slap trade sanctions on Taiwan for undermining global agreements that protect tigers, rhinos and other endangered species.

NUMBER OF TIGERS LEFT IN THE WORLD	
Indian/Bengal Tiger	<3,000
Indochinese Tiger	<1,000
Sumatran Tiger	<600
Siberian Tiger	<250
South China Tiger	<50
Javanese Tiger	Extinct
Caspian Tiger	Extinct
Balinese Tiger	Extinct

Only if the Clinton-Gore Administration imposes trade sanctions by the Nov. 7 deadline can tigers be saved from the threat of extinction by the year 2000.

Taiwanese officials will crack down on the wildlife racketeers if Taiwan's exports are threatened. And poachers won't hunt down the 5,000 tigers left in the wild if the market disappears.

The tiger can be saved.

Taiwanese racketeers pay poachers as much as $15,000 for a single tiger. Sold piecemeal, the tiger's skin, bones, eyes, blood, and penis may go for $60,000. Bears, orangutans, Asian leopards, rhino horns, and panda skins – banned under international agreement – are also on sale in Taiwan. U.S. trade sanctions are the only option left.

So, please, mail the three coupons below. Join the boycott. And stop the men eating tigers in Taiwan.

URGENT! TAKE ACTION BY NOV. 7 DEADLINE!

SAVE THE TIGER. BOYCOTT TAIWAN.

President Bill Clinton
The White House
1600 Pennsylvania Avenue, NW
Washington DC 20500

Taiwan is the #1 threat to endangered species including the tiger and rhino. Your Administration has already certified that Taiwan is subverting global conservation agreements and is subject to U.S. trade sanctions. You have until Nov. 7 to put teeth in conservation—and save the tiger.

NAME

ADDRESS

Pres. Lee Teng-Hui
Chaehshou Hall
Chung King South Road
Ti Pei, Taiwan 10728

Postage:
33¢ postcard
50¢ 1/2 oz. letter

Taiwan's assault on endangered wildlife causes deep revulsion and threatens the foreign trade that is Taiwan's lifeline. Extinction is final. Only your government can prevent it. I will boycott goods labeled "Made in Taiwan" until you comply with global conservation agreements.

NAME

ADDRESS

Sam LaBudde, Earth Island Institute
Endangered Species Project
Fort Mason Center E-205
San Francisco CA 94123

☐ I have mailed the coupons to President Clinton and Taiwan. ☐ I am joining the Taiwan Boycott effective immediately. Keep me posted.
☐ I enclose my tax-deductible support for your campaign: _$25 _$35 _$50 _$75 _$100 _$500 or_____.

NAME

ADDRESS

[NORWAY DEFIES INTERNATIONAL BAN ON WHALING]

They're killing whales again

In the last century, the world's population of whales was systematically decimated by commercial whalers. Hundreds of thousands of blue whales, sperm whales, humpback whales, and others — some of the most magnificent creatures on Earth — were hunted to the brink of extinction. Some whale species saw their numbers reduced so drastically that — even with a total ban on whaling — they may never recover.

Only when it was almost too late did the nations of the world — prodded by an outraged public — join together in an unprecedented agreement to end the wholesale slaughter of whales. In 1982, the International Whaling Commission (IWC) declared a worldwide moratorium beginning in 1986. Under IWC rules, all commercial whaling would end. It was a hard-won victory.

But now, one country, Norway, is turning its back on that agreement. And the brutal, needless commercial slaughter of whales will begin all over again. It doesn't have to be that way. Just as before, we have the power to stop it. But we must act now. Here are the details:

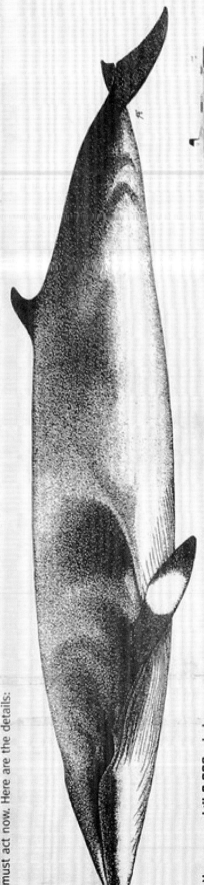

Norway to kill 2,000 whales

Twenty years ago, the world realized that whale populations in our oceans were threatened by the ruthless whaling that had gone uncontrolled for over a century. At the same time, scientists were just beginning to discover the rare intelligence and grace possessed by these extraordinary mammals. The delicate role whales play in preserving the balance of ocean ecology was just exploding. Instead, the harpoons gore the whale, causing it to bleed to death slowly and painfully. Whales that die this way suffer so horribly that some scientists describe it as "gigantic animal torture."

There's no excuse for any of this cruel, mindless slaughter. Originally, whales were hunted for meat, oils, and other minor by-products, all of which have been replaced by cheaper and still holding out, refusing to back away from the impending whale slaughter. Norway's defiant stand marks it as an environmental renegade, recklessly brandishing isolationism at a time when the fate of the Earth turns on global cooperation.

4 "People have short memories"

A Norwegian whaling representative has been

The Killing Begins

This year Norway has already killed 95 whales, claiming it to be for "scientific research." But this is only a prelude to the massive commercial whale killing planned in the coming months, unless Norway can be convinced to reverse its policy.

Save the whales. Boycott Norwegian Cruise Line and Royal Viking Line.

Most cruise ships carry marine

being understood. Joining together, schoolchildren, scientists, legislators and concerned citizens around the world began a decade-long fight to save the whales.

Today, in complete defiance of the International Whaling Commission (IWC) — the global body established to regulate whaling — Norway is resuming its horrific commercial whaling practices. This summer, Norwegian whalers announced their plans to hunt down 2,000 minke whales over the next year. Norway's flagrant violation of the IWC moratorium threatens to undermine all significant whale protections won over the last twenty years.

It isn't just a matter of saving minke whales. If the world doesn't react strongly enough to Norway's decision, Japan and Iceland are likely to resume the commercial killing of whales as well. Japan, in particular, wants to be free of the whaling treaty so it can begin a massive whale "harvesting" operation in Antarctica. Also, Norway's cavalier defiance of the whaling ban threatens to disrupt the spirit of global cooperation and consensus that's essential to other international environmental treaties, such as those concerning ozone depletion, endangered species, and global warming.

There are numerous recorded instances of grenade-tipped harpoons malfunctioning and not

2 "Gigantic animal torture"

Norwegian whalers claim the minke whale population can withstand the harvest of 2,000 whales a year, a statement that's contrary to established scientific consensus. The whalers also claim that their grenade-tipped harpoons cause whales little pain, which not only contradicts all scientific evidence, but also defies common sense.

Ms. Gro Harlem Brundtland
Prime Minister, Kingdom of Norway
c/o His Excellency Mr. Kjeld Vibe, Ambassador of Norway
2720 34th St. NW
Washington, DC 20008

Dear Prime Minister Brundtland,
I am outraged that Norway would unilaterally defy the International Whaling Commission's moratorium on commercial whaling. I am especially shocked that an avowed environmentalist such as yourself would ignore worldwide concern in favor of Norwegian whaling interests. Not only are you courting a boycott of Norwegian fish products and cruise lines, but also possible trade sanctions. With the Winter Olympics to be held in Norway in 1994, you also risk an Olympic boycott by countries and individuals protesting Norway's renewed whale slaughter. Please show real leadership and stop the killing of whales now.

NAME
ADDRESS
CITY   STATE   ZIP

more plentiful substitutes. In fact, Norway doesn't even have a market for the 2,000 minke whales they plan to kill and process into steaks and sausage. According to Steinar Bastesen, a spokesman for the whalers, to create consumer demand, they must first teach Norwegians to enjoy the taste of whale meat. More likely, Norway will sell its slaughtered whales to Japan for a quick profit.

Use the coupons below. Tell the Kloster family, owners of Norwegian Cruise Line and Royal Viking Line, two of Norway's biggest moneymakers, that you won't set foot on their cruise ships as long as the brutal whale slaughter continues.

3 Norway's "green" Prime Minister

The resumption of commercial whaling is strongly backed by Norway's self-proclaimed "green" Prime Minister Gro Harlem Brundtland, who took some of the tougher environmental positions at the Earth Summit this year. Also, in her Harvard commencement address last spring, the Prime Minister called for all nations to overcome their isolationist tendencies for the good of our planet. Either she's forgotten what she said or has had a change of heart. Now she is quoted as saying that Norway will "...stand up straight in the storm we expect to come."

Norway's defiance has shocked even its strongest allies. Representatives of the European Community (EC) have denounced Norway, and there are indications that its future membership in the EC may be in jeopardy.

The outrage over Norway's decision hasn't been confined to Europe. Here in the U.S., Burger King cancelled a multi-million dollar deal for Norwegian cod. Other major restaurant chains are contemplating similar actions. Knowing that it risks an official U.S. embargo on all its fish products, the Norwegian government has hired a big Washington, D.C. law and lobbying firm to block potential trade sanctions.

In Norway — despite strong vocal opposition to whaling — Brundtland's government is

Mr. Knut Ul. Kloster, Jr.
Chairman
Kloster Cruise Ltd.
95 Merrick Way
Coral Gables, Florida 33134

Dear Mr. Kloster,
Norway's defiance of the IWC whaling ban threatens to disrupt the spirit of international cooperation and goodwill that's essential to the global marketplace. It will be Norwegian businesses — such as the Norwegian Cruise and Royal Viking Lines — that will pay a high price for Norway's resumption of commercial whaling. Please use your influence to reverse Norway's decision and save the whales. Until that happens, I — along with my family and friends — won't be doing any business with Norwegian companies, or buying Norwegian products.

NAME
ADDRESS
CITY   STATE   ZIP

quoted as saying that "people have short memories." The whaling interests in Norway — as well as in Japan and Iceland — think they can get away with it because we'll forget. That we just won't care as much this time. It's up to us to prove them wrong.

Use the coupons below. Tell the Kloster family, owners of Norwegian Cruise Line and Royal Viking Line, two of Norway's biggest moneymakers, that you won't set foot on their cruise ships as long as the brutal whale slaughter continues.

Tell EC President Jacques Delors that you support tough sanctions against Norway. And, most importantly, let Prime Minister Brundtland know that Norway can't turn back the clock to a time when the oceans were red with the blood of slaughtered whales. When entire whale species were driven to the brink of extinction.

We can't allow Norway — or any country — to act like an outlaw nation, ignoring with impunity the international agreements protecting whales. We must support the efforts of concerned Norwegians who are fighting to reverse their government's policy.

History has taught us repeatedly that countries that act without any regard for the rest of the world — or their own people — are reckless and dangerous. Not only for the survival of whales but for the rest of us as well.

If we don't act now to save the minke whales in Norway, we'll soon be fighting to save the whales everywhere, again.

President Jacques Delors
The European Commission
200 Rue de la Loi
1049 Brussels, Belgium

POSTAGE $.50

Dear President Delors,
I am shocked that Norway is defying the IWC ban on commercial whaling, despite protests from EC members. Norway's unilateral defiance of the whaling ban is a threat to all international cooperation — alive efforts to address urgent environmental concerns. Insist that Norway reverse its whaling policy before it is allowed to join the European Community or be part of EC fisheries agreements. Thank you for helping protect the Earth's remaining whale populations.

NAME
ADDRESS
CITY   STATE   ZIP

biologists on board to help passengers better understand the marvels of sea life. We wonder what the biologists who work for Norwegian Cruise or Royal Viking Lines will say about Norway's brutal whale slaughter. Or if they'll explain the relationship between the Norwegian Government and the owners of both cruise lines — the powerful and influential Kloster family of Norway. Probably not. Use the coupons below and ask the Kloster family to use their influence with the Norwegian government to save the whales. Or you, your family and all your friends — as well as everyone else you spread the world to — will be sailing with someone else.

The Humane Society
of the United States

Earth Island Institute / Humane Society of the U.S.
Norwegian Whaling Campaign
300 Broadway, Suite 28
San Francisco, California 94133

If we don't act now to stop Norway from breaking the worldwide ban on commercial whaling, the slaughter will begin all over again, threatening once more the survival of these magnificent creatures. Here's my tax-deductible contribution in support of your efforts to stop Norway and protect the world's remaining whale populations: □ $15 □ $50 □ $100 □ $250 or $_____
Please make checks payable to Earth Island Institute.

□ I've sent the coupons. □ Please send me more information on how I can help stop Norway from killing whales again.

NAME
ADDRESS
CITY   STATE   ZIP

For even faster action, call 1-800-999-3866 and the three letters above will be sent out in your name. The charge of $7.95 can be billed to your credit card and will assist our campaign.

[Hundreds of thousands of these graceful, intelligent creatures maimed and killed]

THE DOLPHIN MASSACRE OFF OUR COAST AND WHAT YOU CAN DO TO STOP IT.

"YOU CAN SEE the dolphins fighting up through the mesh. They're unable to breathe. They're drowning. Now a crew member throws explosives to scare the dolphins toward the far end of the net. This plan backfires. Panicked by the bombs, the dolphins pile up in the net next to the ship, churning the water white. You can hear them crying out...

"Now the captain loses patience and commands the operation to continue, even though there are hundreds of animals still in the net. So you see dolphins tangled in the webbing, hoisted twisting into the bright blue sky and dragged through the crushing maw of the power block.

"When the net retrieval is almost finished, the skiff returns and the remaining floats are draped between the two boats, forming a deep bag with a very narrow opening. Mixed in with a hundred dead or dying dolphins is our catch of ten or twelve tuna. You can hear the crew joking as they cast the stunned, dead and wounded dolphins adrift in the sea."

As documented on CBS News, this eyewitness report from a biologist working with Earth Island Institute who shipped undercover aboard a Latin American tuna boat this year confirms our worst fears.

The slaughter of dolphins along the

VIDEOTAPE PHOTO COURTESY OF SAM LABUDDE.

Videotape shot on a tuna ship is eyewitness evidence of dolphin slaughter in 1988. Despite federal laws, trapped, drowned, mangled dolphins are again business as usual off the Pacific Coast.

Pacific coast continues full force.

The documentary evidence shows that between 75,000 and 150,000 dolphins are being massacred each year by U.S. and foreign tuna fleets off the Pacific coast.

It's the largest kill of marine mammals in the world today. Because the law meant to prevent this slaughter is simply not enforced.

Even the officials paid to protect the dolphins admit the fishing fleets are netting dolphins on purpose. Multi-million dollar tuna ships, complete with helicopters and the latest in radar, may "set" their mile-long nets on the same herd of dolphins four times a day in search of the tuna below.

Frightened, maimed, and drowned, dolphins are casualties of high-tech fishing wars.

All the corporate promises and official reassurances are, it turns out, worth nothing.

What can you do to stop the slaughter of the dolphins?

First, stop buying all canned tuna. The dolphins die in the hunt for yellowfin, the most common kind on the shelves. Boycotting all kinds will send the big companies a message they can't ignore.

Second, mail the coupons to Earth Island and to the House and Senate subcommittees in charge of protecting the dolphins.

Dolphins are mammals like us. They breathe air. They nurse their young. They communicate and work together in groups. Graceful and intelligent creatures, dolphins have been known to come to the aid of drowning humans.

We're suing the federal government to enforce existing laws, save the dolphins, and forbid import of tuna netted by our neighbors without regard for dolphin kills.

Your contribution will also let us work for tougher laws, better research and greater protection for the world's dolphins —especially those species in immediate danger of extinction.

Speed is of the essence. Every day you delay, a thousand more wild dolphins— pregnant and nursing mothers, infants and juveniles—could be trapped and drowned in the tuna nets.

Graceful and intelligent creatures we dream of understanding and befriending are dying horribly, needlessly. To stop this crime against the dolphins. . .and against our own humanity. . .please act immediately.

These are the most common kinds of canned tuna you'll see on grocery shelves. You may also see "house brands" and higher-priced bonito and albacore. Keep it simple. Boycott them all. Return the coupon to us and we'll send you addresses to write in protest.

Hon. Gerry E. Studds
Chairman, Subcommittee on
Fisheries, Wildlife Conservation
& the Environment
U.S. House of Representatives
Washington, D.C. 20515

We can't allow the massacre of the dolphins to go on. Renew and enforce the federal Marine Mammal Protection Act and bring the kill down to zero. Future generations won't forgive inaction.

NAME

ADDRESS

CITY   STATE   ZIP

Hon. John F. Kerry
Committee on Commerce,
Science & Transportation
U.S. Senate
Washington, D.C. 20510

We can't allow the massacre of the dolphins to go on. Renew and enforce the federal Marine Mammal Protection Act and bring the kill down to zero. Future generations won't forgive inaction.

NAME

ADDRESS

CITY   STATE   ZIP

I've joined the tuna boycott as of today. Here's my contribution to your fight to rescue the 75,000 to 150,000 dolphins now killed each year. I know you won't rest until the slaughter has been halted.

☐ $25   ☐ $50   ☐ $75   ☐ $100   ☐ $150   ☐ more.

NAME

ADDRESS

CITY   STATE   ZIP

EARTH ISLAND INSTITUTE Save-the-Dolphins Project, 300 Broadway, Suite 28, San Francisco, CA 94133 ATTN: David R. Brower, Chairman

Public Media Center

[NATIONWIDE CONSUMER ADVISORY]

Bumble Bee Tuna's parent company, Unicord, Inc., still sponsors the slaughter of dolphins.

Alone among the three major tuna canners, Bumble Bee has lied about its corporate connection to the netting and drowning of dolphins.

Bumble Bee's publicized claims that environmentalists endorse these practices are completely false.

Our on-site inspection of a Unicord cannery in Thailand confirms that it has continued to process thousands of tons of tuna caught with deadly driftnets.

As a consumer, your choice is now perfectly clear.

You can buy "dolphin-safe" tuna from StarKist, the company that first set the standard for dolphin protection, or from Chicken of the Sea, a company that keeps its promises.

Or you can reward a cynical corporation slaughtering defenseless dolphins while riding the PR coat-tails of more responsible companies.

Claiming its global operations are "dolphin-safe" when they're not, Bumble Bee has undercut firms truly concerned about dolphin deaths and boosted its sales at their expense.

You can take personal action to end dolphin-killing worldwide.

■ Boycott all Bumble Bee Seafoods products. Mail a stinging rebuke to the company's president.

■ Ask your grocer to stop selling tuna caught unsafely. (We'll send you a complete list of dolphin-safe brands.)

■ And, please, if you can, support our work. We launched the canned tuna boycott that led to "dolphin-safe" standards. Now we're monitoring tuna canners around the world.

Bumble Bee announced it was "dolphin-safe" the same day StarKist did. But in the seven months since, Unicord has been responsible for countless dolphin deaths.

Only Bumble Bee has failed to keep its word. There's only one way to hold this giant multinational accountable.

Save the dolphins. Don't buy Bumble Bee canned tuna.

To save dolphins from being killed in tuna nets, you can buy StarKist or Chicken of the Sea.

Mark Koob, President
Bumble Bee Seafoods, Inc.
5775 Roscoe Court, San Diego, CA 94123

Bumble Bee has pulled the environmental sting of the year. You continued to contract with dolphin-killing tuna ships and buy driftnetted tuna in Asia, then fraudulently claim endorsement from environmentalists. This is an outrage. Why should I buy Bumble Bee tuna ever again?

NAME _____

ADDRESS _____ CITY _____ STATE ___ ZIP

David Phillips
Earth Island Institute Save the Dolphins Project
300 Broadway, San Francisco, CA 94133

Keep these killers in line. Keep up the pressure. Make sure the honest companies remain accountable. And get the government to enforce the law to stop the dolphin slaughter. Here's my contribution: __$15 __$35 __$50 __$100 __$250 __$500 or $_____.

NAME _____

ADDRESS _____ CITY _____ STATE ___ ZIP

But don't buy Bumble Bee!

Help us spread the word. Please copy this Consumer Advisory and post it where you work.

55

50,000 DEAD DOLPHINS ARE JUST THE BEGINNING . . .

RALLY TO PROTEST MEXICO'S SLAUGHTER OF DOLPHINS MONDAY SEPT. 30, 11 AM Third & Market Streets, San Francisco Call (415)788-3666 for details!

U.S. & Mexico launch a worldwide assault on endangered species.

Under the cover of "free trade," and with U.S. connivance, President Salinas of Mexico has mounted a campaign to gut vital environmental protection laws in the United States and around the world.

The first victims? 50,000 dolphins expected to be trapped and killed by Mexican-based tuna ships this coming year.

The tuna fleets of Ecuador and Panama have adjusted their fishing techniques to protect nursing dolphins and their young, who are the most common victims (mother dolphins refuse to leave their young behind when they become entangled in the nets).

But Mexico protested to GATT, a secretive

Carla Hills & the GATT-ling Gun:

Every endangered species in the world is suddenly under the gun since GATT (General Agreement on Tariffs and Trade) officials in Geneva decided behind closed doors that sanctions to protect endangered species violate free trade. Unless this ruling is repudiated by the full GATT Council, the U.S. Marine Mammal Protection Act and thirty years of endangered species safeguards will be gutted. **The ruling must be overturned by Tuesday, Oct. 8...and the U.S. must insist that GATT adopt environmental reforms.** Only U.S. Trade Representative Carla Hills can do it. But her boss, President Bush, is reportedly "undecided"! Send a message to Ms. Hills now. **This is your chance to stop the killing.**

trade body based in Geneva, that the U.S. embargo on tuna imports from nations violating the federal Marine Mammal Protection Act was an "unfair trade practice."

And GATT, oblivious to any of the environmental impacts of world trade, upheld Mexico's claims.

If this ruling is allowed to stand, the slaughter of dolphins may be unstoppable.

Worse, all *other* trade sanctions designed to halt traffic in endangered species, stop driftnetting, sustain the rainforests, end the

shameful and dangerous dumping of toxics in the Third World, and ban global trade in ozone-depleting chemicals, will be useless.

Environmental activists worldwide are dismayed by Mexican President Salinas' failure to bring his nation's policies into line with his public pledges on the environment.

And shocked that President Bush, the self-proclaimed "environmental president," sent a State Department team to Mexico to aid and abet a back-room deal gutting the United States' own environmental laws.

This is an emergency. Mail the coupons below...or call the 800 number at left...today. Thank you.

EARTH ISLAND INSTITUTE

Act now to halt the slaughter.

Call 1-800-7-DOLPHIN to send urgent mailgrams in your name to President Salinas *and* Carla Hills... $6.95 will be billed to your credit card for this emergency service.

U.S. Trade Representative Carla Hills
600 17th Street, N.W.
Washington, D.C. 20506

GATT's decision to uphold Mexico's protest of a U.S. ban on imported tuna caught by killing dolphins is an absolutely catastrophic blow to *all* worldwide efforts to guard endangered species and the global ecosystem. The U.S. has the clout to block the Geneva bureaucrats, salvage America's environmental protections, and stop the slaughter at sea. GATT must start recognizing environmental factors in world trade. Make this long-overdue reform your #1 priority.

NAME

ADDRESS

President Salinas de Gortari
Palacio Nacional
Mexico City, Mexico

Despite assurances made during free trade negotiations that there would be no environmental sell-outs, Mexico is winning a reputation as the world's dolphin killer. If Mexico's search for a GATT loophole is any indication, your environmental guarantees have little credibility. Save the dolphins. And listen to Mexico's eco-activist Group of 100: do your part to form a 19-nation Latin American Ecological Alliance to solve the growing problems throughout our hemisphere.

NAME

ADDRESS

Dave Phillips, Co-Director
Earth Island Institute
300 Broadway, S.F., CA 94133

Dolphin Project

Your relentless pressure on the U.S. government to actually enforce the Marine Mammal Protection Act — and the consumer boycott of "unsafe" canned tuna you helped organize — has made powerful corporations and independent nations decide to stop the massacre of dolphins. The GATT ruling is the most critical challenge yet, undermining decades of environmental progress.
[ ] I mailed the other coupons. [ ] I enclose my tax-deductible contribution of _$20 _$35 _$75 or ___.

NAME

ADDRESS

NOTE: First-class postage to Mexico is 45¢ for a typical 1-oz. letter.

PREPARED BY PUBLIC MEDIA CENTER.

"ECONOMICS IS A FORM OF BRAIN DAMAGE"

[An urgent message about restoration to President Bill Clinton from environmental elder David Brower]

[David Brower is or has been — President, Earth Island Action Group; first executive director of the Sierra Club; instigator of the Sierra Club Foundation, Friends of the Earth International (now in fifty countries), the League of Conservation Voters, Environmental Liaison Center International (Nairobi), The Fate and Hope of the Earth Conferences; and Earth Island Institute; decorated U.S. Mountain Division combat veteran; editor of fifty-seven environmental books; awarded nine honorary degrees; honorary member of the Appalachian Mountain Club and American Alpine Club; twice nominated for the Nobel Peace Prize; subject of John McPhee's book Encounters with the Archdruid; married 49 years with four children and three grandchildren].

Futurist Hazel Henderson, well versed in economics, says so. Perhaps you had something like this in mind in your inaugural allusion to our borrowing the Earth from our children – a loan conventional economists ignore. Al Gore considers conventional economics a form of blindness (see *Earth in the Balance*, pages 182-196, 337-45). Hundreds of thousands in my audiences agree – and so would hundreds of millions in yours, given the chance.

Too many economic advisers have been ignoring what their advice to governments and corporations has cost the Earth and the future. Economists continue to ignore it, in effect advising that we trash the Earth.

What kind of trashing?

Having turned 80 much sooner than I expected, I can look back on fourscore years and some disturbing events:

1] The population of the Earth tripled, and is a good ten times more than the planet can sustain over the long run.

2] The population of California is twelve times greater, making it difficult for the state to afford the essentials of a good life.

3] The world as a whole has exhausted four times as many resources as were used up in all previous history.

4] California's six thousand miles of salmon streams in the Great Valley have been reduced to about two hundred.

5] Only four and a half percent of California's unique redwoods remain, and none of its storied sardine fishery.

All that, except for the redwoods, took just eight decades. How about the last two decades?

1] The world's new deserts, created by people, equal all the cropland of China.

2] Enough functioning soil has been lost by other means worldwide (drowned under reservoirs, paved under highways, covered by suburbs, contaminated with chemicals, eroded by wind and water) to equal all the cropland of India.

3] Enough of the Earth's forests have been destroyed to cover the U.S. east of the Mississippi from Canada to the Gulf.

4] We have suffered, too insensibly, an incalculable loss of biodiversity essential to a sustainable life-support system. The loss is incalculable because we don't know how many species we have sent to extinction before we even had time to discover them. (We may already have destroyed the cure for AIDS.)

5] People keep calling for economic growth fed by more of this destruction. They forget the Law of the Minimum. It doesn't matter how much water we have if we run out of air.

6] Conventional economic advice brought humanity to the edge of a precipice. Before we take another step, or force our children to, we had better turn around. The change we need more than any other is a U-turn toward an economy that is sustainable in the long run. Any other economic goal is stupid.

Civilization is marching into the future guided by blind economic growth which the Earth will not allow us to sustain. Our economists continue to forget the costs to the Earth and the costs to the future. And the conscience-free transnational corporations and the Fortune 500 seem determined, in their full-court press for the General Agreement on Tariffs and Trade (GATT), to obliterate all environmental barriers to world trade. This is exactly backwards. There should be no world trade without environmental protection.

There will be no universities, churches, media, customers, or even love, on a dead planet. It is time to realize that we are killing it with apathy, carelessness, and wanton development.

[IT'S HEALING TIME ON EARTH]

Henry David Thoreau asked, "What's the use of a house if you haven't got a tolerable planet to put it on?" Or of a nation, or economy, or jobs?

We can start putting the life-support system of this planet back together. It will require CPR — Conservation, Protection, and Restoration — and TLC thereafter. Take your pick of words for the global goal — restore, renew, repair, regenerate, rehabilitate, replenish, re-create, heal, or just fix it while it runs.

If there is to be a sustainable society, humanity needs to make an attainable, profitable U-turn toward the restoration of both human habitat and the habitat of all the other species sharing this Earth with us.

Excitement and energy are required. A Global Restoration Fair at the Presidio of San Francisco in 1995 is now under discussion. It could help us make a U-turn. The year 1995 is the 50th anniversary of the signing of the United Nations Charter. And a Global Restoration and Conservation Service can help the world pull together in the Green Century. Its world headquarters ought to be in the Presidio, soon to be in the National Park System.

The Restoration Fair and the Service could help us retrace our steps to where we got lost. Applying our science, technology, humanity, and compassion, we can take on the rewarding work of restoring the life-support system that was evolving very nicely until we began carelessly trashing it.

[JOBS AND CAREERS TO END THE TRASHING]

Here is a partial list. Reclaim deserts, regrow forests, revive rivers, renew soil fertility, restore wetlands and vernal pools, rebuild populations of endangered species, remove a few dams (ask for a list!), recycle as much of the waste stream as nature does, put railroads back on the track, rehabilitate broken-down structures or replace them with neighborhood parks, recover the lost skills of honest maintenance, recapture and reuse the nation's junk, reinvest in prosperity.

Put people to work to create better lives for us all.

Existing skills and the jobless can get the healing started. New skills and assignments can carry it on. Let's start with universities and trade schools. For example, students receiving federal financial help for their studies, as you have urged, could repay their debt with a stint in the Global Restoration and Conservation Service. Let the Service include all creeds, colors, classes, ages, and sexes. Putting aside favorite prejudices, they can work globally and locally toward peace on and with the Earth.

Two-thirds of the 300,000 people I've addressed lately on four continents are willing to commit a year of their next ten to

this cause! The force is there. You can help the world focus it.

Academia needs to train students (and itself) for that trip. All professions and skills will have roles.

There is plenty of energy and talent among the present jobless and homeless to be put to work, with optimum supervision.

The U.S. is subsidizing, at 4 billion per year, the energy wasted in poorly insulated homes. Invest that instead in jobs helping poor people insulate their homes.

And there are thousands upon thousands, maintained at heavy expense in jails who, with maximum supervision, can be out of cells and in the open, helping to restore the Earth, the society, and themselves.

Whatever restoration may cost will be far cheaper than failing to undertake it in time. It's OK to tax and spend, or borrow and spend, if the spending is on a sound investment.

Incidentally, those who think there can be no adequate economic return from restoration should take their car to the shop or their body to the doctor. Restoration pays.

Thank you.

DAVID R. BROWER

[HOW *YOU* CAN ACT]

Please use the coupons or write your own letters or call the 800 number and we will send letters in your behalf. If you can, get ten friends from all over to do the same. Let President Clinton know there will be wide support for the bold leader who pilots human society and its associates into the Era of Restoration that will keep the island Earth and its passengers alive.

And throw some parties. Get some fun out of all this. Ask your guests and your organizations to suggest further ways to heal the man-made wounds. Give some awards. And let the President and us know which of our ideas you like, and which of your award-winning ideas you'd like us to like. – D.R.B.

SEND THE COUPONS OR CALL 1-800-4-1-EARTH for information on how to get things moving–including your restoration parties–at little costs and with big benefits.

EVOLUTION: SQUEEZING THE EARTH'S 4.5 BILLION YEARS INTO SIX DAYS OF CREATION

■ **Monday, 12:01 A.M.**
Earth begins.

■ **Tuesday, 12 noon**
Life comes aboard.

■ **Tuesday to Saturday morning**
Millions upon millions of species come and fewer millions leave.

■ **Saturday, 7:00 A.M.**
Enough chlorophyll has been at work to allow fossil fuels to begin to form.

■ **Saturday, 4:00 P.M.**
The great reptiles come on stage.

■ **Saturday, 9:45 P.M.**
They vanish, after a five-hour run.

■ **Saturday, 11:56 P.M.**
Something like us shows up.

[That was four minutes before midnight. Now let's shift to seconds before midnight]

■ **30 seconds to midnight**
Homo sapiens!

■ **1.5 seconds to midnight**
Agriculture begins and the hunter gatherers multiply at will, not having to hunt and gather anymore.

■ **1 second to midnight**
Agriculture has been so successful that the forests which once ringed the Mediterranean Sea are reduced to pitiful fragments. Some religions are invented to help us out of the mess.

■ **1/3 second to midnight**
Buddha is born.

■ **1/4 second to midnight**
Christ is born.

■ **1/20 second to midnight**
Columbus gets lost and the strip search of the Western Hemisphere is under way.

■ **1/40 second to midnight**
The Industrial Revolution. Mozart and Bach begin their creative efforts. (Two caused little harm. Back to Bach!)

■ **1/80 second to midnight**
Oil is discovered.

■ **1/200 second to midnight**
Atomic Age is born. GNP race is started by Russians. U.S. wants no one to have a grosser national product than ours and joins the race, which Japan seems to be winning.

■ **Midnight on Saturday**
Gridlock prevails.

A NEW ERA IS DAWNING. WHAT KIND OF WORLD WILL YOU GIVE YOUR GRANDCHILDREN A CHANCE TO KNOW?

Island came another Brower manifesto. This one was in the form of an open letter to President Bill Clinton, mostly written by Brower himself, with a copy to Boutros-Boutros Ghali, then President of the United Nations:

"ECONOMICS IS A FORM OF BRAIN DAMAGE".

That ad (*page 57*) expressed Brower's overall assessment and critique of the global environmental situation, and included several good suggestions for economic changes that Brower felt might ease the problems. It's a profound and interesting statement. Unfortunately, however, that ad was *not* persuasive in getting either President Clinton or the United Nations to do any kind of early about-face. But it was still an urgent early warning about the new and frightful global economic framework that was rapidly advancing. David Brower was among the first to warn us.

GLOBALIZATION OF CORPORATE POWERS (1991–2001)

As with the momentous emergence of national and global television, the early 1990s were also the time when something brand new and profoundly grim emerged onto the scene: the *globalization* of corporate activity. Suddenly, and without formal announcement, the world's largest corporations were quickly growing beyond nation-state controls. With the new availability of instantaneous global communications, corporate activity became rapidly globalized, enabling them to largely remove themselves from most nation-state controls.

The transitions began in the 1980s and accelerated in the early 1990s via the rapid application, expansion, and deployment of digital electronic communications technologies. Because of that "advance" in technological capability, traditional corporate institutional and nation-state communication boundaries became effectively obsolete. Instantaneous *global* multi-national communication systems became possible and desirable for large corporations. Corporations could now expand their operations far more rapidly anywhere on the planet, while maintaining constant control, contact, and communications among their dispersed parts and activities. This enabled far easier coordinated planetary planning and daily operations.

By the early 1990s, these same revolutionary communications instruments were also finding their ways into ordinary private homes, local marketing, and retailing. At that point, therefore, both sides of the industrial equation were impacted: the production/communications aspect, and the market feasibility aspect.

So, the entire shape, reach, and scale of marketing activity was revolutionized, advancing from local, to regional, to national to global. Meanwhile, regulation and control over these processes was much less within the governing powers of nation-states. In fact, many of these new institutions were increasingly regulated by the participants themselves, via the blossoming of new international trade agreements.

★   ★   ★

Corporations understood the shapes and economic and political potentialities of these technology shifts long before anti-corporate activists did. That remained true into the 1990s, well after many giant new global trade institutions had already been created and begun to assume global authority. These included the World Trade Organization (WTO), the International Monetary Fund (IMF), the General Agreement on Tariffs and Trade (GATT), the North American Free Trade Agreement (NAFTA), and the Association of Southeast Asian Nations (ASEAN), among other new largely *self-governing* global trade agreements.

No longer would democratic nation-states be making the most important decisions about global environmental behavior from corporations. Now it would mostly be the corporations themselves increasingly in control of nation-state decisions, via their increased off-shore communications powers, the fantastic speed of information movement, the financial controls over domestic electoral politics, and the effective operating control of globalized, stateless institutions.

As for the already existing activist communities, regrettably, it took some time for local or nationally oriented economic activists to grasp what was happening *outside* of national boundaries, or to figure out whether, when, and how to fight these new turns of circumstance.

Although many of these transformations were already underway by the late 1980s-early 1990s, the new capabilities and possibilities of global technologies continued to accelerate. And yet, the political and social implications of this change did not fully catch the attention of US or international activist organizations until late into the 1990s. Only then did it become clear that the existing activist focus on anti-corporate local or domestic resistance was inadequate to deal with the new systems and governance situations that were now upon us. New global communications and organizing systems were required.

★   ★   ★

To my knowledge the very first significant formal signs of any organized *international resistance* to the rapid globalization process, now suddenly underway, took place during two extraordinary meetings in 1994. They were hosted in San Francisco at the home of wealthy environmental activist-philanthropist-businessman (former co-owner of ESPRIT, the large international fashion company) Douglas Tompkins. Tompkins was himself, of course, a highly experienced multi-national businessman, and he fully grasped the ominous import of what was going on globally at that time. Unlike most other very wealthy business-people, Doug's deepest love and commitment was not really business; it was the environment, as his later actions totally displayed. He was deeply worried about the environmental and social implications of those accelerating negative global trends.

I'd been a close friend of Doug's since the early 1960s, long before he and his first wife, Suzie, ever launched ESPRIT, and before my later partnership with Howard Gossage. I'll describe much greater detail about Doug, and my *later* collaborations with him, in Chapter Four. But for the moment, the main point is that in 1990, as Tompkins was withdrawing from ESPRIT, he asked me to help introduce him to some of the world's leading environmental and political activists. He hoped they might join in trying to launch new discussions about the implications and probable consequences of an expanding "economic globalization" (still a new term in those days) that was clearly upon us. Doug was very alarmed about the environmental, social, and political implications of what was happening, and wanted to initiate discussions and create connections among leading long-time environmental and political activists from every continent. Tompkins suggested I should help pull together a good international meeting of the best activists on these matters, so we could discuss what to do.

With the help of several other colleagues—(most notably Victor Menotti and Debbie Barker)—we compiled an extraordinary list of many of the world's leading environmental and political activists from that period. Then finally in 1994, we invited and hosted 50 of them to two three-day landmark meetings at Doug's house, on Russian Hill in San Francisco.

The central focus of both of those meetings was to explore, study, and understand the emerging new international trends and their implications, and to discuss what we might be able to do about them. Those invited to these inaugural meetings were all highly engaged economic activists. They came from every continent on the planet. But up to that point, they'd mostly been focused on local and regional economic issues. These meetings announced a big shift in emphasis and attention. Most of the attendees had not even known each other before these meetings. And the announced focus on *globalized* economics was new for most all of us.

Attendees at these first two meetings included Third World leaders, Martin Khor and Meenakshi Raman (from Third World Network, Malaysia), English trade activists Colin Hines, Tim Lang, Simon Retallack; the amazing and powerful Vandana Shiva (India); global Indigenous leader, Victoria Tauli-Corpuz (*Igorot*, from the Philippines), as well as Walden Bello (Philippines), Helena Norberg-Hodge (Sweden), Maude Barlow and Tony Clarke (Canada), and Sarah Larrain (Chile).

Also invited and deeply involved from the United States were John Cavanagh (Institute for Policy Studies), Mark Ritchie (Institute for Agriculture and Trade Policy), and David Korten (*Yes* Magazine, and the Club of Rome). And, very importantly, Lori Wallach (Public Citizen). All of them were soon actively promoting the need for a new level of coordinated *international* resistance. In fact, Lori Wallach of Public Citizen, the DC based activist group, had *already* begun organizing opposition to these new international issues. During 1992 and 1993, Public Citizen led the way, sponsoring three very powerful national advertisements on these issues, well ahead of any other domestic group on these campaigns. *(See example on following page.)*

For many of the attendees at these extraordinary 1994 meetings, these were the first shocking realizations that our battles would no longer be mainly local or domestic. We realized, as never before, the urgent need to begin partnering with activists in other parts of the world.

Our discussions zeroed in on the dreadful potentialities of this new globalization of corporate power and the need for coordinated global opposition beyond local and even national resistance. Sitting across from each other, we all more clearly understood that a giant shift was underway. Our primary attention would now have to be on the new international eco-

(text continued on page 62)

SABOTAGE!

[GEORGE BUSH, GATT, AND THE SECRET SIDE OF "FREE" TRADE]

of America's Health, Food Safety, & Environmental Laws

If talk about "free trade" puts you to sleep, you'd better wake up fast! While we've been dozing, President Bush has been pushing for new international trade rules that give a secretive foreign bureaucracy vast new powers to threaten American laws that protect your food, your health, your wilderness and wildlife, and your job. It's part of the hidden agenda in the big new trade agreements like GATT and NAFTA.

The critical decisions may come soon. Now is the time to speak out against this "free trade" scheme, or your kids and the planet will pay for decades. Here are the details.

I. Sneak Attack on Democracy

body that nobody elected, that nobody knows, and that operates in secret beyond national laws or the democratic process.

III. Faceless Trade Bureaucrats

Under GATT, when one country sues another, a panel of free trade officials is formed to hear the case. The hearings are secret. No testimony from consumer, health, labor, or environmental groups. No press, no public. The manner of the deliberations is unknown. Under NAFTA, the process will be similar.

Who sets the standards that trade panels try to apply? If the *Uruguay Round* is completed, the standards for food safety, for example, will be set by another mysterious unaccountable group, the Codex Alimentarius, located in Rome. Codex will also rule NAFTA. The main advisers to Codex are giant multi-national corporations. A recent U.S. delegation included Coca Cola, Pepsi, Nestle, Ralston Purina, Kraft, and General Foods. *Where are the environmentalists in Codex?* There are none.

What if country refuses to change its laws when the trade panel demands it? GATT can then impose severe international trade sanctions, leaving a country as a kind of trade outlaw, its economy injured. But that's not the end. One of the most disturbing elements of the

HARINE MARSHAL FUND

GATT THREATENS "DOLPHIN SAFE" LAW: *One of the many American laws challenged by GATT is the one that prevents sale or import of tuna caught in a manner that also kills thousands of dolphins. Millions of Americans fought for this law, and Congress passed it by a huge majority. But GATT bureaucrats in Geneva decided it must be rescinded as a "barrier to free trade." Who are these people? And why does George Bush support them? Please read below, and use the coupons.*

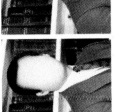
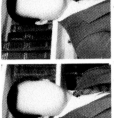
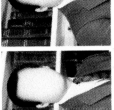
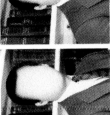

Werner Krutein / PHOTOVALET

"Free trade" sounds good. It has a logical, friendly ring, so few people pay attention. The press accepts it, and Congress goes along with hardly a whimper.

It turns out, however, that the only thing *free* about free trade is the freedom it gives the world's largest corporations to circumvent democracy and kill those "pesky" laws that protect people and the planet. Free trade agreements are the instruments they use.

The immediate threat is the General Agreement on Tariffs and Trade (GATT). Though GATT has existed since 1947, only recently have the Reagan and Bush administrations, on behalf of multinational corporations, been trying to expand GATT's powers. In the present GATT talks, called the *Uruguay Round*, new trade rules may soon give foreign governments the ability to challenge U.S. (and other democracies') laws as "barriers" to free trade. Bush is *also* pushing the new North America Free Trade Agreement (NAFTA), with Mexico and Canada, which could similarly sabotage U.S. laws.

That the laws were created by democratic process is no longer the point. Nor does it matter that the laws protect people's health, jobs, or natural resources. The main question becomes this: *Do multi-national corporations like the law or not?* If not, a secret panel of GATT bureaucrats can demand th... the U.S. laws be cancelled.

If these new sets of trade rules are passed, they could be used against *thousands* of laws in countries around the world that give priority to clean food and clean water, protect sea mammals and wildlife, preserve trees or other resources, restrict poisonous pesticide sprays, save rain-forests and safeguard small farmers from being overpowered by agribusiness.

Are we being alarmist? Consider the recent GATT ruling in the tuna-dolphin case. Here we have a law, the Marine Mammal Protection Act, supported by tens of millions of Americans. It prohibited the sale in the U.S. of tuna that was caught by purse seine nets that also kill tens of thousands of dolphins in the eastern Pacific.

The Bush Administration *opposed* that law but could not stop it. However, in Geneva, under GATT, Mexico was able to sue the U.S., charging *our* dolphin law was a "barrier to trade." The GATT bureaucrats agreed, saying the law has to go. Mr. Bush has asked Congress to follow GATT's order. All this in the name of "free trade."

A similar process may soon threaten the laws forbidding export of logs from the federal lands in the Pacific Northwest — and hundreds of other laws in the U.S. (and in other countries) that safeguard consumers, workers, farmers, and nature.

What conclusions to draw? Simply this: We are witnessing one of the slickest suppressions of the democratic process in history, substituting the will of trade bureaucracies which citizens cannot influence. The beneficiaries are multi-national corporations for whom democracy itself is an impediment to *their* free trade.

II. *Increasing Poisons & Toxics*

Another principle in the *Uruguay Round* of GATT, and in NAFTA, is the *harmonization* of each country's laws to international standards. If a U.S. law has higher standards of health or safety, it could be *harmonized down* to a lower common denominator. For example, present U.S. law strictly limits DDT and other poisonous residues on fruits or vegetables. Another law regulates asbestos use. Those laws could be challenged and *harmonized down* to lower international standards. The same fate probably awaits the California state initiative (Proposition 65) that requires the labeling of products for carcinogens and toxics. This law, which protects food safety, may be nullified.

What applies to U.S. law also applies to laws of other countries. European laws to stop the sale of beef shot-up with carcinogenic growth hormones like DES, may also have to be *harmonized down*. That is, eliminated. Japanese laws that keep out dangerous food colorings and dyes, known to cause cancer, probably won't survive either. And Thailand's anti-smoking campaign was challenged by the U.S. under GATT.

So, you see, it's *not* that the U.S. gains or loses in these trade wars. It's *that the people of every country, North and South, lose when they try to protect their health, their jobs, and their environment.* We all become subject to the veto of an international

PESTICIDE RESIDUES ALLOWED ON YOUR FOOD UNDER NEW GATT RULES		
Import Product	Poison	Percent Increase
Peaches	DDT	5,000
	Aldrin	250
Broccoli	DDT	3,300
	Permethrin	200
	Aldrin	300
	Heptachlor	500
Apples	DDT	1,000
	Permethrin	4,000
Carrots	Benomyl	2,500
	Heptachlor	2,000
	DDT	1,000
Potatoes	Diazinon	500
	Heptachlor	500
	DDT	1,000
Strawberries	Lindane	300
	DDT	2,000
Milk	Endrin	300
Bananas	Aldicarb	160
	DDT	5,000
Grapes	DDT	2,000

Uruguay Round is the proposed creation of a new global super-agency with extraordinary powers: The Multi-Lateral Trade Organization (MTO). This organization would require countries to "take all necessary steps to ensure conformity" to GATT. The Congressional Research Service confirms that, under MTO, our elected representatives "would no longer have control."

What does *that* mean? Are we looking at the New World Order's enforcers? A GATT police? This much we know: The proposed powers of MTO are very great, and very ominous.

IV. *What You Can Do*

If these big trade agreements "succeed," we will truly face a New World Order beyond the control of any citizen democracy. Your jobs, your health, your safety and the environment will all be directly threatened. So will your democracy, and the democracy of other countries. Beyond that, the expansion of GATT represents a new blueprint *and* a new mechanism for the organization and control of resources and life on Earth, under the "benevolent" guidance of bankers and multi-national corporations. But in order to proceed with their vision, they must first eliminate the power of democracies to control their own laws. That is why it's important to stop NAFTA, and the GATT expansion *now*.

Speed is essential. President Bush hopes to conclude these agreements by the fall. Even if he achieves this, Congress must still approve the deal. *Tell them what you think. Please do it today.* Use the coupons below. Thank you.

Public Citizen
National Consumers League
Citizens Trade Watch Campaign
Earth Island Institute
Institute for Agriculture and
   Trade Policy
Rainforest Action Network
American Society for the Prevention
   of Cruelty to Animals (ASPCA)

Sierra Club
Friends of the Earth
Fair Trade Campaign
The Humane Society of the United
   States
National Toxics Campaign
Community Nutrition Institute
Clean Water Action

To: Citizens Trade Campaign, c/o Public Citizen
215 Pennsylvania Ave. SE. Washington, D.C. 20003
[ ] I have mailed the coupons.
[ ] I want to help. Please keep me informed on all developments relating to GATT, NAFTA, and other free trade agreements and their democratic, social and environmental implications.
[ ] To keep up your good work, here is a donation of
$15 ___ $25 ___ $50 ___ $100 ___ $500 ___ Other ___
(Contributions are not tax deductible.)
NAME
ADDRESS

To: Richard Gephardt, Majority Leader,
U.S. House of Representatives, Washington, D.C.
Congress has the ability and the obligation to block the cynical assaults on the democratic process represented by the *Uruguay Round* of GATT, and NAFTA. As you have said, no international trade agreement should ever be permitted to jeopardize laws that protect our food, our environment and our jobs. Where do you stand on the final *Uruguay Round* rules?
NAME
ADDRESS

To: Jacques Delors, President, European Commission of the EC.
200 Rue de la Loi, B-1049 Brussels, Belgium USE 50¢ POSTAGE
As leader of the European trade community, you should know that American environmentalists, farmers, workers, consumer groups and health groups are united against the current proposal for the *Uruguay Round* of GATT, and see NAFTA heading in the same dangerous direction. Though I am not opposed to all trade agreements, it is obvious that citizen democracies all over the world will be directly undermined by this cynical GATT agreement that can circumvent every country's health, environmental and labor laws.
NAME
ADDRESS

To: Samuel Skinner, Chief of Staff.
The White House. Washington, D.C. 20500
American environmentalists, farmers, workers, consumer groups and health groups are united against the current proposal for the *Uruguay Round* of GATT, and see NAFTA heading in the same dangerous direction. Though I am not opposed to all trade agreements, it is obvious that the laws of citizen democracies all over the world will be directly undermined by GATT and NAFTA.
NAME
ADDRESS

nomic structures that were being formed, practically sub-rosa. Meeting together, we grasped that we were about to confront a huge new movement of political, corporate, and economic power that was far beyond the reach of democratic governmental processes. Given all the recent advances in the instruments of globalized mass communications, the globalization of corporate economic powers (and their political influences), were now accelerating rapidly. The main question on the table was, *what if anything, should we do about it?*

From these discussions was born the International Forum on Globalization (IFG), I assumed the role of Executive Director, wonderfully assisted by Debbie Barker and Victor Menotti as the initial executive operating staff. And thus began 25 years of collective international activism on the consequences of corporate globalization, rapidly taking over global economic activities. IFG's collaborative international activism included numerous public "teach-ins" in the US Europe, Asia, and South America, as well as more than forty publications on key aspects, and some very sensational public events. IFG also organized some direct action campaigns targeting the primary globalizers.

Most well known, perhaps, among the direct impacts, was the IFG-led giant protests against a meeting of the World Trade Organization (WTO) in Seattle in November–December 1999. One of the ads which follows *("INVISIBLE GOVERNMENT")*, financed by Doug Tompkins, ran in *The New York Times* and several local Seattle papers just before the WTO meeting was to begin. That ad directly attacked the WTO, and rallied people onto the streets of Seattle where they successfully blocked all entrances to the WTO meeting, leading to its breakdown and suspension.

We will have much more to say on this subject in Chapter Four, when we will elaborate on two decades of Doug Tompkins' activities and impacts, focused on the shocking new reality of the *globalization of corporate* activities and controls, and efforts to battle that.

(Chapter 4 begins on page 67)

Should the People Who Caused the Problems be the Ones to Create the Solutions?

The crisis that put the world economy on the brink of collapse is NOT OVER. *We are only in the eye of the storm. The same "experts" who drove the system to the edge are still in charge. Worse, it's the same system, with the same values. Quick fixes will not suffice for long; the system is inherently flawed.* NEW VOICES ARE NEEDED AT THE TABLE — NOW. *In response to the situation, the Board and Committee on Global Finance of the International Forum on Globalization met in Siena, Italy, during September to produce the document on this page. It was then circulated for signatures; some are shown below. For more background, please use the coupon. (The statement begins at left.)*

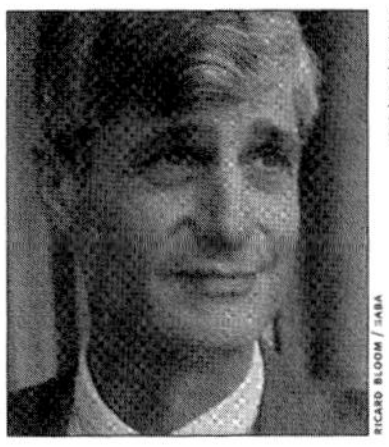

ROBERT RUBIN, SECRETARY OF THE U.S. TREASURY.
Continues to advocate IMF bailouts for former colleagues in banking, while urging even greater freedoms for speculators, global corporations and banks.

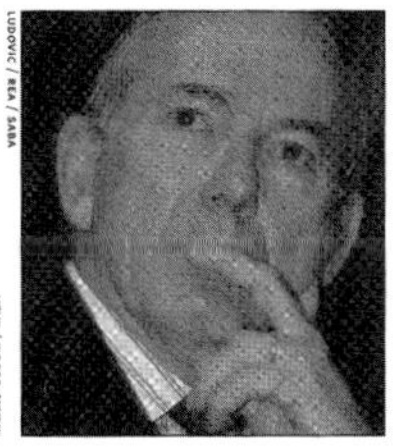

MICHEL CAMDESSUS, MANAGING DIRECTOR, IMF.
Bailed out by U.S. taxpayers (and others), now wants to *institutionalize* the same processes within the IMF that caused the financial chaos.

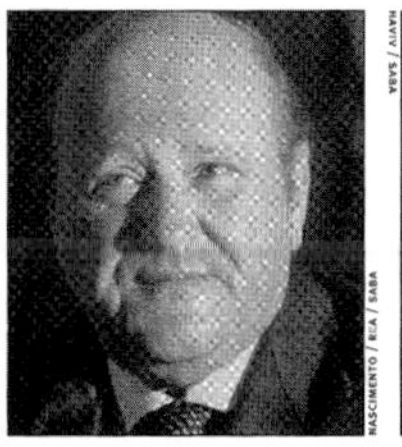

RENATO RUGGIERO, DIRECTOR GENERAL, WTO.
Called the proposed Multilateral Agreement on Investment—which gives vast powers to investors —"the new constitution for a global economy." Don't we have a constitution already?

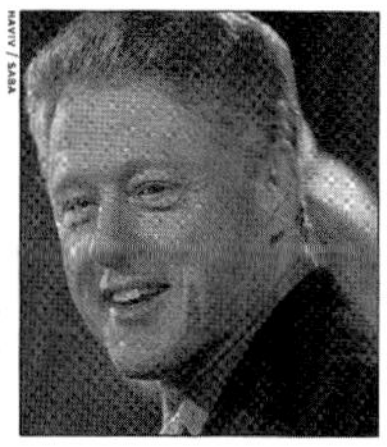

BILL CLINTON, PRESIDENT, USA
The world's top salesman for failed corporate free trade and investment policies that have brought about the global financial crisis.

THE SIENA DECLARATION

1 The undersigned have long predicted that corporate-led economic globalization, as expressed and encouraged by the rules of global trade and investment, would lead to extreme volatility in global financial markets and great vulnerability for all nations and people. These rules have been created and are enforced by the World Trade Organization (WTO), the International Monetary Fund (IMF), the North American Free Trade Agreement (NAFTA), the Maastricht Agreement, the World Bank and other global bureaucracies that currently discipline governments in the area of trade and financial investment. This volatility is bringing massive economic breakdown in some nations, insecurity in all nations, unprecedented hardships for millions of people, growing unemployment and dislocation in all regions, direct assaults on labor conditions, loss of wilderness and biodiversity, massive population shifts, increased ethnic and racial tensions, and other disastrous results. Such dire outcomes are now becoming manifest throughout the world, and are increasing daily.

2 The solutions to the crises that are being offered by the leadership of the trade bureaucracies, and most western industrialized states, as well as bankers, security analysts, corporate CEOs and economists — the main theoreticians, designers and promoters of the activities that have led us to this point — are little more than repetitions, even expansions, of the very formulas that have already proven socially, economically and environmentally disastrous. The experts who now propose solutions to the financial meltdown are the very ones who, only months ago, were celebrating Indonesia, Thailand, South Korea and other "Asian Tigers" as poster-children for the success of their designs. Notably, these experts have been wrong in nearly every predicted outcome of their policies.

Now these "leaders" advocate that we solve the problem by *further* opening markets, *further* opening and liberalizing the rules of investment (via such draconian formulas as the Multilateral Agreement on Investment, and an expanded IMF and/or WTO powers), *further* suppressing the options of nation-states and communities to regulate commerce for the good of their own publics and environments, *further* discouragement of such models as "import substitution" that have the chance to enable nations to feed and care for themselves, and *further* centralization of control within the same governing bodies as at present. In other words, more of the same.

According to these architects of globalization, it is only a matter of "fine tuning" or "first aid" while on the way to continued expansion of their same failed dream. They cite "cronyism" among the Third World's nations as contributing to the problem, but say nothing of the cronyism exhibited by the U.S. Treasury-Wall Street-IMF collaborations by which western bankers bail out other western bankers for their disastrous policies.

Clearly, the architects of the present crisis have not understood what they have wrought, or, if they have understood it, cannot afford to admit it.

3 As for the tens of millions of people who now suffer from this experiment, the expert solutions include no bailouts. Many of these people, formerly self-sufficient in food, are now dependent on the absentee-ownership system of the global economy. Now abandoned, they are left to seek solutions outside the system, from foraging in the (fast disappearing) forests, to barter systems, to social upheaval as means of expression. Many are finding that their attempts to return to prior means of livelihood — such as small scale local farming — are impossible, as their former lands have been converted to industrial corporate agricultural models for export production. Land on which people formerly grew food to eat has been converted to corporate production of luxury commodities — such as coffee, beef, flowers, prawns — to be exported to the wealthy nations. Poverty, hunger, landlessness, homelessness, and migration are the immediate outcome of this. Insecure food supplies, lower food quality, and often dangerous contaminated foods are a secondary outcome. The situation is unsustainable.

4 Its creators like to describe the global economic system as the *inevitable* outgrowth of economic, social and technological evolution. They make the case that centralized global economies that feature an export-oriented free trade model, fed by massive deregulation, privatization, and corporate-led free market activity in both commodity trade and finance — free of inhibiting environmental, labor and social standards — will eventually bring a kind of utopia to all people of the planet. Now it is clear that it is a *utopia for corporations* that they have in mind. But even this will fail to achieve its goals, as the entire process is riven with structural flaws. No system that depends for its success on a never ending expansion of markets, resources and consumers, or that fails to achieve social equity and meaningful livelihood for all people on the planet, can hope to survive for very long. *Social unrest, economic and ecological breakdown are the true inevitabilities of such a system.*

> "These experts have been wrong in nearly every predicted outcome of their policies."

5 It is appropriate to recall that the present structures of globalization did not grow in nature as if they were part of an evolutionary process. Economic globalization in its present form was deliberately *designed* by economists, bankers, and corporate leaders to institute a form of economic activity and control that they said would be beneficial. It is an invented, experimental system; there is nothing inevitable about it. Globalization in its recent form even had a birthplace and birthdate: Bretton Woods, New Hampshire, 1944. It was there that a design was agreed to by the leading industrial nations. The WTO, the IMF, the World Bank, et. al. were instruments that grew out of the design plan.

Great expectations have led to despair. After more than 50 years of this experiment, it is breaking down. Rather than leading to economic benefits for all people, it has brought the planet to the brink of environmental and social catastrophe. The experiment has failed.

6 With the crisis now obvious in Asia, Russia, Brazil, Mexico and soon, predictably, in other places, including western industrial nations, many peoples and nation-states have begun to recognize the failure of the globalization experiment. They have begun to ask specifically if globalization — especially free trade in financial flows — is in the best interest of their own nation, or any nation. We have seen serious corrective actions recently taken by China, India, Hong Kong, Malaysia, Russia and Chile which, by various means, have tried to counter the destabilizing force of unregulated private investment that has proved to benefit no one but the people who advocate it. As we write, many more nations are showing renewed interest in these expressions of resistance and withdrawal from uncontrolled global capital. Importantly, the nations that have put, or maintained, controls on capital have demonstrated a higher degree of stability, and are better able to act successfully in the interests of their own resource and economic bases and in the interests of their own populations.

We applaud such actions and urge more nations to investigate and adopt currency and investment controls, as appropriate to their unique situations, rather than continuing to take dictates from distant bureaucracies who have proved they do not know what they are doing.

7 Though the current crisis tends to be reported as strictly "financial" in nature, it is worth noting that the problems are deeper and more endemic to the inherent flaws in the design of the global economy itself. All peoples of the world have been made tragically dependent upon the arbitrary self interested acts of giant corporations, bankers and speculators. This is the result of the global rules that remove real economic power from nations, communities and citizen democracies, while giving new powers to corporate and financial speculators; and rules that suppress the abilities of local economies, and nations to protect resources, public health and human rights. This has left the peoples of the world in a uniquely isolated, vulnerable condition, dependent upon the whims of great, distant powers. This too is unsustainable.

8 Any truly effective solution to the current financial crisis, and the larger crises of economic globalization, must include the following ingredients among others:

A) Recognition and acknowledgment that the current model, as designed and implemented by present-day, corporate led global trade bureaucracies is fundamentally flawed, and that the current crises are the inevitable, predictable result of these flaws.

B) Convening of a new Bretton Woods type international conference which would bring to the table not only representatives of nation-states, bankers and industry, but an *equal* number of citizen organizations from every country to design economic models that turn away from globalization and move toward localization, re-empower communities and nation-states, place human, social and ecological values above economic values (and corporate profit), encourage national self reliance (wherever possible) including "import substitution," and operate in a fully democratic and transparent manner.

C) Create efforts to build on the experiences of Chile, Malaysia, India and the other countries that have placed controls on capital investment and currency speculation. Encourage all activity that reverses present policies that expand the freedoms of finance capital and transnational corporations, while suppressing the freedoms of individuals, communities, and nation-states to act in their own behalf.

D) Immediately *cancel* all efforts toward completion of the Multilateral Agreement on Investment (MAI), or the expansion of the International Monetary Fund, and/or the WTO to include ingredients of the MAI that give added freedom to finance capital to operate free of national controls.

Finally, the undersigned wish to state that we are not opposed to international trade and investment, or to international rules that regulate this trade and investment, so long as it complements economic activity that nation-states can achieve for themselves, and so long as the environment, human rights, labor rights, democracy, national sovereignty and social equity are given primacy.

INTERNATIONAL FORUM ON GLOBALIZATION
1555 Pacific Ave., San Francisco, CA 94109
phone: (415) 771-3394 *fax:* (415) 771-1121
email: ifg@ifg.org *web:* http://www.ifg.org

❍ Please send a packet of information about the global economic crisis. (*Enclose $10 within U.S.; $15 abroad*)

❍ Here's a donation to continue your public education campaign: $500 ___ $100___ $50 ___ $25 ___ other ___________ *(donations are tax deductible)*

NAME ______

ADDRESS ______

CITY ______ STATE ______ ZIP ______

PHONE ______

INTERNATIONAL FORUM ON GLOBALIZATION

BOARD OF DIRECTORS AND COMMITTEE ON GLOBAL FINANCE

(organizations shown for identification purposes)

Maude Barlow, Council of Canadians, Ottawa
Walden Bello, Focus on the Global South, Bangkok
Brent Blackwelder, Friends of the Earth, Washington, D.C.
John Cavanagh, Institute for Policy Studies, Washington, D.C.
Tony Clarke, Polaris Institute, Ottawa, Canada
Herman E. Daly, University of Maryland
Susan George, Transnational Institute, Amsterdam
Edward Goldsmith, The Ecologist, London
Martin Khor, Third World Network, Penang
Andrew Kimbrell, International Center for Technology Assessment, Washinton, D.C.
David Korten, People-Centered Development Forum, New York
Jerry Mander, Public Media Center, San Francisco
David Morris, Institute for Local Self Reliance, Minneapolis
Helena Norberg-Hodge, International Society for Ecology and Culture, UK
Carl Pope, Sierra Club, San Francisco
Mark Ritchie, Institute for Agriculture & Trade Policy, Minneapolis
Vandana Shiva, Third World Network, New Delhi
Steve Shrybman, West Coast Environmental Law Association, Vancouver
Victoria Tauli-Corpuz, Indigenous People's International Centre for Policy Research, Philippines
Lori Wallach, Public Citizen, Washington, D.C.

Also signed by (partial list)

John Acquay, Friends of the Earth (Ghana)
Thomas Akabzaa, Third World Network (Ghana)
Miguel Altieri, UC, Berkeley
Louis Lefeber, York University, (Canada)
Harriet Barlow, Blue Mtn. Center
Tom Barry, Interhemispheric Resource Center
Medea Benjamin, Global Exchange
Wendell Berry, farmer and author
Agnés Bertrand, Observatoire Globalisation Economique (FR)
Beth Burrows, Edmonds Institute
Leslie Byster, Silicon Valley Toxics Coalition
Bruce Campbell, Canadian Centre for Policy Alternatives
Church World Service
Kevin Danaher, Global Exchange
Committee for New Priorities
John Davis, Wild Earth
Chris Desser, Migratory Species Project
Oronto Douglas, Environmental Rights Action (Nigeria)
Richard Douthwaite, Foundation for the Economics of Sustainability (Ireland)
Fiona Dove, Transnational Institute (Netherlands)
Ulrich Duchrow, Kairos Europa (Germany)
Ramón Durán, AEDENAT (Spain)
Jan Eastman, Canadian Teachers' Federation
Tewolde G. Egziabher, Institute for Sustainable Development (Ethiopia)
Chowdhury Farouque, Friends of the Earth (Bangladesh)
Paige Fischer, Pacific Environmental Resource Center
Alan Fricker, Sustainable Futures Trust (New Zealand)
Jeanne Gauna, Southwest Organizing Project
Larry Goodwin, Africa Faith and Justice Network
Alan Griffiths, 'STOP MAI' Campaign (Australia)
Ricardo Grinspur, Centre for Research on Latin America & the Caribbean (Canada)
Richard Grossman, Program on Corporations, Law and Democracy
Randall Hayes, Rainforest Action Network
Hazel Henderson, economist
Tim Hermach, Native Forest Council
Colin Hines, Protect the Local, Globally (UK)
Olivier Hoedeman, Corporate Europe Observatory (Holland)
Liz Hoskin, GAIA Fndn., (UK)
Mikulas Huba, Society for Sustainable Living (Slovakia)
Mika Iba, Network for Safe & Secure Food and Environment (Japan)
Wes Jackson, Land Institute
Wendy Johnson, Friends of the Earth (New Zealand)
Jim Jontz, American Lands Alliance
Ib Jorgensen, Aalborg University (Denmark)
Tom Kane, Centennial College of Applied Arts and Technology
Josh Karliner, Transnational Resource & Action Center
Danny Kennedy, Project Underground
Charles Kernaghan, The National Labor Committee
Joo Young Kim, People's Solidarity for Participatory Democracy (Korea)
Fred Kirschenmann, Northern Plains Sustainable Ag Society
Brewster & Cathleen Kneen, The Ram's Horn (Canada)
John Knox, Earth Island Institute
Marek Kurinec, Organization of the Slovak Union of Nature & Landscape Protectors (Slovakia)
Tim Lang, Center for Food Policy (UK)
Valerie Langer, Friends of Clayoquot Sound (Canada)
Sara Larrain, Chilean Ecological Action Network (Chile)
José Lutzenberger, Fundação Gaia (Brazil)
Marianne Manilov, Ctr. for Commercial-Free Public Education
Rocio Mejia Flores, RMALC, (Mexico)
Aileen Mioko Smith, Green Action (Japan)
Anuradha Mittal, Institute for Food & Development Policy
John Mohawk, Seneca Nation
Sid L. Mohn, Heartland Alliance for Human Needs & Human Rights
Pat Roy Mooney, RAFI (Canada)
David Morris, Institute for Local Self-Reliance
M.D. Nanjundaswamy, Karnataka State Farmer's Assn. (India)
Ricardo Navarro, Friends of the Earth (El Salvador)
Njoki Njoroge Njehu, 50 Years is Enough
Richard B. Norgaard, Intl. Society for Ecological Economics
John Passacantando, Ozone Action
Ignacio Peón Escalante, Mexican Action Network on Free Trade
Dave Phillips, Earth Island Institute
Kika Pitsillidou, Friends of the Earth (Cyprus)
Carlos Quesada, CIEDES (Costa Rica)
Carolyn Raffensperger, Science and Environmental Health Network
Simon Reeves, Tamaki Makau Rau Auckland (New Zealand)
Peter Richardson, Catholic Office for Social Justice
Heather-Jane Robertson, Canadian Teachers' Federation
Atila Roque, Brazilian Institute for Socio-Economic Analysis
Wolfgang Sachs, Wuppertal Institute (Germany)
John Seed, Rainforest Information Center (Australia)
Mira Shiva, Peoples Health Network (India)
Kavaljit Singh, Public Interest Research Group (India)
John Stauber, Center for Media and Democracy
Todd Steiner, Sea Turtle Restoration Project
Rosalie Steward, Green Party of Aotearoa (New Zealand)
Jonathan Tasini, National Writers Union
Patricia Thomas, Alliance Party (New Zealand)
Quincey Tompkins Imhoff, Foundation for Deep Ecology
Myriam vander Stichele, Transnational Institute (Netherlands)
Dra. Ella Vazquez Dominguez, Instituto de Ecologia (Mexico)
Steve Viederman, Jessie Smith Noyes Foundation
Alejandro Villamar, Mexican Action Network on Free Trade
Casey Walker, Wild Duck Review
Cam Walker, Friends of the Earth (Austrailia)
Thomas Wallgren, Alternative to the EU (Finland)
Tracy Worcester, Soil Assn. (U.K.)
Miriam Young, Asia Pacific Center for Jusitice and Peace
Juraj Zamkovsky, Center for Environmental Public Advocacy FoEI (Slovakia)

[DON'T LET CONGRESS TRADE AWAY OUR RIGHTS]

JEOPARDIZED *by* GATT–
100 *U.S. Environmental Laws*

A MAZINGLY, WITH ALMOST NO DEBATE, the U.S. Congress may soon approve an international trade agreement (GATT) that threatens hundreds of popular laws created by Congress and state legislators. These include the Nuclear Non-Proliferation Act, the Marine Mammal Protection Act,

gas-guzzler laws, pesticide laws, laws that keep lead out of food and toxics out of water...federal laws and state laws that protect wildlife and natural resources as well as human rights, workers' rights and consumer safety. BUT THE BIGGEST VICTIM IS DEMOCRACY ITSELF. So

what's going on? Why is Congress about to trade away our rights? You can stop it. Please read below.

Last year's NAFTA debate nearly ripped our country in half. Now comes the General Agreement on Tariffs and Trade (GATT) and its enforcement arm, the World Trade Organization (WTO). It's similar to NAFTA, but 30 times bigger, and worse.

[GATT MEETS DEMOCRACY]

though the U.S. was able to block the outcome. But now the Europeans have sued again, and won. *And under the new GATT/WTO rules, the U.S. will have to comply by eliminating the law, or face serious trade sanctions.* Bad news for dolphins. Bad news for wildlife.

standards. They are angry that the U.S. can refuse their exports, so they will sue under GATT. The GATT panels may demand that the U.S. "conform" to *lower standards* by saying that ours are not "based on sound science." But many scientific findings are inconclusive; U.S. *precautionary standards* protect the public far more. After GATT rules, we may find DDT back on our tomatoes.

▲ CHALLENGE SIX:
PROP. 65 - CALIFORNIA'S SAFE DRINKING WATER & TOXIC ENFORCEMENT ACT

Created by a massive popular initiative, this act requires warning labels on products that contain substances known to cause cancer or reproductive harm. The Europeans object because Prop. 65 "imposes stricter California standards in place of [weaker] federal standards." This same rationale applies to Europe's objections to California's law restricting lead content in wine.

▲ CHALLENGE SEVEN:
CALIFORNIA'S GLASS RECYCLING PROGRAM

The Europeans plan to challenge literally dozens of California laws (and many from other states) because they impose certain requirements on imports that Europeans fear could become national standards, such as the requirement that all glass be recyclable. Welcome back to the throwaway lifestyle.

▲ OTHER CHALLENGES:

The above list is a tiny fraction of the over one hundred laws that will be jeopardized by GATT. Included will be California laws that (1) reduce waste in packaging; (2) require newspaper recycling; (3) restrict smog-causing emissions; (4) require labeling of dangerous additives; (5) control air fresheners, floor polishes, hair care products and insect repellents in New York State, laws that emit polluting compounds.

Every state is affected. In New York State, laws that limit the amount of lead, mercury and other toxics in containers are threatened. So are New York smog control laws, insecticide laws, organic compound restrictions, phosphates in detergent. and the sale of certain wild animals (including leopards, cheetahs and alligators).

Connecticut laws that require recyclable newsprint, recycling of nickel cadmium batteries and prohibit the sale of certain wild animals and plants, and laws that set standards for safe packaging are all under the scrutiny of the European challenge.

Ralph Nader has put it this way: "Nothing is more likely to pull down our present U.S. consumer and environmental protections and derail future advances than the proposed expansion of GATT."

The corporate pressure to pass GATT is immense. An advertising blitz has already started. The Clinton Administration has already caved-in, and if NAFTA is any example, Congress will too. *But what's truly alarming here is the willingness of our elected leaders to undermine the democracy that put them in power, and the laws they helped create.* Don't let Congress trade away America's ability to make its own laws by putting our lives in the control of faceless foreign bureaucrats in Geneva.

Please use the coupons below. Thank you.

SIERRA CLUB

▲ CHALLENGE TWO:
THE NUCLEAR NON-PROLIFERATION ACT

Nuclear accidents and terrorism would be the ultimate environmental disaster. The U.S. adopted this law to control proliferation. But European countries, who want the right to sell nuclear weapons technology to "outlaw" countries, have challenged the U.S. law which requires "consent" on issues of reprocessing, enrichment and storage of dangerous nuclear materials originally obtained from the U.S.. *Countries like North Korea will leap for joy at this challenge.*

▲ CHALLENGE THREE:
CORPORATE AVERAGE FUEL ECONOMY (CAFE) STANDARDS

Minimum gas mileage rules and "gas-guzzler" taxes were designed to promote production of more fuel efficient cars that protect the air we breathe and reduce fuel imports. European carmakers don't like the rule, because their cars don't meet the standards. If they win, we will all breath the result.

▲ CHALLENGE FOUR:
MAGNUSON ACT AND PELLY AMENDMENT

Europe has targeted these laws that protect fisheries and the global ocean commons from overfishing and disastrous methods of fishing like driftnetting. The EU challenge will be based on GATT rules that prevent the U.S. from rejecting imports based on the way fish are caught or environmental harm.

▲ CHALLENGE FIVE:
FOOD SAFETY LAWS

The United States has many laws, both state and federal, that require inspection of food for contaminants, pesticides, bacteria and other undesirable ingredients. Most countries have far less stringent

---

Environmentalists are unified in opposition. GATT clearly represents the gravest threat to environmental laws since the turn of the century. Here's how it works:

If GATT is ratified, any of 117 signatory countries — *mostly non-democracies, few with any environmental laws* — can challenge other countries' laws as barriers to free trade under GATT's rules.

Once a challenge is lodged, a secret panel of GATT officials is convened in Geneva; faceless bureaucrats not elected by any democratic process. *Their deliberations are closed, they permit no testimony from citizens groups, and no democracy can overrule them.*

The members of these panels are geared to serve transnational corporations. Yet, once they have ruled, *any country* is bound to "conform" its laws to these GATT standards, however low they may be. The "conformity" applies to federal, state and even local city and county laws.

Can the U.S. refuse to comply? Let's say we did try to resist "conforming" our dolphin protection laws to Mexico's standards, or our pesticide laws to Poland's standards. The World Trade Organization could then apply severe sanctions against the U.S., as though we were an international outlaw, like Iraq or Haiti.

All this is done in the name of "free trade." But the real goal is deeper: *To homogenize the world's laws at the common denominators which gigantic transnational corporations find comfortable.* The GATT is really designed to help these corporations circumvent the rule of democracy; getting rid of pesky environmental and other laws that protect resources, workers, consumers, public health, human rights and similar democratic standards. So it's "free trade" for corporations but control and conformity for the rest of us.

THE ABOVE THREAT IS NOT THEORETICAL. Just one month ago, the European Union circulated a list of the laws it wants to force the U.S. to eliminate, if GATT is okayed. Here are a selected few of those:

▲ CHALLENGE ONE:
THE MARINE MAMMAL PROTECTION ACT

One of America's most popular laws, it protects dolphins by restricting import of tuna that is caught in a manner that also kills thousands of dolphins. Mexico challenged this law under the old GATT rules in 1991, and won,

Techno-Utopianism

Our society has placed all its bets on technology, but it may be time to reconsider. Far from paradise-on-earth, we're nearer ecological collapse. Now, a terrifying new generation of technologies — from eugenics to robotics — is raising the stakes. Here's the question: When did we okay these? In a democracy shouldn't there be national debate, and referenda, before such profound commitments?

Descriptions of new technologies are invariably optimistic, even utopian. That's because most technology news originates from corporations who profit from it. Whether through millions of dollars in advertising or futuristic Disneyworld exhibits, the information they provide is always in *best-case* terms. Negative possibilities are left out. This has been so since the Industrial Revolution. For example:

At the turn of the 20th century, the *automobile* was introduced as "clean, safe, convenient, private, fast, non-polluting [unlike horses]." No mention of pavement covering the landscape, air pollution, noise, deaths on the highway, or oil wars.

In mid-century, *pesticides* were going to save our crops and "feed a hungry world." No mention of poisoned food, land, wildlife, water, or growing rates of cancer.

Nuclear energy was promoted as a "clean, safe" energy source. No mention of radioactivity lasting 250,000 years, the impossibility of safe disposal of wastes, or the chance of catastrophic accidents.

Television was going to "democratize information," educate the poor, and promote world peace. No mention of mind-numbing commercialization, or the global homogenization of consciousness and culture.

Antibiotics were going to stop diseases, and *have* slowed some. But they've also caused antibiotic resistance in bacteria, and *superbugs*, raising new fears of unstoppable pandemics.

The *internet* was sold as a boon for democracy, "empowerment," and education. But it's also brought bankruptcy to thousands of bookstores, retail shops, and small businesses; an unprecedented invasion of privacy; computers in classrooms replacing teachers; and growing personal isolation and depression. *Empowerment?* That's apparently meant more for e-commerce titans and global corporations than anyone else.

Genetic engineering is supposed to replace pesticides, end disease, and also feed the world. No mention of risks from escaping genetically modified organisms, health risks from "frankenfoods," or the looming specters of eugenics, human cloning, and "designer babies." (See below.)

※ ※ ※

It's logical that marketers of technologies present only *best-case* scenarios. Corporations have no legal requirement and surely no financial stake in exposing *worst-case* scenarios. So the public is deprived of the information we need about the pros *and* cons of technical evolution.

(Nuclear power is an exception. It's had a rougher time finding public approval since we understood its *worst-case* potential in the first moment we heard of it, at Hiroshima. The chemical industry had a similar setback in the 1960s at Love Canal, when horrible toxic materials bubbled up onto people's lawns.)

But in a democracy, shouldn't we have full disclosure *before* awful things happen? Is it okay that only corporations get to predict technology's impacts? *In today's world, technology is arguably more important than whom we elect to office; shouldn't we vote on technology too?*

This much is sure. A century after the industrial revolution, the planet is hurtling toward an ecological breakdown of unprecedented scale: climate change, ozone holes, species extinctions, pollution of air, land and water, and industrially caused cancers. *All are directly rooted in technological excess.* Neither has technology solved hunger or disease, or provided a minimally satisfactory life for most people on earth.

Nonetheless, we stay the course. Our commitment is total. So here's what's coming next.

"Improving" Nature

Rather than bringing unintended consequences upon the natural world, the new generation of technologies is changing nature itself. Three examples:

- **Human Eugenics.** Just as biotechnology is changing the gene structures of plants, animals, microbes, etc., *eugenics alters people.* After the Human Genome Project completed sequencing the human genetic structure, the media loudly trumpeted the presumed medical benefits of re-engineering hereditary human characteristics.

  But most media left out the likelihood that human genetic alteration would be used for other purposes such as: "more desirable" cosmetic, emotional, or mental traits. (Tall, blonde, blue-eyed? Smarter? Dumber? Submissive? Can work long hours?) Ultimately,

For a century, we've been trained by futuristic imagery of technical perfection, like this techno-Oz/computer-biotech-agriculture vision. From Buck Rogers to Star Wars; from World's Fairs to Disney's Tomorrowland, technology is our panacea. Has it lived up to its billing? Are we now ready for eugenics, human cloning and Metaman? Has anyone asked if you want them?

the use of eugenics may depend on fashion, or worse; who's in charge. "Designer babies" are possible. So are "chimeras," part human/part animal. *And someday, will someone seek to create and clone a superior new race?* It's been proposed before.

Princeton's Dr. Lee Silver, an advocate of human genetic engineering, predicts that society might eventually be divided into genetic classes: the "naturals" who have not been genetically improved, and the "GenRich" (about 10% of society). The GenRich will run businesses and institutions while the naturals are laborers. Since these genetic changes will become part of the hereditary germline, class divisions will be permanent.

So, where do *you* stand on this? Has anyone ever asked?

- **Nanotechnology.** This goes beyond genetics to the atomic structures of all things, living and non-living. According to Dr. Richard Smalley of Rice University, nanotechnologists hope to "reverse the harm done by the industrial revolution." They will do this by *improving* nature, i.e., isolating and re-positioning atoms and molecules into entirely new products, machines, weapons, trees, plants, people, *whatever*. (At the atomic and molecular level there's little difference between "living" and "non-living" matter; everything is subject to re-creation.)

  The nanotechnologists' promises include among others: safer and cheaper space travel and colonization, and microscopic nanomachines that cure diseases.

  Other nanomachines, called "assemblers" will re-create anything made in factories. No workers needed! Nanomachines can be plopped into a soup of primary molecules to re-assemble them in new ways.

  Impossible? Maybe not. Chief Scientist at Sun Microsystems, Bill Joy, recently wrote that given the "progress in molecular electronics" we might achieve that level of technology by mid-century. (*Wired*, April, 2000.) But Joy has grave doubts about proceeding, citing dangers from escaping self-replicating nanomachines, and from military applications. (There are also terribly frightening surveillance and privacy concerns.) So far, Joy is one of few major scientists to be openly critical.

- **Robotics.** Everybody loves the idea of cute robots freeing humans from labor, though so far they mainly free humans from *jobs*. But robotic science is moving quickly beyond workplace issues, and toward a "post-biological" future. That comes when robots have physical *and* cognitive capabilities approaching human beings, and can *self-replicate.* At that point will humans no longer be necessary?

  Dr. Hans Moravec, Director of the Mobile Robot Lab at Carnegie Mellon University says we'll soon pass the present limits on artificial intelligence, robotic mobility and computational speed, thus making possible a kind of merger between humans and robots. He envisions that humans will eventually be able to "download" the contents of our brains and "consciousness" into mobile, self-replicating, autonomous robots.

Moravec says this is good because humans can now only record a small percent of what we know. Worse, our knowledge is stored within decaying biological entities. Moravec imagines a society that lives beyond the limits of flesh. Organic life can be abandoned to a higher "post biological" species. Here's what he says in his book *Mind Children*: "Such machines could carry on our cultural evolution, including their own construction and increasingly rapid self-improvement, without us, and without the genes that built us. When that happens, our DNA will find itself out of a job, having lost the evolutionary race…Our culture will then be able to evolve independently of human biology and its limitations, passing instead directly from generation to generation of ever more capable intelligent machinery."

Dr. Gregory Stock of UCLA also praises the "merging of humans and machines into a global superorganism." He calls it "Metaman" and says it will "take control of human evolution."

※ ※ ※

It is difficult to gauge the ultimate viability of such technologies as these, but what is truly alarming is that anyone would actually propose them. Great universities, the military and corporations fund and patent them. Lawmakers dutifully promote them. *Meanwhile no one tells the public what's at stake: The profound, irreversible alteration of all life on earth, and the proposition that nature has become irrelevant.* Right now, the only hindrance to deployment of this new generation of technology is whether or not corporations can profit, or the military can make weapons. Are those the right standards? Bill Joy has recommended "relinquishment," as far as eugenics, nanotechnology and robotics are concerned. Just say no? That's a good start. *But in a democratic society, we must also demand active public participation, full disclosure, debate, and referenda on every technological development beyond a certain scale.* Who controls new technologies, and to what end? How will they affect jobs, health, social structure, governance, and the natural world? Do we want them at all? Should they be scrapped?

Clearly, we can no longer afford to give corporations and scientists free reign to reshape our lives, and to destroy the earth and creation itself! It's time we got organized!

Many public interest groups are already alarmed about these issues. To contact them, or get involved yourself, please call us.

International Center for Technology Assessment
Earth Island Institute
Nature Institute/NetFuture
Silicon Valley Toxics Coalition
The Loka Institute
Foundation on Ethics and Meaning
Council for Responsible Genetics
Center for Commercial-Free Public Education
Tikkun Magazine
Edmonds Institute
New York Open Center
Center for Media and Democracy
Collective Heritage Institute/Bioneers Conference
Rainforest Action Network

Signers are all part of a coalition of more than 80 non-profit organizations that favor democratic, localized, ecologically sound alternatives to current practices and policies. This advertisement is the final one in the Megatechnology series. Other ad series discuss extinction crisis, genetic engineering, industrial agriculture and economic globalization. For more information, please contact:

**Turning Point Project, 666 Pennsylvania Ave. SE,
Suite 302, Washington, DC 20003 • 1-800-249-8712
www.turnpoint.org • email: info@turnpoint.org**

4

DOUG TOMPKINS &
THE TURNING POINT PROJECT

—◆—

Deep Ecology: From ESPRIT to Arne Naess
Turning Point Project, a Philosophical Legacy
Kristine Tompkins Continues the Work

IN MANY WAYS, the most remarkable extended ad campaign that I ever helped produce was a series of 25 ads that were sponsored and largely conceived by Doug Tompkins. He called it the Turning Point Project. The ads ran in 1999 and 2000, full-page *New York Times* ads, every other Monday for one year. (We generally chose Monday for *Times* insertions because that's the day of the week when the paper typically has the fewest retail advertisements competing for readers' attention. And Mondays are usually less expensive.)

The Turning Point ads were entirely paid for by Doug's Foundation for Deep Ecology, which I'd helped manage for him during much of the 1990s. Public Media Center co-produced the ad series in partnership with Deep Ecology and with the avid participation of Andrew Kimbrell of the Center for Food Safety, part of the Center for Technology Assessment. Each of the ads was co-signed by several dozen leading non-profit organizations of the period, as you will notice. Several of those ads appear later in these pages.

But, before getting into the full story of the Turning Point campaign, I'd like to focus a bit on Tompkins himself, definitely one of the few most remarkable people and activists I have ever known: brilliant, daring, dedicated, brave, dogged, and amazing. In Chapter Three, I briefly described Tompkins' crucial role in the early 1990s, hosting groundbreaking meetings that helped launch a new international movement

against the globalization of corporate powers. Out of that emerged the International Forum on Globalization, and two decades of dynamic and effective international economic and environmental activism. But there's much more to Doug's story.

FRIENDLY NEIGHBORS

I first met Doug in the early 1960s, when, by chance, we were neighbors on Russian Hill in San Francisco. We'd often chat on the street, grab a coffee someplace, and watch our young kids playing together on the lawn. At that point in his life, Doug was primarily dedicated to outdoor physical activity: mountain climbing, kayaking, downhill ski racing, etc. He had already accomplished quite a few "first ascents" of peaks in South and North America, usually accompanied by his great friend Yvon Chouinard, who later founded Patagonia, the sportswear company. Doug hoped to win a place on the US Olympic downhill ski-racing team. He tried out, came close, but didn't make the final cut.

In 1965, Doug opened the North Face Ski Shop in San Francisco's North Beach. It was only a half block from my own very popular theatrical publicity client, "The Committee," where I spent a lot of time. So, Doug and I were easily able to continue to drop in on each other and go sit around with coffee at Café Trieste. Since my publicity career in those years placed me well inside the "show-business" world, Doug had

The Internet & the Illusion of Empowerment

The computer revolution has been no boon to democracy. It has threatened personal privacy like nothing before, and it's a serious toxics hazard, too. As for empowerment, let's call it "corporate empowerment" because they gain far more than you do.

The communications revolution is an odd revolution since all sides agree about it. The conservatives and the liberals, the George W. Bushes and Al Gores, the engineers and the artists, the corporations and the activists who oppose them, accept computers and the internet as empowering to individuals and democracy. But are they?

Corporations are most articulate in these matters. They use "empowerment" and "freedom" as sales points in millions of dollars worth of advertising. A decade ago, we saw TV commercials showing lines of depressed men in grey suits, marching in a dreary world. *Computers would set them free.* Now the ads show happy monks in Asia, happy children in Africa, happy farmers in Japan, all joining the internet revolution—which you'd better do, too. Everyone should think different together.

Meanwhile, political leaders advocate subsidized "information superhighways" that wire all classrooms to the internet—costing taxpayers about $100 billion. This, despite research that immersing kids into high technology doesn't make them happier, more creative, alive, or smarter. It may do the opposite: make them lonely, alienated, and depressed. Kids don't learn better from computers; they learn best from people, nature, and live play. But officials pay little attention to such evidence. We are in the midst of a technological stampede. We are in technological freefall.

Contrary Factors

Are computers "empowering?" Yes, and no. They serve us well in many ways. They help us organize our work, write and edit. We can communicate with like-minded colleagues and be part of global networks. We can disseminate ideas, and create and visit web sites. We can play video games. That's the good news. We've heard about those.

What's the rest of the story? Here are some points that advertisers have left out:

■ *Privacy and surveillance.* When you make an online purchase, or just hit a web page, you could be automatically adding to the huge *accessible* data banks that store information about you, your family, your job and salary, your buying patterns, your credit status, and other facts and habits you might rather strangers didn't know. Computers have let loose the greatest invasion of privacy in history. And there's a thriving industry of companies in business just to sell this information about you.

The same technology is used in the workplace for a kind of surveillance impossible till now. For example, if you're in any kind of clerical job, your employer may be measuring your key strokes per minute or month; or, how long it takes you to complete a phone transaction, etc. Millions of Americans are no longer job-rated by humans, but by computer systems, often in another state. Is this empowering?

■ *Toxics.* They call it a "cleaner" industry than the old smokestack industries, but unfortunately, it isn't so. The high tech industries use massive amounts of toxic chemicals that damage the environment and threaten the health of workers. Silicon Valley (Santa Clara County, CA) has more Superfund toxic dump sites than any other county in the U.S.: 29 sites, 80% of which are due to electronics manufacturing. Similar patterns are showing up in Austin, Phoenix, and Albuquerque, where high-tech industries are locating. Who's paying to clean up their mess? You are, with other taxpayers.

Silicon chip manufacturing needs huge amounts of pure water, while also producing serious contamination of groundwater. Underneath Phoenix, a 15-mile plume of contamination, mostly caused by the electronics industry, has cut available groundwater by 25%. At a time when the planet is experiencing a fresh water shortage, chip manufacturing is becoming a grave threat to life on Earth.

■ *E-commerce.* Suddenly, we are being pushed to convert the economy to e-commerce. The government wants to subsidize e-commerce activity

"THINK DIFFERENT" has been the theme of one computer company's ads, using photos of Einstein, Gandhi, and King, et al. What do these ads mean? That by joining the internet generation with everyone else, you'd become unique like these heroes—none of whom needed computers? Or, are the companies promoting the idea that conformity is somehow creative? For that, George Orwell would be a better selection.

by banning taxes on it, and by working for global trade deals that outlaw tariffs on e-commerce. They call this The New Economy.

However, banning taxes on e-commerce directly threatens the tax base of most states and cities. You may soon see reduced health, education, fire, police, sanitation, and other services, just to feed the coffers of e-commerce titans. In the end, this corporate package will be worth hundreds of billions of dollars for one part of the economy (the "virtual" part, run by computer giants) while subverting the old "brick and mortar" economy: small businesses, retail shops, bookstores, even malls, where humans physically gather, talk and "touch the goods." Is it legal for the government to favor only one kind of economic activity? Is it a good idea? Are we empowered yet?

There's still more to the story:

Corporate Empowerment

The editors of *Wired* magazine—the internet bible—say the computer revolution has brought a new political structure to the planet. The symbol of today is no longer the atom, it's the web, a *decentralized* form. The political "center" is diminished, they say, and the new web structure "elevates the power of the small player." This idea is widely accepted.

But if the political center has been stifled by the internet, somebody forgot to tell the transnational corporations in New York, Tokyo, Brussels, and Geneva. The news might surprise the 200 global corporations that now control nearly 30% of all economic activity on the planet, or the 51 companies that number among the 100 largest economies in the world. Mitsubishi, General Motors, Exxon, to name only a few, are each larger than many countries, including New Zealand, Portugal, Malaysia, Israel, Singapore, Venezuela, Chile, Ireland, *etc.* Such companies seem oblivious that their power has now been contained by our personal computers. They keep cutting down forests, building huge dams, monopolizing oil, dominating communications, and controlling politicians. And with the recent explosion of global mergers, *they* seem to think their powers are growing!

Computers have had a central role in encouraging corporate giantism. In fact, *modern global corporations could not exist at their present scale, or operate at their speed, without global networks to keep their thousand-armed enterprises in constant touch, seven days each week, 24 hours per day.* And, they use these same networks to instantaneously, at the touch of a key, move billions of dollars of assets around the world, without the ability of any nation-state to observe it, or regulate it.

So what kind of revolution is this?

❦ ❦ ❦

To use a term like "empowerment" to summarize the effects of computers-in-society may be misjudging the ultimate social, political, and economic outcomes of this revolution. The internet and computers may help us *feel* powerful, but while we're e-mailing and networking among our virtual communities, global corporations use these instruments at a scale that makes our use pale by comparison. When *they* hit their

computer keys, they can move billions of dollars instantly from banks in Geneva to, say, Sarawak, and a forest gets cut down. Or, they may buy billions in national currencies only to sell them again a few hours later, causing wild market fluctuations and currency crashes, like a few years ago. While we move *information*, they express *power.* There's a difference. It's not just who benefits from this technology; it's who benefits *most?* It's not the small player. It's the big player. Someday, we may conclude that global computer networks that we celebrate for their democratic potential, that we call empowering, are helping facilitate the greatest centralization of unregulated, unaccountable corporate power ever. It's crucial for democracy that we think this through.

❦ ❦ ❦

Some groups are beginning to be concerned. No-one says don't use this technology, but major questions—social, political, environmental—are emerging about the outcome of this trend. Many of the groups have good ideas about how to improve things.

Think different. (Think *differently,* actually.) Start asking questions about how this revolution is going. For inspiration you might check the work of, well, Gandhi, who actually spent his life working *against* the kind of centralizing technology that global computer systems represent. Or, Dr. King, who said this: "Mammoth productive facilities with computer minds…Gargantuan industry and government, woven into an intricate computerized mechanism, leave the person outside…man becomes separated and diminished…democracy is emptied…This process produces alienation—perhaps the most pervasive and insidious development in contemporary society."

For more information about how to get involved, please call.

International Center for Technology Assessment
The Loka Institute
Cultural Environment Movement
Center for Media and Democracy
Independent Media Center
Center for Commercial-Free Public Education
Rainforest Action Network
International Society for Ecology and Culture
Earth Island Institute
The Nature Institute/NetFuture
Whole Earth Magazine
Silicon Valley Toxics Coalition
Association of Waldorf Schools of North America
Collective Heritage Institute/Bioneers Conference
Media Alliance
Planet Drum Foundation
YES! Magazine
Jacques Ellul Society
We, The World
The Ecologist Magazine

Signers are all part of a coalition of more than 80 non-profit organizations that favor democratic, localized, ecologically sound alternatives to current practices and policies. This advertisement is #3 in the Megatechnology series. Other ad series discuss extinction crisis, genetic engineering, industrial agriculture and economic globalization. For more information, please contact:
Turning Point Project, 310 D St. NE, Washington, DC 20002
1-800-249-8712 · www.turnpoint.org · email: info@turnpoint.org

asked me if I knew any good local bands that he could hire to play at the Grand Opening launch of his ski shop. I suggested one that I thought was pretty good—a new, still little known local band called The Grateful Dead. They were happy to play at the party. I think we paid them $50. (I have wonderful pictures from the party of their drummer, Pig Pen, standing with Susie Tompkins, Doug's wife and business partner at that time.) It was a great party; Joan Baez showed up, with her younger sister Mimi Farina, who would soon also be performing on stage with The Committee comedy troupe, down the block.

A few years later, Doug finally decided to quit the ski shop. He joined with Susie in a new women's clothing company she had started, together with her friend Jane Tise. Their brand was called Plain Jane. But after awhile, Doug and Susie decided to branch out and launch a new clothing company of their own. They called it ESPRIT, which quickly became an enormously successful global enterprise. That effort took most of Doug and Susie's time and attention in the 1970s and 1980s. And ultimately, it made both of them very wealthy.

Nonetheless, Doug and I found some time to get together, hang out in cafes, gossip, and talk things over. He would often complain to me that he wished he could just drop all the business stuff and live far away in the mountains somewhere, preferably South America, and devote himself solely to hiking, climbing, and environmental campaigning.

Tompkins was also a huge fan and admirer of the ads we'd done with David Brower in the mid-1960s to save Grand Canyon. Doug asked me if I would introduce him to Brower. I did. They got along extremely well. Their common bond was their great love and engagement with *wild* nature. Doug and Dave spent long hours talking to each other about nature and what it meant to them. They inspired each other.

In those years, while still devoted to business, Doug was nonetheless a voracious reader, and he followed environmental issues very closely. He eventually immersed himself in a new international movement called "Deep Ecology." This was a Europe-based, very radical environmental trend launched by Norwegian scholar Arne Naess. Doug poured through all of Arne's books and writings, and then flew to Norway several times to meet with him and learn more about Deep Ecology. Doug also brought Arne to San Francisco for several visits in the late 1980s and 1990s, where I was also able to meet him—a charming, laid-back, and humble man.

Also by the late 1980s, Tompkins began talking to me (privately) about how he was thinking of quitting ESPRIT. He'd decided he wanted to concentrate solely on environmental issues. Soon after that, he announced he was going to sell his interest in the company to his wife, Susie. And alas, Doug and Susie also announced that their marriage was splitting up.

DEEP ECOLOGY

Once he exited ESPRIT, Tompkins indicated he wanted to devote the rest of his life to environmental causes and actions. He soon formed the Foundation for Deep Ecology, an activist, grant-making foundation for environmental projects. He invited me to join the founding Board of Directors, and to be Executive Director as we launched the project. Soon after, I was partnered in that work by Doug and Susie's enthusiastic and talented daughter, Quincey, who took over the Executive Director work so that I could concentrate solely on funding and campaigning aspects.

Deep Ecology began a very aggressive grant-making program, which put us directly in touch with most of the key activist groups of those years. This was also the period, as briefly mentioned in Chapter Three, that Doug hosted, at his home, a landmark series of 1994 private gatherings among dozens of environmental and political activists from every continent. Those meetings enabled Doug and the whole group to get to know each other, share ideas, and begin collaborative action within the new International Forum on Globalization.

By 1993, Doug had decided to fully follow his dream. While still operating the Foundation for Deep Ecology from the house on Russian Hill, he pulled up roots and moved himself to a huge ranch in a glorious, remote, mountainous area of south-central Chile, near Renihue. There he began the next part of his life: a 20-year process of buying huge tracts of open lands in southern Chile—several million acres—and then also doing likewise in Argentina.

Doug's announced goal was to prevent those lands from ever becoming *commercially* logged or "developed," while he also worked passionately to restore them, as needed, to their natural wild state. He called the process, "bringing them back to beauty." He used that term repeatedly, with obvious pleasure and passion.

After a year or so in South America, Doug was joined in his work and his life by his soon-to-be second wife,

"The Next World War Will Be About Water."

[– The World Bank]

The planet is running out of fresh water, but not because of thirsty people. 90% goes to global industry: mostly high tech manufacturing and industrial agriculture. Now corporations want to ship river and lake water across the ocean to Asia, in giant "bladders." It's for thirsty computer companies.

We'd like to believe there's an infinite supply of water on the planet. But the assumption is false. Available fresh water equals less than one half of one percent of all the water on Earth. The rest is sea water, or polar ice. Fresh water is renewable only by rainfall, at the rate of 40-50,000 cubic KM per year. The supply is finite. *That's all there is.*

Global *consumption* of fresh water is doubling every 20 years. *That's more than twice the rate of human population growth.* But human beings actually use only 10% of the planet's fresh water.

65% of the world's fresh water goes to industrial agriculture, which uses water at a much higher rate than the small self-sufficient family farmers who are being replaced. The rest goes to other industrial uses, like high-tech and computer manufacturing. (Silicon chips require massive supplies of pure water.)

According to the United Nations, more than one billion people on Earth already lack access to clean fresh drinking water. Still, *industrial* water users expect to double *their* consumption within the next twenty-five years. By then, two-thirds of the world population will be suffering from severe water shortage.

❧ ❧ ❧

As the water crisis becomes worse, one would anticipate that governments and global bureaucracies, conscious of the planet's limits, would advocate conservation. Instead, some propose a new solution: *Privatize and globalize the remaining fresh water.* Sell it to corporations, and let the global market decide who gets to drink it, or use it. New trade agreements like NAFTA and the WTO already define water as a "commodity" and have rules that *require governments to permit water exports under certain conditions.*

Corporations are excited. Water may soon be more valuable than oil, so there are billions to be made. Among their schemes is to ship North American lake water across the Pacific. *Picture a gigantic supertanker crossing the ocean while towing a humongous floating balloon carrying part of Lake Superior.* The water will be sold to Asia's high-tech industries (and U.S. companies in Asia). Very few thirsty people can afford to buy the water for drinking. As for environmental consequences from such shipments, and the further depletion of American lakes and rivers, no one is asking.

State of the world's waters

This new form of fresh water diversion is only the latest in a century of water projects — dams, aquifer pumping, canals and other diversions — that have left the world's water resource in a desperate state. Here's a quick summary:

■ In the U.S., only 2% of rivers have *not* been dammed. The Colorado and the Rio Grande rivers are so over-tapped that little of their waters reach the sea. The High Plains Ogallala aquifer, stretching 1,300 miles from Texas to South Dakota, is being depleted eight times faster than nature can replenish it.

■ In Mexico City, pumping exceeds natural recharge by 50-80% per year. Arabian Peninsula groundwater use is three times greater than recharge. Saudi Arabia may be completely depleted in 50 years. Israel's extraction exceeded replacement by 2.5 billion meters in the last 25 years; 13% of its coastal aquifer is contaminated by agricultural chemicals or sea water.

With the world running out of water, is the best solution to privatize and globalize the remaining supply, letting the market decide who drinks and who does not?

■ In Africa, *the aquifers barely recharge at all.* Water is being depleted by some 10 billion cubic meters a year. Northern China has eight regions of aquifer overdraft, while the water table under Beijing dropped 37 meters over the last 40 years. The land under Bangkok has actually *sunk* due to overpumping. And the Nile River, the Ganges, and the Yellow River in China, like the Colorado in the U.S., are so dammed and diverted that the waters do not reach the sea.

■ Cities and industrial zones are now in direct competition for water with industrial agriculture. In "free trade zones," like the Maquiladoras of Mexico, nearly all water goes to manufacturing. Babies are drinking Coke and Pepsi. (During one drought, Mexican authorities cut off water supplies to everyone *but* industrial users.)

■ Some countries are near *war* over water. Namibia and Botswana are arguing about diversions of the Okavango River. Israel, Jordan and other mid-East countries are also arguing. Malaysia has threatened to cut off Singapore's water supply (which flows from the north). And Turkey opposes Kurdish independence, precisely because Kurds live in the mountains, where the water is.

■ In India, families pay 25% of their income for drinking water. Poor residents of Lima, Peru, pay $3 for a cubic meter of often contaminated water. More than five million people, mostly children, die every year from bad drinking water.

■ The effects on wildlife and biodiversity is beyond tragic. The United States has lost 50% of its wetlands. So has Canada. California has lost 95% of its wetlands, and populations of migratory birds and waterfowl have dropped from 60 million in 1950, to 3 million now. 37% of America's freshwater fish are at risk of extinction; 51% of crayfish; 40% of amphibians; and 67% of freshwater mussels, mostly from poisoned waters that run off from the agriculture industry. 40% of U.S. rivers and streams are too dangerous for fishing, swimming or drinking.

■ In England, 30% of the rivers are down to one-third their average depth. Egypt's Aswan Dam reduced harvestable fish by 67%. 75% of Poland's rivers are so contaminated that their water is unfit even for industrial use.

Do we get the point yet? There is simply no way to overstate the water crisis of the planet today.

Clear choices

What now? There are few rivers left to dam. Aquifers are in crisis. *So then, is the best solution to let global corporations export lake and river water by towing it in balloons across the oceans, for profit?* Does anyone really believe that will solve more problems than it causes?

Though we are not in the habit of facing the truths about the limits of our planet, we must. There's only so much water. Once we accept that, we can make some logical moves:

1) *Recognize that water is life to all species.* Water should not become a commodity; it is part of the commons, owned by all of us forever. It should not be privatized or traded or globalized.

2) *Leave water where nature put it,* in its own watershed, as part of larger ecological systems. Decisions about its use should be localized.

3) *Full conservation and reclamation programs should begin now.* Industrial users should pay.

4) *Industrial agriculture should be phased out.* It's too toxic, and energy and water intensive. A return to small-scale local farming will save water and energy, and it will keep our rivers clean. Strict controls are needed on water use by high-tech manufacturing.

5) International agreements should determine where emergency fresh *drinking* water is needed. *Non-profit* organizations, like the Red Cross, should supply such regions, as needed. *Free.*

For more information and to obtain a complete report on the global water crisis (*Blue Gold*, by Maude Barlow, International Forum on Globalization), please contact us.

The Council of Canadians
Friends of the Earth
International Forum on Globalization
Earth Island Institute
David Suzuki Foundation
Global Exchange
Pacific Environmental Resources Center
People Centered Development Forum
YES! A Journal of Positive Futures
Project Underground
Rainforest Action Network
Research Foundation for Science, Technology and Ecology
International Center for Technology Assessment
International Forum on Food and Agriculture
Institute for Agriculture and Trade Policy
Native Forest Council
50 Years is Enough: U.S. Network for Global Economic Justice
Forest Guardians

Signers are all part of a coalition of more than 60 non-profit organizations that favor democratic, localized, ecologically sound alternatives to current practices and policies. This advertisement is #4 in the Economic Globalization series. Other ad series discuss the extinction crisis, genetic engineering, industrial agriculture and megatechnology. For more information, please contact:
Turning Point Project, 310 D St. NE, Washington, DC 20002
1-800-249-8712 · www.turnpoint.org · email: info@turnpoint.org

Kristine McDivitt. She had been the CEO of Patagonia, Inc.—the progressive outdoor clothing company founded by Doug's long-time mountain-climbing friend, Yvon Chouinard. Kris also spent much of her time in South America, particularly in the Patagonia region; and she too was fully involved in very expansive conservation activities. Once together, Doug and Kris moved rapidly to buy more huge tracts of land in both Chile and Argentina that would otherwise have surely been logged and/or developed.

Doug and Kris protected their lands from any and all commercial development. They re-planted with native trees and brought back the wild-life that had lived there earlier. After only a few years, Doug and Kris were being acknowledged as being among the largest private land-owners in the world.

Once their lands were fully restored to their natural state, Doug and Kris began *donating* lands to the governments of Chile and/or Argentina, but with a mandatory contracted condition: the lands must become protected as National Parks and must *never* be commercially developed. Doug and Kris continued this work together until Doug's shocking death in 2015, ironically, inconceivably, tragically, from a kayaking accident!! Kris has continued their remarkable work to this day. She was lately widely celebrated for donations of a million acres toward new national parklands in Chile, and also millions of acres of parklands and ocean shoreline on the eastern coast of Argentina.

TURNING POINT PROJECT: PHILOSOPHICAL LEGACY

Land conservation represented only one side of Doug's passions, dedication, and activity. He also remained, throughout, a truly radical activist on a broad range of environmental issues. Through the Foundation for Deep Ecology, Doug would use any tool possible to support environmental battles on a large scale, in the US, Europe, or anywhere.

Tompkins was also very interested in the advertising approaches that he'd witnessed from Freeman, Mander & Gossage, as well as PIC and PMC, going back to the Brower days, and also including the more recent environmental campaigns that emerged in the 1990s. The Foundation for Deep Ecology provided funding for many of those campaigns.

Tompkins was always eager to stimulate campaigns that effectively argued for protection of *wild nature*,

and *wildlife*. In fact, he became so excited by this form of campaigning that he began personally writing and producing ads himself on key environmental issues in South America, with very positive results. He produced and placed several of those ads in Chilean newspapers on important local and regional issues, with great success.

One of Doug's first and most successful South America campaigns was the effort to shut-down a large commercial salmon-raising enterprise in a bay near his Renihue home. Then, a few years later, Tompkins personally wrote, designed, and created an excellent ad campaign to block Chilean government efforts to run hundreds of miles of power lines atop the mountain chain that separates Chile from Argentina. Absent Doug's personal efforts, both of those projects would have proven devastating to environmental protection in the region.

Doug's South American ad campaigns carefully followed the advertising style and forms he had watched being developed in San Francisco, including the use of multiple coupons. He was a very fast learner. These two big ad campaigns—he wrote them both in Spanish with help from a local team—were both 100% successful in creating a movement to block the projects he opposed. In some ways, the Chile ads enabled him to personally articulate the grandest expressions of his overall worldview—including his celebration of "deep ecology."

Then, in the late 1990s, Doug told me that he would really like to sponsor and help create a full ad series to run in the United States, expressing a broad critique across a full range of core issues that were threatening the world. Tompkins appreciated that battling his own favorite local issues was only part of the story. Much larger capitalist economic and conceptual frameworks dominated our globalized industrial growth society; these needed broader articulation. Thus was born the Turning Point Project.

Doug and I were joined in the conception, discussions, planning, and execution of this mega-project by Andrew Kimbrell from the Center for Food Safety. Kimbrell had also been wanting to devote more of his organizational activism toward *root causes* of what was clearly the coming breakdown of our society, and possibly the planet. After long discussions at Doug's house in Chile, we three agreed on a campaign expressing a comprehensive focus on the dreadful state of the natural world, and the role of technologies, economies, and societies that are leading us quickly down the path to disaster.

THIS ADVERTISEMENT IS #3 IN A SERIES ON
ECONOMIC GLOBALIZATION

Invisible Government

The World Trade Organization (WTO) is emerging as the world's first global government. But it was elected by no one, it operates in secrecy, and its mandate is this: To undermine the constitutional rights of sovereign nations. How could this happen? What can we do?

Starting tonight, the World Trade Organization (WTO) begins its Ministerial Meeting in Seattle. Just created in 1994, it is now the principal rule-making body of the global economy. 134 nation-states have ceded it powers that once firmly resided within nations. The WTO is already among the most powerful, secretive, and undemocratic bodies on Earth. Its authority extends deeply into the *internal* political processes of sovereign countries, forcing them to alter laws and priorities. It is fast becoming a *bonafide* global government for the new millennium. WTO former Director-General Renato Ruggiero called it the "new constitution for a single global economy." And a European trade minister said: "It's not undemocratic, it's *anti-democratic.*"

The central idea of the WTO is that *free trade*—actually the values and interests of global corporations—should supersede all other values. Any obstacles to global trade are viewed with suspicion. In practice, these "obstacles" are the laws of nation-states that protect the environment, small businesses, human rights, consumers, labor as well as national sovereignty and democracy. The WTO views these as possible impediments to "free trade," and they become subject to challenge within closed WTO tribunals. Unlike other global bodies (including the UN), the WTO enjoys unique *enforcement powers*. Offending countries *must* conform with WTO rules, or face harsh sanctions.

Secret tribunals

The WTO's judicial system ("Dispute Resolution Body") operates in *secret*: no press, no public, no public interest organizations. Three bureaucrats (former corporate or government trade officials, with no social or environmental training) make profoundly important judgements affecting human health, jobs, agriculture and food, and the environment. The only standards these invisible judges apply concern consequences to the freedom of corporate trade. *They have never once ruled in favor of the environment.*

It would be impossible to list the *many dozens* of cases they have heard (though we can send you information about them; see number below). But, here are a few:

■ The WTO ruled that the U.S. must rewrite parts of its Clean Air Act to permit imports of less pure gasoline; the result may be more air pollution and lung disease.

■ The European Union was told it *cannot* ban imports of beef products (from the U.S.) that had been treated with potentially cancer-causing hormones.

■ Japan was told to lift its import ban on certain fruits that carry dangerous invasive insects. Such products require heavy doses of harmful pesticides at the border. The WTO ruled Japan must import the fruits, regardless.

■ And, after a challenge by the U.S., Europe was told to stop favoring bananas grown in the Caribbean by small independent farmers over Chiquita Bananas grown by corporate, plantation-style, agriculture.

Do you begin to see a bias in this?

Chilling effects

Actually, the WTO achieves most of its purposes by a "chilling" effect. The mere *threats* of actions have been sufficient to get most small nations to *voluntarily* change their laws and legal structure to be "WTO compliant." For example, Guatemala decided voluntarily to lift a ban on advertising by Gerber Infant Formula that claimed it was healthier than breast milk. Canada removed its ban on a suspected neurotoxin, MMT, under threat of a challenge (under a NAFTA rule that's now proposed as a WTO rule). Thailand quit manufacturing its own low cost AIDS drug after the U.S. threatened a WTO suit to help American drug companies. (Thailand's AIDS victims can't afford to pay American drug prices. The U.S. is also threatening South Africa.)

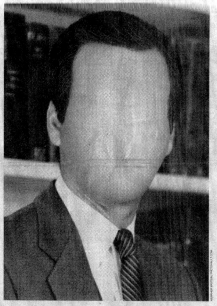

WTO decisions are made in secret, closed tribunals—like the old "star chambers"—where unelected faceless bureaucrats sit in final judgement over the constitutional rights of nations. Their decisions effect your job, human rights, public health, food safety, the environment and democracy.

Here's what's most important: Whether challenges are brought by the U.S. against a country, or by another country against the U.S., or by other countries against each other, the composite effect is "cross-border deregulation" which ratchets-down standards for safety, health and the environment *everywhere. That is the WTO's goal:* Free trade for corporations, but severe controls upon nations and citizens that try to protect the safety of their food, their jobs, small businesses or Nature.

New expansions

In Seattle, the WTO will propose a new "Millennium Round" of negotiations. One proposal for this round would make it nearly *impossible for any government to ban the import of genetically engineered foods.* Another would permit global corporations to enter "public sectors" like education, healthcare, public broadcasting, water delivery. We might find Mitsubishi controlling American schools, or Exxon running BBC. There's also a move to cut tariffs on wood products, which would ravage the world's last pristine forests.

But the Godzilla of WTO plans is to revive some of the old, discredited Multilateral Agreement on Investment. Those rules would impose restrictions on *every* level of government; down to states, counties and cities. Foreign companies would have to be given "national treatment," i.e., treated exactly as if they were local companies. So, let's say your city now favors local or minority owned businesses to build municipal buildings, roads, or to provide school lunches. This would be illegal.

Let's say your state wanted to stop the cutting of forests, or fishing for endangered species; a foreign company could sue, saying this deprives them of profits that *local companies had already enjoyed.* Let's say your state requires new investors to use "domestic content," or to hire local workers, or to *not* send their profits back to Europe (but to reinvest some in the community). Such local rules would be illegal.

It would also be impossible for any country to regulate rapid capital entry or exit, leaving all countries vulnerable to currency speculators and financial crashes. *Neither would your country, state or city be able to "discriminate" against countries with terrible human rights or environmental records, as was done against South Africa during apartheid.* If this law had existed back then, South Africa would not have democratized. Nelson Mandela would still be in jail.

Winners & losers

There *is* an ideological rationale for free trade. It supposedly benefits all segments of society. The homily goes like this: "A rising tide will lift all boats." So far, however, it's only lifting yachts.

Following 20 years of the most rapid expansion ever of global trade, only a tiny group at the top of the corporate pyramid has experienced significant benefits. Gaps between rich and poor have been widening, even in the U.S. For example, American CEOs are now paid, on average, 419 times more than line workers, and the ratio is increasing. Median hourly wages for workers is *down* by 10% in the last ten years. The top 20% of the U.S. population owns 84.6% of the country's wealth. And the wealth of the world's 475 billionaires now equals the annual incomes of more than 50% of the world population *combined.* Lifting all boats, indeed.

WHAT CAN YOU DO?

Right now, hundreds of public interest groups are in Seattle to protest the WTO. *Most want the WTO to stop in its tracks:* No Millennium Round. No expansion of powers. A full public re-assessment of the WTO's performance till now. *Many feel the WTO can never be democratically reformed.*

Meanwhile, there are many ways you can participate. Lots of information is available. Please contact us.

International Forum on Globalization
Institute for Policy Studies-Global Economy Project
Friends of the Earth
Global Exchange
Sierra Club
Greenpeace USA
International Center for Technology Assessment
United Steelworkers of America
Alliance for Sustainable Jobs and the Environment
Defenders of Wildlife
People Centered Development Forum
Rainforest Action Network
The Council of Canadians
Earthjustice Legal Defense Fund
Sea Turtle Restoration Project
The Humane Society of the United States
Pacific Environmental Resources Center
Earth Island Institute
Institute for Local Self-Reliance
Polaris Institute
Tikkun Magazine
International Forum on Food and Agriculture
International Society for Ecology and Culture

Signers are all part of a coalition of more than 60 non-profit organizations that favor democratic, localized, ecologically sound alternatives to current practices and policies. This advertisement is #3 in the Economic Globalization series. Other ad series discuss extinction crisis, genetic engineering, industrial agriculture and megatechnology. For more information, please contact:

Turning Point Project, 310 D St. NE, Washington, DC 20002
1-800-249-8712 • www.turnpoint.org • email: info@turnpoint.org

The 25 Turning Point ads that ran in *The New York Times* were not all focused specifically on wilderness or land issues, as had been Doug's prior efforts—although the natural world was certainly a direct victim of current industrial and economic policies. The primary goal of the Turning Point campaign was to influence the contexts of thought that were leading countries, the United States especially, into terrible new terrain.

The 25 ads in the series expressed our joint view of the most dangerous behaviors steering the world toward a likely collapse, and what we ought to do about them.

The problems were broken into five broad categories: The Extinction Crisis, Megatechnology, Genetic Engineering, Industrial Agriculture, and Economic Globalization. Each Turning Point ad was targeted against some specific prevailing economic, political, or industrial belief system and practices "that are driving the beast" as Doug liked to say. The campaign attempted to critique fundamental operating assumptions of technological, industrial, globalist, expansive capitalist society, which were bringing disastrous global consequences of the kind we face today. Our hope was to present an alternative worldview and conceptual framework that could guide organized resistance.

Most of those ads were not written to target specific narrow issues and key players nearly as much as other ad campaigns I have described in this book. Neither did they attempt to specifically generate direct mail, coupons, phone calls, or other organized responses on specific issues. They had a broader intent: to influence fundamental thought and understanding of the larger, desperate situation we now face and its primary ingredients, along with an urgent necessity to reform our economic and political assumptions. All this in addition to taking direct action.

Several of the Turning Point ads did have direct activist intent, and they did in some cases produce enormous public responses with immense political impacts. Most notable among those was *Invisible Government*. That ad followed two others that attacked corporate economic globalization and the birth of the World Trade Organization (WTO). The three ads, including *Globalization vs. Nature* (*page 77*), ran in *The New York Times* beginning two weeks before the scheduled Ministerial meeting of the WTO in Seattle in late November 1999, when government leaders from around the world were planning to convene their "Millennial Round" and expand the WTO's powers.

"Globalization vs. Nature" called to join WTO resistance groups that were sponsoring public events in Seattle just prior to the Ministerial meeting. This included a three-day "teach-in" organized by the International Forum on Globalization, to analyze and to react to the WTO's plans and agenda. Our teach-in was held at Seattle Symphony Hall, packed to overflowing with nearly 3,000 attendees each day. It became the flagship event to share inside intelligence and align strategies.

When *"Invisible Government"* appeared the day before the meetings were to start, presenting the now iconic image of a faceless bureaucrat, announcing that "right now," hundreds of public interest groups were in Seattle and *"Most want the WTO to stop in its tracks,"* it produced a powerful, catalyzing effect.

Those ads and the teach-in were widely credited with laying the intellectual groundwork that prevented the opening of the official WTO meetings. On the scheduled launch day of the WTO, 50,000 angry protestors jammed onto the streets of Seattle. They blocked all entrances to the WTO meeting and overwhelmed the local police response. Finally, the WTO was forced to announce that their event was suspended. A new, articulate, anti-globalization movement was awake.

Several other Turning Point ads also had direct political impacts, especially those which attacked NAFTA, and several that attacked biotechnology. Under the techno-utopian framework of "Megatechnology" the ads aroused, for the first time, public discussions over that still emerging issue.

★   ★   ★

All of the Turning Point ads were born from those extensive conversations over several weeks in Chile, between Tompkins, Kimbrell, and myself. We had thereafter worked back and forth between Chile and the US over the next year, with many good ideas also coming from Tom Turner, one of Doug's primary colleagues and advisors in San Francisco.

The overall coordination of the Turning Point ad production process was by Miyoko Sakashita of the Turning Point Project and Katie Kleinsasser of Public Media Center. (Two decades later, Miyoko is now a

If computers in schools are the answer, are we asking the right question?

The Clinton administration proposes to spend about $100 billion taxpayer dollars to bring computer technology to every classroom. Who benefits from this? Our kids? Or just the computer industry? Some parents and teachers feel this will do more harm than good. They are getting organized.

Millions of children have become unwitting participants in a massive social experiment. It involves the radical restructuring of the education system, and the way our children learn to experience the world. Most shocking is how little thought is going into it. The assumption seems to be that computerizing things automatically improves them. Is this true?

1. What is gained and what is lost?

This much is sure. Billions toward computers means fewer teachers, less teacher training, larger classes, fewer athletic programs, lunch programs, music, art, nature classes, recreation, libraries, and books. It means more "distance learning," less face-to-face, human-centered or environmental experience. Are computers worth that loss?

One segment of society surely gains: the computer industry. It has a direct stake in addicting kids to computers, and emphasizing machines over teachers. Now we see the companies donating computers to classrooms; a tax deduction for them, and a long-term business stimulant. ("The first one is always free," says the pusher.) The question remains: *Are your children better off?*

Many educators don't think so. They believe that children learn to be full, intelligent, competent human beings through *human* contact, *nature* contact, lots of play, diversity of experience, and a rich sensory environment. Kids need to experience themselves as creative, reflective, grounded, curious, engaged people.

So far, there is no persuasive evidence that children learn or feel better from using computers. Educational psychologist Dr. Jane Healy says, "An atmosphere of hysteria surrounds the rush to connect [children] to electronic brains…research shows that computer 'learning' for young children is less brain-building than even such simple activities as spontaneous play or playing board games…'Connecting' alone has yet to demonstrate academic value…Just because children—particularly young ones—are performing tasks that look technologically sophisticated does not mean they are learning anything important."

The American Academy of Pediatrics argues that "time spent with media often displaces involvement in creative, active, or social pursuits." It recommends that no electronic media be permitted in kids' rooms, and that children below the age of two not watch TV.

Sitting alone with machines—TV or computers, at school or at home—is no fast track to long-term learning. It may be the opposite.

2. Recent findings

- According to the *Washington Post*, a study by the Educational Testing Service, Princeton, of 14,000 fourth and eighth graders "showed that students who spent more time on computers in school actually score worse on math tests than students who spent less time with computers." The *Post* added that "several earlier studies provided no conclusive evidence that the new technology was any better as a tool than pencils and paper in teaching children to read, write, and do mathematics."

- A report by the Third International Math and Science Study showed that, although U.S. fourth graders used computers in school three times more than youngsters in five other countries, the other countries outperformed the U.S. in math skills. Meanwhile, in five nations that have more computers at home than U.S. children do, the foreign students did no better than the U.S. students in science.

- A third study, at Carnegie Mellon University (1998), said that the more hours people spend on the internet, the more depressed, stressed, and lonely they become. "People are substituting weaker social ties [virtual relating] for stronger ones," said the lead author of the study. "They're substituting conversations on narrower topics with strangers for conversation with people who are connected to their life."

Do computers really help children learn better? Or to be more creative? Are they more alive? Happier? Smarter? There's evidence to the contrary.

- And a survey of 4,113 people by Stanford University's Institute for the Quantitative Study of Society said this: "the internet could be the ultimate isolating technology…even more than television before it." The study warns of a fragmented world where people spend more time "home, alone, anonymous." Is this what we want for our kids?

3. Training for adulthood

There is also the issue of jobs. One computer company's ads, worth millions of dollars, are showing kids in Europe and Asia saying: "Are you ready for the internet generation?"

Parents feel tremendous pressure about this.

But does a child need to learn computer skills at five years old to get a job at 21? Computers are quite easy to learn at any age. Anyway, computer programs they might learn today in third grade will likely be obsolete by seventh grade. What's the rush?

More important is that young kids learn the kinds of things that computers do not teach: how to get along and cooperate with real people of all ages. How to *experience* one's own imagination and creativity. How to be comfortable and calm in themselves. How to experience nature. How to play. Research shows that brain development continues throughout childhood, and that *diverse* activity, play and human contact are crucial to intelligence, creativity and emotional stability. Teaching tools that are right for 14 year olds may not be right for four year olds. Young children would be far better served if the government funded safe playgrounds.

Some say "let's not shield children from reality; computers are what's happening now. Even if there are weird people online; even if kids are inundated with commercials." But isn't a parent supposed to protect a child? Don't we see the value of preserving the innocent, playful, imaginative "culture" of kids? Must we allow small children to be turned into commodity-craving adults?

4. Information and perspective

We are told that computers bring access to information, and no one denies this. But is more information what our children desperately need? N.Y.U. education professor Neil Postman has written: "If a nuclear holocaust should occur someplace in the world, it will not happen because of insufficient information… if crime terrorizes our cities, marriages are breaking up, mental disorders are increasing, and children are being abused, none of this happens because of a lack of information…The fact is that our children, like the rest of us, are now suffering from information glut, not information scarcity."

If we need to know something, it's easy to find. We still have libraries. We have teachers. The problem is not a lack of information, it's the domination of one form of information—the kind that gets passed through machines like TV and computers: cerebral, non-sensory, non-experiential, *non-touch.*

Education writers Alison Armstrong and Charles Casement: "When children learn computers, they are not just learning a skill, they are changing the equations between themselves and the sources of knowledge about the world around them." On the loss of reading skills, the authors add this: "Computer use changes perceptions in a radically different way from print. Unlike print, which encourages reflection and a careful consideration of various points of view, computer software urges immediate action. Speed and control are emphasized at the expense of thoughtfulness, understanding, and a slower, more deliberate formation of ideas."

Portland State University professor Chet Bowers says heavy use of computers by children may be producing a generation of kids with less feeling for nature. Digital learning, he says, *amplifies* objective knowledge forms while distancing kids from the sense-world required to truly grasp the nuances and subtleties of nature, or human relationships. *Data substitutes for feeling, awareness, and wisdom.*

As we switch from prior modes of learning to technological modes, we are creating different kinds of children, and ultimately, a different society. Have we thought this through? Do we know what we want? Are we going too fast? Shouldn't we take time to discuss this?

These are only a few issues that should have been addressed *before* politicians and school officials joined forces with computer companies. But it's not too late to slow down. *The crucial step is that you must get involved, at the family, school and community level.*

Step one is to learn to ask tough questions of school superintendents and political candidates. *Where is the research that computers improve learning, or happiness? What is being sacrificed in this doubtful pursuit? Aren't the arts, sports and playgrounds ultimately more important to young kids?* There are many organizations that can help you on these matters. Contact us, and we will send you a list of groups and some ideas they're proposing. In twenty years, your children will thank you.

Alliance for Childhood
Association of Waldorf Schools of North America
The Center for Commercial-Free Education
The Loka Institute
Silicon Valley Toxics Coalition
International Campaign for Responsible Technology
TV Turnoff Network
International Center for Technology Assessment
Jacques Ellul Society
Computer Professionals for Social Responsibility
The Nature Institute/NetFuture
International Society for Ecology and Culture
Lapis Magazine
Center for Plain Living
Earth Island Institute
Rainforest Action Network
Tikkun Magazine
The Ecologist

Signers are all part of a coalition of more than 80 non-profit organizations that favor democratic, localized, ecologically sound alternatives to current practices and policies. This advertisement is #1 in the Megatechnology series. Other ad series discuss extinction crisis, genetic engineering, industrial agriculture and economic globalization. For more information, please contact:

Turning Point Project, 310 D St. NE, Washington, DC 20002
1-800-249-8712 • www.turnpoint.org • email: info@turnpoint.org

74

leading attorney at the Center for Biological Diversity in San Francisco, fighting many of these same issues in the courts.) They worked closely with Mark Mazziotti of Public Media Center, who was the lead graphic designer of the whole series with support from the Foundation for Deep Ecology.

As for whether that ambitious campaign actually changed public consciousness and action on this range of issues, it's hard for me to assess. We do know that some of the ads produced enormous public response—in addition to that Seattle response—and contributed to a movement of techno-skeptics, then still in its infancy. The anti-tech ads were accompanied by two public conferences on 'Techno-Utopianism'—one in New York City, and one in Berkeley—produced by the International Forum on Globalization. Each three-day conference gathered 3,000 people a day for detailed critiques of the entire direction and virtues of our new techno-logically dominated societies.

Looking back now on that ad series, I think we made one major mistake. This entire group of ads did not feature any of the response mechanisms that characterized most other ads we did in this period—cut-out coupons, etc. Looking back, and judging by the giant public turnout after the *Invisible Government* ads in Seattle, as well as some other ads of that period, I think we may have failed to take sufficient advantage of people's eager desire to respond and *engage* in a new movement of this kind. People were obviously eager to express themselves and to try and influence the powers-that-be on these matters. Perhaps, if we'd used the normal response mechanisms, we could have expanded the expression and impacts in several new directions. Nonetheless, I have been told by many people that they felt that they'd learned a lot from those ads, and that they broadened their worldview. I hope, for Doug's sake, my sake, your sake, and the planet, that it may be true.

(Chapter 5 begins on page 81)

E-Commerce &
The Demise
of Community

The government seeks billions in tax subsidies for e-commerce, though it means bankruptcy to thousands of non-dot-com businesses, neighborhood stores, even malls; real places where people gather. It will also mean less tax revenues for public services like schools, transportation, hospitals, fire and police. Why such official prejudice—one business over another? Is it fair? Is it legal?

You have heard about "planned obsolescence," a corporate strategy that creates products that wear out fast, so customers buy new ones. Now we have corporations, *shamefully* backed by federal officials, working a similar strategy on the entire economic system. They call it "The New Economy," and make it seem that anything that's not online is passé, and somehow grungy. Their apparent goal is to make obsolete as much as possible of the old "brick and mortar economy," i.e., the physical economy of real stores and real products, where people actually gather, talk and "touch the goods." In the process, they are also making obsolete the fundamental basis of American community and culture.

It's a bipartisan effort. Fueled by high tech campaign donations, Republicans *and* Democrats are fighting each other over who can give away more tax breaks to help e-commerce companies. A few years ago, Congress created a moratorium on new internet taxes. And a new report from the official Advisory Committee on Electronic Commerce wants the e-commerce moratorium extended five more years. By then, maybe Americans will get used to such favoritism. *(Already now, sales taxes have become impossible for states to collect on e-commerce; the Supreme Court ruled that businesses that do not have a physical presence in a state need not collect taxes. This ruling is being applied to e-commerce, and the government is doing nothing to fix it.)*

Dot-comers are being given insurmountable advantages over normal businesses that are too small to have lunch with politicians or to make donations. We are observing one of the greatest big business boondoggles in our history.

If the main beneficiaries are clear—the giant, trendy internet and high tech industries—the sacrificial victims are also clear: (1) all small neighborhood and retail businesses that relate people-to-people rather than online, (2) state and local public services that rely heavily on tax revenues: health, education, sanitation, parks, transportation, water, power, fire, police, etc., and (3) a value system, and way of life, that places community and people above *virtual* community. *Is it worth this cost?*

Doing the numbers

1. Forrester Research, Inc., reports online consumer shopping in the U.S. will increase from $13 billion in 1998 to $108 billion in 2003, about 6% of overall U.S. retail spending. Business-to-business online shopping will reach nearly 10% by 2003.

Moody's Investors Service warns that if U.S. retailers lose a mere 7% of their sales to the internet (equal to the impact of a moderate recession) profitability may decline by 50%. Some categories of retail—books, music, videos, computers—will reach 10% market penetration by the end of *this year*, thus threatening the survival of thousands of retail shops. *But you knew that already;* neighborhood bookstores and other shops are already closing before our eyes.

2. Forty-five states now have taxes on normal retail sales. These taxes generate about $150 billion annually, accounting for one-third of overall state revenues. As shopping moves online (with no taxes on sales) revenues will plummet. Forrester Research says that internet sales already cost state and local governments about $525 million in revenues in 1999 alone. Here's how a few states fared:

New York	26.6 million *lost*
Florida	30.3 million *lost*
Illinois	32.6 million *lost*
Texas	51.9 million *lost*

You may soon experience this loss via disappearing school sports or arts programs, unrepaired highways, closed museums and libraries, pileups of garbage on the streets, or even fewer busses than now.

Boarded-up shops, cafes, bookstores and other human-to-human business may soon be the norm in your neighborhood. E-commerce is leading us to a new culture of isolation; "virtual communities" replacing communities. Why this crusade against small business, while we subsidize trendy titans of e-commerce?

3. The National Governors' Association is very alarmed. It predicts that online sales will reach $200 billion by 2004, and $1 trillion ten years hence. Forty-two of American's fifty governors recently issued letters opposing an extension of the ban on e-commerce taxes. The NGA said it would "immediately reduce state and local tax revenues by more than $30 *billion* per year…make state and local tax systems more complex, more biased in favor of the wealthiest corporations, and unfair to individual taxpayers and small business…[and] would force either reductions in education, transportation and public safety programs, or [cause] offsetting revenue increases on every other taxpayer."

In other words, *your taxes might increase* in order to effectively subsidize the biggest, richest e-commerce companies.

4. *Meanwhile,* internationally, the U.S. is leading the push to ban *all tariffs and new taxes* on e-commerce activity. In fact, one of the victories of the anti-WTO movement in Seattle, last year, was to *prevent* passage of a U.S. proposal to *permanently codify a global ban on e-commerce tariffs and new taxes.* Now the U.S. is negotiating privately with individual countries to ban new taxes and tariffs on e-commerce. Some call the proposal, "the Bill Gates rule." Most threatened will be Third World economies which are now almost entirely based on small, local, traditional businesses and shops; artisanal and self-sufficient activity, all vulnerable to dominating global corporations.

Even at the International Monetary Fund—no enemy of big business—an economic study has warned that The New Economy would threaten services in industrial countries: "Ballooning electronic commerce, and increased mobility of the factors of production will likely cause significant falls in tax revenue…states need to look for alternative ways to provide social protection."

The culture of isolation

More important than which businesses gain and lose, is what it all means for American community life. Subsidizing one economy while trashing another, *replacing one culture with another,* will put American community life, as we have known it, on the brink of extinction.

Not long ago we lamented the loss of Main Street, and its replacement by malls. But one thing Main Street and malls have in common is *physical presence.* People gather in public places, make contact with each other, and sustain a sense of community cohesion.

Real community has a *geographic* basis; it's about people and neighbors seeing one another, engaging with each other's families,

building personal trust. Being involved. "Virtual community" (via the internet) is *virtual.* It is placeless and out of context. It's not community; it's the absence of community. And it has negative consequences for people and democracy.

The utopian dream of the dot-com economy is to have millions of people isolated at home, living life through machines. They have social relations through machines; they shop via machines. Now they can even seek psychiatric help over the internet, and it looks like they'll need it.

Recent studies by such institutions as Carnegie-Mellon and Stanford University, among others, are finding that Americans who rely heavily on the internet are becoming more isolated, alienated, lonely and depressed. We see it among school children who are trained too early in computers, and we see it among adults, too. *Is anyone really surprised?*

❦ ❦ ❦

What can be done? As an individual, you can do the following: First, shop local; if you can find what you need in your neighborhood, buy it. Don't buy online unless absolutely necessary. The momentary convenience is not worth killing your local bookstore, specialty market, wineshop, drugstore.

Second, oppose special deals to attract dot-com business to your town; it may drive out local business and raise your rent, too.

Third, ask your elected officials where they stand on tax subsidies for e-commerce, and their impact on your community.

Fourth, contact the growing number of organizations, like those listed below, who are alarmed about favoritism for e-commerce, and the toll it is taking. *Contact us,* and we will send you information about groups working on this issue and their programs.

Fifth, tell your friends.

Institute for Policy Studies/Global Economy Project
International Center for Technology Assessment
International Forum on Globalization
Earth Island Institute
The Nature Institute/NetFuture
Silicon Valley Toxics Coalition
Center for Commercial-free Public Education
The Loka Institute
Center for Media and Democracy
The Foundation for Ethics and Meaning
Institute for Food & Development Policy/Food First
Rainforest Action Network
Collective Heritage Institute/Bioneers Conference
Planet Drum Foundation
We, The World
YES! Magazine
Jacques Ellul Society
The Ecologist Magazine

Signers are all part of a coalition of more than 80 non-profit organizations that favor democratic, localized, ecologically sound alternatives to current practices and policies. This advertisement is #4 in the Megatechnology series. Other ad series discuss extinction crisis, genetic engineering, industrial agriculture and economic globalization. For more information, please contact:

Turning Point Project, 666 Pennsylvania Ave. SE, Suite 302, Washington, DC 20003 • 1-800-249-8712 www.turnpoint.org • email: info@turnpoint.org

Globalization
vs. Nature

The World Trade Organization (WTO) has been granted spectacular powers to challenge every nation's environmental laws. So far, its victims include dolphins, sea turtles, clean water, clean air, safe food, family farms and democracy itself. But it's just getting started.

I n a democratic society, we presume the right to make laws that reflect the deepest values of citizens. But this is no longer the case. With the emergence of the World Trade Organization (WTO), democracy has moved to the back burner. It no longer matters what democratic societies want; what matters is what global corporations want, as expressed and enforced by global trade bureaucracies in Geneva.

Created in 1994, the WTO is already among the most powerful, secretive, undemocratic and *unelected* bodies on Earth. It has been granted unprecedented powers that include the right to rule on whether laws of nations — concerning public health, food safety, small business, labor standards, culture, human rights, or *anything* — are "barriers to trade" by WTO standards. If so, the WTO can demand their abrogation, or enforce very harsh sanctions.

Here's the tradeoff: Nation-states and their citizens sacrifice their democratic rights. Corporate interests gain them. Commercial values are the only ones that count.

I. Against the environment

The very first ruling of the WTO held that regulations under the U.S. Clean Air Act, which set high standards against polluting gasolines, was non-compliant with WTO rules. It was ruled unfair to foreign oil companies that produce dirty oil. As a result, the U.S. government rewrote our regulations so that autos can emit dirtier exhaust. Because of this ruling thousands of people may become sick; some may die.

The very popular Marine Mammal Protection Act — specifically the provision that protects dolphins from being slaughtered by tuna fishermen — was found non-compliant (under a GATT rule; now part of the WTO). And the sea turtle protections under the Endangered Species Act were found "WTO illegal." The U.S. may have to rewrite those protections too. Millions more animals may die.

Soon, we can expect challenges to American laws controlling pesticide use, protecting community water rights, and banning raw log exports, by which both forests and processing jobs are saved. (See photo caption.)

Is this a conspiracy against American laws? No. The WTO has made similar rulings against Japan for refusing imports of fruit products that carry dangerous invasive species. And the European Union (EU) was told it could not forbid imports of beef from animals fed potentially carcinogenic hormones. *(In its entire history, no WTO ruling has ever favored the environment.)*

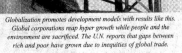
Globalization promotes development models with results like this. Global corporations reap hyper growth while people and the environment are sacrificed. The U.N. reports that gaps between rich and poor have grown due to inequities of global trade.

Examples abound. Laws in *all* countries are being homogenized to the lowest common denominator, penalizing countries with higher health and environmental standards.

Such rulings also have secondary, "chilling" effects. Nation-states are increasingly frightened to stand-up to corporations. Guatemala recently *cancelled* a health law that forbade baby food/infant formula companies from advertising their products as healthier than breast milk. And Canada *cancelled* its ban on the gasoline additive MMT, a well-known potential neurotoxin. (This was under a NAFTA rule now proposed for the WTO.) Canada and Guatemala hoped that by cancelling their public health laws, they would save their taxpayers the costs of a legal battle. But whatever is saved may later be spent on medical

Globalization is the number one threat to world resources. Now the U.S. wants a "Free Logging Agreement" for the WTO's meeting in Seattle. If accepted, the world's last forests may soon look like this.

treatments. It's no conspiracy against the U.S.; it's a conspiracy against the environment. And it's a conspiracy in *favor* of freeing corporations from democratic laws that regulate their excesses.

II. The deeper problem

These attacks on environmental laws are symptoms of a larger environmental problem: globalization itself. Under globalized free trade, countries as diverse as Sweden and India, Canada and Thailand, Bolivia and Russia are meant to merge their economies, and homogenize their values toward maximum commodity accumulation. This puts the whole planet in a single giant economic (and political) structure, with global corporations in charge.

Such corporations depend on never-ending resource supplies, never-ending growth, ever-expanding markets, and constant supplies of cheap labor. So, WTO rules give top priority to such goals. Older values like preserving nature, or protecting workers, or public health, or communities, or democracy are viewed as impediments to global corporate growth.

But how long can this go on? Already we see serious ozone depletion, global warming, habitat and species destruction, epidemic pollution; we are on the brink of a global environmental collapse. How long can we keep growing on a finite earth? *This system is unsustainable.* And one of its *most* unsustainable aspects is the emphasis on *export* production, as the following case shows.

III. The case of globalized food

Any nation's people are most secure when they can produce their own food, using local resources and local labor. This creates livelihoods, minimizes costly transport and waste,

and solidifies communities. It also helps make countries more self-reliant.

Until recently, most people in the world were fed by small farmers, producing diverse staple food crops to serve local communities and local markets. But under WTO rules small farmers are disappearing. In much of the world (including the U.S.) global corporations have taken over most aspects of farming, using chemical-intensive methods, and now biotechnology. Small farmers have given way to miles of single crop luxury *monocultures*, for *export to foreign markets*. Today the average meal Europeans and Americans eat travels about 1,500 miles from source to plate. Instead of eating food grown ten miles away, we eat food from overseas. *And every mile the food travels causes environmental havoc.* The increase in ocean, road, and air transport to ship food back and forth across the planet massively increases energy use, ocean and air pollution, and climate change. It also increases refrigeration, with negative effects on the ozone layer. And it requires far more packaging, putting added pressure on forests. It also requires new infrastructures: roads, ports, airports, and canals, often built in pristine places. Anyway, *industrial food is less healthy*; heavy with chemicals that pollute soil and water and cause public health problems.

Self-sufficiency is giving way to dependency. The situation is already bad, but the proposed new expanded agriculture rules of the WTO will make it far worse, codifying globally the export-oriented agriculture model.

SEE YOU IN SEATTLE?

So much for the bad news. The good news is that hundreds of groups are now protesting what's going on. *This year, many will be focused on the World Trade Organization's Ministerial meeting in Seattle, November 30-December 3.* They are demanding an immediate *halt to WTO expansion* and a total *reassessment of its performance.* For information about public events these groups are sponsoring (from Friday Nov. 26th to Dec. 3rd), and new publications, please contact us.

Sierra Club
Greenpeace U.S.
Friends of the Earth
Food First / Institute for Food & Development Policy
Defenders of Wildlife
David Suzuki Foundation
International Forum on Globalization
Rainforest Action Network
The Humane Society of the United States
Institute for Policy Studies-Global Economy Project
50 Years Is Enough: US Network for Global Economic Justice
Earthjustice Legal Defense Fund
Native Forest Council
People Centered Development Forum
YES! A Journal of Positive Futures
Pacific Environment & Resource Council
Institute for Agriculture and Trade Policy
Global Exchange
Heartwood
Sea Turtle Restoration Project

Signers are all part of a coalition of more than 60 non-profit organizations that favor democratic, localized, ecologically sound alternatives to current practices and policies. This advertisement is #2 in the Economic Globalization series. Other ad series discuss the extinction crisis, genetic engineering, industrial agriculture and megatechnology. For more information, please contact:

Turning Point Project, 310 D St. NE, Washington, DC 20002
1-800-249-8712 · www.turnpoint.org · email: info@turnpoint.org

Three ways industrial food makes you sick.

Industrialized agriculture puts animals in concentration camps where they become crazy and diseased. It puts chemicals on our vegetables and fruit. It slips bacteria genes into our lettuce and biotech growth hormones into our milk without telling us. Then we serve it all to our kids for "dinner."

1. Increased cancer risk

It is not possible to say with certainty that any particular cancer in your family or community has been directly caused by the massive use of chemicals in industrial food production. But many studies implicate pesticides in incidences of leukemia and lymphoma, as well as cancers of the brain, breast, testes and ovaries.

According to the U.S. Food and Drug Administration (FDA), over 35% of the food that they tested in 1998 contained pesticide residues. 53 pesticides classified as "carcinogenic" are presently registered for use on major crops, including apples, tomatoes, and potatoes. 71 different ingredients in pesticides have been found to cause cancer in animals and humans. Consumers Union reported that tests of apples, grapes, green beans, peaches, pears, spinach and winter squash have shown toxicity at hundreds of times the levels of other foods. And many U.S. products have tested as being more toxic than those from other countries.

A National Cancer Institute study found that farmers who used industrial herbicides had six times greater risk than non-farmers of contracting non-Hodgkin's lymphoma, a type of cancer. (American farms use nearly a billion pounds of pesticides each year.) The Environmental Protection Agency (EPA) says it has identified 165 pesticides as potentially carcinogenic.

The EPA also reports that more than 1,000,000 Americans drink water laced with pesticides that have run-off from industrial farms. Agricultural chemicals have also leeched into hundreds of rivers, making fish unsafe to eat, water unsafe to drink or to swim in. Toxic sludge is another worry: heavy metals, chemicals and low-level radioactive wastes are now used as fertilizers in industrial farming. Eventually these find their way into groundwater.

Industrial agriculture advocates argue that the link between pesticides and cancer is not proven; but corporations have said things like that about everything from cigarette safety to asbestos to global warming. We are dealing with the health of families here; *shouldn't the precautionary principle be the standard to apply?*

2. Increase in food-borne diseases

Every week the media carry stories about people becoming sick from bacteria in food. Researchers at the Centers for Disease Control (CDC) estimate that food-borne pathogens infect up to 80 million people a year, and cause over 9,000 deaths in the U.S. alone. The bugs are passed to humans through beef, chicken, or pork, but sometimes from cheese, fruit and vegetables that are carelessly processed.

Food-borne diseases have increased in recent years largely because of the industrialization of animal-raising. Most animal products now come from animals raised in *concentration camp* conditions: thousands are jammed together in tiny cages or on the floors of poorly ventilated stadium-sized buildings; covered with each other's excrement; gone crazy from the crowding; injected with growth-inducing hormones and antibiotics. The CDC says that reported cases of diseases from *Salmonella* and *E. coli* pathogens are ten times what they were two decades ago, and cases of *Campylobacter* are more than double. The CDC saw

These are "factory farm" pigs. Like cows and chickens they are raised in horrendous conditions, crazy from confinement, injected with massive amounts of hormones and antibiotics. The increase of food-borne diseases caused by such treatment has led the industry to suggest nuclear irradiation to solve the problem. Wouldn't healthy animals be a better answer?

none of these bugs in meat until the late 1970s when factory farming became popular.

The use of antibiotics in animal-feed may also be accelerating the alarming growth of antibiotic resistance. *Infections resistant to antibiotics have now become the 11th leading cause of death in the US.* Most reports blame doctors for over-prescribing antibiotics for people. But nearly 50% of U.S. antibiotics are given to animals, not people.

Antibiotics fed to animals eventually cause disease organisms to mutate stronger. *Salmonella, E. coli, Campylobacter* now have antibiotic resistant strains. If you eat a chicken with antibiotic resistant *E. coli*, you might become very sick, and antibiotics may not be able to help. If we don't immediately stop using antibiotics on factory farm animals, we could eventually produce an uncontrollable "supergerm," even a global pandemic.

Scarier still is "Mad Cow Disease." In England, more than 4 million cattle were destroyed, because of fear of infection. No such outbreak is yet admitted in this country, but what of the 100,000 "downed cows" that die each year for unexplained reasons? Since "downed cows" have previously been ground-up and fed to other cows, serious concern is appropriate. The CDC is studying them.

The response from the industrial food industry is to build hundreds of nuclear irradiation stations to kill the bugs. The average pound of hamburger may receive the equivalent of millions of chest x-rays. But is the proliferation of nuclear power stations the right answer to a problem that could be solved by raising animals in a healthy environment? We don't think so.

3. Biotechnology is not the answer

An alarming percentage of our food has been genetically engineered (GE): nearly 50% of US soybeans (and soybean products)

and cotton; 35% of corn and canola. Some estimates are that 50% of packaged foods contain at least one GE ingredient, *but none are labeled for consumers.* Certain tomatoes have virus genes; certain lettuce has bacteria genes; among hundreds of other examples.

Why are no genetically engineered products labeled? The companies refuse to do it, asserting the foods are safe. (None have had independent long-term testing.) And the FDA, intimidated by industry, does not require testing or labels. But wouldn't you like to be informed?

The FDA *has* warned that some genes contain toxins whose effects can be amplified by gene splicing; and that certain GE foods can produce serious allergic reactions. There is also the possibility of "horizontal gene transfer," where viruses spliced into one gene sequence "infect" other species, bringing grave risks. Why doesn't the FDA warn us of these?

Finally, the point is this: The massive change-over from farming to *corporate* farming — with its corresponding change in values — has produced a level of health risk that never existed before.

But you can protect yourself: (1) Buy *"certified organic" foods.* (2) *Call us* at the number at the bottom of the page. We will send you lists of genetically engineered products. 3) *Call the FDA.* (1-888-463-6332). Tell them you want mandatory testing and labeling on all genetically engineered foods, and an end to factory farming of animals.

Center for Food Safety
The Humane Society of the United States
Organic Consumers Association
Mothers & Others for a Livable Planet
Food & Water
EarthSave International
Sustainable Cotton Project
Food First / Institute for Food and Development Policy
Humane Farming Association
David Suzuki Foundation
Earth Island Institute
Institute for Agriculture and Trade Policy
International Forum on Food and Agriculture
The Land Institute
Organic Farming Research Foundation
GRACE Factory Farming Project
Corporate Agribusiness Research Project
Grassroots International
International Society for Ecology and Culture
International Forum on Globalization

Signers are all part of a coalition of more than 60 non-profit organizations that favor democratic, localized, ecologically sound alternatives to current practices and policies. This advertisement is #3 in the Industrial Agriculture series. Other ad series discuss the extinction crisis, genetic engineering, economic globalization and megatechnology. For more information, please contact:
Turning Point Project, 310 D St. NE, Washington, DC 20002
1-800-249-8712 · www.turnpoint.org · email: info@turnpoint.org

Clearcutting in Your National Forests?

It comes as a shock to most people, but your National Forests are not protected from logging. Smokey the Bear is selling off the trees to timber companies at fire sale prices. You can help stop it. Support an end to commercial logging on public lands.

95% of the original forests in the continental United States have already been destroyed. Most of those that remain are on public lands, *your* lands, including National Forests.

These American forests contain some of the most magnificent wilderness areas left in the world, and the most spectacular stands of old-growth forests. There are the great Cathedral Forests of the Pacific Northwest, the Ponderosa Pine forests of the southwest mountains, and the eastern hardwood forests of New York and New England. National Forests are also the country's prime reservoir of biodiversity, and are habitat for thousands of imperiled species. These include: the Gray Wolf, Grizzly Bear, Spotted Owl, Indiana Bat, Coho Salmon, and countless others. When the habitat is gone, so are the animals.

Two-thirds of the big game left in the western United States is on public land. 80% of U.S. rivers have their sources in the National Forests. Tens of millions of people visit the forests every year.

Most Americans assume these forest lands are well protected for posterity by the U.S. Forest Service. But the dreary fact is, the Forest Service protects the trees only long enough to sell them to giant transnational timber companies, who clearcut them, as in the photo above.

Oddly, the Forest Service doesn't get much for them; it sells them at subsidized prices—well below market value. The cost to taxpayers is over $1 billion every year, and you lose your national forests, too.

※ ※ ※

Every year, more than 450,000 acres of trees are cut down within your National Forests. That's about two square miles of deforestation every day. Since 1960, in California and the Pacific Northwest alone, over three million acres of old-growth forests have been cut down by commercial timber companies.

To accommodate this deadly activity, 440,000 miles of logging roads have been jammed through formerly pristine areas. That's more road than the U.S. Interstate Highway System: enough road to drive back and forth from California to New York 150 times. These roads can be as devastating as the logging itself, wreaking terrible damage to wildlife habitat of all kinds.

This kind of commercial logging also has secondary effects. For example, logging and clearcutting on steep slopes and along rivers causes extensive landslides and soil erosion, and increases downstream flooding. One Forest Service study in Six Rivers National Forest in California confirmed that slides and erosion had lately increased 500-2,000 percent. Siltation from this erosion has had catastrophic effects on native fish populations, drastically reducing recreational

The greatest danger to our National Forests is not fire. It's commercial logging at fire-sale prices, as shown in this photo of Gifford Pinchot National Forest. The public is mostly unaware that the U.S. Forest Service is auctioning off vast tracts of trees far below market value. Taxpayers essentially pay for private interests to destroy our public forests. And the loss to biodiversity and the environment is beyond price.

fishing opportunities. In the Pacific Northwest alone, 103 salmon stocks are already extinct, with another 214 at risk.

※ ※ ※

Such abhorrent behavior has not always been the case. When the Forest Service was established in 1897, its mission was to save the forests from uncontrolled exploitation. But pressure soon increased in Congress to open the forests to timber interests. In 1899, the first commercial timber cutting began on National Forest land. In the years after, away from the public eye, a cozy partnership developed between the logging industry and the Forest Service. Timber companies got a cheap wood supply, the Forest Service got a bloated budget from timber sales, and Congressmen got huge campaign donations from the industry. Everybody gained, except the trees, and the public. Meanwhile, Smokey the Bear cried about forest fires.

Things turned a lot worse during the Reagan years, and have continued badly since. Timber interests routinely lobby Congress to authorize more logging, on more acreage, on steeper slopes, in more pristine areas. They argue the country needs the wood, and the jobs, but neither argument is true.

National Forests contribute only 3.3% of U.S. timber consumption: we can live without it. Even a minimum effort put into conservation and recycling would more than make it up. For example, should we be throwing away wooden construction pallets after only one use? (Amazingly, wood pallets account for half of the hardwood lumber production in the U.S.)

As for jobs, timber cutting accounts for less than 3% of all jobs in our National Forests. There would be far more jobs if we stopped all the logging, and put the loggers to work closing the roads, repairing the devastation, and increasing services for recreation. For forest communities, recreation in

our National Forests already provides thirty times as many jobs as logging does. In fact, logging destroys sources of the recreation. The Forest Service has everything backwards.

What you can do

The U.S. National Forests are among our last hopes for wildness on this continent; as they are diminished, we lose species, we lose biodiversity, we lose the opportunity to break out of our urban confines. You can help protect these forests, and the wildlife habitat they provide, by becoming active in the campaign to end all commercial logging on public lands—in your forests. The groups listed in the coalition below are already working to convince the U.S. Forest Service that it's in America's best interests—ecologically and economically—to stop cutting now and to begin repairing and restoring the nation's forests. Please contact us. We will direct you to the groups working on the issue, and provide you with further information.

John Muir Project
Native Forest Council
Native Forest Network
National Forest Protection Alliance
National Ministries-American Baptist Churches
Rainforest Action Network
Religious Campaign for Forest Conservation
RESTORE: The North Woods
Southern Appalachian Biodiversity Project
U.S. Public Interest Research Group
Wild Earth
Biodiversity Legal Foundation
California Wilderness Coalition
Center for Biological Diversity
Christians Caring for Creation
Consumers Choice Council
Earth Island Institute
Forest Guardians
Forest Watch
Friends of the Earth
Grassroots Environmental Effectiveness Network
Greenpeace U.S.
Heartwood
Idaho Sporting Congress

Signers are all part of a coalition of more than 50 non-profit organizations that favor democratic, localized, ecologically sound alternatives to current practices and policies. This advertisement is #3 in the Extinction Crisis series. Other ad series will discuss genetic engineering, economic globalization, industrial agriculture and megatechnology. For more information, please contact:
Turning Point Project, 310 D St. NE, Washington, DC 20002
1-800-249-8712 • www.turnpoint.org • email: info@turnpoint.org

79

The Second Massacre
Of Wounded Knee
Is Taking Place In The Courts.

After the Massacre of Wounded Knee, 1890.

This Time We Can Help Prevent It.

In 1868 the United States Government signed the Fort Laramie Treaty, guaranteeing for all time the sovereignty of the Sioux Nation and its right to South Dakota west of the Missouri River. Almost immediately the white man broke that promise too, and the Sioux lands quickly shrunk to almost nothing. Then in 1890 government forces brutally massacred nearly three hundred Sioux men, women and children after they had surrendered all but one of their weapons. It was to be the last massacre of the Indian Wars, but perhaps only the first at the village of Wounded Knee.

JUST LAST FEBRUARY Wounded Knee was retaken by a group of Indian people belonging to different tribes but with a single immediate goal: that of returning the village to the control of the Oglala Sioux Nation.

Immediately Wounded Knee was surrounded and blockaded by federal marshals, the FBI, the Bureau of Indian Affairs police, the federal border patrol, and elements of the U.S. Army.

[LEGAL MASSACRE]

THE SECOND MASSACRE of Wounded Knee is about to take place in the courts. The U.S. Government is now conducting one of the most massive legal assaults ever waged upon the Indian people as hundreds of members and supporters of the Oglala Sioux Nation are being arrested, indicted and held in excessively high bail.

And for what?

For the crime of demanding once again that the U.S. Government honor its legal agreement with the Sioux Nation.

For the crime of demanding once again that they be allowed to live in accordance with traditional tribal ways and to govern themselves free of outside control and exploitation.

"WHAT TREATY that the whites have kept has the red man broken? Not one. What treaty that the white man ever made with us have they kept? Not one. When I was a boy the Sioux owned the world; the sun rose and set on their land; they sent ten thousand men to battle. Where are the warriors today? Who slew them? Where are our lands? Who owns them? What white man can say I ever stole his land or a penny of his money? Yet, they say I am a thief. What white woman, however lonely, was ever captive or insulted by me? Yet they say I am a bad Indian. What white man has ever seen me drunk? Who has ever come to me hungry and unfed? Who has ever seen me beat my wives or abuse my children? What law have I broken? Is it wrong for me to love my own? Is it wicked for me because my skin is red? Because I am a Sioux; because I was born where my father lived; because I would die for my people and my country?" —Chief Sitting Bull

For the crime of demanding once again the return of their tribal and legal birthright; the sacred lands which gave rise to a magnificent culture and sustained life for thousands of years before being ruthlessly stolen by foreign settlers.

And some merely for the crime of transporting food, medical supplies, clothing and blankets to the sick and starving occupants of the besieged village of Wounded Knee.

Wounded Knee has become a symbol of a much larger issue, a symbol of the abuse which all Native Americans have endured at the hands of the Bureau of Indian Affairs and the Department of the Interior. (Three hundred and seventy-one treaties with various tribes have been signed and broken by the United States Government.) It has demonstrated once again that the policies of this government in dealing with Native Americans have remained essentially unchanged in over four hundred years.

QUALITY OF LIFE:

Here's a sample of the quality of Native American life under the "Care" of the Bureau of Indian Affairs:
—Indian male life expectancy is 44.5 years.
—Suicide is 15 times the national average.
—Malnutrition on reservations is common.
—Unemployment is 90 percent.
—The school dropout rate is 75 percent.
—The average annual Indian family income is $1000.
—95 percent of housing is substandard.

[WE MUST PUT AN END TO IT]

IT WILL BE a long road back for the millions of Native Americans living under the heel of corrupt and uncaring government officials. But the court battles on behalf of the Oglala Sioux Nation and their supporters will go a long way toward dramatizing the plight of Indian peoples throughout the United States.

These trials will involve millions of dollars in legal expenses for the Oglala Sioux. With-

PREVENTING THE LEGAL MASSACRE

At this moment an understaffed and under-financed legal defense committee is feverishly preparing for hearings and trials, the results of which will affect not only the occupants of Wounded Knee, but *every* American for years to come:

✱ Some 450 people were arrested for attempting to bring food and medicine to the beleaguered village, 150 of them outside South Dakota. Some have been indicted under U.S. Code Sec. 231 A 3 (disturbing an arresting officer during time of civil disturbance) and others under the "Rap Brown" act (crossing state lines to incite a riot)—both of questionable constitutionality.

✱ Defense attorneys have had to enter a motion asking a federal judge to dismiss himself from further cases after he offered one leader a "deal" if he would inform on others.

✱ Excessive bonds have been set in gross violation of the Bail Bond Reform Act, and bonds have been revoked for talking to the press.

✱ Attorneys have filed suits resulting from beatings and the destruction and confiscation of residents' property by government and tribal police during and after the occupation.

✱ There have been numerous firings and denials of child care and welfare benefits as reprisals for the occupation.

✱ And the White House negotiators who agreed to meet and discuss grievances with the occupants as part of the "settlement" of the Wounded Knee occupation? They sent a telegram to say they couldn't make it.

out adequate funds the struggle will be useless, the courtroom massacre of Wounded Knee will succeed, and the sickness, poverty and disgrace will continue.

Please give what you can afford to help a proud and courageous people regain the dignity and freedom which is rightfully theirs.

Ramon Roubedeaux, Treasurer
WOUNDED KNEE LEGAL DEFENSE FUND
919 Main Street, Suite 112
Rapid City, South Dakota 57701

I would like to help prevent the legal massacre of Wounded Knee. Enclosed is my contribution for the legal defense of the hundreds indicted for the "crime" of seeking dignity and freedom for Native Americans:

$_____ , $500_____ , $100_____ , $50_____ , $10_____

NAME_____

ADDRESS_____

CITY_____ STATE_____ ZIP_____

Make checks payable to Wounded Knee Legal Defense Fund.

Signed: Vernon Bellecourt, A.I.M.; Stewart Udall, Representative Shirley Chisholm (D-N.Y.); Representative Ron Dellums (D-Calif.); Representative Robert Drinan (D-Mass.); the Rev. David Hunter, National Council of Churches.

5
INDIGENOUS PEOPLES' ISSUES

Centuries of Invasion; Cross-Culture Campaigning;
Successes & Failures; Victory in Hawaii: Pele Defense Fund

ADVERTISING ON INDIGENOUS PEOPLES' issues is often very difficult. It requires arguing *across* cultures and ways of seeing and understanding history and the world. For most Americans, Indigenous cultures, their histories, and belief systems—and the complex details of their nation-hoods—are not familiar. And yet they are relevant to many subsequent conflicts, issues, and engagements in North America over the last five centuries, as we will amplify. We offer this discussion in two parts: history and current events.

PART ONE: HISTORY

Most of us are well aware, of course, that peoples lived in many parts of what is now called "America" before Europeans landed and took over. Across the North American continent, these Indigenous tribes lived in dozens of distinct separate nations. In most cases they'd been living on those lands for hundreds, or in some cases, thousands of years before the Europeans landed here, killed a high percentage of the native inhabitants, appropriated most of the lands, established rules and controls over them, and strictly confined Indigenous sovereignty, behavior, and authority. Nonetheless, many of the surviving Indigenous peoples have continued their struggles for centuries; arguing for their sovereign rights, national recognition, and independence, a battle that continues today.

The problem began in 1492, when Christopher Columbus landed. He came armed not only with guns and cannons, but he was supported by the prevailing *"Inter Caetera Bulls"* rulings of Pope Nich-

olas V and Pope Alexander VI. Those ruling Popes asserted a *"Law of Nations"* that specifically declared that *non-Christian* peoples should *never* be allowed to be owners of the lands their ancestors had lived on for millennia.

The name "America" derived from Amerigo Vespucci, a Spanish businessman who landed on this continent in 1497, five years after Columbus, seeking new resources and properties to develop.

Christian rulings by subsequent Popes on these matters evolved over hundreds of years into the presently prevailing European *"Doctrine of Discovery."* This doctrine asserts and justifies that invading nations have full take-over rights over all Indigenous lands right up to and through the present day. But it's definitely not a settled issue. Details follow.

INDIGENOUS NATIONHOOD

Before the "Americans" came along, there were dozens of separate Indigenous "nations" on this continent, some of which joined in large federations. These included, for example, the Iroquois Confederacy which covered what later became several eastern states. And also the Dakota Confederacy covering most of the mid-west. But none of the dozens of Indigenous nations that lived here ever imagined their nationhood as covering areas nearly as vast as what became the United States. No Indigenous nation ever proposed that the entire continent should be one unitary "nation."

Meanwhile, for hundreds of years, Europe's Christian rulers continued to assert that all lands that had been invaded by Christian nations, anywhere on earth, gained permanent *sovereign land title* which could never be granted back to the original Indigenous tribes. Only to invading European powers.

As more and more Europeans continued to arrive in "America," successions of Indigenous peoples, coast to coast, were militarily overpowered, and their nationhood and traditional systems of self-governance were undermined, diminished, or destroyed. Nonetheless, some of those conquered Indigenous nations—many of whom had been living autonomously on their own lands for 500-5,000 years—do still exist today, albeit in very reduced versions. All are now contained entirely *within* American ruling systems.

Sometimes, formal contracts, or partial "self-rule" agreements, were concluded between the new Americans and the Indigenous nations. Those deals articulated varying degrees of autonomous governance for the surviving Natives, *but no permanent land ownership and no political autonomy* beyond American rule. Tribes were permitted limited *self-governance* only within the legal rules and boundaries of the larger American nation.

Possibly most notable among the still-existing Indigenous nations are the Iroquois Confederacy lands and peoples within New York State. An often noted scholarly fact about the Iroquois is the significant influence their system had upon the original authors of the first US Constitution.

The ancient Iroquois governance system was an elaborate, sophisticated, highly democratic process— which is widely accepted as the oldest living system of participatory democracy on Earth, with accounts of its foundation dating back to the 12th century. Many Scholars believe that this system had a significant influence on the US Constitution's framework. We will come back to this issue later in this chapter. Nonetheless, despite this, the Iroquois were never allowed full national independence.

Some other Indigenous "nations" were also permitted to sustain small "reservations" within US borders, and they too were often allowed to remain "self-governing" to a very limited degree. Those reservation agreements have been officially "authorized" over the last few hundred years via contracts between various Indigenous nations and the *occupying* governing power, the "United States."

In 1978, the US Indian Claims Commission published an astonishing map confirming the exact traditional territories of some 90 separate Indigenous Tribal nations on what is now US land. Many of those nations actually continue to exist today, albeit at a much smaller size, in various status conditions, and under US law. Those nations do retain a limited degree of local "self-governance." And many of them continue to speak of and hope for eventual independence, and recognition, as the *separate independent nations* they once were. But, *none* of these Indigenous tribes have yet been permitted to "own" their lands as separate entities. And none of their internal laws are allowed to super cede any American laws. To this day, not one single Indigenous "nation" has been permitted to return to its former "independent national entity" status, that it enjoyed over many prior centuries.

Forced Removal

While some Indigenous nations do still live on their traditional lands, there have been cases over the past several hundred years where Indigenous peoples have been forcibly moved en-masse *off* their ancient lands. Having sometimes been required to move hundreds or thousands of miles away from their ancestral homeland territories.

Notable among those forced removals was the displacement in the 1800s of thousands of the Dakota peoples from their ancient homelands in what is now the United States mid-west. They were forcibly marched to new lands hundreds of miles south and west of their original lands. Similar dreadful events happened in the early 1900s to the Navajo people, forced to leave their homelands and march about 1,500 miles, to the Utah desert region, where their survivors remain today, sharing desert lands with the Hopis.

And more recently, within the 20th century, there was the forced removal of dozens of Hawaiian and Alaskan Indigenous communities from lands they'd lived on for 500-1000 years before the Europeans invaded and took control. In the case of Native Hawaiians, for example, starting in the mid 1900s, Hawaiians were pushed, by the US military, off their oceanfront arable pasturelands where they'd been living for many centuries. They were forced to move up mountainsides they'd mostly never lived on before.

That forced relocation in Hawaii was accomplished to make way for a vast invasion of sugar plantations, owned and operated by incoming Asians and "Americans," who, with the help of the US military, turned Hawaii into an "occupied" nation. Then, in the late 1990s, the Americans engineered the final overthrow of Hawaii's Queen Liliuokalani and the complete destruction of what was left of Hawaii's government. Sixty years later, in 1959, Hawaii was given "statehood" and has since been mostly governed by its now dominant Caucasian American officials. (We'll come back to the Hawaii and Alaska stories, and some ads that ran in the behalf of Native Hawaiians, later in this chapter.)

Much of the above history, its nuances, and the grim struggles and current efforts of Indigenous nations attempting to retain and affirm their nationhood are beautifully reported in a magnificent book, *Basic Call to Consciousness* (first published in 1978), which I strongly recommend. The book offers brilliant contributions from the great Iroquois scholar, Chief Oren Lyons, as well as the late Indigenous scholars John Mohawk and Jose Barreiros. Their book details the history, its effects, and the legal status of Indigenous peoples of the Americas today, and their continuing efforts to retain or recover true sovereignty over their ancient lands and governance. *(Updated editions of that book are available from the publisher, Akwesasne Notes.)*

I had the great pleasure and good fortune to meet and befriend all three of the activists/authors of that book, and to work with them and several other Indigenous activists. (Some added details about the resistance efforts of Chief Lyons and his colleagues are reported in my own 1989 book, *In the Absence of the Sacred.)*

Unfortunately, few Americans today have been sufficiently well briefed on the detailed histories and impacts of the newly arrived Europeans—mostly Spanish, English, Dutch, or French—which began with Columbus and accelerated into the 17th century up to the present day. Neither do they know many details about the complexities of the formal contracts for "reservation" agreements made between the new Americans and the surviving Indigenous peoples.

The dominant factor in all this, of course, is that the Americans were driven by a corporate-capitalist system which is forever obliged to seek ever more land and more access to more resources. So, continued Indigenous nationhood (or rights), over traditional lands soon became obviously incompatible with American economics and values.

For resource hungry corporations, all accommodation deals with Indigenous peoples tended to be viewed as only *temporary* impediments, that would eventually be overpowered. The net result is clear: the original native inhabitants of the North American continent have had to sacrifice 80-90% of their territories, their rights to self-governance, and their rights to make decisions about land ownership, land use, political rights, cultural practice, economic practice, etc. In the process, they found their cultures and internal political systems profoundly undermined, and grossly misunderstood.

NEW POLITICAL VALUES, RELIGIONS, CULTURES

Beyond the loss of political control, Indigenous religious, political, and cultural practices were all enormously impacted by the domination of the new Americans. Indigenous communities had obviously never been Christian, Jewish, or Muslim, so they were instantly "alien" to new-coming Americans. Among Indigenous peoples, all religions tend to be "nature-based." Worship and respect also tend more toward natural elements: lands, volcanoes, bodies of water, winds, wildlife, mountains, etc., each of which was typically revered as a source of religious perspective and guidance.

As for systems of governance among Indigenous nations, these were far different from the practices of the invading Americans, who had nearly always before lived under Europe's nobility. Traditional Indigenous governance systems tended toward non-hierarchical, community-based, locally-oriented systems; mostly *collective* governance, with primary importance given to an integration, or "partnership," with nature.

For example, in traditional Indigenous communities, there was/is very little "private property." Except for household items, most "ownership" is generally by the whole community. The concept of "private land ownership" never existed in traditional Indigenous communities. Land is viewed as a *primary* environmental factor, like air or water. One can live on it (or drink it, or breathe it) but definitely never "own" it, as Americans seem to demand.

Similarly, economic concepts like economic growth (or capitalism) were generally nowhere visible among Indigenous communities. Decision-making among Indigenous nations, as said, always tended toward *collective* processes, without hierarchical leadership. This was particularly the case among the Iroquois Six Nations peoples, or *Haudenosaunee*, who were among the main Indigenous communities living on the lands of the Eastern part of North America, in and around what became the states of New York and Pennsylvania in the late 1700s.

As mentioned above, it is believed that traditional Indigenous governance systems had a substantial influence on the new Americans, particularly Benjamin Franklin, Thomas Jefferson, and James Madison, the leaders (commonly referred to as the "founding fathers") of a core group charged with seeking alternative systems of government, free from unelected monarchs. Franklin and others were particularly impressed by the Iroquois Confederacy's Great Law of Peace, which united their five (later six) independent tribal nations as a single body while maintaining some of each individual nations' rights. It ultimately encouraged a democratic model to federate the thirteen original American colonies—culminating in the Articles of Confederation, the Constitution, and the United States of America.

The Iroquois Confederacy political processes included consensus decision-making among clans, nations, and ultimately "houses" of governance comprised of each nation. An assembly called the Grand Council would be held, where Chiefs acting as representatives of their clan's interests would meet in an attempt to achieve a joint consensus on all issues. A consensus was reached only if and when all three decision-making bodies were in agreement: the Elder Brothers, Younger Brothers, and Keepers of the Fire. This idea of equal and collaborative governing houses also became a crucial element of the American model and remains so today.

In the Iroquois system, none of the clan Chiefs had top-down authority. Each Chief was primarily a representative or "facilitator" over some particular function: agriculture, hunting, spiritual practice, etc. While all Chiefs were male, they were appointed by their respective Clan Mothers. If or when the Clan Mother or larger clan deemed it desirable that a Chief should be relieved of his role, the Clan Mother would appoint a new Chief in his place. At the local level, clans maintained both a women's and men's council to the Clan Mother that were equal in representation and rights.

Notably, the Indigenous systems did not feature any single "executive" leader, such as a king or queen, while the American system *did* retain a European style single leader with significant top-down authority. However, this leader was no longer "king" but "President," and could be installed or removed by public voting. Thus retaining far fewer authoritarian powers than monarchs in Europe.

But, unlike the Iroquois, the new American governance system did not include *any* participatory rights or any representation for women. Women's participation was not achieved in American governance until about one and a half *centuries* later, in the 1920s.

PART TWO: CURRENT EVENTS

As America's corporate resource needs continue to grow, American forces are *still* invading Indigenous lands, albeit usually via "legal" means rather than military. Current US policy always leans heavily toward primary support for the desires of US corporations, who are ever hungry for more development land, or more oil or coal or other urgent contemporary resources. Just recently, for example, under Donald Trump, protections for wildlife in Alaska, on Indigenous Gwich'in lands, were directly threatened. And Trump (whose family migrated to the US from Germany and whose father was an outspoken Nazi supporter; and Trump himself who is a white "American nationalist") accelerated these land takeover policies, viciously arguing against non-white immigrants who negatively affect our "great white culture". . . as if Americans actually were the original peoples of these lands, which is farcical.

According to new Americans like Trump, "American purity" has been threatened by invading Mexicans, Hondurans, Africans, Asians, as well as those goddamn Natives. But of course, if the point of Trumpism were to actually confirm prior rights for "first Americans," neither Trump, or I (whose parents were born in Europe), nor many of you readers, would be here at all.

So then. Given present circumstances, asking Americans to hold off capitalist land exploitation and development just to preserve the lands, cultures, and religious rights of the native peoples of these lands can lead to confusion. To an average American audience, or, for that matter, to audiences in other parts of the world, Indigenous arguments about their ancient lands and cultures are alien to mainstream media, if not downright weird. So, most do-gooder efforts to argue in behalf of those causes often lead only to indifference.

To an average American, it's the Indigenous people who are the aliens. European Americans have become the "natives" for many people, and so are Euro-based cultures, legal systems, and stances in the larger modern world. The fact that the "Americans" only arrived a few centuries ago, and stole land from societies that were already here, and who'd been living on their lands for a thousand years or more, is shoved under the rug. Indigenous religious or cultural or historic arguments may occasionally be viewed as "charming" or "quaint" but not relevant to the needs of the wider (American/colonial) society.

Part three:
Cross-Culture Campaigns,
Successes & Failures

I have mentioned all the above at the beginning of this chapter because I have long felt that this elemental background needs inclusion when arguments concerning Indigenous rights and issues take place.

The question then becomes: should one really try to argue in behalf of Indigenous causes from the perspective of those little known historic realities, citing agreements that were supposed to protect Indigenous rights? Or, would it be more practical and effective (given how little is generally understood about the legal history) to stick with more contemporary understanding of rights, justice, and freedom; to argue the Indigenous cause within regular mainstream American economic values and frameworks. Historic agreements? Legal rights? Private Property? Contractual terms? Etc.

It's a difficult decision, and it varies from case to case. Later in this chapter, for example, I will discuss in detail all the back-and-forth that was involved in choosing which path to use to fight the multi-dimensional case of the Pele Defense Fund, an Indigenous Hawaiian activist group on the Big Island of Hawaii. They were trying to stop a monstrous development project on their traditional sacred lands. And, with the help of some advertising, they succeeded! I'll come back to that longer complex discussion in a moment.

But first, let's quickly discuss the several ad campaigns that relied on traditional cultural references. Only half of them led to victories.

Winning Campaign:
Gwich'in People of Alaska

Among the most positive campaigns in the group was that of the Gwich'in people. After millennia living in what is now northern Alaska and Canada, in the late 1980s, the Gwich'in found themselves in a desperate battle to protect their Native lands, resources, and culture against the development visions of the Reagan administration—their fortune weighed against speculative oil in the Coastal Plain of the Arctic National Wildlife Refuge. As part of Public Media Center's longtime involvement in the campaign to prevent oil drilling in the Refuge, it played an important role in helping the Gwich'in prepare and place some very timely, effective ads. That ad campaign helped the Gwich'in to survive and maintain most of their traditional way of life. That's the good news. For now.

The Gwich'in, who call themselves the Caribou People, lead a subsistence way of life that has centered around the Porcupine Caribou Herd since the Ice Age, 200 centuries ago. So intertwined are they with the herd—relying on caribou for food, clothing, tools, shelter, and rituals—that they call the herd's calving and nursery ground in the Coastal Plain *Iizhik Gwats'an Gwandaii Goodlit*, or, The Sacred Place Where Life Begins. Gwich'in life and culture, it is said, are tied to the caribou much like the Indigenous people of the Great Plains relied on the buffalo.

The Arctic National Wildlife Refuge is protected wilderness, but only partly. Its biologically sensitive Coastal Plain, coveted by oil companies as the nation's best chance to boost domestic oil production, is *not* permanently protected. So, in the mid-1980s, Reagan's Interior Department advocated opening the territory to exploitation, involving continuous invasive road-building, construction, noise, pollution, and people. This was a typical case of global extractivist culture, with its capitalist value system, threatening the way of life of a traditional, subsistence-based culture advocating for sustainability.

The Gwich'in have always spoken for their inherent human rights. In 1988, tribal chiefs, Elders and youth in Alaska united with those in Canada and formed the Gwich'in Steering Committee to collectively defend their interests.

In 1991, as the Senate prepared to vote on opening the area to development, the Gwich'in Steering Committee and PMC produced huge, striking posters with a beautiful close-up photograph of Gwich'in elder, Isaac Tritt, and placed them in strategic bus shelters and Metro stations in Washington, DC. One ad charged: "Don't let Big Oil send us the way of the buffalo."

The measure was defeated. PMC and the Gwich'in then capitalized on the momentum by running the full-page ad in the New York Times, *"Our Arctic way of life has endured 20,000 years, must we now die for six months of oil?"*(*page 118*) to persuade other Americans to reject Arctic drilling. Amplifying the voice of the Gwich'in people, the ads written by Jono Polansky played a role in informing the US public about the Gwich'in resistance, and ultimately in fending off—for decades—the continuing assault on the Refuge.

In 2017, three decades after Reagan, President Donald Trump strongly advocated the exact same project on the very same lands, just as he did with a lot of Reagan's failed, disgusting ideas. This time, the measure passed; Congress opened the Refuge's Coastal Plain to

" PLEASE STOP YOUR AIRFORCE — IT IS DESTROYING OUR PEOPLE "

1 NITASSINAN

The Innu people have lived in what is now called northern Quebec and Labrador for more than 9,000 years. Until recently, there was little claim on their land or its resources, so they have been able to maintain their traditional life.

The Innu are a nomadic people who spend much of each year moving among their fishing and hunting camps. They never had cities. They had no roads. In their region of thickly forested hills, and magnificent lakes, the Innu hunt caribou, beaver, mink, ducks and geese and they fish. In their camps, they prepare the furs, tan hides, smoke their foods, make snow shoes, and train the younger generations in the ancient Innu knowledge of how to live in the north. This knowledge has been passed this way for hundreds of generations. This is the Innu life. When it is disrupted by outside forces, the Innu existence is threatened.

Canada began to invade Nitassinan after World War II. Hydro-electric projects put dams on the rivers. Mining operations were opened in many areas. Logging began. Roads and communications systems were built on Innu land. And all the while, the Canadian government urged the Indians to give up their ways and become wage-earners and consumers; to become Canadians; to become like everyone else.

The Innu have resisted, insisting they are a sovereign nation that has no treaty with Canada ceding land, or that permits Canada to operate on Innu territory. The Innu want to maintain their lives as they always have. They want their sovereignty recognized.

2 NATO TRAINING

Canada built a military base near Goose Bay in 1946. But it was not until 1980 that it invited NATO countries to participate in low level bomber training flights from that airfield. West Germany and England joined. In 1986 Holland did, too. The United States may soon also participate.

At present, about 10,000 sorties fly over Innu land (some at night) using late model supersonice aircraft that zoom low over the

"We are the Innu people of Nitassinan. Others call our land Labrador or Canada. We have always lived here on our land. It has passed from generation to generation. We spend our time fishing and hunting. Our Nation is 10,000 people.

"Canada has built a military airfield on our land and invited other countries to train their bomber pilots here. Holland is among others that do this. Each year more than 10,000 screaming jets fly only 50 feet above the trees and over our heads. The sudden, terrible noise and shock is scaring our people. It is driving the animals away, and is destroying the fabric of all life here. It is killing us. Imagine if such a thing happened to you. You would fight it.

"We are the rightful owners of this land. We have never ceded any of it away, and yet Canada uses the land without our permission.

"Our request is simple, but it is a matter of life and death for us. Please contact your government and ask that it stop these violations to our way of life and to nature. Thank you." Representative, Innu Nation.

trees. By 1996, the number of flights will increase to 19,000. (If Belgium or Italy joins, the number will increase further.) In addition to just flying, the exercises include high-speed pursuit, target practice, and night vision training for such missions as were recently undertaken in Iraq.

Low level flight training was once held over western Holland and parts of Germany. But the public outrage was so great that the practice was discontinued; exported to the Indian lands in Canada. There, the resistance is just as strong, but it is out of range of mass media. Anyway, Indians have no political power; few non-Indians are concerned for the cause.

The F-16 jets the Dutch airforce use produce a noise of 145 decibels, about 50% higher volume than produces pain in the ear of a listener one mile away. Canada says it enforces rules that aircraft may not fly near Innu hunting camps, though the Innu say this is a lie, that the rule is ignored. In any case, Innu camps are not fixed; people move within about a one hundred mile radius, following the animals, along riverbanks and lakeshores, and through valleys. This is the way the Innu have done for millennia.

The effect of low level flights is devastating. Great caribou herds, upset by the shock and the noise, have abandoned their migration routes. Exhaust fumes damage vegetation and poison the waters. Migrating birds become confused and breeding birds disappear, sometimes abandoning their young. Innu hunters have reported seeing their cattle stampede, waterfowl leave their habitat, and female mink and fox eat their young. Among the people, tension, fear and anger have replaced the serenity and peace of traditional life. Families hesitate to continue their migrations. There is pressure to move to cities; those that do often fall into alcoholism and despair. The traditional way of Innu life is threatened as never before.

3 WHAT CAN BE DONE

Innu leaders have protested to the Canadian government and military at the scene. There have also been occupations of the airfield runways, where hundreds of Indians were arrested and taken to jail. But these have scarcely been noticed by media, and have had little effect. The Innu need help from us. We need to end our participation in these arrogant military exercises.

A few years ago, a delegation of Innu leaders came here to ask our leaders to withdraw Dutch participation in the program.

They were met with disinterest and cynicism. One of our leaders (Van Vlijmen, Christian Democrat) said: "I understand they (the Innu) are going through a sad period. We all have to change: that is evolution." Another (Ploeg, Liberal Party) told the visiting Indians: "We apologize for the noise, but we fly for your freedom."

It is obvious that what we are doing to the Innu would never be accepted here by our own people. To do it to others is the apex of arrogance and irresponsibility. That it means the death of an ages-old culture, which lives by a philosophy of peaceful collaoration with the natural world, and does no harm to us or any other people, makes the matter much more serious and tragic.

Please join us in demanding that all Dutch participation in these flight training programs be ceased at once. Please use the coupons below. They will bring an important message to our leaders. Also send mail and telegrams. Thank you.

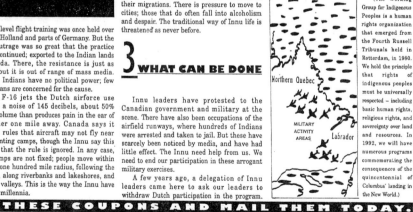

W.I.P.
(Working Group for Indigenous Peoples)
Postbus 40066,
1099 BB Amsterdam

(The Working Group for Indigenous Peoples is a human rights organization that emerged from the Fourth Russell Tribunals held in Rotterdam, in 1960. We hold the principle that rights of indigenous peoples must be universally respected – including basic human rights, religious rights, and sovereignty over land and resources. In 1992, we will have numerous programs commemorating the consequences of the quincentennial of Columbus' landing in the New World.)

oil and gas leasing by a provision snuck into Trump's 2017 Tax Cuts and Jobs Act. (*Let's again repeat Dave Brower's famous warning: "There are no environmental victories; only holding actions. Capitalist economic interests never give up."*)

Meanwhile, former PMC staff approached the Gwich'in again to advise them that the successful ads they ran in 1991 should run again now, almost exactly as written three decades before. As we go to press, that still has not yet happened, but there has been some very good news. In 2021, the Biden administration temporarily halted the extraction plans, and the lease rights are being challenged in the courts. Let's hope permanent protection of the Refuge will be forthcoming.

ANOTHER WIN: INNU PEOPLE, LABRADOR

Another one-shot Indigenous campaign that was eventually successful included an advertisement that I first wrote in English, translated into Dutch, that ran in one of the Netherlands' main newspapers.

The ad was in behalf of the Innu people of Nitassinan, an Indigenous community in Labrador, Quebec. The Innus had been trying for years to stop the Dutch air-force from continuing to fly their very noisy practice bombing flights over Indigenous lands in Labrador. Dutch military planes were making daily runs, zooming low over this isolated thousand-year-old Indigenous community, which was very upset about the practice.

A group of great Dutch activists in Amsterdam, led by Govert de Groot and Jan van Boeckel, had been fighting this cause for years, but not succeeding. They contacted me about trying to do an opposition advertisement, which I wrote in English. They translated to Dutch. That one ad, which ran in the *Volkskrant* in 1992, caused great public outrage in all corners of Dutch society. The issue was raised at the national parliament and on prime-time television. Thousands of people sent in their coupons to the Dutch government and also pledged financial support. The widespread exposure enabled the Innu Support Group to organize a high-visibility symposium at the University of Limburg in Maastricht, entitled "How Can One Own the Sky?" Eventually, the Dutch air-force flight training over Goose Bay stopped, with the official reason that it had become too costly. However, the power of the ad campaign's impact on public opinion should not be underestimated in its influence on the government's final decision.

The ad was later translated and adapted for other campaigns about overflights sponsored by other nations, over similar Indigenous territories. In all such cases, the flights have now been stopped.

PARTIAL VICTORY: CREE PEOPLE, JAMES BAY, QUEBEC

Another partly successful campaign included two ads, one sponsored by Greenpeace, and another sponsored by a coalition of 42 Indigenous groups and leaders in the US and Canada. The ads focused on a giant two-dam project that was planned to be built on Cree and Inuit lands near James Bay, within Quebec. The dams were being constructed by Hydro-Quebec, and the success of the dam-building project was eventually to be measured by how much power the company would be able to sell (and send) to US customers, most notably to the states of Vermont and New York.

The ads ran in New York City, Albany, and Burlington, Vermont, and were hotly debated in the Montreal Press. The campaign was not 100% successful, but the public outrage stimulated by the ads did persuade New York's Gov. Andrew Cuomo to back out of the deal, causing one of the dams to be canceled. That notably diminished the scale and impacts of the whole project, and protected a portion of the Indigenous lands. The other dam is now operating.

FAILED CAMPAIGNS: MAYANS OF GUATEMALA; NAVAJO AND HOPIS, UNITED STATES

Not all of our campaigns on these matters have been successful. A notable failure was the advertised effort by the Tribal Sovereignty Project—a marvelous coalition of 40 US Indigenous groups—in behalf of the Indigenous people of Guatemala. It was an effort to expose the dreadful plight of Guatemala's Mayans, who are by far the majority population of that country and who've lived on that land for 10,000+ years. About 500 years ago, the Mayans were routinely invaded by a murderous religious/military minority from Spain which had more recently been enjoying the political help and commercial support of several US governments and corporations.

I regret to report that the plight of the Mayan majority in that country was not improved in any way by the ad we prepared. In fact, it's arguable that the ad had the opposite effect, angering the Guatemala government which then clamped down still further on the Mayans. By now, those military leaders in Guatemala are mostly gone, but the civilian government is only slightly

MARIO CUOMO, AMERICAN EXPRESS AND — *CATASTROPHE AT JAMES BAY*

[DESTROYING A WILDERNESS THE SIZE OF FRANCE]

© JOHN McHUGH

© DAN BUDNICK/WOODFIN CAMP

The Great Whale River, and the entire James Bay region of Quebec, will soon fall victim to one of the largest, most destructive and most senseless development projects in history. Please urge Governor Cuomo and American Express to reverse their present course.

The developer of the James Bay dams, Hydro-Quebec, says it is sensitive to environmental issues, but look at this photo. More than 10,000 caribou were killed by a torrent of water from a Hydro-Quebec dam, built in the early stages of the project. More caribou, beluga whales, polar bears and hundreds of other species are threatened by new construction.

New York State has signed an electricity deal that will produce an ecological catastrophe on a scale with the devastation of the Amazon: dozens of huge dams, thousands of square miles of flooded lands, mercury poison in lakes and rivers, death to caribou, whales, polar bears, seals and migratory birds. It will shatter the culture of the Cree Indians and Inuit. **It will not provide lower electric rates. It will not bring jobs to New York. And we don't need the electricity.**

Now for the good news: Governor Cuomo can still save the day, and you can help him. Please read below:

1. The James Bay hydroelectric dam development in Canada (see map) is the *largest*, most expensive (about $40 billion) and most destructive energy project *ever* in North America. Created by Hydro-Quebec, the project divides into two phases: Phase I is already complete, with horrendous effects on the land and wildlife. James Bay II was delayed for a time so financing and new markets for electricity could be found. That's when Governor Cuomo and the New York Power Authority came in, saying New York would buy some power. And Shearson Lehman/American Express arranged financial backing for Hydro-Quebec.

2. If the entire project is completed, a system of 650 dams and dikes will block almost every wild river in a wilderness watershed the size of France. Flooding alone will cover five million acres (the size of New Hampshire). Including roads rammed through the wilderness, as well as airports, power lines, power plants and other buildings and facilities, the overall impact will compare with the destruction of the Amazon. Environmentalists call James Bay "the Amazon of the North."

3. We are speaking of one of the great wild areas on the Earth. It's a land of thousands of pristine lakes and rivers. Here is the largest caribou herd in North America. Here is the home of an extremely rare population of freshwater seals. Here is the calving ground of thousands of beluga whales. Polar bears, black bears, lynx, beaver, moose, snow geese, and hundreds of kinds of ducks and migrating birds live here.

4. James Bay is also home to 15,000 Cree Indians and Inuit who have lived peacefully here for 5,000 years, fishing and hunting in an ages-old balanced relationship with nature. But since Hydro-Quebec came on the scene, their world has abruptly changed. The floods have released vast amounts of mercury into their crystal-clear lakes and rivers, poisoning the trout, the white fish and char. All are now inedible. Caribou migration routes have been disrupted by construction and water releases. Thousands have been killed.

5. The Grand Chief of the Cree, Matthew Coon Come, has put it this way:
"The lands of my people have begun to look like a battle-field after a bomb raid. Wildlife habitats are flooded. Rivers and lakes are poisoned by mercury. We can no longer eat the fish. Animals are dying by the thousands. Our values are oriented to nature. If you destroy the land you destroy the Cree people. Parents can no longer teach the children out on the land. We're losing our way of life. We don't want your money. Where can you buy a wilderness so vast and beautiful?"

6. The James Bay project is a virtual Death Warrant for the great Cree Nation. The flooding has stressed their economy. The Natives fear that *new* construction will bring an influx of 20,000 non-natives, further impacting the fragile land and the wildlife, while also bringing prostitution and alcohol. All of this will be a grave threat to Native family life.

7. The government of Quebec says the projects are supported by the Natives. That is not true. The Indians never heard of this project until Phase I construction was secretly started in a remote area. They found out on the radio. Later, they were coerced into signing a retroactive agreement which was supposed to protect their hunting and fishing rights, their land rights and the environment. Like most treaties with Indians, this one has been ignored. The Natives had to go to court to demand enforcement.

8. Finally, however, the keys to the project lie here in the U.S. Both New York state and Vermont have said they would buy power. If they reverse course, the project will not be financially feasible and will be delayed for many years. The only mystery is why the states signed on at all.

9. Energy studies have clearly shown the following: (1) New York and Vermont will not need new energy for at least a decade. (2) Conservation of energy and alternate energy sources would be non-destructive, would reduce air emissions, and would be at least 20% cheaper. (3) Alternate energy sources and investment in energy efficiency are far more labor intensive than hydro: *more jobs!* (4) Transmission of energy by high-powered lines marching across the state is inefficient and potentially dangerous.

10. Why *did* Governor Cuomo back James Bay? Chief Matthew Coon Come of the Cree has said he believes the governor was simply not well advised. In any case, Mr. Cuomo could still become a hero. The governor can have the deal cancelled without penalty. He has asked for a year to decide. *But he needs to cancel now, to send a message to other markets.*

11. As for the financial institutions behind the project — Shearson Lehman/American Express — joined by Merrill Lynch and First Boston — they should be told there are better ways to profit than by devastating a great wilderness, destroying animals, and killing a traditional culture that has shown how to live well without destroying nature. *Please help stop the James Bay project. It makes no sense environmentally or economically. Write letters. Tell your friends. Mail the coupons. Please act now.* Thank you.

James Bay Coalition:
Earth Island Institute
Environmental Planning Lobby
Friends of the Earth
Grand Council of the Cree
Greenpeace
The Humane Society of the United States
National Audubon Society
Native American Council of New York City
Natural Resources Defense Council
Rainforest Action Network
Sierra Club
Student Environmental Action Coalition of New York

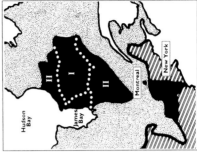

PAID FOR WITH A GRANT FROM GREENPEACE

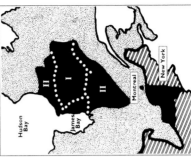

LIONEL DELEVINGNE

Some 650 dams and dikes and thousands of square miles of flooded lands will take a terrible human toll. 15,000 Native people, like the Cree Indian child above, will see many of their lands submerged, communities disrupted, and wildlife endangered. The Cree are suing to block the project.

The James Bay Project, c/o Greenpeace
P.O. Box 2032, New York, NY 10013
I want to help block the James Bay dams:
[ ] I have mailed the other coupons. [ ] Please send me more information about what I can do.
[ ] I am enclosing a tax deductible donation for continued public education about the James Bay dams issue. O$10 O$25 O$50 O$100 OOther _____
[ ] I am an American Express cardholder.
NAME
ADDRESS

Mr. James Robinson III, Chairman, American Express Company
American Express Tower, World Financial Center, 200 Vesey St., New York, NY 10285
There are far better ways for your Shearson Lehman Brothers division to act than by backing the most socially and environmentally irresponsible development project on this continent. Please inform your partners on this project, Merrill Lynch and First Boston, of my opinion, and that you will withdraw all backing from this environmental disaster.
[ ] I am an American Express cardholder. [ ] I am not an American Express cardholder.
NAME
ADDRESS

Governor Mario Cuomo
Executive Chamber, State Capitol, Albany, NY 12224
We don't need more studies to know that the massive James Bay project is the most devastating development project ever in North America. The economic effects are also bad: higher electric rates and fewer jobs than alternative energy schemes. Please have the Hydro-Quebec agreement cancelled now, and help send the message that New Yorkers don't want to destroy nature for expensive electricity that we don't need.
NAME
ADDRESS

PREPARED BY PUBLIC MEDIA CENTER

89

Help Stop The War Against THE MAYAN INDIANS OF GUATEMALA

Despite the attention on Central America there's little reporting of the terrible events in Guatemala: A half million Indian people, descendents of the great Mayan Nation, have been driven from their homes by military regimes gone insane. 15,000 have been killed in massacres. 50,000 have fled, near starvation, to Mexican refugee camps. And it's getting worse.

American Indian organizations have joined to publicize what is going on, and to try to stop it. You can help. Here are the details.

1. Of seven million inhabitants in Guatemala, *a majority are Mayan Indians.* They are part of the oldest continuing civilization on Earth, which has lived on that land since ten thousand years before Columbus "discovered" America.

2. Only 400 years ago, the Spanish Conquistadores arrived. Though the Spanish killed thousands of Mayans and eventually established a country (Guatemala), most of the Mayans survived. The Indians continued to live in traditional ways, in small farming communities. Even today in Guatemala, 22 Mayan languages are spoken. Spanish is the "first" language for a *minority.* A minority with guns.

3. In 1900, new colonists arrived from Europe and the U.S. seeking plantation lands. Indians were driven off their land by subterfuge and force, just as here in the United States. By 1965, 70% of Guatemalan farmland was controlled by 2% of the population. *(Source: UN Food and Agriculture Organization.)*

4. On land where Indians had successfully grown all their own food for thousands of years, there are now only cash crops, owned by foreign corporations and exported abroad: coffee, bananas, cotton and sugar. No food for the local people.

Some Indians work as pickers for $3.00/day. Most live in the highlands where they attempt to survive by farming tiny plots. *More than half the children die of hunger before they reach five.*

5. This system has been maintained by force. Plantation owners installed fierce military regimes and encouraged generals to enrich themselves. (See box II.) But in the 1970s there were signs of hope. The Indians organized farm co-ops, health programs, schools and unions.

6. The landowners and military couldn't stand this. They called the co-ops, schools and unions "communism." They cited a tiny guerrilla movement (500 members nationwide

I. THE INDIANS AND THE ARMY

As in South Africa, where a minority rules a majority by force, the Mayan Indians of Guatemala (60% of the population) live under military siege. According to Survival International, "The Guatemalan government has decided that by definition all Indians are guerrillas ...[The government] seeks to destroy Indian languages, clothing, religious fiestas, even musical instruments." △ Indian families are moved off their farmland to military enclaves "for their own protection." Cornfields and crops are often destroyed, "so guerrillas won't get them," leaving the Indians dependent on handouts. Indian men are forced to join paramilitary "civil patrols." Those who decline are called "guerrillas" and shot. △ Tens of thousands of Indians have fled abroad or become exiles in their own land.

at that time) and launched a terror campaign. Hundreds of union leaders, professors, teachers and agricultural workers were killed. Mountain Indian villages were destroyed and scores of people (mostly Indian) were murdered in the most depraved ways:

"First they came in helicopters and gathered the people together. Then one by one they took them away and killed them...They carry guns but they don't use them on children: [they] grab the children by their feet and smash their heads against a post, or take a rope, tie it around the child, and three pull in one direction, three in another."

7. That report (from *America's Watch: "Human Rights in Guatemala–No Neutrals Allowed"*) is typical of hundreds of sworn statements taken from Indian refugees by such other organizations as Amnesty International, Oxfam America, Survival International.

Rather than driving out guerrillas, such tactics created more of them, often leaving Indian people "caught between two fires." Civil liberties are now nonexistent in Guatemala. Secret executions have been routine. The military can arrest and detain people without charge. The media is banned from criticizing. And conscription is at the point of a gun. (See box I.) The net effect is to reinforce the power of the small clique of landowners, while destroying a traditional Mayan society which has lived on that land for millenia.

8. Where is the U.S. in all this? American helicopters do much of the killing. American fruit, sugar, coffee and textile companies operate plantations. American oil companies are on Indian land. American banks are backing them.

9. In 1977, President Carter stopped aid to Guatemala because of its human rights performance. But Ronald Reagan, who speaks of "freedom" and "human rights" when the subject is Poland, is not concerned about those for the Indian majority in Guatemala. He approved the sale of helicopter equipment used by the Guatemala military. He

urged huge international bank loans to the murderous military regime. He stood for more economic and military aid. (Only when *American* A.I.D. workers were also murdered a few weeks ago did Mr. Reagan show pause in his support.) As for the slaughter and dislocation of the Mayan people, made exiles in their own land, he has yet to utter a word.

▽   △   ▽

To the American Indian people who sign this ad, all of this is old news. We have observed the destruction of Indian populations many times. The process of separating people from their lands, destroying their self-sufficiency, making them dependent, shattering their traditional ways has been known to us for hundreds of years. We could cite a thousand examples. *But in Guatemala it's happening now.*

Here is what you can do: Use the coupons below. Send money to help pay for this ad and to aid the refugees. Work for the following: (1) No more U.S. military or economic aid, (2) creation of a human rights commission under the UN or OAS to monitor events in Guatemala, (3) UN monitors at the Guatemala-Mexico border, to prevent raids against the refugees, and (4) granting asylum to refugee Mayans in the U.S. *Don't let the U.S. send Indians back to Guatemala to be slaughtered.* Please act today. Thank you.

III. FOOD WAR
In Guatemala, more than half the children die of hunger before they reach the age of five. Why? A handful of plantation owners and their military surrogates have driven the Mayan Indians off farmlands they've occupied for 10,000 years. Now, 70% of the farmland is controlled by 2% of the people, who grow only export crops like coffee and sugar. Self-sufficient Indian societies are being destroyed.

II. MINORITY RULERS
A succession of military dictators has been extremely violent towards the Indian majority. △ General Lucas Garcia (left) initiated the 1978-1982 terror campaigns in the Indian highlands which left 15000 dead and caused tens of thousands to flee their homes. In the process, Lucas stole for his personal use thousands of acres of Indian land. △ Lucas was overthrown in 1982 by General Ephrain Rios Montt (center) a fundamentalist preacher. He proclaimed "God's Will" and then killed some 5000 more Indians, caused 30,000 to flee to Mexico, and made homeless another quarter of a million. △ Now, General Oscar Humberto Mejia Victores has overthrown Rios Montt. Mejia was Vice Minister of Defense under Lucas and Minister of Defense under Rios Montt. So he was the actual supervisor of the massacres. He has called all Indian leaders "subversives." △ Who's next? To the Indians, it scarcely matters. What's needed is the end of military rule and a government which is responsive to the majority: Indians.

Please clip and mail

<table>
<tr>
<td>

To: *Kenneth Dam,* Deputy Secretary of State, State Dept., Washington, D.C. 20520

The U.S. must protest the brutal treatment of the Mayan Indian majority in Guatemala. Instead, we've supported dictators who've made the Indians exiles in their own land. *Please:* Demand a halt of Guatemala's raids on refugee camps. Maintain the new ban on military and economic aid, and on commercial military sales. Grant the Indian refugees in the U.S. political asylum.

Name

Address

</td>
<td>

To: *General Oscar Humberto Mejia Victores,* President of Guatemala, c/o Guatemala Embassy, 2220 "R" St., NW, Washington D.C. 20008

Indian people are not "subversive" for demanding land to grow food and a halt to military siege. The Indians are a majority in Guatemala, and have been there for 10,000 years. Stop removal of Indian people from their traditional lands. And stop the murderous raids on refugee camps in Chiapas, Mexico.

Name

Address

</td>
<td>

To: *Tribal Sovereignty Program,* (Daniel Bomberry, Coordinator), Guatemala Project, P.O. Box 10, Forestville, CA 95436

☐ I mailed the coupons.
☐ Please mail me a list of organizations and activities, so that I may participate further.
☐ Here is a donation of $_____ to help place this ad elsewhere, and/or to aid refugees.

Name

Address

</td>
</tr>
</table>

Signed by: American Indian Lawyers Training Program *(Oakland),* American Indian Movement *(Oakland),* Americans for Indian Opportunity *(Wash. DC),* Assembly of First Nations *(Ottawa, Ont.),* Dene Nation *(Yellowknife, NW Territories),* Indian Law Resource Center *(Wash. DC),* Indigenous People's Network *(Wash. DC),* International Indian Treaty Council *(New York),* Lakota Treaty Council *(Pine Ridge, SD),* National Coalition to Support Indian Treaties *(Seattle),* National Congress of American Indians *(Wash. DC),* National Indian Youth Council *(Albuquerque),* Native Nevadans for Political Action and Education *(Nixon, NV),* Northwest Indian Women's Circle *(Tacoma, WA),* Oglala Sioux Tribe *(Pine Ridge, SD),* Tribal Sovereignty Program *(Forestville, CA),* Winnebago Tribe *(Winnebago, NE),* World Council of Indigenous Peoples *(Lethbridge, Alberta). Also Endorsed by:* Anthropology Resource Center *(Boston),* Cultural Survival *(Cambridge),* Institute for Food and Development Policy *(San Francisco),* Oxfam America *(Boston),* Plenty International *(Wash. DC).*

Produced by Public Media Center

improved from the 1980s, when we ran that ad. Also unsuccessful was the actually very interesting ad in behalf of the Hopi and Navajo peoples of the southwest desert of the US who have been in a century-long struggle with the US, attempting to hold-off continuous incursions from America. Although these ads were not successful, they contain excellent discussions of the most relevant values and issues that continue today. I particularly love the quote from John Lansa, a Hopi chief, speaking against the commercial strip-mining projects that invaded the sacred Black Mesa area of the Hopi reservation:

> "Nature is everything to the Hopis. It is the land, all living things, the water, the trees, the rocks—it is everything. It is the force that comes from these things that keeps the world together . . . . This is the spiritual center of this land. This is the most sacred place, right here on this mesa . . . . Before the white man came, all the Hopi were happy and sang all the time. The Hopi didn't have any class structure at all—no bosses, no policemen, no judges; everything was equal . . . . Our lives were very rich and humble. We never take more than we need. We live close to the earth, as laid out by the great spirit. When the white men came, everything started getting out of balance. The white brother has no spiritual knowledge, only technical . . . . Now there is a big strip mine where coal comes out of the earth to send electricity to the cities. They cut across our sacred shrines and destroy our prayers to the six directions . . . . Peabody is tearing up the land and destroying our sacred mountain . . . It's very hard that Peabody takes away the water because it upsets the balance of things. You can't do things like that and have nature in balance."

As the author of those ads, I felt badly about their failures. However, there were some major successes, notably in Hawaii. One ad tells the full and interesting story on that.

MAJOR SUCCESS: NATIVE HAWAIIAN PELE DEFENSE FUND

This story concerns the 1988 campaign by the Native Hawaiian's Pele Defense Fund. They were attempting to save the revered virgin Puna Rainforest on the south-central part of the Big Island of Hawaii. This is old-growth forest land that had been recognized and codified more than a century ago in agreements between the American invaders of the Hawaiian islands and the Indigenous peoples of those lands, who considered those forests to be among their most sacred. *Off-limits* for any form of development.

But, in the mid 1980s, the government of the state of Hawaii decided to ignore the decades-old Puna rainforest agreement, and announced a plan to cut down the forest and mine the lands for geothermal energy. The goal was to then ship the energy over to Waikiki to serve rapidly expanding tourist hotels and amusements. Pele Defense Fund was horrified by this prospect and fought back hard, including publishing two advertisements that ultimately achieved 100% success. The details of that story present a good illustration of the importance of carefully choosing correct campaign arguments.

Pele Defense Fund was then and still is led by three dedicated Indigenous practitioners: Palikapu Dedman, a local fisherman on Big Island, Lehua Lopez, a writer and public spokesperson for Indigenous issues, and Emmet Aluli, a Native Hawaiian practicing MD from the island of Molokai.

I had first met Aluli back in the mid-1970s. I had joined him in an earlier protest movement to stop the US military from continuing to use the small and sacred island of Kahoolawe, off the coast of Maui, for bombing practice. The bombing had been going on there since World War II.

In the early 1970s, Native people started protesting against the bombings. They began taking armadas of canoes and small row-boats overnight from Maui, then landing and occupying parts of Kahoolawe for weeks at a time before the US military could evict them. Two protestors died in the process from stepping on live ordinance on the grounds.

Eventually, after some legal battles, a group of Native Hawaiian protesters were permitted to spend occasional weekends camping and attempting to restore Kahoolawe. Pathways were cleared among the rubble so one could hike carefully over the central hills and around the island. At the invitation of Dr. Aluli and another great Indigenous Hawaiian activist, Colette Machado, I was among a few non-Indigenous people permitted to join the protests. Finally, in the late 1970s, the US military announced it would no longer use the island for training exercises or practice bombings, and it completely withdrew. But, they left behind a mess of bombed-out trees and lands, and mountains of military rubble. Native Hawaiians were given permission to restore the islands, and they received some federal funding support towards the cleanup. They've been making impressive progress ever since.

But that's *not* the main story I want to tell in this section. Let's go back over to the Big Island of Hawaii.

A decade after Kahoolawe, in the mid 1980s, Aluli and Dedman came to San Francisco to meet with me. They told me about their efforts to fight a massive new geothermal project planned for their sacred Puna forest area on the Big Island. This was

91

COME TO HAWAII

Swim in polluted water; Breathe toxic fumes; See ugly electric towers.

Help us prevent the industrialization of Paradise. Here are the details:

1. The largest and most expensive energy development ever on the Big Island of Hawaii is now getting underway—geothermal drilling on the slopes of the active Mauna Loa volcano, at Kilauea. One drilling site sits in the midst of a glorious and unique Hawaiian rainforest. (See Box A) The whole project is only a few miles upwind from Hawaii Volcanoes National Park and from neighborhoods where thousands of people live. *None of these places will ever be the same.*

2. To Native Hawaiians, the drilling itself is a brutal violation of our religious beliefs. (See Box B) For us, the volcano is a manifestation of Pele, the living Goddess sacred to Native Hawaiian religion. To violate Pele by drilling into her body is as outrageous to us as someone bulldozing the Sistine Chapel would be to Christians. But *you* don't have to be religious to be horrified.

3. The developers say geothermal drilling does not harm the environment. Nothing could be less true. For example, geothermal production releases into the air a toxic

THE NEW HAWAII?

Here is an artist's conception of what the Big Island of Hawaii may look like if plans proceed for the new geothermal energy development, undersea cable, and industrialization. Thousands of electrical towers, 87 feet tall, marching across the land. Noxious fumes. Huge trucks barrelling through serene neighborhoods. A metals smelting plant pouring toxic waste into the sea. Rainforest destruction. Pollution of the sea. Overbuilding of cities. Higher utility rates, higher taxes, destruction of our quality of life. And for Native Hawaiians, the ultimate insult to Pele. Is this what you want for Hawaii? Is this the Hawaii you love? If not, you can help change the future. Please mail the coupons.

Illustrations and photos by Elizabeth Garsonnin

To: Senator Daniel Inouye, 722 Hart Office Bldg., Washington, DC 20510

I love Hawaii, and so ask you to join me in opposing geothermal drilling on the Big Island. As senior Senator from Hawaii, please fight this assault on the quality of life and the environment, as well as the higher taxes and utility rates it causes. And as Chair of the Senate Indian Affairs Committee, I ask you to support Native Hawaiian religion as you have Native American religion.

Name _____
Address _____

To: Mayor Dante Carpenter, Hawaii County, 25 Aupuni Street, Hilo, Hawaii 96720

Please withdraw your support for geothermal development on the Big Island. It will lead to further industrialization and destruction of the natural beauty and quality of life which all Americans have admired, till now. I feel you should support the Native Hawaiian people who are fighting to protect their land and culture.

Name _____
Address _____

To: Governor John Waihe'e, State Capitol, Honolulu, Hawaii 96813

Industrialization of Hawaii, via massive geothermal energy projects and undersea pipeline boondoggles —which we all pay for—will destroy the quality of life that made Hawaii a vacation paradise for Americans. Please withdraw your support for such counterproductive developments, and instead support the Native Hawaiians who are fighting to preserve their culture, religion and environment.

Name _____
Address _____

To: Pele Defense Fund, P.O. Box 404, Volcano, Hawaii, 96785

I support your efforts to preserve the Big Island's beauty and your traditions and culture.
☐ I have mailed the coupons.
☐ Here's a tax deductible donation of $10 —, $35 —, $100 —, $100C —, other ___ for education and litigation. (Checks payable to: *Protect Kahoolawe Fund/Pele Defense.*)

Name _____
Address _____

corrosive gas called hydrogen sulfide, which smells like rotten eggs or stinking sewage. At very low levels the odor is annoying, and can be sickening to the very young, the ill, the elderly, and pregnant women. At higher levels, the gas can kill. Depending how the wind is blowing, even normal operations may make life unpleasant for nearby communities. These include the National Park, where two million visitors come each year, a major economic resource. How do you think visitors will react to the stink? And what of *non-normal events?* What if there's an accident?

4. Remember, the drilling is into an *active volcano.* Earth movements are common. So are lava eruptions and cracks in the Earth. Only one such event could break-up the wells and pipelines, releasing a toxic cloud over thousands of homes. It could also blow over the spectacular black sand beach at Kalapana, and around the bend to Kona. The developers say this risk is small, but they are gambling with our homes, our future, and as we'll see, our money.

5. Then there's the noise. When geothermal wells are first vented, the closest sound to it is a 747 taking off. *Except this takeoff can last eight hours for several days per week.* Then there'll be clanging pipes and huge tractor-trailer trucks climbing up and down the once serene hills, night and day. For people who moved to this place for its wonderful rural quality, and for a peaceful future for their kids, that dream might be destroyed.

6. Power lines. Huge new electrical towers and power lines will crisscross the southern part of Hawaii. Worse, if the *next* stage proceeds (an undersea cable), more than 1,000 electrical towers, 87 feet tall (as tall as a nine-story building) will march across the island. The route is directly over The Saddle between Mauna Loa and Mauna Kea. Right now that route offers visitors one of the most magnificent, unusual and uncrowded scenic drives in the world.

7. One of the developers, Campbell Estate, says it hopes to generate *at least 300 megawatts* of electricity from their geothermal projects. Other developers will add to this total. But as the Big Island only uses about 110 MGW, the big question remains: What on earth is such excess energy for? Two things: the rampant industrialization of *this* island, and, via the underwater cable, to ship power to Oahu and Maui so *they* can develop even more.

8. Here on the Big Island, the plans include a missile launching facility, expanded resort and condo development, expanded cities and worst of all, a metals smelting plant. This will service the ocean mining industry, converting metal-bearing ocean crust into manganese, cobalt and nickel. The plants will also produce a huge toxic waste problem, with the poisons to be dumped into ocean trenches. These same trenches are now among our richest fishing grounds. So much for our local fishermen. And so much for our coastline. And for Hawaii, it will be a step from which there's no going back.

9. The developers tell us new jobs will result. But none of these industries are labor intensive. Anyway, the few high paying *skilled* jobs will be filled by people imported from the mainland. The *local* people will wind up with jobs as janitors, sweepers, bus boys and maids. Is that the economic help we need? Miserable jobs in an industrial slum? No. What we need is this: Clean water and air. Our fishing grounds and our beaches preserved. And if it's our economic welfare that's the goal, then we'd greatly appreciate the release of some Hawaiian Homelands for agriculture, as was promised long ago.

10. Now for the science fiction part; transmitting the surplus power to Maui and Oahu by an undersea cable. Here's the problem: The Big Island-Maui portion of the cable must cross a deep, treacherous, geologically unstable channel, 6,500 feet deep. *That is seven times deeper than any cable has ever been laid.* So far, no one has any idea how to build such a cable, but they're going for it—funded by the power company, the State of Hawaii and the U.S. government. For Hawaii residents that means much higher utility rates, and higher state and federal taxes. (Mainlanders pay only once.)

11. The developers claim that building this fantasy cable will cost "only" one and three quarters billion dollars. (If true that would cost every family in this state more than $6,000 in new interest and taxes.) But independent analysts put the real cost much higher—more than *four* billion. And when the money is spent, what will we have? We'll have a fragile undersea cable (maybe) that could be destroyed at any time. We'll have the further overdevelopment of Oahu and Maui. On Hawaii, we'll have toxic fumes, noise, ocean and air pollution, fields of electrical towers, higher rents, higher taxes, higher utility bills and a decimated rainforest. We'll have a direct blow at tourism and at our lifestyle. What a deal.

12. Do alternatives exist? Of course they do if only we reject that industrial vision of Hawaii. Our true energy needs can be met by expanded use of wind, biomass, solar energy, waste heat recovery, more efficient architecture and most of all, conservation. (Merely converting Oahu residences to solar water heating would save 140 MGW). Such steps would not destroy our islands' beauty, the land, the ocean, or the quality of life.

Until now, Native Hawaiian people who sponsor this ad, acting to protect our religion, have not sought outside support. But two geothermal projects are blazing forward. We need your help. Everyone who lives in this state has a stake in the outcome. In fact Hawaii is part of the dreams of every American. So please join us. Send the coupons. Help with a donation. Post this ad in a public place. Keep in touch. *Mahalo.*

PELE DEFENSE FUND
P.O. Box 404
Volcano, Hawaii 96785

Box A.

RAINFOREST BODY COUNT

'OU Hawaiian Honeycreeper

'IO Hawaiian Hawk

LANALANA Happy Face Spider

The Hawaiian rainforest is unique in the world. 98% of the native plants, insects, birds and animals can be found nowhere else on the planet, but here. But many of these are now endangered as are all three above. With geothermal drilling, the destruction will be vast and permanent. You can stop it.

Box B.

DESECRATION OF PELE
The Hawaiian Religious Viewpoint

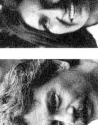

The United States is supposed to guarantee freedom for all religious worship, but it looks like it doesn't apply to all religions. The Hawaiian religion, still observed by thousands of us, is different from Christianity, or Judaism or Buddhism. Like Native Americans, our religion is in Nature. To Hawaiians, our Gods and Goddesses are alive and with us. On the Big Island, the Goddess Pele appears to us daily in all her forms. She is the volcano, the lava, the steam, the heat, the vapor. Her family is present in the fern, certain shrubs, certain native trees. She is the land itself. We pray to her daily. Many of our chants and hula are for her and about her. We believe some of us are descended from her. This is the way we have believed for thousands of years. For us it is a sacrilege to drill holes into Pele's body, to capture her steam, to destroy her rainforests, all so some people can make money. Such things should never be done to sacred places. But when we argue that point in courts or commissions they don't take us seriously. We are ignored. This is not right. It is not respectful of our religion or of Hawaiian people. It is also a violation of American law protecting religious worship. So we are struggling to stop geothermal drilling of Pele. We are taking our case to the U.S. Supreme Court. And we are running ads. Please join our campaign. Use the coupons.

Ralph Palikapu Dedman, fisherman, Punalu'u, Hawaii (President, Pele Defense Fund)
Noa Emmett Aluli, physician, Kaunakakai, Molokai (Vice President, Pele Defense Fund)
Lehua Lopez, environmental activist, Hilo, Hawaii (Secretary-Treasurer, Pele Defense Fund)

especially alarming, given that those lands had already been officially recognized and formally protected decades earlier as "sacred lands" for Indigenous peoples. Now the Hawaii government was trying to reverse itself. The preserved forested land was suddenly to be *clear-cut* and *deep-mined* for geothermal energy.

Pele Defense Fund had managed to raise sufficient money for an advertising campaign. So, after excellent discussions, we proceeded. But then we came face to face with some difficult strategic choices, and found we disagreed on a central point.

My first instinct was to produce an ad that put this entire project into a broad educational and historical perspective, from the Native Hawaiian viewpoint. It's a very good example of a typical negative story about the history of American invasion and takeover, and the negative impacts on Indigenous peoples within what became US boundaries. I thought it would be important to enlighten American tourists, headed for their vacations in "Paradise," about what had happened in Hawaii over the last centuries. I planned to trace the whole history of a self-sufficient, autonomous, thriving territory of Hawaii, that had then been invaded by a brutal US military less than a century earlier, then occupied and dominated, primarily in behalf of gigantic US sugar plantation corporate interests.

The original populations of Hawaii and their traditional governance and cultural and religious practices—and their relationships to land—had already been violently undermined and shoved-back off most of their traditional lands. This, despite agreements to the contrary that had been made a century before between the native Hawaiians and the advancing Americans' interests.

American economic and military forces were, at first, largely pushing forward mainly in behalf of the rapidly growing Hawaii sugar plantations' export production. Those enterprises then brought large new populations of foreign plantation workers and compatible businesses: Chinese, Japanese, Koreans, Filipinos, Portuguese, Puerto Ricans, and others, as well as Americans. The rights of Native Hawaiians were being ignored.

By 1893, American sugar plantation interests, supported by a massive US military presence, decided they needed to accelerate the inevitable. That was the year the military supervised the overthrow of the remaining Hawaiian monarchy, thus throttling the little that was left of traditional governing systems on the islands. Then, in 1894, the United States mainland government formally declared that Hawaii was no longer an independent nation. It was thenceforth a "US territory," and was to be ruled by the US military. All vestiges of Hawaiian traditional governance were

wiped out, as well as any recognitions of sacred lands which had been so important for traditional religious practice. Most Native populations were shoved off their traditional oceanfront lands and forced to go "mauka," up the mountain-sides, to new territory. Hawaii then evolved beyond just sugar industries into a mecca for glorious tourism.

Seventy years later, in 1959, with no remaining remnants of self-governance for Native Hawaiians, the "new" immigrant population of Hawaii—supported by the US military who'd been stationed there since World War II—officially voted to become the 50th US state. That decision was notably *opposed* by Native Hawaiians, who strongly voted against it. But they were by now disempowered and outnumbered by the far larger population of new "Americans," now living in Hawaii and ran the businesses that catered to and promoted Hawaii's elaborate tourist industry, monetizing the island's remaining beauty and sugar industry.

But now, a half century later, when tourists vacation on the "Big Island" or stroll the beaches of Waikiki or Hanalei, they have very little knowledge of that history, and no idea whose ancient lands and sacred places they're actually walking on. And no-one is telling them. And yet, the whole story that happened on these once paradisaical islands of Hawaii has been every bit as grim as anything that happened to other Indigenous peoples on the US "mainland" throughout the 18th, 19th, and into the 20th centuries.

So, I assumed that's what the advertisement that we were preparing should cover. But then, after discussions with Palikapu, Lehua, and Emmet, it was clear that *their* most urgent goal was very different than mine. They were less aimed at the grim history of US-Hawaiian relations, but more aimed at focusing on and saving this one important ancient forest, *now*! They argued for practicality. We had to choose an approach that had the best chance of complete victory on that issue, even without totally re-educating the average US citizen. They did not want to water down the central argument by broadening it to other issues.

We decided on a practical compromise. The ad would put much less attention on the bitter Native Hawaiian history of subjugation or on the nuances of Indigenous religious values that the forests and the sacred volcano represented. Instead we'd take a *direct path to victory*.

We would focus our arguments on telling American tourists that their beloved vacation paradise was being rapidly destroyed in many ways, notably including cutting down that beautiful, sacred, Pele forest. We would urge Americans to demand that the forest they loved should be saved. So, instead of raising all those nuanced spiritual, cultural, and historic arguments about Indigenous peoples that risked boring Americans, we'd concentrate on the rapid environmental destruction of a glorious Pacific Paradise in behalf of petty commercial motives. And, we would warn potential tourists from the mainland that maybe they should be re-thinking their plans of coming to a dying Hawaii. That approach notably also had the best chance to *scare the hell* out of Hawaii's government and its tourism industries.

The ad was inserted in the most important mainland newspapers that spoke to potential tourists to Hawaii: *The New York Times* and *San Francisco Chronicle,* with the *Los Angeles Times* and other papers across the country reporting on its content.

We also ran a slightly altered version of the ad in the *Honolulu Advertiser,* Hawaii's most important newspaper, so local people and governments could also see it. But we changed the main heading to address more local concerns. It is otherwise exactly the same ad as ran in the mainland newspapers.

Both ads went on to describe the giant geothermal energy project that was on the verge of being built in the magnificent ancient Puna Rainforest in the Southeastern part of the Big Island. An elaborate illustration by Elizabeth Garsonnin showed how the proposed new project would destroy the ancient forest, as well as putting criss-crossing gigantic 87-foot-tall electrical towers across a hundred miles of the otherwise gorgeous central region of the Big Island. It would destroy one of the world's most spectacular landscapes. Then the gas would be piped deep undersea to Oahu—a process that had never been successfully tried and had once been thought too dangerous. The developers' goal was to feed still more development energy toward expansion of Waikiki's tourism, while ignoring the added pollution of the oceans off Oahu.

Geothermal production also releases terrible toxic smells, like stinking sewage. And drilling into live volcanoes on the Big Island can potentially bring on giant eruptions, earthquakes, and also waste products that will pour down to the sea. And it was all very costly. Taxes would have to be raised to pay for it!

The ads did include one large box with photos of the Pele Defense Fund leadership, who did express a far more direct Native viewpoint and motive. The box went on to describe traditional Native Hawaiian religious and cultural arguments, which were being ignored by the government. They pointed out that Puna was a place that had been protected as an Indigenous sacred zone for many decades, but not any more:

> "The United States is supposed to guarantee freedom for all religious worship, but it looks like it doesn't apply to all religions…. To Hawaiians, our

> Gods and Goddesses are alive and with us. On the Big Island, the Goddess Pele appears to us daily in all her forms. She is the volcano, the lava, the steam, the heat, the vapor….she is the land itself. We pray to her daily….For us it is a sacrilege to drill holes into Pele's body, to capture her steam, to destroy her rainforests, all so some people can make money. …But when we argue that point in courts, they don't take us seriously. We are ignored. This is not right."

The ad suggested that tourists should re-consider whether they wanted to come to Hawaii at all!

When the ads ran in New York and California, they produced an instant mountain of coupon complaints mailed to Hawaii's governor and to Senator Daniel Inouye. The mail poured in from the continental metropolises that provided most of the tourism dollars for the Hawaii economy. We then also informed Hawaii's government that we planned to run this ad again, and again, and that they'd be followed by more ads directed against tourism to Hawaii. We said the campaign would continue for several months.

In fact, we didn't know for sure if that was true. We had no idea, as yet, where we might get additional money for repeated insertions. But that was our intention.

As soon as the ads appeared, the Hawaii government freaked-out, fearing the effects all this might have on long-run tourism, Hawaii's number one economic source. Major local protests of the development followed, and the entire project was halted. The developers were forced to start from scratch, and to build on a less culturally and environmentally sensitive site. The land later became one of the first significant parcels to be returned to Hawaiian control.

So, there you have a religious cultural group, acting in behalf of its traditional cultural and religious values, while using arguments that could speak across a massive cultural divide, directly to thousands of tourists who visit Hawaii. The ad was basically telling them: "Please, don't come here anymore. Your vacation paradise is being ruined!"

A schoolroom of California kids shot dead every two weeks.

Isn't that enough?

Handguns have become the leading killer of California's children... the murder weapon of choice and the #1 teen suicide method. California is selling a thousand more each day and more kids are getting their hands on them with tragic results. Many responsible Californians agree on four steps that must be taken:

1 **Ban Saturday Night Specials.** These cheaply-made, cheap-to-buy handguns are disproportionately represented in homicides and other crimes. Imports were banned 25 years ago. Domestic Saturday Night Specials, 80% now made in Southern California, weren't.

2 **Let communities decide what rules to live by.** Most states preempt local gun controls with looser state laws, California among them. But where sensible laws rule, handgun violence declines. Twelve California counties account for most youth killings in the state. Wouldn't home rule make our streets and our children safer?

3 **Increase the potential penalty for carrying a concealed handgun.** Right now, it's a misdemeanor to carry a non-permitted, loaded pistol in your jacket pocket or tucked in your waistband — like jaywalking, or dropping a gum wrapper — while brass knuckles can be prosecuted as a felony.

4 **Treat handguns like other consumer products.** There are now more safety rules on teddy bears than on handguns, and basic devices that could prevent most accidental shootings are not required. Why not bring safety standards for handguns under the jurisdiction of the Bureau of Alcohol, Tobacco and Firearms?

These proposals were presented as part of a recent videoconference among 1,500 Californians and others who want to prevent handgun violence against kids. It looked at handgun violence as a public health menace, and how to reduce it.

As Donna Shalala, U.S. Secretary of Health and Human Services, noted "...gun violence against children is not an inner city problem. It's not a problem of poor people. It's not a problem confined to certain genders or ethnic groups. And, most important, it is not — nor will it ever be — somebody else's problem. It is our problem."
In response to the tragic consequences of violence in our society, The California Wellness Foundation is dedicating more than $35 million over five years to support a comprehensive Violence Prevention Initiative. To learn more about the Campaign to Prevent Handgun Violence Against Kids and other projects of the Initiative, please write us.

The California Wellness Foundation
6320 Canoga Avenue, Suite 1700
Woodland Hills, California 91367

PUBLIC MEDIA CENTER

6
MISCELLANEOUS *ONE-SHOT* AD CAMPAIGNS

Getting Personal Issues Noticed, Trying for the "Hole-In-One"
Desperation Efforts, Little Noted Issues,
Against Guns, Rolling the Dice

MOST OF THIS BOOK till now has described sustained campaigns that consist of multiple ads from individuals or organizations, inserted over periods of time, from weeks to months to years. This was the case with Sierra Club, Planned Parenthood, Friends of the Earth, Earth Island, Public Citizen, Douglas Tompkins, and others we are describing. Similarly, the Alvin Duskin campaigns were sponsored by a single passionately devoted individual, who had sufficient funds to make it possible for advertising efforts to break-through media passivity on certain urgent local issues.

And the two ads by Joan McIntyre on animal rights—regarding whale intelligence *and* the commodification of wild animal skins—were both efforts to break out, or burst through, with something beyond the usual range of mainstream media perception. Those are subjects that mainstream media would certainly not likely select or amplify. The same might be said of *most* Indigenous efforts per our earlier discussion.

Not every do-gooder organization has the organizational capacity, or sufficient funding, to take such expensive routes through media. But there *are* occasions where an individual or organization feels sufficiently frustrated by circumstances, or passionate on issues, to risk throwing enormous amounts of money toward somehow being heard, at least one time. This was surely the case of Matthew Fox, OP, the priest who was silenced by the Catholic Church in a clearly unjust manner. *(His personal protest ad appears on page 98.)*

In fact, there are a significant number of one-shot do-gooder advertising efforts that are rooted in a powerful sense of *frustration* with the media. They express a feeling that if the media was properly paying alert attention, dangerous negative outcomes could sometimes be averted, whether from environmental catastrophes or social-political deprivations. It's of course true that one-time negative events often take place in zones of behavior not usually focused upon by mass media. In such cases, extraordinary one-time public responses may be the only way to expose a negative situation and seek public support. Private individuals or small organizations will sometimes decide to take extraordinary steps to be noticed and seek help.

Of course protest demonstrations can also be mounted. And of course *physical* protests have the potential to incite media response. But organizing sufficiently large public protests to be impactful is not always possible. And if not, then advertising offers one last-chance opportunity. If enough funds can be gathered, there is the option to *buy* a page (or two) of media, and successfully expose information and opinions and/or news that media has not noticed, or has ignored.

But there are some problems.

As mentioned, problem #1 is that it's very expensive to use ads. Nevertheless, there are certain individuals, and/or small groups, who do decide to "roll the dice" as it were; to take the gamble that raising funds for a one-time extraordinary effort is warranted, and worth the effort and risk. They decide that the issue is

THE NEW YORK TIMES, WEDNESDAY, DECEMBER 14, 1988

z   A11

"MY FINAL STATEMENT BEFORE BEING SILENCED BY THE VATICAN"

 atthew Fox is a Dominican priest, ordained in 1967. He holds a doctorate from the Institut Catholique in Paris, is the author of twelve books and the founder of the Institute in Culture and Creation Spirituality, Oakland, California.

Effective December 15, 1988, Father Fox is being officially silenced. For one year, he will be forbidden to "teach, preach or lecture." The action against Father Fox was initiated by the Congregation for the Doctrine of the Faith at the Vatican, headed by Cardinal Joseph Ratzinger. This is the same office that was known for centuries, until 1965, as the Holy Office of the Roman Inquisition. At no time during the investigation of Father Fox's teachings was he permitted the opportunity to directly respond to the Vatican's charges against him. Here is his statement on the matter.

1 Fundamentalism in the Church

In 1971, the Synod of the Bishops declared: "The Church recognizes everyone's right to suitable freedom of expression and thought. This includes the right of everyone to be heard in a spirit of dialogue which preserves legitimate diversity within the church."

This openness, and the spirit of outreach to other faiths originally promised by the Second Vatican Council and Pope John XXIII, is far too precious to permit it to be aborted by the present regime in the Vatican.

There is a grave danger that by recent actions against American priests, sisters and bishops, including the Liberation Theologians working with the poor in Latin America, and culminating in its action against me, the Vatican is doing to Catholic Americans what it has already done to the church in Holland: (1) silencing creative thinkers, (2) creating a climate of intimidation among theologians, (3) expelling dissenters, (4) dismantling episcopal collegiality, and (5) appointing bishops who are "yes men" to Rome.

I am deeply concerned, not only as a priest and a theologian, but also as an academician. The American tradition of academic freedom is endangered by such direct interference from the Vatican. That I was given no "day in court" to respond to the charges makes the situation still more alarming.

Finally what such actions reflect is a new fundamentalist zeal at large in the Catholic church. Like recent fundamentalist movements in other religions, such as Islam and Judaism, it now threatens to take control.

2 The Charges: "Dangerous, Deviant, Feminist"

Cardinal Ratzinger first requested an investigation of me in 1985, asking my own order, The Dominicans, to undertake it. Three distinguished theologians were appointed. In their report, they found no heresy. In fact the report commended my "hard work and creativity." Cardinal Ratzinger overruled the Dominican Order, citing my book,

Original Blessing, as "dangerous and deviant." He instructed the Dominicans to silence me.

At no time did the Vatican speak or correspond directly with me. But from correspondence between Cardinal Ratzinger and the Dominicans, I conclude that his charges against me are mainly these:

*I emphasize "original blessing" at the expense of "original sin."
*I do not condemn homosexuality.
*I refer to God as Father *and* Mother.
*And, as Cardinal Ratzinger charged, I am "a fervent feminist," critical of the church's position against the ordination of women.

In fact I do not deny these "charges." The question remaining is this: why are these positions so threatening to

ment it brings, the human species can begin to act on its divine gifts rather than wallowing in its sins.

Creation Spirituality is also the oldest tradition on this continent, since the Native peoples *lived* it for thousands of years until the arrival of the Europeans.

Hundreds of thousands of people in the world today are ardent supporters of this movement. Our own organization numbers more than 25,000 adherents.

Unlike Fall and Redemption theology, which is dominant today, Creation Spirituality is not patriarchal, it is feminist. It believes ecstasy, eros, and passion are not curses, but blessings. Creation Spirituality emphasizes beauty, not self-denial. It believes compassion, justice and celebration are the goals of spirituality. It emphasizes creativity over obedience. It believes humans are essentially divine. Its psychology is one of trust. Its champions include Hildegard of Bingen, Meister Eckhart, Francis of Assisi and Julian of Norwich. It believes we are all prophets.

4 Why is this important?

Mother Earth is in jeopardy, caused by the anthropocentrism of religion, education, and science during the past three centuries. A new beginning is required centered on the *sacredness of the planet*: its rainforests, oceans, soil, air and *all* the creatures of the Earth.

We believe that religion, science and art must overcome their antagonisms and

ping into that power. We must unleash the wisdom of all religions —Western and Eastern, as well as Native American and Goddess traditions — to reveal the Cosmic Christ. This cannot happen until Western religion recovers its mystical heritage.

We believe that worship that bores people is a sin. Worship is meant to astonish, to challenge, to delight and to empower. We believe all adults can touch the divine child that exists within us.

With the expansion of mindless fundamentalism, *healthy* religion *must* stand up and be heard; religion that is not anti-intellectual; religion that teaches mysticism as well as morality and struggles for justice as the prophets did.

We believe that the youth of the world, so many of whom dwell in "Third World" countries, have an absolute right to a future with healthy soil, forests and air; with good work and a vision of how and why the universe gave them birth.

For all people who believe as we do, Creation Spirituality furnishes common ground. We see ourselves as a form of Liberation Theology for *First* World peoples, whose poverty is less material than it is spiritual and psychological. Addiction, loneliness and fear, so rampant in the West, are rooted in our alienation from the Earth and from God. Creation Spirituality, we believe, offers an antidote to this condition.

5 What can you do?

I am being silenced, but you are not. Please speak out. Here are three ways to begin.

1. Write to the Apostolic delegate: Most Rev. Pio Laghi, Apostolic Pro-Nuncio, 3339 Massachusetts Avenue, N.W., Washington, D.C. 20008. (Send us a copy please.)

2. Post this ad in a public place; ask your friends to read it and to respond.

3. If you are interested, learn more about Creation Spirituality. Mail the coupon below. Thank you.

Matthew Fox, O.P.

This advertisement is sponsored by Friends of Creation Spirituality.

VICTIMS OF THE ROMAN INQUISITION

ARCHBISHOP RAYMOND HUNTHAUSEN   FATHER CHARLES CURRAN   FATHER LEONARDO BOFF

Established in the 13th Century to root out heretics, the Holy Office of the Roman Inquisition acted against such luminaries as Galileo, Meister Eckhart, Teresa of Avila and John of the Cross. In 1965, for public relations reasons, the name was changed to the Congregation for the Doctrine of the Faith, but its purpose remained the same. Its most recent victims are Bishop Pedro Casaldaliga and Leonardo Boff (for their Liberation Theology work in Brazil among the poor), Archbishop Raymond Hunthausen of Seattle (for liberal policies opposed by Rome), and Dr. Charles Curran of Washington, D.C. (for dissenting on questions of sexual ethics). Matthew Fox is the latest in this distinguished company. The question remains: should the modern Catholic church be succumbing to such fundamentalist zeal?

Cardinal Ratzinger that he would overrule the Dominican Order and deprive me of my freedom to speak or teach? Clearly, the case against me is more political than it is theological.

3 What is Creation Spirituality?

Creation Spirituality did not begin with me. It is the oldest tradition in the Bible. All of the prophets were creation-centered, including Jesus.

Creation Spirituality asserts that the creation of the Universe is a blessing from God: the *original* blessing. And with this blessing and the empower-

work together to awaken the human imagination and to heal the planet. The survival of the Earth depends upon "reinventing our species" (Thomas Berry) so that we live more harmoniously with Nature. The new cosmology that science, art and mysticism unite to teach is the ancient spiritual and ecological lesson: all things are connected.

We believe, as Albert Einstein did, that "mysticism is the basis of all true science and the person who can no longer stand rapt in awe is as good as dead."

Meister Eckhart taught that "God is a great underground river," and that the world's great religions are all wells tap-

To: Friends of Creation Spirituality, P.O. Box 19216, Oakland, CA 94619

☐ I would like more information on your programs and activities. (Friends of Creation Spirituality organizes workshops, promotes a Master's Degree program, distributes audio/video resources, and publishes a bi-monthly magazine, *Creation.*)
☐ I would like to become a Friend of Creation Spirituality. Here is a $35 donation which will include a one-year subscription to *Creation.*
☐ Here is a tax-deductible donation of _$20, _$50, _$100, _$500, _$1000.

NAME

ADDRESS

sufficiently important that they must somehow manage to *buy* a full-page of a newspaper or magazine to tell the story—a one-shot intervention—even in cases where the issue is highly "personal" (as you will see from several ads in this chapter).

In that way, a person can, at least once, project their issue into a visible public view. And, sometimes, one highly visible effort *does* get the ball rolling. In fact, David Brower's very first ad in 1966 about Grand Canyon is a great example of this process. Brower took an issue that was already, effectively, "lost." The Grand Canyon dams already had the announced support of President Johnson and Secretary of the Interior Stewart Udall, and were very close to being approved in Congress. And yet, at the very last minute, as discussed in Chapter One, Brower used a couple of spectacular ad insertions to turn it around.

Sierra Club had never once in its prior history poured money into such an expensive and high-risk media approach. But the effort was so successful that Brower and the club went on to use similar approaches to address other environmental issues, sometimes with great success.

But, a grim reality remains. Given how very expensive mainstream media advertising is, and how difficult it is to create effective ads, anyone seriously thinking of trying to take that approach faces the prospect of spending tens of thousands of dollars—sometimes of personal funds—and yet still failing to change anything. Despite the risk, some people feel so strongly and urgently, they go for it anyway. Sometimes it works. Sometimes it doesn't. (We will discuss this point in greater detail in Chapter Seven).

So, in this chapter we present a mixed display of *one time insertion* ads—dealing with issues and viewpoints that their sponsors felt had not been sufficiently reported upon in the media. Or perhaps they'd been poorly reported. But which some people considered so urgent that they needed special effort and attention, seeking a breakthrough. These issues included, for example, the little noted but significant environmental effects of eating beef, or, the goings-on within unfamiliar nations where political subjugation is rampant, or, the little noted threats to lesser known wilderness areas, or insufficiently expressed reactions to public events, etc., etc.

Various groups, or individuals, may sometimes feel that drastic efforts are justified to bring such subjects forward. Often, this impulse results in that "one shot" effort, trying for what Gossage used to call "the

hole in one." Sometimes it's a recognized, important public issue, and sometimes it's just an effort to make a personal or "individual" comment. The effort may be on a national issue, or on a specific local situation that the media has not sufficiently exposed—at least not in the views of the ad's sponsor(s). For example, whether the Pope had made an egregious mistake by silencing a local priest; or concerning a poorly understood public event (like the shooting down of KAL 007); or the urgent question of whether Dan Quayle was really too stupid to be Vice President of the United States!

In that latter case, for example, you will see an ad that was actually composed by three well-published authors, who were appalled at the unpreparedness and personal ignorance of a Vice Presidential candidate. That ad is beautifully written by well-known author Orville Schell, joined together with writers Peter Coyote and Paul Hawken, and is itself very interesting and entertaining. And yet, despite the quality of the effort, its one-time insertion in one local newspaper was not nearly enough to prevent Quayle from being elected (with George Bush, Sr.).

Sometimes, larger organizations—normally used to having sufficient funds and good entry to the media—might seek to express a critique of the way information has been handled in the mass media. Such was the case with one ad from Greenpeace *(see page 102)* and another from *The Nation* magazine *(page 101)*. Both of those expressed frustration with the way mainstream media were portraying an important public event. And each of those ads did achieve some media impact, causing expanded critical discussions within the industry.

In a few other cases, local environmental groups were trying to expose major impacts on little-noticed wilderness areas, and upon nature itself. One ad, for example, articulates and amplifies (then) little known subjects, such as the environmental effects of meat-eating, an issue which still has not gained effective public impact.

In another very significant case, there has been the effort to discuss proliferation of guns in the US. Despite the ad that opened this chapter, the public has been left very frustrated by a lack of action on this issue. Some large efforts have been made to gain momentum against handgun proliferation, and against the National Rifle Association—the dominant political player on that issue—but there was little progress. Public Media Center worked closely with several organizations to attempt to mount effective national campaigns against the legality of privately owned pistols and rifles. One series of ads, in fact, was produced in behalf of Sarah Brady, whose husband, the press secretary for President Reagan, was shot in the same assault that wounded Reagan. Those ads sought at least a ban on "mail order" gun purchases, or a seven day waiting period, so background checks could be completed (*see page iv*). It took years of Congressional wrangling, however, for the Brady Bill requiring background checks on handgun purchases to be enacted into law.

Unfortunately, this battle did not gain much ground over the decades, and the problem has since magnified, beyond one-on-one killings. Now mass murders of high school students, party-goers, or religious groups have become a frequent occurrence. The anti-gun movement needs a much more accelerated, multi-dimensional media campaign to achieve the paradigm shift required to end gun violence in the United States.

There are some recent signs that this is beginning to take hold, but obviously not fast enough, and not yet within a single focused group, such as a Sierra Club or Planned Parenthood. But, someday, this is going to work.

★   ★   ★

Among the other ads you will also find in the following pages are expressions from little-known groups in Japan, New Zealand, and Tibet, who were fighting against grim possibilities in their region. Among that group, the Tibet ad was most successful. But in all those cases, the expression is mainly an effort to fill information gaps that the mass media have otherwise permitted. So, this chapter offers a few such varied one-time efforts along the above lines.

(Chapter 7 begins on page 111)

THE NEW YORK TIMES, THURSDAY, OCTOBER 25, 1984

(Memorandum to the press and the public, from the The Nation)

K.A.L. 007:
After a year's investigation, The Nation Magazine believes that the official U.S. version is not credible.

W**hen the plane flew off** *course, it entered one of the most intensely monitored zones in the world. The U.S. Navy, the Air Force, the Army, the CIA and NSA all maintain multiple surveillance stations and satellites aimed at Kamchatka and Sakhalin, capable of instant communication with Washington. A baseball could not fly through without alerting the top levels in our Defense Department. The central question is this: Why did we not warn the plane it was headed for danger? We had hours to do it. There are only two possible answers: (1) U.S. electronic defenses had the most mind-boggling breakdown in history, or (2) we allowed the plane to fly into danger (or worse, sent it). In either case, we have a national scandal. Why is Congress not probing this? And where is the American press? For our part, The Nation offers to open our files to all accredited investigators.*

WHAT DID WE KNOW AND WHEN DID WE KNOW IT?

This shows the intended and actual flight paths of K.A.L. 007. It also shows the flight path (figure eight pattern) of a U.S. RC-135 reconnaissance plane, which has powerful radar and which closely approached K.A.L. 007. There are several important U.S. surveillance stations in the region, including "over the horizon" radars at Wakkanai, Japan and aboard the U.S.S. Observation Island. In addition, there are 27 Japanese radars within range. That the U.S. did not know K.A.L. 007 was off-course defies belief. Why didn't we warn it? Who decided not to?

T**he K.A.L.** incident may have been the most important event of the last four years. 269 people died. It widened the chasm between two nuclear nations. It produced a wave of patriotic fervor. It gave Mr. Reagan the edge he needed to increase the arms budget. It shattered hopes for arms control. It scared the whole world. But if all this resulted from misleading reports, hiding U.S. complicity, don't Americans need to know that?

The investigation was undertaken by David Pearson, a doctoral candidate at Yale University, using documents and statements largely in the public record. It was reported in full in *The Nation,* August 18. Since then, some news-media have picked-up the story, including NBC's "The Today Show," the *Seattle Weekly,* and *N.Y. Times* columnist Tom Wicker, twice. But in the year that has passed since the incident, no mainstream medium has published results of its own investigation. As far as we know, none has undertaken an investigation.*

Our purpose in taking this advertisement, the first such in the 120 year history of *The Nation,* is to try to get this story off the back burners. We wish we could reproduce it whole right here but it's 13,000 words. If you would like to read it in full, use the coupon and we'll send you a free reprint. Meanwhile, here are summaries of a few of the questions raised:

1. Why did we not warn the Korean airliner?
As indicated above, K.A.L. 007 flew through dozens of U.S. military and civilian, and Japanese radars. These radars were *especially* attentive that day, apparently because of an expected Soviet missile test. It is normal practice for the military to inform civilian aircraft and air controllers when a commercial flight is off course. This time they did nothing. Why?

2. When did Washington know?
We have never been told when Mr. Weinberger or Mr. Shultz were informed of the crisis, or how long they

waited before telling the President. We do know that several communications systems, including World Wide Military Command and Control, and Critical Intelligence Communications System are designed to inform the Pentagon and the President within minutes of a crisis. According to the President's press secretary, Mr. Reagan was first told of the K.A.L. incursion at 10:30 PM (EDT), August 31, 1983. He received an update at 1:30 AM, September 1. That morning, at 10:10 AM, he learned that the plane had been shot down by the Soviets. If this sequence is true, then the President was not informed of the crisis until eight hours after it was over. He wasn't fully informed until twenty hours after the fact. Can this be so? (The prime minister of Japan was informed many hours earlier though the Japanese have far less extensive intelligence capability.) Is it possible there was a simultaneous breakdown in the communications systems critical to national security? Or, was the news deliberately withheld from the President? If so, why? Who was responsible? Finally, there's the possibility the President *was* told earlier but has not admitted it.

3. Why did the Korean plane behave oddly?
The pilot delayed his takeoff from Anchorage by twenty minutes for no apparent reason. He also added 9,800 pounds of extra fuel, which he never reported as he is required to do.

By the time the plane passed Bethel, Alaska, its first checkpoint, it was twelve miles off course. The pilot falsely reported he was on course. Military radar operators noted the deviation but did not correct the pilot.

K.A.L. 007 gave false positions several other times, and also changed course and altitude without reporting the changes as required. One of the course changes occurred as the plane approached Sakhalin Island; the airliner flew abruptly *north* toward sensitive Soviet military positions. (See map.) Could *that* have been a mistake? Meanwhile, another K.A.L. flight, 015, was apparently giving false reports on behalf of 007.

For some of its route, K.A.L. 007 was flying without its lights on, a violation of international law. And when finally intercepted by the Soviet fighter, the Korean plane refused all inquiries and took evasive action.

4. What was the role of the RC-135?
The White House said the reconnaissance plane was never closer than 75 miles to K.A.L. 007, and that the RC-135 was back at its base when the Korean plane was downed. The U.S. has not backed these statements by releasing the exact route of RC-135 or the places it inter-

sected K.A.L. 007. Reconstruction of the usual reconnaissance flight paths from Shemya Island, overlayed with U.S. and Russian statements, suggests strongly that the planes were much closer. (The Russians say the planes flew parallel for ten minutes, causing the two to merge on radar. This is one explanation for why the Soviets did not realize they were tracking a commercial airliner, as the U.S. has recently conceded.) Even if the planes were 75 miles apart, the radar and sophisticated electronic equipment of the RC-135 would have made it aware of 007. The questions remain: Why did it not warn the Korean plane? Did RC-135 have a control function in the K.A.L. mission?

5. Why were the Soviets confused?
All reports affirm that the Soviets could not find the Korean airliner for hours after first spotting it on radar, suggesting a possible Russian communications breakdown. Author David Pearson thinks such a total breakdown is as unlikely for the Russians as for the U.S. One possibility is that the confusion was caused by deliberate U.S. electronic jamming. An RC-135 can do that; so can many ground stations. If so, was K.A.L.'s intrusion orchestrated? Was the jamming an effort to shield the plane?

6. What about the tapes?
Numerous tapes exist which could unravel mysteries. The U.S. routinely records Soviet air-ground communications, and knows what the Russians saw. Why are these tapes not released? The Japanese Defense System has publicly stated it has tapes of Russian ground to air conversations, but they too refuse to make them public. Why? Secretary Shultz says the U.S. intercepted Soviet radar data from Kamchatka. These data could shed light on 007 and RC-135. But the U.S. will not release those either. Is someone hiding a "smoking gun?"

O**n** the basis of all the evidence—we have only touched the surface in this ad—David Pearson concluded this: "At the minimum, it appears that the President and his Administration misled the press and the world concerning what they knew about the K.A.L. 007 incident and when they knew it. Beyond that, it appears probable that they risked 269 lives in the hope of gathering information about Soviet defense systems. If those surmises are unwarranted, then…security that the U.S. built over decades suffered an unprecedented and mind-boggling breakdown."

We at the Nation find the implications of the Pearson report staggering. It does not condone Soviet behavior. *They* shot down the plane, and they too withheld critical information. But in a free society, such questions as Pearson raises must not go unanswered. If his report can be refuted, we should know it. If his report *is* accurate, as we believe, then it raises the gravest possibilities of U.S. complicity. What's needed now is in-depth investigative reporting, seeking to discover exactly what happened, when, and who made the decisions. Congress and the press must find out. We offer to help in any way we can.

The Nation

Hamilton Fish, 3rd, *Publisher*
Victor Navasky, *Editor*

President Reagan · Secretary Shultz · Secretary Weinberger

*The only major official investigation was by the International Civil Aviation Organization. But the ICAO did not attempt "firm conclusions," as the U.S., Japan and Russia all refused to provide critical information. The findings that did emerge were tentative, and were directly refuted by ICAO's own Air Navigation Commission.

Produced by Public Media Center

The Militarization of Paradise

Why They Blew Up the Rainbow Warrior.

While the world is worrying about nuclear war, there's been one going on in the Pacific for forty years. On lush, fragrant islands, the United States, Britain and France have exploded 200 nuclear bombs, populations have been forcibly moved, there is radiation sickness and pollution. ¶ Pacific islanders have had enough. They want it stopped. No more tests. No more nuclear bases. They want their homes back. ¶ Greenpeace went out there to help. So our ship was sabotaged and Fernando Pereira, our photographer, was murdered. What now? With your help, we can still complete the work the Rainbow Warrior began. Here are the details.

I. Spy Story.

To follow it in the media, you'd think the sinking of the Greenpeace ship was part of a sexy little spy novel: BEAUTIFUL FRENCH SABOTEUR. GOVERNMENTS NEAR COLLAPSE. What the stories don't explain is *why* our ship was there. Or, they reduce it to "protesting a French nuclear test." But there's a lot more news than that, involving *more* than France.

In this most heavenly part of the world, with its gorgeous tropical islands and peaceful people, nuclear bombs have been going off since 1946. First by the United States, joined later by Britain, then France.

The French tests (about 110) are conducted at Moruroa, in "French" Polynesia, with negative effects on wildlife, coral reefs and the island people of the region. Governments of a dozen Pacific nations have asked the French to stop. International agencies have sought to measure the radiation level of the air, water and land. But France has stonewalled everyone.

A Greenpeace ship has gone to the test zone five times since 1972, hoping to focus world attention. This year, the French government sank our ship and killed our photographer. Why? Are they saying it will now cost lives to engage in peaceful protest?

II. Nuclear Guinea Pigs?

The United States conducted 66 atmospheric nuclear tests at Bikini and Enewetak Atolls, between 1946-1958. To do these tests, the U.S. had to move all the people. The islanders were told if they moved it would be "for the good of all man-

Evacuation from Rongelap.

These women are among 304 people from Rongelap Atoll who were evacuated from their irradiated homes in May, by the Rainbow Warrior. Rongelap was 100 miles downwind from the huge United States' "Bravo" nuclear test in 1954, but the people were never warned. The U.S. had moved populations of several other Pacific islands, so why not these? Apparently to give scientists a chance to study the effects of radioactive fallout. It was research. (See Part II.) The people have suffered high rates of thyroid cancer, leukemia, miscarriage and the birth of "jellyfish babies." Shapeless blobs that live for a few hours then die. Thirty-one years later, Rongelap is still "hot." The people have asked the U.S. for help, but have been refused. To do so, would publicly admit complicity. So Greenpeace was asked, and we helped the people move. Six weeks later our ship was blown up by the French. The man who took this photo was killed.

Last Voyage of the Ship that Saved the Whales.

The Rainbow Warrior, the same ship that travelled the world to help save the whales, had a different goal this year: to intervene in a forty year nuclear testing nightmare in the Pacific. Two hundred explosions which have left many islands uninhabitable, people homeless and suffering radiation sickness. From Hawaii, the Greenpeace ship went first to Rongelap to evacuate people whose island is still radioactive from a test thirty years ago. Next stop was Kwajalein to protest Star Wars testing there. Then New Zealand. It would have gone to Polynesia to protest the French nuclear tests, but the French blew up the ship. Every country in the world has expressed anger and sorrow at the bombing except the United States and England. Why? Read the details below. Want to change how the story ends? Use the coupons.

kind." Then their islands were bombed. Now, the people want to go back. But the radiation is still too high to permit it.

One of the tests, named "Bravo" (1954) was the largest U.S. atmospheric test ever. One hundred miles away the people of Rongelap Atoll felt the fallout rain upon them. Why were *these* people *not* moved? One government paper (from Brookhaven Labs) says: "the habitation of these people on the island will afford most valuable ecological radiation data on human beings." So this was research? The people were guinea pigs? For the research results, see photo caption.

III. Star Wars Testing.

Meanwhile, on nearby Kwajalein, one of the Pacific's largest and best fishing lagoons, which supported thousands of people for centuries, the U.S. has moved the whole population. Not to spare them from nuclear bombs, but to use the lagoon for target practice for missiles launched from California, 4,500 miles away. It's part of the Star Wars testing range. So Kwajalein today is home to an American military base with golf courses, suburban houses, and swimming pools.

As for the Kwajalein people they have been jammed onto the tiny island of Ebeye: 66 acres, no water, few coconut trees. The population density is greater than Washington, D.C. With their subsistence lifestyle destroyed, the people are reduced to accepting U.S. handouts. The place is now known as "the slum of the Pacific." The people want to go home.

IV. The Pacific: An "American Lake?"

South and West of the Marshall Islands, a tiny new nation, Belau, has been refused its promised independence from America. Why? Because on four successive occasions, the Belauans went to the polls and affirmed their wish for a constitution which bans all nuclear arms. The U.S. rejected all four votes, insisting that Belau must permit a U.S. nuclear

base, covering one third of that nation's territory. That's the price of Belau's "freedom."

There are similar goings-on in New Zealand. Last year that nation banned all warships containing nuclear weapons from its ports. And then a few months ago, New Zealand joined thirteen Pacific countries in a South Pacific Nuclear Free Zone Treaty. So New Zealand became the first allied Western democracy to take a *moral* stance against nuclear weapons. For this expression of sovereignty, the U.S. government threatened major sanctions, including expulsion from ANZUS. And many Pacific people believe that the French bombed the Rainbow Warrior, *while in New Zealand,* to embarrass that nation for stepping out of line, and to put all others on notice.

While the U.S. seeks *more* Pacific ports and bases, there are already bases on Wake, Johnston, Midway and Tinian Islands, as well as Guam, the Philippines, Japan, Australia, the Aleutians and in Hawaii. The U.S. has so many battleships, carriers, nuclear bombers and subs roaming the once peaceful Pacific, that some have begun to call it, "An American lake." But is it really? Is the Pacific American property? Does the U.S. no longer acknowledge sovereign rights of other nations?

Big military powers get away with such behavior because the Pacific is far away, there is little news about it, and Pacific nations are small and powerless. So these gentle people, on their fabled island paradises, get to be victims of a nuclear holocaust that supposedly hasn't begun. For them, it has.

The people of the Pacific want this situation to change. They want an end to a thirty year radiation nightmare. They want their once magnificent islands cleaned-up and returned to their control. They want medical help. They want no more nuclear testing, and no more nuclear bases. They do not want to be pawns in a Big Power arms race that has nothing to do with them.

The members of Greenpeace are dedicated to helping make these changes by non-violent direct action. It is sometimes dangerous work, but we have many people ready to do it. Hundreds of Greenpeace campaigners have intervened between whalers and whales, hunters and seals. We have blocked ships from dumping toxins. We have climbed smokestacks, we have blocked offshore oil and gas developments.

To Greenpeace, all ecological threats are of a piece. They are all expressions of a terrifying loss of balance between humans and the natural world. They are iron-fisted statements that all creatures must bend to commercial and military purposes. In the end, these acts become threats to all life on Earth.

In years past, Greenpeace ships and campaigners have been threatened. In 1980, the Rainbow Warrior was seized by the Spanish while protesting whaling activities, and three years later a Soviet gunship chased us. *But until this year, no government has ever tried to kill us.* Perhaps the stakes are getting higher. Or perhaps the message is meant for all environmentalists, for all who work for peace, for *you.* It is a warning not to cross some invisible line of involvement.

Obviously, this will not work. Greenpeace is more committed than ever to the protection of all species. And we will continue to oppose *all* nuclear testing by every nuclear power, whether in the Pacific, or in Nevada (where there've been fifteen tests this year.) Or by the English, the Russians or the Chinese. We will also continue our lobbying in world capitals, seeking a Comprehensive Test Ban Treaty. We need your help. Please mail the coupons. Post this ad in a public place. Tell your friends. Get involved. Join Greenpeace. Thank you.

GREENPEACE
1611 Connecticut Ave. N.W. Washington D.C. 20009

TO: Mr. Michael Gartner, President, NBC News, 30 Rockefeller Plaza, New York, NY 10112

Though I am writing to you, I ask that you inform your counterparts at CBS, ABC and CNN that my appeal applies equally to them. The public has a right to know fully about Dan Quayle's background. I don't understand why the press has not been able to get the story. This man could someday be in control of our nuclear arsenal. If there are skeletons in his closet — the use of money or family influence for favors, plagiarism, disciplinary action in college — the public should be informed. Please be more aggressive in seeking the story.

NAME
ADDRESS

TO: Mr. Tom Greer, Editor, *Cleveland Plain Dealer*, 1801 Superior Avenue N.E. Cleveland, OH 44114

Your newspaper has broken several stories about Dan Quayle's background but you have been unable to reveal the details of his college records. The public has a right to know Mr. Quayle's background. He might someday be in charge of our economy, negotiations with the Soviets, and our nuclear arsenal. People are frightened of the possibility of his election. If there are skeletons in his closet — the use of money or family influence for favors, surrogates to take his exams, disciplinary action in college — we need to know *before* he's elected to office. Please help us get the rest of the story.

NAME
ADDRESS

TO: Ms. Katherine Graham
The Washington Post and Newsweek
1150 15th Street, NW, Washington, D.C. 20071

It would be unprecedented if Dan Quayle was elected to office before the public was informed about his background. He might someday be in charge of our economy, negotiations with the Soviets, and our nuclear arsenal. This possibility frightens people. If there are skeletons in his closet, we need to know the answer before he becomes Vice-President, and possibly President.

NAME
ADDRESS

To: Independent Committee on
Presidential Qualifications
466 Green St., Suite 200, San Francisco, CA 94133

☐ I have mailed the coupons.

☐ You may use my name in further advertising.

☐ Here is a donation of ☐ $25☐ $50☐ $100
☐ $500 ☐Other $_____.

NAME
ADDRESS

(What is he hiding? When will the press get the story?)

RELEASE DAN QUAYLE'S COLLEGE RECORDS *NOW.*

The polls are now confirming what has been obvious for six weeks. Republicans, Democrats and Independents are all in agreement on one point: *The most frightening thing about this election is Dan Quayle.*

✳✳✳

Whether you prefer George Bush or Michael Dukakis, it is clear that either is qualified to run for President. They are both experienced. They have paid their dues. The same can be said for Lloyd Bentsen. You take your choice.

Only one person, Dan Quayle, is in a different category. Moreover, he has neither the stature, the judgment, or the achievements that are expected of a President. He has never had a significant job that wasn't arranged or funded by his family, including his National Guard service and his election to the U.S. Senate. He achieved very little as a lawyer, a public servant in Indiana, or a U.S. Senator, save one bill he co-authored with Senator Ted Kennedy.

✳✳✳

What worries us most is the way he has consistently evaded full disclosure concerning his admission to university; his employment in Indiana; and his military service.

Most alarming is his staunch refusal to inform the public about his performance in college and law school — or to provide his academic and his disciplinary records. He has admitted "mediocre grades," but he won't release the records. If he has nothing to hide, why has he permitted rumors to

persist, not only about poor grades, but disciplinary actions for plagiarism and the hiring of surrogates to take his exams?

Dan Quayle could stop these rumors instantly, by simply allowing

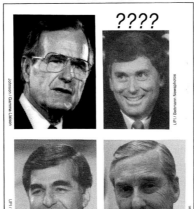

????

Why won't Dan Quayle finally put to rest the controversy about his college days? Having acknowledged "mediocre grades" why won't he show the public his actual records? Applicants for U.S. Civil Service jobs routinely provide their records. So do applicants to the F.B.I., law firms, schools and corporations. Why not Dan Quayle?

the universities to release his records. Why doesn't he do this? And why doesn't George Bush insist he do it?

Finally, why has the press been so uncharacteristically shy about pursuing these issues?

Look here. We are speaking about a man who could become President of the United States. Since Franklin Roosevelt, one in three Vice Presidents has become President. We have at least as much right to know Dan Quayle's character as that of Gary Hart or

Geraldine Ferraro's husband.

We want to know his college grades. We want the details concerning his family's donations to his college and law school. We want to know if the university is still receiving donations from the Quayle family, and if any special deals were made. We want to know why Quayle was given a second chance on special exams that others had to pass the first time. We want to know why he was admitted under an affirmative action program designed for disadvantaged and minority applicants. *We want to know if he was ever disciplined by the university and, if so, for what actions.*

✳✳✳

If George Bush is elected and then dies in office, Dan Quayle will be Commander-in-Chief of the Armed Forces of the United States. He will represent this nation and conduct our international affairs. Dan Quayle will control the world's most awesome nuclear arsenal, and we don't know who he is. He *is* obviously a man who has often received special treatment. This is no time for *more* special treatment. We urge the press and the Republican Party to get the story out. If you agree, please mail the coupons. Thank you.

INDEPENDENT COMMITTEE ON PRESIDENTIAL QUALIFICATIONS
c/o 466 Green St., Suite 200, San Francisco, CA 94133
Orville Schell; Paul Hawken; Peter Coyote, Co-Chairmen

This advertisement is not paid for by any candidate, nor have the contents been discussed with either the Bush or Dukakis campaigns.

(NEW INTERNATIONAL COALITION: BEYOND BEEF)

The Goal: A 50% Reduction of Beef Consumption by 2002

FROM A GLOBAL VIEWPOINT, one of the gravest threats to the Earth's ecology, as well as to human health, is the overconsumption of beef. Now, for the first time in history, ecology groups are joining animal protection, anti-hunger, human rights, family farm and health groups to launch the first worldwide campaign to reduce the population of cattle and the consumption of beef. Please join us. It will benefit your health and the planet too. Here are eight reasons why:

1. Personal Health

The U.S. Surgeon General has reported that 70% of deaths in the United States are related to diet, especially the overconsumption of beef and other saturated fats. Americans now eat 25% of all the beef consumed in the world, a habit that all reputable research has linked to heart disease, colon and breast cancers and strokes. Foreign countries that have lately adopted American diets have shown similar accelerating disease rates. Aside from smoking, there is no greater personal health risk than eating meat. But if you are not concerned about your *personal* health, consider the rest of this story.

2. Animal Suffering

In the United States, more than 100,000 cows are slaughtered every day. The great majority of these are *not* raised by family farmers but by the Factory Farm and Factory Feedlot system; giant corporate conglomerates that raise the animals just as if they were assembly-line parts. Their treatment of the creatures is one of the great horror stories of our time.

of the total methane released. Also, to grow the feed the animals eat requires intensive use of petro-chemical fertilizers that emit *nitrous oxide*, another greenhouse gas. NO_2 alone accounts for six percent of global warming.

Unless checked, global warming may cause a 4-9 degree rise in the earth's surface temperature over the next decades; the greatest climate change since the Ice Age. Should that happen, the polar ice caps will melt, lowland and coastal regions will flood, farm lands will become parched, certain plant species will die, forests will be disrupted and so will the lives of billions of people. Reducing beef consumption worldwide will help avert this catastrophe.

5. Water: Pollution & Scarcity

One of the least known negative aspects of our cattle culture is its effect on our water. In the United States, beef cattle produce nearly one billion tons of organic waste each year. Much of this finds its way to our rivers and streams.

An average steer produces 47 pounds of manure every day. A typical 10,000 head Factory Feedlot produces waste equivalent to the human waste from a

Consumers must demand that whatever beef they continue to buy comes only from farmers who raise them humanely, under sustainable or organic standards. In reality, only family farmers can meet such standards since all Factory Feedlots are intrinsically inhumane, and use vast amounts of chemicals, hormones and pesticides.

Finally, government policy must be reoriented to reward real farmers for growing food for people, rather than feed for corporate cattle. Government farm

CHICHESTER / AUDUBON PRODUCTION

herbicides and pesticides, with much of that stuff winding up in your dinner steak.

(Veal calves are especially brutalized, taken from mothers at birth, forced to live their lives in tiny wooden crates, force-fed, permitted no exercise, sociability or sunlight. They often become anemic and suffer chronic diarrhea; all to produce the treasured "white veal" of restaurants.)

After being fattened at feedlots, the cattle are jammed into giant truck trailers with no room to move. Some fall during travel and are trampled. Broken legs, backs and pelvises are common, but no treatment is given. These animals are called "downers" by cattlemen. Though in great pain, they are chained and dragged from the trucks to the killing rooms. As for cattle that do survive the death rides, they are often ravaged by stress-related disease, until led to their own violent ends.

Meanwhile, back home on the range, the U.S. government uses your tax dollars to subsidize cattle industry programs that exterminate millions of wild animals: wolves, bears, mountain lions, coyotes, bobcats, foxes. They are poisoned, shot or gassed in their dens to make room for our hamburger supply. The result is a tragic loss of wildlife diversity. The only animals left on the American range these days are millions of doomed cattle.

3. Rain Forest Destruction

When you eat your last fast-food hamburger, it may have come from land that was, until recently, rain forest. Since 1960, some 25% of Central American rain forests have been burned and cleared to create pasture for beef cattle, usually destined to become hamburger. Similar activity is underway in the Amazon. It has been estimated that every four ounce hamburger made from rain forest beef destroys 55 square feet of tropical rain forest.

The rain forests are now disappearing at a terrifying rate. With them are going some of the richest wildlife habitats on earth, rare pharmaceutical plants, as well as the homelands of hundreds of thousands of Native peoples who have lived in and protected these forests for millennia. All of this traded in for hamburgers.

4. Global Warming

The number of cattle on the earth has now reached 1.3 billion and is growing. This has become a major factor in the increase of three greenhouse gases: *carbon dioxide, methane* and *nitrous oxide.* The burning of Central and South American rain forests to clear pasture lands has released billions of tons of carbon dioxide into the atmosphere. But that's only the beginning.

Beef cattle, like other ruminant animals, *belch* large amounts of methane gas as part of their digestive processes. This is seen as amusing in some quarters, but not by atmospheric scientists, because worldwide it adds up to 60 million tons of methane each year. That's 12%

water pollution both here and elsewhere in the world.

Cattle production also requires a staggering amount of water. In fact, *nearly half the water consumed in the United States* now goes to grow feed to raise cattle and other livestock. In the American west, where a long drought is underway, the impact of cattle is particularly serious. A recent study of the problem in California shows how wasteful beef production is:

GALLONS OF WATER USED TO PRODUCE ONE POUND OF:	
Lettuce	21
Tomatoes	29
Melon, cantaloupe	40
Broccoli	42
Milk	90
Corn (grain)	119
Alfalfa (hay)	129
Whole wheat bread	139
Oats	197
Barley	216
Soybean tofu	219
Brown rice	251
Pasta (white flour)	287
Eggs (chicken)	660
Cheese	896
Butter	2057
Beef	2464

Source: Water Education Foundation, Sacramento, California

In California, people are being told to restrict their toilet flushing, take fewer showers, and not to wash their cars. *But producing one pound of beef uses water equivalent to eight months of daily showers.* Such waste is appalling. If Americans cut their consumption of beef by half, then enormous amounts of water and land would be freed-up to grow more practical, less wasteful, and more healthful foods while preventing the loss of our scarce fresh water supply.

6. Desertification

The overpopulation of cattle is a major cause of desertification on the planet, diminishing arable lands, decreasing food supply and effecting climate changes. Here's how it happens.

More than 1.3 billion cattle are stripping much of the vegetative cover from the earth's grasslands. Each animal eats its way through 900 pounds of vegetation a month. Without plants to anchor the soil, absorb water, and

recycle nutrients, land becomes increasingly vulnerable to wind and water erosion. In addition, with nearly *five billion hoofs* stomping on the ground, compacting it with 24 pounds of pressure per square inch, the soil is less able to absorb water and more prone to erosion.

In the Western United States, the story is especially grim. According to a report prepared for the U.N., 430 million acres of western rangeland are suffering a 25-50% drop in yield, due partly to overgrazing by cattle.

7. World Hunger

Few people are aware of the direct effects of beef consumption on world hunger. The first effect (as described above) comes from the loss of arable land to desertification. But there is more.

Nearly one billion people suffer hunger and malnutrition, and over 40 million die annually of starvation, mostly children. Despite this, *more than one third of the world's grain harvest is not used to feed people, but to feed livestock.* In the U.S. alone, cattle and other livestock consume 70% of all grain produced in the country. If our farmlands produced *food, not feed,* the nutritional needs of one billion people could be met.

A related issue is that millions of peasants in developing countries are being driven from their ancestral lands — where they formerly grew their *own food* — so that *more* grain can be grown for livestock. The net effect is that millions of Third World people become homeless, hungry and angry.

8. Preserving Family Farms

The present emphasis on *corporate farming* has been devastating to small family farmers. The big beef conglomerates have such a vast lobbying program in Washington, D.C., that they have skewed public policy in their favor, while hurting small farmers. For example, agribusiness companies and the beef-packing giants have successfully lobbied to secure subsidies for their feed grain, while leaving small farmers unable to profit. Corporate cattle ranchers have also been able to collectively manipulate prices to the small farmers' detriment.

Family farmers are the backbone of America and must be supported against the voracious conglomerates.

that is driving the family farmer off his land.

So much for the bad news. The good news is we *can* do something about it.

The Beyond Beef coalition is a broad-based international group of environmentalists, animal protectionists, and people who work toward human health, nutrition, and the survival of the family farmer. We have three specific goals: (1) Reduce individual beef consumption by at least 50%; (2) Replace our beef diet with grains, fruits and vegetables; and (3) For those who maintain beef in their diets, refine cattle production practices to promote humanely treated, sustainably raised cattle.

You can help. You can start personally by cutting your own beef consumption by at least 50% and urging your friends to do likewise. And, by joining the Beyond Beef coalition, you can take part in projects, working with schools, restaurants and other institutions, toward a more healthful diet for people and the planet. All members will receive a newsletter to keep you up to date and give you more ideas of what to do. *Join today.* Please sign the coupon. Thank you.

BEYOND BEEF COALITION

Jeremy Rifkin, President   Howard Lyman, Executive Director

MEMBERS: *The Greenhouse Crisis Foundation: Public Citizen: Rainforest Action Network: Greenpeace. U.S.A.: EarthKind: The National Coalition Against the Misuse of Pesticides: Earth Island Action Group: Food First / The Institute for Food and Development Policy: Physicians Committee for Responsible Medicine: Peoples Medical Society: Public Lands Action Network: Rest the West: EarthSave: Free Our Public Lands: International Rivers Network: Fund for Animals: Farm Sanctuary: Parents for Safe Food. England: Earthcare in World Farming. England: Earthwatch. Ireland: Die Verbraucher Initiative. Germany: KAG. Switzerland: Erklärung von Bern. Switzerland: VELT. Belgium: NOAH. Denmark: Alternative Konsumenten Bond. Holland: Lega Per L'Ambiente. Italy: Network for Safe and Secure Food and Environment. Japan: União Protetora do Ambiente Natural (UPAN). Brazil: Walhi. Indonesia: Sahabat Alam Malaysia. Malaysia: Research Foundation on Science, Technology and Natural Resource Policy. India: Rainforest Information Centre. Australia: Tanzania Environmental Society. Tanzania*

TO: Beyond Beef, 1130 17th St., NW, Suite #300
Washington, D.C. 20036

O Yes, please sign me up as a member of the Beyond Beef Coalition. I understand I will receive your newsletter, updates, briefing materials, and organizing packets for schools and restaurants.

To make a tax deductible donation make check payable to: GPC / BEYOND BEEF CAMPAIGN

O Here is $30 membership fee.

O Here is my donation to help spread the message:
___$50 ___$100 ___$500. Other ___

NAME

ADDRESS

[On the Award of the 1989 Nobel Peace Prize to the Dalai Lama]

Will the world let Tibet disappear?

Miraculously rare are those nations which have withstood the ferocious storms of world history for 2,000 years, as Tibet has.

In our lifespans alone, from Central Europe to Southeast Asia, holocausts have swept whole peoples to the brink of annihilation.

Now China threatens to erase Tibet from the map. Will the world once again wait until the victims have turned to dust before it decries the crime? This is your chance to come to the rescue...*before* it's too late.

Occupied by the Chinese army, alone at the roof of the world, remote from the world's attention, Tibet has survived agonies of oppression with its independent spirit intact.

Now the time has come to seek your help. The six million of Tibet do not want to disappear. They want to live.

Will you hear them? *Will you answer?*

A rainbow strikes the Potala Palace, Lhasa. Photographs by Galen Rowell.

Four months before the Tiananmen Square massacre in Beijing, there was a massacre in Lhasa, Tibet. It was also perpetrated by the Chinese Army. But no TV cameras were present.

The shootings were "excessive, unpredictable, indiscriminate," reports a statement signed by thirty-six foreigners present in Lhasa on March 5, 1989, when troops fired on peaceful demonstrators.

It was only one in a series of atrocities committed since the Chinese military occupied independent Tibet in the 1950's.

Hundreds have been killed this year. In our generation, more than one million Tibetans — 1 out of 6 — has been tortured, executed or starved to death.

Chinese violations of human rights and international law in this remote, once-peaceful land have been denounced in three United Nations resolutions, and by the U.S. Congress, the European Parliament, Asia Watch and Amnesty International.

Now, the nation itself is about to vanish from the face of the planet.

More than seven million Chinese have been moved into occupied Tibet in violation of the Geneva Convention.

The Tibetans, a distinct people with their own language, Buddhist religion, cultural tradition and a national history dating to 127 B.C., are outnumbered in their own country.

Over six thousand of their temples and monasteries have been destroyed. Ten thousand political prisoners are held incommunicado. More than half of sovereign Tibet has been carved off and attached to Chinese provinces.

The remainder is a Chinese military reserve, with one Chinese soldier for every ten Tibetans.

As many as a quarter of China's nuclear missiles are based in Tibet. And China has threatened to dump radioactive and chemical wastes in Tibet.

Shangri-La was never entirely a myth. Tibet was once a spiritual sanctuary in the heart of Asia. War was renounced, hunting and capital punishment were banned. The entire population followed the ideals of compassion and nonviolence embodied in their Buddhist faith.

Now Tibet is impoverished, oppressed and exploited.

With Namibia free and the nations of Eastern Europe recovering their autonomy, will once-independent Tibet, brutally occupied by China for forty years, be the last colony left on Earth?

Will the world let 2,000 years of Tibetan civilization disappear in a genocidal campaign of repression?

The Dalai Lama, legitimate head of state of the Tibetan people, inheritor of a leadership tradition dating unbroken to the Fourteenth Century, last year proposed a five-point plan (see box) to facilitate a peaceful resolution for Tibet.

This year, he was awarded the Nobel Peace Prize for his commitment to nonviolence.

What we ask now is your support.

Tibet must be the test for China to rejoin the world community.

Let Tibet live. Please mail the coupons.

HIS HOLINESS THE DALAI LAMA'S FIVE POINT PEACE PLAN

1. *Transformation of the whole of Tibet into a zone of peace.*
2. *An end to China's population transfer, which threatens the survival of Tibetans as a people.*
3. *Respect for fundamental human rights and democratic freedoms.*
4. *Protection of Tibet's natural environment, including an end to nuclear weapon production and nuclear waste dumping in Tibet.*
5. *Earnest and direct negotiations on the future status of Tibet and relations of the Tibetan and Chinese people.*

Javier Peréz de Cuéllar
Secretary General of the United Nations
New York, New York 10017

Please do everything you can to implement the U.N. General Assembly resolutions condemning China's brutal human rights violations in Tibet and calling for Tibetan self-determination. With the award of this year's Nobel Peace Prize to the Dalai Lama, the moment has come for the U.N. to facilitate a peaceful resolution to the tragic situation in Tibet. The fate of the Tibetan people is in your hands. Please act now.

NAME

ADDRESS

Secretary James Baker
U.S. Department of State
2201 C Street NW,
Washington, D.C. 20520

No nation that cherishes freedom and peace can turn a blind eye to China's brutal military occupation of Tibet and its massive campaign of terror. With the award of this year's Nobel Peace Prize to the Dalai Lama, it's time our government officially recognized his leadership of Tibet's government-in-exile and supported U.N. efforts to facilitate a peaceful resolution.

NAME

ADDRESS

TIBET FUND
107 East 31st Street
New York, N.Y. 10016

We can't allow China to erase Tibet from existence. It's time our government recognized the Dalai Lama as Tibet's leader-in-exile and supported U.N. efforts to end China's campaign of terror against the people of Tibet. I've mailed the other coupons and I enclose a tax-deductible contribution to help save Tibet. __ $25 __ $35 __ $50 __ $100 __ $500 or more $_____ .

NAME

ADDRESS

Prepared by Public Media Center.

OZONE SHOCK

[TELL DU PONT TO STOP DESTROYING THE OZONE LAYER NOW!]

The world's leading atmospheric scientists, including those from NASA, are agreed: The ozone layer that protects life on Earth from excessive ultraviolet radiation has been dangerously depleted by CFCs and other chemicals, and it's getting worse. The Director of the United Nations Environment Programme has called it, "A danger as big as humanity has ever faced." The government has already begun daily ultraviolet alerts, due to dangerous depletion of the ozone shield. Before long ALL LIFE ON EARTH WILL BE IN FOR A TERRIFYING SHOCK. At a time like this, can you believe that Du Pont Corporation and its major shareholder, Seagram, continue to profit from these deadly products? Don't let them get away with it. Please read below:

Today

The Future?

I. Future Life

When Du Pont advertised that it brings "better things for better living," it did not say this meant "better living" in fear of the sun, staying indoors, or donning ultraviolet radiation suits. For that's what the future may hold.

Du Pont is the world's largest producer of chlorofluorocarbons (CFCs), the main culprit that causes ozone destruction. The chemicals work their way slowly to the stratosphere, break apart, and release ozone destroying chlorine. When this occurs, the ozone layer thins, and sunshine becomes increasingly toxic to life. In many parts of the southern hemisphere, Canada, Europe and the U.S., the problem has gone beyond the danger point.

According to NASA scientists, the ozone problem is worse than was ever predicted, and is accelerating. Here's why: it takes about 20 years for CFCs to rise to the ozone layer and cause damage. CFC production did not peak until the 1980s, so the majority of CFCs produced to date have not yet begun to reach the ozone layer. When they do, an already terrible crisis will get much worse. The whole Earth will be affected, and the danger will last for more than a century.

Even if all production stopped today, the damage could not be undone. The U.S. Environmental Protection Agency has predicted that 12 million Americans will suffer skin cancers over the next 50 years due to ozone depletion. 200,000 will die. It will also mean increased cataracts and blindness, and a serious weakening of the human immune system for millions of people, which, in turn, will increase vulnerability to infectious diseases.

Overall, it may mean that neither you, nor your children, nor theirs will, in their lifetime, go safely again to beaches or parks. In some places it could be dangerous to *ever* go outdoors without 100% skin coverage. *Normal life could be interrupted for generations.*

II. Corporate Denial

Scientists first linked CFCs with ozone destruction in 1974. Du Pont denied these links and fought efforts to regulate CFCs. In 1978, when CFCs were finally banned for use in aerosol sprays, Du Pont promoted these chemicals for auto air conditioning, refrigeration, industrial cleansers and foams. Eventually Du Pont had to admit the problem, dubbed itself a champion of the environment, and proudly announced it would stop *some* production of *some* ozone destroying chemicals by 1996. *Some production by 1996?* Given that millions of additional people will get cancer and cataracts, and experience immune suppression, by what standard is the continued production warranted? *Corporate profit.*

It turns out that in 1996 Du Pont will partly convert to hydrochlorofluorocarbons (HCFCs) which are only marginally better, since they *also* destroy the ozone layer, albeit somewhat less. Alternative technologies do exist, but Du Pont does not profit from them, so it does not promote them. So much for your "green" corporation.

As for Seagram Corporation (Tropicana juices, Chivas Regal, Crown Royal), it owns 24.5% of Du Pont and has seven members on Du Pont's Board of Directors. Seagram's Chair, Edgar Bronfman Sr., has said, "We think Du Pont is doing a superb job environmentally." Here's the question: if you were a Director of Seagram, sitting on Du Pont's Board, would you say such a thing? Wouldn't you demand the company stop producing this horrible stuff *now?*

III. Effects on Non-Human Life

We have emphasized the effects on human beings: increased rates of skin cancer deaths, cataracts, blindness, and suppression of the immune system. These only begin to tell the story. We humans, at least, can try to cover ourselves. *Animals, plants, crops, and trees cannot do this.* They remain totally exposed to increased ultraviolet radiation. In southern Chile, for example, where the ozone hole has been open for over a decade, there has been increased incidence of rabbits and sheep with malformed eyes and impaired vision, as well as deformed tree buds, among other occurrences.

Even worse, however, are the apparent effects on oceanic phytoplankton, which live near the surface of the sea. These creatures are the base of the marine food chain. When plankton populations decline, so will the populations of the fish that eat plankton, and the mammals that eat the fish: seals, dolphins, whales *and human beings.* When you combine this effect with the fact that soybean and rice crops — which are the staple food for most of the Earth — are especially vulnerable to ultraviolet radiation, we may be looking at the greatest starvation the world has ever seen. And the greatest destruction of wild nature as well. This is why the U.N. calls it, "a danger as big as humanity has ever faced."

Alternatives To Du Pont's CFCs and HCFCs

When Du Pont Corporation is challenged for continuing to produce CFCs and HCFCs, the company says there are no viable alternatives. *This is not true.* In fact, there are many alternatives, with new ones being developed. The problem for Du Pont is only that it does not profit from the safer alternatives. Here is a *partial* list:

1. Aerosols.
CFCs are already banned for this use in the United States and Canada, but abroad they may still be sold for use in deodorants, sprays, paints, polishes and cleaners. Effective alternatives include solid stick and roll-on dispensers, mechanical spray pumps, brushes and pads. There are also alternative chemical spray propellants as well as compressed gases, like air and CO₂. Even in the case of asthma inhalers, dry powder inhalers are in wide use in Sweden and the Netherlands.

2. Foams.
The use of polystyrene foam cups and food containers and foam packaging can be drastically reduced or eliminated. (Paper cups or mugs, will do the job as well.) As for insulation for appliances, vacuum insulation panels are superior. Fiberglass, rock wool and cellulose easily substitute for rigid foam.

3. Solvents.
The electronics industry has already decided that water-based cleaning processes work as well as, and often more cheaply than, CFC-based methods. Citrus-based solvents are also being used effectively.

4. Refrigeration and cooling.
New safe technologies include passive and active solar technologies, evaporative air conditioning, ammonia compression systems, as well as water and alcohol, or helium used as refrigerants. These systems are already in use. Also, air conditioning technologies based on waste heat recycling from on-site generation have the potential to eliminate CFCs while reducing energy use by 20%.

IV. Four Point Action Plan

The full effects of ozone destruction will be upon us in our lifetime. There is no way around this. But we *can* try to minimize the effects on our children and the Earth. Here are a few ways to start:

1. Demand that Du Pont immediately halt all production or licensing of CFCs and HCFCs, as well as the global warming gases, HFCs. Continued production of these deadly substances condemns your children and theirs to even more terrible problems. Write the Du Pont and Seagram Chairmen and telephone them. (Du Pont: 1-800-441-7515; Seagram: 514-849-5271). And use the coupons below.

2. Demand that Du Pont and Seagram put all the profits they have made from these ozone depleting chemicals into a new fund to: 1) provide a transition to environmentally safe alternatives; 2) recapture and recycle existing CFCs, to prevent their release to the atmosphere; 3) assist non-industrial countries in procuring safe alternatives and avoid the deadly dependence on CFCs.

3. Demand that Du Pont and Seagram, and individual directors of these companies, be held accountable to the fullest extent of the law for damages to people who develop disease caused by ozone depletion, as well as damage to property and the environment.

4. Change your consumption habits. Do not buy polystyrene foam, or any products packaged with polystyrene foam. Demand that your local appliance dealer sell only safe alternatives like helium, or water and alcohol refrigerators, and air conditioners that run on evaporation. If your home or office air conditioners or refrigerators require servicing, insist that all CFCs and HCFCs be recaptured rather than vented to the air. Demand that your community establish local CFC recapture and recycling centers. And, bring back windows that open.

* * *

Finally, of course, we must face a basic fact. With ozone destruction and global warming, it is obvious that human life is just as endangered as the rest of nature. Uncontrolled, industrial society is no longer enhancing human life, it is beginning to destroy it. We cannot pollute our own nests forever. *It is not a question of jobs vs. environment. There will be no jobs on a dead, scorched Earth, and no people either.*

You can help. Join the Greenpeace campaign to save the ozone layer from further destruction. *Mail the coupons.* In turn, we will send you more information, and tell you how you can participate in further actions. Please do this today. Thank you.

GREENPEACE

ADVERTISEMENT

CAN NEW ZEALAND STOP THE JAPANESE DEATH SHIP?

Claiming it is doing so for "peaceful" reasons, Japan is building up a massive stockpile of plutonium, the essential element in nuclear warheads.

How does this affect New Zealand?

To get tonnes of toxic, radioactive plutonium from factories in Europe back to Japan for its nuclear energy program, the Japanese government has launched the plutonium freighter *Akatsuki-maru*.

This ship has just embarked on what could be the most dangerous voyage in human history. Already, the governments of Argentina, Brazil, Chile, Uruguay, South Africa, Malaysia, Singapore, Indonesia and the Philippines have barred access to the ship. And many Pacific nations are strongly protesting.

That leaves the Japanese government with only one uncontested route. Around the Cape of Good Hope — and straight for New Zealand and Australia.

[**What nuclear experts say:** *A mere 8 kgs. of plutonium missing from a Japanese shipment measured in tonnes would give terrorists all they need to make a crude atomic bomb equal in power to the explosion (above) that flattened Hiroshima in 1945.*]

The secrecy-shrouded voyage of a Japanese freighter loaded with 1.5 tonnes of the most deadly substance known to mankind is only the first of what will be dozens of trips over the next twenty years.

Unless New Zealand refuses to accept this cargo and its colossal risks right now, your children will grow up never knowing when — or if — their world could end in atomic disaster.

We are Japanese citizens concerned about plutonium. With this advertisement, we are breaking our own government's blackout on this explosive story.

We want you, as a New Zealander, to have the facts you need to make your own decision:

1] Despite huge technical problems and insurmountable security risks, a faction inside Japan's government has promoted the shift from low-grade uranium to bomb-grade plutonium for reactor fuel.

2] Japan's plutonium policy is the greatest long-term threat to nuclear disarmament and non-proliferation efforts worldwide. While headlines fret about this or that nation being able to acquire *ounces* of plutonium, some 45 *tonnes* of plutonium reprocessed from U.S.-supplied uranium will be shipped from Europe to Japan starting this year.

3] Japan already has the plutonium and plutonium production capacity to sustain its existing energy R&D efforts. Acquiring even greater quantities from reprocessing plants in France and the U.K., Japan's civil nuclear program will possess more nuclear bomb material

THE START OF A NEW COLD WAR?

PLUTONIUM LEFT IN U.S. ARSENAL	PLUTONIUM LEFT IN FORMER SOVIET ARSENAL	JAPAN'S PLUTONIUM SUPPLY BY 2020

SOURCE: CNIC, TOKYO

Because plutonium breeder reactors are uneconomical and dangerous, the U.S., U.K., Germany and France have given them up. Only Japan is rushing to power nuclear reactors with bomb-grade plutonium. While the U.S. and Russia are trying to dismantle their plutonium arsenals, Japan is building a gigantic stockpile of plutonium. Why?

than any military in the world.

4] History has come to a crossroad. The Cold War is over. We finally have a chance to end the nuclear nightmare. As Japanese, we are deeply saddened that our government's plutonium policy, as it now stands, would disrupt Pacific regional stability and deter nuclear disarmament.

We are equally concerned that sea shipments of Japanese plutonium will put the globe in danger of severe environmental contamination. We cannot let this happen.

5] In an accident off the New Zealand coast, one Japanese plutonium shipment could release as much radiation as 10-20 Chernobyls. A single ounce of plutonium, dispersed in the air, can cause tens of thousands of human cancers. If a plutonium ship burns, collides or sinks, spilling its contents in the coastal currents, radioactive contaminants with a half-life of 24,000 years could make the shores of New Zealand a wasteland.

6] According to a study by independent U.S. marine safety experts, the casks which will carry Japan's plutonium are not designed to survive severe collisions or ship fires. A report by the French nuclear authorities who packed the plutonium in La Hague discloses that the casks would fail after ninety minutes at 1,000°c. *Since ship fires*

[**Route of the death ship:** *With air shipment barred for safety reasons, Japan has three choices. Shove right through more than a dozen protesting nations in the Caribbean and Pacific. Trust this Cook Straits ferry-size plutonium freighter on the treacherous Tasman Sea. Or give up the whole crazy idea.*]

commonly burn for a day or more at temperatures higher than 1,000°c, it is highly questionable whether the plutonium casks would survive a severe accident off New Zealand's coast.

7] Plutonium in transit is also considered to be the world's most tempting terrorist target. According to the U.S. Defense Department, "even if the most careful precautions are observed, no one could guarantee the safety of the cargo."

8] The *Shikishima*, the sole Japanese Maritime Safety Agency vessel escorting the plutonium freighter, has its own problems. On its way to France, it twice made unexplained returns to Japan — the reasons kept secret. What would happen if it now had to abandon the *Akatsuki-maru* mid-voyage?

9] Frightened and angry official protests about emergency ports-of-call from nations en route have all but ruled out sending the ship through the Panama Canal or the Straits of Malacca. That leaves the Japanese government with only one route: around the Cape of Good Hope, near stormy Antarctic waters south of Australia, then right between New Zealand and Australia

to Japan. Despite your Prime Minister's pledge to keep New Zealand nuclear-free, he has not as yet officially come out against the death ship. It is now virtually certain that the plutonium shipments will pass your shores. And New Zealand or Australia would be the only ports-of-call in an emergency.

10] As Japanese, we profoundly respect your nation's Nuclear Free Zone, Disarmament and Arms Control Act. The *Akatsuki-maru* carries nearly 200 nuclear bombs' worth of plutonium. It violates the spirit of New Zealand's nuclear-free policy for this ship to pass by your waters, threatening your people and your environment.

It is in your power to block this plutonium trafficking— and spare the world 20 years of nuclear terror on the high seas. As a citizen, you have the right to protest against a policy so dangerous to New Zealand and to the security of the entire Asian-Pacific region.

While we are pressuring our own government, please urge yours to go on record against this global threat.

Join the many other nations who have already said NO. For yourself, for your children, for the future of New Zealand, please mail the coupons below.

JAPANESE CITIZENS CONCERNED ABOUT PLUTONIUM

Representatives: Asaishi Koji, Ayukawa Yurika, Ikejima Fukiko, Kawada Masaharu, Ogiso Miwako, Ōshita Yumiko, Aileen Mioko Smith, Takagi Jinzaburo. This warning is made possible by the contributions of men and women throughout Japan who are opposed to our government's irresponsible plutonium policies. We welcome your inquiries. Fax our Kyoto office at 81-75-702-1952. Thank you.

SOUND THE ALARM...MAIL THESE MESSAGES.

PRIME MINISTER JIM BOLGER
Parliament Buildings
Wellington, New Zealand

The Japanese government must reverse its policy of stockpiling tonnes of plutonium. For the sake of every New Zealander, demand — as other nations have demanded — that the Japanese government forbid its plutonium freighter *Akatsuki-maru* to approach our shores. Put New Zealand's welfare first.

NAME

ADDRESS

AMBASSADOR DELLA M. NEWMAN
American Embassy,
#29 Fitzherbert Ter Thorndon,
Wellington, New Zealand

Just when the U.S. and Russia have stopped making plutonium for weapons, Japan has started recycling U.S.-supplied reactor fuel into weapon-ready plutonium and stockpiling it. The U.S. has the right, by treaty, to veto anything this irresponsible. Please tell Washington.

NAME

ADDRESS

HONORABLE MICHIO WATANABE
Japanese Minister for Foreign Affairs
c/o Embassy of Japan, 7th Floor,
Norwich Insurance House, 3-11 Hunter St.
Wellington 1, New Zealand

We cannot allow you to risk our lives by sending your plutonium freighter *Akatsuki-maru* past our coast. We want good relations with Japan, but I am compelled to strongly protest this threat.

NAME

ADDRESS

JAPANESE CITIZENS CONCERNED ABOUT PLUTONIUM
1-59-14-302 Higashi-nakano, Nakano-ku,
Tokyo 164, Japan

As a New Zealander, I share your concerns about plutonium and challenge the Japanese government to abandon its plan to transport and stockpile tonnes of bomb-grade material over the next two decades. The death ship must be stopped.

NAME

ADDRESS

AUTHORIZED BY: JAPANESE CITIZENS CONCERNED ABOUT PLUTONIUM

How to win an argument with a meat eater.

The Hunger Argument

Number of people worldwide who will die of starvation this year: 60 million

Number of people who could be adequately fed with the grain saved if Americans reduced their intake of meat by 10%: 60 million

Human beings in America: 243 million

Number of people who could be fed with grain and soybeans now eaten by U.S. livestock:1.3 billion

Percentage of corn grown in the U.S. eaten by people: 20

Percentage of corn grown in the U.S. eaten by livestock: 80

Percentage of oats grown in the U.S. eaten by livestock: 95

Percentage of protein wasted by cycling grain through livestock: 90

How frequently a child starves to death: every 2 seconds

Pounds of potatoes that can be grown on an acre: 20,000

Pounds of beef produced on an acre: 165

Percentage of U.S. farmland devoted to beef production: 56

Pounds of grain and soybeans needed to produce a pound of feedlot beef: 16

The Environmental Argument

Cause of global warming: greenhouse effect

Primary cause of greenhouse effect:: carbon dioxide emissions from fossil fuels

Fossil fuels needed to produce a meat-centered diet vs. a meat-free diet: 50 times more

Percentage of U.S. topsoil lost to date: 75

Percentage of U.S. topsoil loss directly related to livestock raising: 85

Number of acres of U.S. forest cleared for cropland to produce meat-centered diet: 260 million

Amount of meat U.S. imports annually from Costa Rica, El Salvador, Guatemala, Honduras and Panama: 200,000,000 pounds

Average per capita meat consumption in Costa Rica, El Salvador, Guatemala, Honduras and Panama: less than eaten by average U.S. housecat

Area of tropical rainforest consumed in every

quarter-pound hamburger: 55 sq. ft.

Current rate of species extinction due to destruction of tropical rainforests for meat grazing and other uses: 1,000 per year

The Cancer Argument

Increased risk of breast cancer for women who eat meat four times a week vs. less than once a week: 4 times

For women who eat eggs daily vs. less than once a week: 3 times

For women who eat butter and cheese 3 or more times a week vs. less than once: 3 times

Increased risk of fatal ovarian cancer for women who eat eggs 3 or more times a week vs. less than once a week: 3 times

Increased risk of fatal prostate cancer for men who consume meat, cheese, eggs and milk daily vs. sparingly or not at all: 3.6 times

The Natural Resources Argument

User of more than half of all water used for all purposes in the U.S.: livestock production

Amount of water used in production of the average cow: sufficient to float a destroyer

Gallons to produce a pound of wheat: 25

Gallons to produce a pound of meat: 2,500

Cost of common hamburger if water used by meat industry was not subsidized by the U.S. taxpayer: $35 a pound

Current cost of pound of protein from beefsteak: if water was no longer subsidized: $89

Years the world's known oil reserves would last if every human ate a meat-centered diet: 13

Years they would last if human beings no longer ate meat: 260

Barrels of oil imported into U.S. daily: 6.8 million

Percentage of fossil fuel energy returned as food energy by most efficient factory farming of meat: 34.5 percent

Percentage returned from least efficient plant food: 328 percent

Percentage of raw materials consumed by U.S. to produce present meat-centered diet: 33

The Cholesterol Argument

Number of U.S. medical schools: 125

Number requiring a course in nutrition: 30

Nutrition training received by average U.S. physician during four years in medical school: 2.5 hours

Most common cause of death in U.S.: heart attack

How frequently a heart attack kills in U.S.: every 45 seconds

Average U.S. man's risk of death from heart attack: 50 percent

Risk for average U.S. man who avoids the meat-centered diet: 15 percent

Risk for average U.S. man who consumes no meat, dairy products or eggs at all: 4 percent

Amount you reduce risk of heart attack if you reduce consumption of meat, dairy products and eggs by 10 percent: 9 percent

Amount you reduce risk if you reduce consumption by 50 percent: 45 percent

Amount you reduce risk if you eliminate these foodstuffs from your diet entirely: 90 percent

Meat, dairy and egg industries claim you should not be concerned about your blood cholesterol if it is: "normal"

Your risk of dying of a disease caused by clogged arteries if your blood cholesterol is "normal": over 50 percent

The Antibiotic Argument

Percentage of U.S. antibiotics fed to livestock: 55

Percentage of staphylococci infections resistant to penicillin in 1960: 13

Percentage resistant in 1988: 91

Response of European Economic Community to routine feeding of antibiotics to livestock: ban

Response of U.S. meat and pharmaceutical industries to routine feeding of antibiotics to livestock: full and complete support

The Pesticide Argument

Percentage of pesticide residues in the U.S. diet supplied by grains: 1

Percentage of pesticide residues in the U.S. diet supplied by fruits: 4

Percentage of pesticide residues in the U.S. diet supplied by vegetabies: 6

Percentage of pesticide residues in the U.S. diet

supplied by dairy products: 23

Percentage of pesticide residues in the U.S. diet supplied by meat: 55

Pesticide contamination of breast milk from meat-eating mothers vs. non-meat eating: 35 times higher

What USDA tells us: meat is inspected

Percentage of slaughtered animals inspected for residues of toxic chemicals including dioxin and DDT: less than 0.00004

The Ethical Argument

Number of animals killed for meat per hour in U.S.: 500,000

Occupation with highest turnover rate in U.S.: slaughterhouse worker

Occupation with highest rate of on-the-job injury in U.S.: slaughterhouse worker

Cost to render animal unconscious with "captive bolt pistol" before slaughter: 1¢

Reason given by meat industry for not using "captive bolt pistol": too expensive

The Survival Argument

Athlete to win Ironman Triathlon more than twice: Dave Scott (6 time winner)

Food choices of Dave Scott: Vegetarian

Largest meat eater that ever lived: Tyrannosaurus Rex

WILL 1968
GO DOWN IN HISTORY
AS THE YEAR THE POLITICIANS
STARTED IMITATING HONESTY?

(It could be. Eugene McCarthy has shown them the *real* thing works.)

You hear a lot of this lately:

"I think McCarthy is great myself, but he'll never, never, never be nominated."

Why? Because the "experts" have told us for years that honesty is fine and so are wit, intelligence, reasonableness, courage, thoughtfulness, idealism, and the rest of it, but a man like that could never be nominated for President. What *really* matters, the pros have said, are these:

1) The backing of old-line party politicos;
2) A flamboyant manner of speechmaking, and
3) Great, great wealth.

As though any of the three had something to do with democracy, or for that matter, the Presidency.

Senator McCarthy has not followed those rules on How-To-Get-Ahead-As-An-Aspiring-President. Instead, he has behaved as though in a democratic system the way to go about getting nominated and elected is to present specific solutions to our great problems *directly to the people.*

It has not been a calculated political decision to behave that way; it is the way he is.

And so far, just a few months into the campaign, he has already accomplished these:

1) He has changed the political mood in America.
2) He has been *the* major factor in altering a disastrous and presumably irreversible trend in Vietnam.

3) He has brought thousands of our young people back into society.
4) He has presented concrete plans to enable Black People to end their "Colonial Status."
5) And also, along the way, he has gotten himself to the position where he stands quite a good chance of becoming President of the United States. You bet he does.

It is *that* realization which may just start a new trend among politicians. (If there's anything you can say about your *standard* politician, it's he's adaptable.)

Anyway, America will be better off for it. Candidates who find *imitative* honesty expedient will be better than those who find no use for it at all.

And now to the money part.

As you know, Mr. McCarthy was raised on a farm, and was a college teacher before his twenty years in Congress. He is *not* a rich man.

Running for President costs 5 million dollars and getting nominated costs almost that, even if you ignore half of what experts tell you. (You *do* have to fly around a lot, and you must get onto television now and then.)

Mr. McCarthy has said, "I can win in California with one fifth of Mr. Kennedy's budget."

If he says it, it must be so.

7
SECRETS OF SUCCESS
STYLE IS CONTENT

Media of Record; Complexity Over Simplicity: Multiple Entry Points
Pathways to Engagement & Clip-Out Coupons

THE FIRST OBVIOUS THING to say about most of the non-profit ads we've displayed in this book, is that they have a lot more words than 90% of other advertisements you are likely to see.

This is because the ads are often "one-shot" insertions, or "low budget campaigns" as presented in the prior chapters. Very few non-profit organizations have the funds to invest in multiple placement advertising campaigns. In fact, as indicated in earlier chapters, many of the do-gooder ad campaigns can barely get the money together for just *one* insertion. So the information in that one-shot ad has to be extensive, clear, instructive, and persuasive. It's often a non-profit organization's best or *only* chance to make a comprehensive, appealing, convincing, and successful argument to a large public audience, and to win out over much larger, well-financed campaigns. It's a tough assignment—especially considering that corporations have sufficient funds to run their ads today, and again tomorrow, and the next day. And then again on television!

The good news is that many of the ads we've displayed actually did achieve their results despite their "one-time-only" appearance. The fact that it's a rare one-time appearance actually helps create at least one moment of surprise and curiosity in a reader—*"What's this?"* This may ultimately help in stimulating interest and engagement in a reader and potential respondent.

Anyway, good or bad, that's the reality. Low budget political advertisers are stuck with this. We've got to

score with a one-shot effort. That's our task. We do not have budgets beyond one-time. So, how *can* we catch attention sufficiently in *one shot* to successfully implant ideas that will attract, engage, and activate a reader? Something that might keep readers sufficiently aroused, so that they're willing to pour through a 1,500 word ad rather than the more familiar 75 words that corporate sources employ. If we can get the reader to do that . . . we've got 'em! They will thenceforth pay attention to the rest of the story.

So, following below are a few details about how to construct *one-time shots* that *do* have a chance to prevail against huge odds, and that can accelerate under-funded political movements. Simply realizing and accepting the stark reality of the above, is step one in the process.

MEDIA "OF RECORD"

The first, and possibly most important decision when contemplating advertising campaigns, is this: *which medium to choose?* If you attempt to use "moving image" media—like television (or even radio)—you will need to deploy dozens of multiple entries of 30 seconds or 60 seconds so as to explain complex histories and details, and their consequences. In our campaigns we are obviously not selling the simple virtues of dish soap or gasoline, but of ideas! The issues we need to address can only rarely be satisfactorily dealt with in one-shot TV appearances of 30 or 60 seconds.

Theoretically you could use broadcast media to concentrate on raising money, or seek donations to halt, say, an intrusive urban over-development project, or improper polluting governmental behavior, etc. But, with broadcast media you are very unlikely to succeed without having sufficient funding to amplify, in a one-shot placement, the enormous, complex background details that fully explain the issues, and are capable of competing with larger commercial entities.

Print media on the other hand, offer something entirely different: *space*, not limited by time. In a single printed page, there is plenty of room to explain complexities. So, the ultimate task is far more do-able. We need to choose media that are serious enough, and which deliver information *slowly* enough, so that full expression and full ingestion are possible. Secondly, we need to choose media that can reach deeply into difficult areas, and which are respected, by both the people causing the problems, and the ones who are fighting to fix them.

The obvious choices are selected print media—certain newspapers and magazines. For our purposes, newspapers are usually the most obvious choice.

As you have seen in this book, most of our political advocacy ads were originally placed in at least one of three major "national newspapers:" *The New York Times, Wall Street Journal*, and/or *Washington Post*. Those three newspapers speak everyday most directly to the key publics that we usually need to reach, and who thrive on in-depth reporting. Those newspapers are also the country's most important "media of record," i.e., the ones that tend to be read closely by the country's most powerful government and corporate interests.

"Media of record" tend to focus daily on the most serious debates among key audiences: businesses, governments, universities, and all ranges of activist communities, from environment to social justice, to battlers on the political stage.

★   ★   ★

In addition to those big three newspapers there are a few other urban papers, with a regional focus, that can often be very relevant. These might include the *Los Angeles Times, San Francisco Chronicle, Chicago Tribune, Miami Herald*, and *The Boston Globe*, among others.

And, there are certain magazines that also offer similarly serious in-depth reporting directed toward equally engaged audiences (*New Yorker, Harpers,*

Atlantic, et. al). But those are not published daily, but weekly or monthly, so their impacts are slower, and usually lower.

The choice of which medium to use for the greatest effect will of course vary from case to case. Most ads you see in this book were run in one or all of the first three major newspapers we've indicated, but also, sometimes, a local paper or key magazine that speaks to similar reactive audiences, such as the *The New Yorker*.

Okay! Now that we know the key media, what can we say about how we should construct our arguments (the Rules of Engagement, as it were)?

COMPLEXITY OVER SIMPLICITY: MULTIPLE ENTRY POINTS

Imagine you are home drinking morning coffee while reading the Sunday newspaper. You turn the page and there's a full-page *advertisement* that covers the page with words, pictures, and charts. Very dense. Very complicated.

Your first instinct is probably to turn the page. *But* the ad really does offer an unusual potpourri of multiple images, plus multiple sub-headings and boxed sections, including photos and/or charts, or extra highlighted graphs, and numbered paragraphs. Unusual and intriguing. It may also contain 4-6 opinionated clip-out coupons. You are invited to fill those out and mail them to a public official who has power to do something about a public issue that the ad has raised.

A reader's first impulse may often be to escape that page. *But wait a second*. The headline is actually interesting, and the subheadings and images also alluring. Something about it all leads us to at least glance through—a heading, a photo, or the main headline—expressing at least that moment of curiosity. That moment may be just enough to implant one thought: *"What the hell is this about?"* That's it. You got 'em!

One normal rule of *commercial* ad-writing, as Howard Gossage once described it, is to provide "just enough string to go around the package." You make a case, just enough to implant one thought or image or desire. For normal commercial advertising, one image or thought is sufficient.

On the other hand, when you are dealing with complex information on major public issues, and you need to get a response—and you only have enough money for a one-time insertion—you need to offer a considerable amount of stimulating information. You've somehow got to get the reader more deeply engaged than in ads that are for shoes or nice dresses, where one image will suffice. It's an entirely different problem.

Here's another important point: If you have gone through the ads in this book, you've maybe noted that in many of the cases (though not all) the full page ad tends to contain *multiple entry points*. The central headline remains, of course, usually at the top of the page. That's intended to have a primary initial appeal. But if the ad has a "do-gooder" purpose, the ad is also designed to *not* allow you to easily leave the page. Reading the headline is not enough. It's only meant as an inducement.

So, beyond the main heading there will likely be more detailed sub-headings, plus one or two or three photos, and perhaps a chart of some kind, and/or another unusual image, secondary side-discussion, map, or added subheadings. The goal is to deliberately add complexity and variety to the message, and (hopefully) build curiosity about a page that offers so much varied, interesting stuff.

For example, in Joan McIntyre's ad, *"KILLING-OFF THE WHALES AND DOLPHINS" (pages 38-39)* there are 7 alternative entry points. The main headline is very direct. But then there's a picture of a *dead* 100-foot whale with humans walking on it, and a sub-heading about whales as the "intelligent non-human life" we've been wondering about. And there's also a charming child's drawing celebrating whales. Then there's a self-contained sub-article, with its own headline and astonishing photos, comparing the brain sizes and the complexities of whale brains vs. human brains. (We learn that humans may not be, after all, the smartest creatures on Earth!)

And then another box focuses on the repulsive practice of the tuna-fish industry which finds their fish by first locating swarms of dolphins who tend to swim just above the tuna herds, an apparently friendly arrangement among the animals. But, it's ultimately *most* helpful for tuna companies gathering their products. Just spot the dolphins and then kill them all. Then you can get the tuna, cut them up, and shove them into little cans! The ad also offers a useful bibliography, and two coupons for further engagement. And a text of about 4,000 words. *On one page!*

In some other ads there may be an added box within the page with its own distinct heading—a self-contained mini ad—containing maybe 30-40 added words. For example, in the ad headlined *"HAS THE*

NRA GONE OFF THE DEEP END?" (page viii) there are two parallel (related) story lines, zeroing in on different details of the subject, plus a photo/statement by Sarah Brady whose husband was left permanently disabled by a gunshot wound. *Plus*, up-close photos of beautiful machine guns and hand-guns. Disgusting, but engaging. Plus, one urgent coupon. You can enter the discussion at any of these points, as each point leads you to others.

There are sometimes also powerful images of devastating visual content, such as in *"LEGISLATION BY CHAIN-SAW"* attacking the giant US corporation, Georgia-Pacific *(page 20)*. G-P had been racing to cut down the last redwoods, preventing them from being saved for a proposed new national park. In addition to terrible images of devastated forests, there's an impressive image of a beautiful redwood forest, plus *five* coupons to be clipped and mailed to some key person(s) who had leverage on the situation. (In just a moment, I will have more to say about the amazing powers of coupons, for both senders and receivers.)

In all the above examples the reader is offered "multiple entry points," i.e., a variety of appeals in the same ad that try to draw-in a diverse audience. The worry, of course, is that the page may look too crowded or dense or stand-offish because of all these additional entries. And there's the risk that the reader may not enter at all. So, it's a balancing act. And you need the help of a very smart graphic designer who grasps the multi-faceted unusualness of the approach. Most advertising emphasizes simplicity. But if you offer many bridges to cross, complexity may actually be of great service. The issues themselves are actually complex; dealing with them from various angles is inherently helpful.

Here are some further examples you have seen earlier in this book:

"SHOULD WE ALSO FLOOD THE SISTINE CHAPEL SO TOURISTS CAN GET NEARER THE CEILING?" This ad *(page 14)* contains a truly astonishing, illuminating time chart, basically showing the history of life on earth, from the earliest sponges, and then dinosaurs, through the present moment. On this chart—devised, by the way, in 1966 by George Dipple of Freeman & Gossage—the tiny line showing the earliest appearance of human beings is so recent it represents the skinniest possible line at the tip of the billions of years' chart. Isn't that a bit too recent to take our supposed superiority for granted? (That chart shocked a lot of respondents.)

"NINE REASONS WHY ABORTIONS ARE LEGAL" (page 40) features photos of two women who suffered from illegal abortions, one of them a physician. They appear on a page with 9 *numbered* paragraphs. Numbering paragraphs tends to stimulate a greater connection with readers, as they realize they can learn something new from each paragraph. Each one tells a slightly different story. *And* there's a photo of anti-abortion bombings, *and* also of a young pregnant woman—plus three coupons at the top of the page, that you are invited to clip, fill-out, and mail to someone who has actual power over the situation, negative or positive.

"JEOPARDIZED BY GATT" (pages 64-65) ran in 1994. This Sierra Club ad reacted to corporations' attempts to undermine the sovereignty of popular, hard-won, US environmental protection laws. The concerns expressed were very much in line with those of Lori Wallach of the Citizens Trade Campaign, seen earlier. A wonderful cartoon drawing shows a businessman stepping on and gleefully hacking the US capital building. And the ad amplifies the situation with eight sub-stories and four small, emblematic, eye-catching photographs.

Just to be clear, none of the above means that it's impossible to present very powerful smaller ads, with only one image, when an important point can be made that way. One of my favorite ads for example, written by Jono Polansky, is the gorgeous single drawing of a beautiful young woman and man as she hands him a loving gift: *"OH DARLING, YOU HAVE EVERYTHING I'VE ALWAYS WANTED IN A MAN, EXCEPT THESE . . . "* A gift-wrapped pack of condoms *(see page 116).*

Or, that moving photo of a sea turtle with the heading *"THIS EXOTIC SEA TURTLE MAY BE HEADED FOR EXTINCTION, BUT IT'S STILL AVAILABLE AS A JAPANESE CIGARETTE LIGHTER."* Which makes its point quickly, directly, powerfully, and offers three response coupons *(page v).*

So, in the end it comes down to specific circumstances and messages. In most cases, however, do-gooder complaints involve whole systems and need to be fully explained in a single one-shot ad. Multiple entry points and response systems can lead the reader carefully through the terrain, stimulate a complexity of thoughts, and awaken a strong response.

Pᴀᴛʜᴡᴀʏs ᴛᴏ Eɴɢᴀɢᴇᴍᴇɴᴛ & Cʟɪᴘ-Oᴜᴛ Cᴏᴜᴘᴏɴs

I have dedicated several prior passages of this book to the memory of Howard Gossage. He was the first person ever to articulate the benefits of this style of advocacy advertising, and he was also my greatest teacher.

But I particularly want to dedicate *this* section to Gossage, for what I think were amazingly brilliant ideas and practices, way back in the early-mid 1960s, specifically on the effects of coupon cutouts on both the senders and receivers. I think they actually had a lot to do with movement-building for do-gooders in the latter half of the 1900s.

As far as I know, Gossage was the first person who advocated putting *multiple* response coupons into print advertising placed by non-profit organizations who were attempting to advocate and influence an important issue. Those response mechanisms have proven to be *very* important in several unusual ways.

First of all, there've been the impacts on the government and/or corporate persons who've been recipients of these coupon messages, especially if the coupons arrive in the tens of thousands as they often do. Showing up to his/her office one morning, he or she may find a giant mailbag (or two of them) sitting up on their desks, with thousands of coupons—*filled-out by hand*, and then *signed by a human being*, and then *sent by ordinary post,* not a tweet—asking the recipient to consider, or reconsider, some stance or policy on an urgent issue.

Howard Gossage felt strongly that the effect of these thousands of filled-out coupons, dumped on the desk of law-makers and/or corporations, complaining about some unforgiveable act, requires that the recipient *must* at least think-over whatever proposal or policy had been put into question. Gossage felt this was far more powerful than, say, picketing or marching while holding signs.

Well, perhaps it's not as powerful as if 5,000 people had instead shown up at the recipient's front door, to make a protest. But it is still a concrete personal written expression on some-kind of controversial issue with which the recipient had gotten involved. The recipient absolutely *must* take it seriously and give it further thought and response.

But that's only the most obvious effect of this process. There is another aspect which is arguably at least equally important: the impact upon the people who are the mailers of those coupons. We are speaking often of tens of thousands of newspaper *readers* who first see the advertisement in the newspaper, with its cutout coupons, and who then must decide if they want to respond. That decision might require them to go through a fairly long process: clip out, fill out, and mail out those coupon messages to the corporate or government officials who are targeted to be impacted.

Clipping and mailing is not such an easy thing to do. And doing it, radicalizes the sender at least as much as it impresses the receiver.

For example, if you get the urge to participate, you must take quite a few steps to do so. First, you've got to get up and go find a scissor and a pen someplace in the house. Then cut out the 4-5 coupons. Then fill them in with your name, address and perhaps your scrawled added comments. Then go find five envelopes and postage stamps. Then write the addresses of the corporate or government people who are doing the cited harms. Then pop the five coupons into separate envelopes, seal them, address them, and go outside to find a mailbox, and send them.

These are trivial activities, of course, but it's actually a fair amount of effort. It's much more personal investment than, let's say, just forwarding a tweet on your iPhone. This process might take, maybe, 15-20 minutes start to finish. And, once you go all the way through, you have invested yourself in the issues in a way that, say, tweeting does not require. You have been a bit more radicalized. Ultimately, that aids movement building.

Meanwhile, back on the receiving end, a person of power or authority receives 5,000 hand-written coupons in the postal mail, filled out by pencil or pen, and addressed specifically to him or her. That may actually have far greater impact, and bring far more attention, than, for example, thousands of tweets, that require very little personal time or engagement to send or to receive.

Howard Gossage felt the coupon-sending process had very significant positive impact on *both* the receiver and the sender. I think he was right. And it helps to explain the notable success of that process over the years, and of the many ads you see in this book.

Sensitivity, strength, security, intelligence. All the qualities women look for in a man can also be found in a foilpack of condoms.

They're an extremely effective way to prevent pregnancy. Especially when they're used with contraceptive foam.

They're fun to put on, if you use your imagination.

And they make a fantastic gift for that special occasion when words... just aren't enough.

You can get them at any drugstore or your local Planned Parenthood.

So next time, show how much you care. With foam for her. And condoms for you.

It might take a sense of humor. But it's part of getting serious.

Planned Parenthood®
Federation of America

810 Seventh Avenue
New York, NY 10019

Protect your love with condoms.

70 ADS TO SAVE *the* WORLD

Our Arctic way of life has endured for 20,000 years. Must we now die for 6 months of oil?

We have learned something about the Arctic in the 20,000 years we have lived up here.

One must not disturb the place where the caribou come to bear their young, even in hard times. Or else nothing will remain for future generations.

This is a lesson some Washington politicians have not yet learned.

Oil development in the Arctic National Wildlife Refuge, promoted by Chevron, Arco, and BP, will end the way of life that has sustained us for a thousand generations ... for six months of oil.

How will America survive the next fifty years, let alone the next thousand years, if our leaders keep acting like this?

There is a better way and many people in Congress know it.

It is to preserve the Porcupine Caribou range as wilderness ... and keep oil drillers out.

Contact the real decision makers now. Begin with the coupons below.

Help protect the Arctic National Wildlife Refuge. Help us protect our children and grandchildren.

Experience tells us such wisdom will safeguard your children as well.

THE GWICH'IN PEOPLE

Help us keep the oil companies out of our Arctic home.

Photos: Taro Yamasaki; Karen Jettmar; Jim Brandenburg/Minden Pictures

---

Mr. James Ross, Chairman
BP America, Inc.
200 Public Square
Cleveland, OH 44114-2375

I strongly oppose your efforts to open the Arctic Refuge to oil exploration. British Petroleum has no right to profit from the destruction of a way of life that has existed for 20,000 years. As a foreign-owned company, BP has an even greater obligation to respect our environment and native people.

NAME _____

ADDRESS _____ CITY _____ STATE/ZIP _____

Mr. Robert Wycoff, Chairman
ARCO, 515 South Flower Street
Los Angeles, CA 90071

Officials admit there's only a 15% chance of finding significant amounts of oil in the Arctic Refuge. And onshore exploration will ruin it. The West Sak field, west of Prudhoe Bay, is a sure thing. Go where the real oil is. Leave the Arctic Refuge alone.

NAME _____

ADDRESS _____ CITY _____ STATE/ZIP _____

Gwich'in Steering Committee
P.O. Box 202768
Anchorage, AK 99520

I want to help the Gwich'in people and protect the Arctic National Wildlife Refuge for future generations. Please keep me informed. Here's my tax-deductible donation of:

___ $25   ___ $35   ___ $50   or $___

NAME _____

ADDRESS _____ CITY _____ STATE/ZIP _____

Prepared by Public Media Center

This is an appeal from the Gwich'in chiefs and people of Arctic Village, Venetie, Chalkytsik, Fort Yukon, Old Crow, Fort McPherson, Arctic Red River, Aklavik, and other traditional communities in northeast Alaska and northwest Canada. To learn more, please call (907) 258-6814 in Anchorage, Alaska. Thank you.

CREDITS

While every effort has been made to identify those directly involved in writing and design, each of these ads was the product of wider collaboration. Advocacy ads involved policy researchers, campaign organizers, funders, and others. Photographers and illustrators are often credited within the ads themselves. Uncredited are the resourceful account executives at Public Media Center who counseled countless organizations on tactics and strategy and helped launch many emerging issues into the mainstream. Dates of ad insertions in newspapers and magazines are recorded, where known; however, the publication list is not complete.

Page viii:
"Cop-killer Bullets . . . "
Writer: Jono Polansky
Designer: Jono Polansky
Agency: Public Media Center
Client: Handgun Control, Inc. (now Brady United)
Appeared: 1987-88

Page ix:
"This Exotic Sea Turtle . . ."
Writer: Jono Polansky
Designer: Jono Polansky
Agency: Public Media Center
Client: Todd Steiner, Sea Turtle Restoration Project, Earth Island Institute
Appeared: *Los Angeles Times,* 20 May 1991

Page x:
"To Many of Our Daughters . . . "
Writer: Jono Polansky
Designer: Jono Polansky
Agency: Public Media Center
Client: National Abortion Rights Action League & the NARAL Foundation
Appeared: *The New York Times,* 22 January 1989 (anniversary of Roe vs. Wade)

Page xi:
"Monocultures of the Mind"
Writer: Jerry Mander, title after Vandana Shiva
Designers: Mark Mazziotti, Ellen Visser
Agency: Public Media Center
Client: Turning Point Project (The Center for Commercial Free Public Education + 15 others)
Appeared: *The New York Times,* 19 June 2000

Page xiv:
"We Will No Longer Buy Anything ... "
Writer: Jerry Mander, Joan McIntyre
Designer: Freeman, Mander & Gossage
Agency: Freeman, Mander & Gossage
Client: Friends of the Earth
Appeared: *Women's Wear Daily,* 2 June 1970

Page 3:
"Contest: Will Yours Be War Toy of the Week?"
Writer: Jerry Mander
Designer: Barbara Stauffacher
Agency: Jerry Mander & Associates
Client: The Committee
Appeared: *The San Francisco Chronicle,* 30 January 1966; *The San Francisco Examiner,* 30 January 1966; *The Stanford Daily,* 4 February 1966

Page 4:
"Computer Commuting"
Concept: Howard Gossage
Writer: Jerry Mander
Designer: Freeman, Mander & Gossage
Agency: Freeman, Mander & Gossage
Client: Rover Division, British Leyland Motors
Unpublished, circa 1967-1969

Page 5:
"KLH & Love"
Writer: Jerry Mander
Designer: Freeman & Gossage
Agency: Freeman & Gossage
Client: KLH
Appeared: *The San Francisco Chronicle,* 19 May 1968

Page 6:
"The Land-Rover and Crime"
Writer: Howard Gossage
Designer: Freeman & Gossage
Agency: Freeman & Gossage
Client: Rover Motor Co. of North America
Appeared: *The New Yorker,* 2 November 1963; *The Wall Street Journal,* 12 November 1963

Page 7:
"1st International Paper Airplane Competition"
Concept: Howard Gossage
Writer: Jerry Mander
Designer: Freeman & Gossage
Art director and illustrator: George Dippel
Agency: Freeman & Gossage
Client: Scientific American magazine
Appeared: *The New York Times,* 12 December 1966; *The San Francisco Chronicle,* 15 December 1966; *The New Yorker,* 17 December 1966; *The Signal* (Santa Clarita, CA), 21 December 1966

Page 8:
"1st International Paper Airplane Competition"
Concept: Howard Gossage
Writer: Jerry Mander
Designer: Freeman & Gossage
Agency: Freeman & Gossage
Client: Scientific American magazine
Appeared: *The New York Times,* 23 March 1967

Pages 12-13:
"Now Only You Can Save Grand Canyon . . . "
Writer: Jerry Mander
Designer: Marget Larsen
Agency: Freeman & Gossage
Client: David Brower, Sierra Club
Appeared: *The New York Times,* 9 June 1966; *The Washington Post,* 9 June 1966

Page 14:
"Should We Also Flood the Sistine Chapel . . . "
Writer: Jerry Mander
Designer: Marget Larsen
Illustration: George Dippel
Agency: Freeman & Gossage
Client: David Brower, Sierra Club
Appeared: *Ramparts,* October 1966; *The New York Times,* 16 April 1967

Page 17:
"Dinosaur and Big Bend . . . "
Writer: Jerry Mander
Designer: Marget Larsen
Agency: Freeman & Gossage
Client: David Brower, Sierra Club

Appeared: *The New York Times,* 25 July 1966

Pages 18-19:
"Grand Canyon National Monument . . . "
Writer: Jerry Mander
Designer: Marget Larsen
Agency: Freeman & Gossage
Client: David Brower, Sierra Club
Appeared: *The New York Times,* 13 March 1967

Pages 20-21:
"History Will Think It Most Strange . . . "
Writer: Jerry Mander
Designer: Marget Larsen
Agency: Freeman & Gossage
Client: Edgar Wayburn, Sierra Club
Appeared: *The New York Times,* 25 January 1967; *The San Francisco Chronicle,* 25 January 1967; *The San Francisco Examiner,* 25 January 1967

Page 22:
"Legislation by Chain-saw?"
Writer: Jerry Mander
Designer: Marget Larsen
Agency: Freeman & Gossage
Client: Edgar Wayburn, Sierra Club
Appeared: *The New York Times,* 18 January 1968

Page 23:
"Earth National Park"
Writers: Jerry Mander, David Brower
Designer: Marget Larsen
Agency: Freeman, Mander & Gossage
Client: David Brower, Sierra Club
Appeared: *The New York Times,* 14 January 1969; *Whole Earth Catalog* supplement, March 1969

Page 24:
"Suing California"
Writer: Jerry Mander
Designer: Freeman, Mander & Gossage
Agency: Freeman, Mander & Gossage
Client: Alvin Duskin, The Legal Committee to Stop the California Water Plan
Appeared: *The San Francisco Chronicle,* 16 June 1970

Page 27:
"As Big A Steal As Manhattan Island"
Writers: Jerry Mander, Warren Hinckel, Alvin Duskin
Designer: Freeman, Mander & Gossage
Agency: Freeman, Mander & Gossage
Client: Alvin Duskin
Appeared: *The San Francisco Chronicle,* 9 October 1969

Page 28:
"You Can Help Decide If Our City..."
Writer: Jerry Mander
Designer: Freeman, Mander & Gossage
Agency: Freeman, Mander & Gossage
Client: Alvin Duskin, The San Francisco Opposition
Appeared: *The San Francisco Chronicle,* 31 January 1971; *The San Francisco Examiner,* 31 January 1971

Page 30:
"Alcatraz, The Bay, Water . . . "
Writer: Jerry Mander
Designer: Freeman, Mander & Gossage
Agency: Freeman, Mander & Gossage
Client: Alvin Duskin
Appeared: *The San Francisco Chronicle*, 2 February 1970

Page 32:
"Breaks Windows, Cracks Walls . . . "
Writer: Jerry Mander
Designer: Freeman, Mander & Gossage
Agency: Freeman, Mander & Gossage
Client: David Brower and Gary Soucie, Friends of the Earth
Appeared: *The New York Times*, 5 March 1970; *The Modesto Bee and News-Herald*, 8 May 1970

Page 33:
"Ecology & War"
Writer: Jerry Mander
Designer: Public Media Center
Agency: Public Media Center
Client: David Brower and Rafe Pomerance, Friends of the Earth
Appeared: *The New York Times*, 23 August 1982

Page 34:
"Ronald Reagan, the Health of Humans . . . "
Writer: Jerry Mander
Designer: Public Media Center
Agency: Public Media Center
Client: David Brower and Rafe Pomerance, Friends of the Earth
Appeared: *The New York Times*, 2 February 1982; *The San Francisco Chronicle*, 9 February 1982

Pages 38-39:
"Killing-Off the Whales and Dolphins"
Writers: Jerry Mander, Joan McIntyre
Designer: Public Interest Communications
Agency: Public Interest Communications
Client: Joan McIntyre, Project Jonah
Appeared: *The New York Times*, 11 June 1973; *The San Francisco Chronicle*, 11 June 1973; *The San Francisco Examiner*, 11 June 1973

Page 40:
"Nine Reasons Why Abortions Are Legal"
Writer: Jerry Mander
Designer: Jessie Bunn
Agency: Public Media Center
Client: Planned Parenthood Federation of America
Appeared: *The New York Times*, 21 May 1985; *The Washington Post*, 21 May 1985; *Los Angeles Times*, 21 May 1985; *Chicago Tribune*, 29 May 1985; *The Press-Tribune* (Roseville, CA), 29 May 1985; *Santa Cruz Sentinel*, 23 January 1986; *The Washington Post*, 6 October 1988; *The New York Times*, 17 October 1988

Page 42:
"Then I Got That Awful Phone Call"
Writer: Jono Polansky
Designer: Jessie Bunn
Agency: Public Media Center
Client: Planned Parenthood Federation of America
Appeared: 1986

Page 42:
"If They're Old Enough to Get Pregnant . . . "
Writer: Jono Polansky
Designer: Jessie Bunn
Agency: Public Media Center
Client: Planned Parenthood Federation of America
Appeared: 1986

Page 43:
"Some Women Are Silent on the Horrors . . . "
Writer: Jono Polansky
Designer: Jono Polansky
Agency: Public Media Center
Client: Planned Parenthood Federation of America
Appeared: *The New York Times*, 27 April 1989; *The San Francisco Chronicle*, 27 April 1989; *The South Bend Tribune*, 22 June 1989; *The Miami Herald*, 5 October 1989; *The Tampa Tribune*, 5 October 1989; *The Orlando Sentinel*, 5 October 1989; *Tallahassee Democrat*, 5 October 1989; *The Naples Daily News*, 10 October 1989

Pages 44-45:
"Robert Bork's Position on Reproductive Rights"
Writer: Jono Polansky
Designer: Jessie Bunn
Agency: Public Media Center
Client: Planned Parenthood Federation of America
Appeared: *The New York Times*, 14 September 1987, *The Washington Post*, 14 September 1987; *Los Angeles Times*, 21 September 1987

Page 46:
"Forty Years Ago I Had a Back-alley . . . "
Writer: Jono Polansky
Designer: Jessie Bunn
Agency: Public Media Center
Client: Planned Parenthood Federation of America
Appeared: *Time*, 14 October 1985 (variant); *The Atlantic Monthly*, 1 November 1985 (variant); *Ladies' Home Journal*, February 1986 (variant); *Chatelaine*, March 1987 (Canadian variant); 1989

Page 47:
"When JR Took Mandy ... "
Writer: Public Media Center
Designer: Public Media Center
Agency: Public Media Center
Client: Planned Parenthood Federation of America
Appeared: *Los Angeles Times*, December 8, 1986

Pages 48-49:
"They Did it 20,000 Times on Television . . . "
Writer: Jerry Mander
Designer: Jessie Bunn
Agency: Public Media Center
Client: Planned Parenthood Federation of America
Appeared: *The Washington Post*, 25 November 1986 ("9,000 Times" version)

Page 51:
"A Bowl of Tiger Penis Soup . . . "
Writer: Jono Polansky
Designer: Jono Polansky
Agency: Public Media Center
Client: Sam LaBudde, Endangered Species Project, Earth Island Institute
Appeared: *The New York Times*, 31 October 1993; *Los Angeles Times*, 27 December 1993

Pages 52-53:
"They're Killing Whales Again"
Writer: Jerry Mander
Designer: Daniela Sklan
Agency: Public Media Center
Client: Norwegian Whaling Campaign, Earth Island Institute / Humane Society of the US
Appeared: *The New York Times*, 18 November 1992

Page 54:
"The Dolphin Massacre Off Our Coast . . . "
Writer: Jono Polansky
Designer: Jono Polansky
Agency: Public Media Center
Client: Save the Dolphins Project, Earth Island Institute
Appeared: *The New York Times*, 11 April 1988; *The San Francisco Examiner*, 25 April 1988; *Santa Cruz Sentinel*, 22 June 1988

Page 55:
"Don't Buy Bumble Bee! . . . "
Writer: Public Media Center
Designer: Public Media Center
Agency: Public Media Center
Client: David Phillips, Save the Dolphins Project, Earth Island Institute
Appeared: *Los Angeles Times*, 1 December 1990, *The New York Times*, 5 December 1990

Page 56:
"US & Mexico Launch a Worldwide ..."
Writer: Jerry Mander
Designer: Public Media Center
Agency: Public Media Center
Client: David Phillips, Save the Dolphins Project, Earth Island Institute
Appeared: *The New York Times*, 30 September 1991

Page 57:
"Economics Is a Form of Brain Damage"
Writers: David Brower, Jerry Mander
Designer: Public Media Center
Agency: Public Media Center
Client: Earth Island Institute
Appeared: *The New York Times*, 17 February 1993

Pages 60-61:
"Sabotage! of America's Health . . . "
Writer: Jerry Mander
Designer: Daniela Sklan
Agency: Public Media Center
Client: Citizens Trade Campaign, Public Citizen
Appeared: *The New York Times*, 20 April 1992; *Wisconsin State Journal*, 26 May 1992; *The Washington Post*, 14 December 1992

Page 63:
"Should the People Who Caused . . . "
Writer: Jerry Mander
Designer: Daniela Sklan
Agency: Public Media Center
Client: International Forum on Globalization
Appeared: *The New York Times*, 20 November 1998

Pages 64-65:
"Jeopardized by Gatt . . . "
Writer: Jerry Mander
Designer: Daniela Sklan
Illustrator: Ward Schumaker
Agency: Public Media Center
Client: Sierra Club
Appeared: *The New York Times*, 27 June 1994

Page 66:
"Techno-Utopianism"
Writer: Jerry Mander
Designers: Mark Mazziotti, Ellen Visser
Agency: Public Media Center
Client: Turning Point Project (International Center for Technology Assessment + 13 others)
Appeared: *The New York Times*, 28 August 2000

Page 68:
"The Internet & the Illusion of Empowerment"
Writer: Jerry Mander
Designers: Mark Mazziotti, Ellen Visser
Agency: Public Media Center
Client: Turning Point Project (International Center for Technology Assessment + 19 others)
Appeared: *The New York Times*, 10 July 2000

Page 70:
"The Next World War Will Be About Water"
Writer: Jerry Mander
Designers: Mark Mazziotti, Ellen Visser
Agency: Public Media Center
Client: Turning Point Project (The Council of Canadians + 17 others)
Appeared: *The New York Times*, 6 December 1999

Page 72:
"Invisible Government"
Writer: Jerry Mander
Designers: Mark Mazziotti, Ellen Visser
Agency: Public Media Center
Client: Turning Point Project (International Forum on Globalization + 22 others)
Appeared: *The New York Times*, 29 November 1999

Page 74:
"If Computers in Schools Are the Answer . . . "
Writer: Jerry Mander
Designers: Mark Mazziotti, Ellen Visser
Agency: Public Media Center
Client: Turning Point Project (Alliance for Childhood +17 others)
Appeared: *The New York Times*, 12 June 2000

Page 76:
"E-Commerce & The Demise of Community"
Writer: Jerry Mander
Designers: Mark Mazziotti, Ellen Visser
Agency: Public Media Center
Client: Turning Point Project (Institute for Policy Studies / Global Economy Project + 17 others)
Appeared: *The New York Times*, 24 July 2000

Page 77:
"Globalization vs. Nature"
Writer: Jerry Mander
Designers: Mark Mazziotti, Ellen Visser
Agency: Public Media Center
Client: Turning Point Project (Sierra Club + 19 others)
Appeared: *The New York Times*, 22 November 1999

Page 78:
"Three Ways Industrial Food Makes You Sick"
Writer: Andrew Kimbrell
Designers: Mark Mazziotti, Ellen Visser
Agency: Public Media Center
Client: Turning Point Project (Center for Food Safety + 19 others)
Appeared: *The New York Times*, 31 January 2000

Page 79:
"Clearcutting in Your National Forests"
Writer: Jerry Mander
Designers: Mark Mazziotti, Ellen Visser
Agency: Public Media Center
Client: Turning Point Project (John Muir Project + 23 others)
Appeared: *The New York Times*, 27 September 1999

Page 80:
"The Second Massacre of Wounded Knee . . . "
Writer: Jerry Mander

Designer : Public Interest Communications
Agency: Public Interest Communications
Client: Wounded Knee Legal Defense Fund
Appeared: *The New York Times*, 27 June 1973

Page 86:
"Please Stop Your Airforce . . . "
Writer: Jerry Mander
Designer: Declan Buckley
Agency: Public Media Center
Client: Werkgroep Inheemse Volken (Working Group for Indigenous People), Amsterdam
Appeared: *de Volkskrant*, 3 March 1992 (Dutch version); English version unpublished

Pages 88-89:
"Catastrophe at James Bay"
Writer: Jerry Mander
Designer: Daniela Sklan
Agency: Public Media Center
Client: The James Bay Project, Greenpeace
Appeared: *The New York Times*, 21 October 1991

Page 90:
"Help Stop the War Against the Mayan. . ."
Writer: Jerry Mander
Designer: Public Media Center
Agency: Public Media Center
Client: Daniel Bomberry, Tribal Sovereignty Program
Appeared: *The New York Times*, 3 January 1984

Pages 92-93:
"Come to Hawaii…"
Writer: Jerry Mander
Designer: Ellen Toomey
Agency: Public Media Center
Client: Pele Defense Fund
Appeared: *The San Francisco Chronicle*, 1 February 1988; *The New York Times*, 21 September 1988

Page 96:
"A schoolroom of California kids shot . . . "
Writer: Jono Polansky
Designer: Public Media Center
Agency: Public Media Center
Client: The California Wellness Foundation
Appeared: *The Washington Post*, 14 March 1995 (variant); *The New York Times* Western Edition, 15 March 1995

Page 98:
"My Final Statement Before Being Silenced . . . "
Writers: Jerry Mander, Matthew Fox
Designer: Public Media Center
Agency: Public Media Center
Client: The Friends of Creation Spirituality
Appeared: *The New York Times*, 14 December 1988

Page 101:
"KAL 007: After a Year's Investigation . . . "
Writer: Jerry Mander
Designer: Public Media Center
Agency: Public Media Center
Client: The Nation Institute
Appeared: *The New York Times*, 25 October 1984

Page 102:
"Why They Blew Up the Rainbow Warrior"
Writer: Jerry Mander
Designer: Public Media Center
Agency: Public Media Center
Client: Greenpeace
Appeared: *The New York Times*, 16 December 1985

Page 103:
"Release Dan Quayle's College Records Now"
Writers: Orville Schell, Peter Coyote, Paul Hawken
Designer: Public Media Center
Agency: Public Media Center
Client: Independent Committee on Presidential Qualifications
Appeared: *The New York Times*, 13 October 1988

Pages 104-105:
"The Goal: A 50% Reduction of Beef . . . "
Writer: Jerry Mander
Designer: Daniela Sklan
Agency: Public Media Center
Client: Beyond Beef
Appeared: *The New York Times*, 23 April 1992

Page 106:
"Will the World Let Tibet Disappear?"
Writer: Jerry Mander
Designer: Public Media Center
Agency: Public Media Center
Client: Tibet Fund
Appeared: *The New York Times*, 11 December 1989

Page 107:
"Ozone Shock"
Writer: Jerry Mander
Designer: Mark Mazziotti
Agency: Public Media Center
Client: Greenpeace
Appeared: *The New York Times*, 5 October 1992; *The San Francisco Chronicle*, 6 October 1992

Page 108:
"Can New Zealand Stop the Japanese . . . "
Writer: Jono Polansky
Designer: Jono Polansky
Agency: Public Media Center
Client: Japanese Citizens Concerned About Plutonium
Appeared: 1992, New Zealand print media

Page 109:
"How to Win an Argument with a Meat Eater"
Writer: Jono Polansky, after John Robbins
Designer: Daniela Sklan
Agency: Public Media Center
Client: EarthSave
Appeared: 1989, poster distribution

Page 110:
"Will 1968 Go Down in History . . . "
Writer: Jerry Mander
Designer: Freeman & Gossage
Agency: Freeman & Gossage
Client: San Francisco Citizens for McCarthy
Appeared: *The San Francisco Chronicle*, 23 April 1968

Page 116:
"Oh Darling . . . "
Writer: Jono Polansky
Designer: Jessie Bunn
Agency: Public Media Center
Client: Planned Parenthood Federation of America
Appeared: 1986

Page 118:
"Our Arctic Way of Life…."
Writer: Jono Polansky
Designer: Cecilia Brunazzi
Agency: Public Media Center
Client: The Gwich'in Steering Committee
Appeared: *The New York Times*, 5 November 1991